A
S0-AWS-662
Mrs. Richmond
Honors English 10
2B

Five Great Comedies

DOVER • **GIANT THRIFT** • EDITIONS

Five Great Comedies

Much Ado About Nothing, Twelfth Night,
A Midsummer Night's Dream,
As You Like It,
and
The Merry Wives of Windsor

WILLIAM SHAKESPEARE

DOVER PUBLICATIONS, INC.
Mineola, New York

DOVER GIANT THRIFT EDITIONS

GENERAL EDITOR: MARY CAROLYN WALDREP

EDITOR OF THIS VOLUME: T. N. R. ROGERS

Copyright

Copyright © 1994, 1996, 1998, 2000 by Dover Publications, Inc.
All rights reserved.

Theatrical Rights

This Dover Thrift Edition may be used in its entirety, in adaptation, or in any other way for theatrical productions, professional and amateur, in the United States, without fee, permission, or acknowledgment. (This may not apply outside of the United States, as copyright conditions may vary.)

Bibliographical Note

This Dover edition, first published in 2005, contains the unabridged texts of five plays: *Much Ado About Nothing* as published in Volume II of *The Works of William Shakespeare*, Second Edition, by Macmillan and Company, London, in 1891, and republished as a Dover Thrift Edition in 1994; *Twelfth Night, or, What You Will* as published in Volume VI of *The Caxton Edition of the Complete Works of William Shakespeare* by Caxton Publishing Company, London, n.d., and republished as a Dover Thrift Edition in 1996; *A Midsummer Night's Dream* as published in Volume III of *The Caxton Edition of the Complete Works of William Shakespeare* and republished as a Dover Thrift Edition in 1992; *As You Like It* as published in Volume V of *The Caxton Edition of the Complete Works of William Shakespeare* and republished as a Dover Thrift Edition in 1998; and *The Merry Wives of Windsor* as published in Volume IV of *The Caxton Edition of the Complete Works of William Shakespeare* and republished as a Dover Thrift Edition in 2000. Introductory Notes were written, and footnotes revised or written anew, specially for the Dover editions.

Library of Congress Cataloging-in-Publication Data

Shakespeare, William, 1564–1616.
    [Plays. Selections]
    Five great comedies : Much ado about nothing, Twelfth night, A midsummer night's dream, As you like it, and The merry wives of Windsor / William Shakespeare.
        p. cm. — (Dover thrift editions)
    ISBN 0-486-44086-9 (pbk.)
    1. Title. II. Series.

PR2761 2005
822.3'3—dc22

2005041275

Manufactured in the United States of America
Dover Publications, Inc., 31 East 2nd Street, Mineola, N.Y. 11501

Contents

Much Ado About Nothing

Much Ado About Nothing

FIRST PERFORMED in 1598, *Much Ado About Nothing* focuses on the love story of Claudio and Hero, but the volatile relationship between Beatrice and Benedick is much more compelling. Critic Dover Wilson calls Beatrice "the first woman in [English] literature . . . who not only has a brain, but delights in the constant employment of it." Her sharp wit leads her to wage a war of words with Benedick, supplying much of the comic energy of the play. But when Hero is cruelly wronged by Claudio, Beatrice's wit and intelligence cannot defend her cousin's reputation; outraged at such injustice, she can only exclaim, "O God, that I were a man!" and convince Benedick to challenge Claudio. Though the couples are united in a conventionally comic ending, *Much Ado About Nothing* goes much deeper in exploring the tensions between the sexes in a society where female chastity is equated with virtue, and that virtue serves as the measure of a woman's worth.

Dramatis Personæ

DON PEDRO, prince of Arragon.
DON JOHN, his bastard brother.
CLAUDIO, a young lord of Florence.
BENEDICK, a young lord of Padua.
LEONATO, governor of Messina.
ANTONIO, his brother.
BALTHASAR, attendant on Don Pedro.
CONRADE, } followers of Don John.
BORACHIO, }
FRIAR FRANCIS.
DOGBERRY, a constable.
VERGES, a headborough.[1]
A Sexton.
A Boy.

HERO, daughter to Leonato.
BEATRICE, niece to Leonato.
Margaret, } gentlewomen attending on Hero.
Ursula, }

Messengers, Watch, Attendants, &c.

Scene — *Messina.*

---

1. *headborough*] a kind of village-mayor.

ACT I.

SCENE I. *Before* LEONATO'S *house*.

Enter LEONATO, HERO, *and* BEATRICE, *with a* Messenger.

LEON.   I learn in this letter that Don Pedro of Arragon comes this night
to Messina.

MESS.   He is very near by this: he was not three leagues off when I left
him.

LEON.   How many gentlemen have you lost in this action?

MESS.   But few of any sort, and none of name.

LEON.   A victory is twice itself when the achiever brings home full
numbers. I find here that Don Pedro hath bestowed much honour
on a young Florentine called Claudio.

MESS.   Much deserved on his part, and equally remembered by Don
Pedro: he hath borne himself beyond the promise of his age; doing,
in the figure of a lamb, the feats of a lion: he hath indeed better
bettered expectation than you must expect of me to tell you how.

LEON.   He hath an uncle here in Messina will be very much glad of it.

MESS.   I have already delivered him letters, and there appears much
joy in him; even so much, that joy could not show itself modest
enough without a badge of bitterness.

LEON.   Did he break out into tears?

MESS.   In great measure.

LEON.   A kind overflow of kindness: there are no faces truer than those
that are so washed. How much better is it to weep at joy than to joy
at weeping!

BEAT.   I pray you, is Signior Mountanto[1] returned from the wars or no?

---

1. *Mountanto*] a fencing term for an upward thrust.

5

MESS. I know none of that name, lady: there was none such in the army of any sort.

LEON. What is he that you ask for, niece?

HERO. My cousin means Signior Benedick of Padua.

MESS. O, he's returned; and as pleasant as ever he was.

BEAT. He set up his bills here in Messina and challenged Cupid at the flight;[2] and my uncle's fool, reading the challenge, subscribed for Cupid, and challenged him at the bird-bolt.[3] I pray you, how many hath he killed and eaten in these wars? But how many hath he killed? for, indeed, I promised to eat all of his killing.

LEON. Faith, niece, you tax Signior Benedick too much; but he'll be meet with you, I doubt it not.

MESS. He hath done good service, lady, in these wars.

BEAT. You had musty victual, and he hath holp to eat it: he is a very valiant trencher-man;[4] he hath an excellent stomach.

MESS. And a good soldier too, lady.

BEAT. And a good soldier to a lady; but what is he to a lord?

MESS. A lord to a lord, a man to a man; stuffed with all honourable virtues.

BEAT. It is so, indeed; he is no less than a stuffed man: but for the stuffing,—well, we are all mortal.

LEON. You must not, sir, mistake my niece. There is a kind of merry war betwixt Signior Benedick and her: they never meet but there's a skirmish of wit between them.

BEAT. Alas! he gets nothing by that. In our last conflict four of his five wits[5] went halting off, and now is the whole man governed with one: so that if he have wit enough to keep himself warm, let him bear it for a difference between himself and his horse; for it is all the wealth that he hath left, to be known a reasonable creature. Who is his companion now? He hath every month a new sworn brother.

MESS. Is't possible?

---

2. *flight*] long-distance shooting.
3. *bird-bolt*] a short, blunt, stumpy arrow used for killing birds.
4. *trencher-man*] a trencher is a plate; Beatrice is making fun of Benedick's appetite.
5. *five wits*] distinguished from the five senses, the five wits were common wit, imagination, fantasy, judgment and memory.

BEAT.   Very easily possible: he wears his faith but as the fashion of his hat; it ever changes with the next block.

MESS.   I see, lady, the gentleman is not in your books.

BEAT.   No; an he were, I would burn my study. But, I pray you, who is his companion? Is there no young squarer[6] now that will make a voyage with him to the devil?

MESS.   He is most in the company of the right noble Claudio.

BEAT.   O Lord, he will hang upon him like a disease: he is sooner caught than the pestilence, and the taker runs presently mad. God help the noble Claudio! if he have caught the Benedick, it will cost him a thousand pound ere a' be cured.

MESS.   I will hold friends with you, lady.

BEAT.   Do, good friend.

LEON.   You will never run mad, niece.

BEAT.   No, not till a hot January.

MESS.   Don Pedro is approached.

Enter DON PEDRO, DON JOHN, CLAUDIO, BENEDICK, *and* BALTHASAR.

D. PEDRO.   Good Signior Leonato, you are come to meet your trouble: the fashion of the world is to avoid cost, and you encounter it.

LEON.   Never came trouble to my house in the likeness of your Grace: for trouble being gone, comfort should remain; but when you depart from me, sorrow abides, and happiness takes his leave.

D. PEDRO.   You embrace your charge too willingly. I think this is your daughter.

LEON.   Her mother hath many times told me so.

BENE.   Were you in doubt, sir, that you asked her?

LEON.   Signior Benedick, no; for then were you a child.

D. PEDRO.   You have it full, Benedick: we may guess by this what you are, being a man. Truly, the lady fathers herself. Be happy, lady; for you are like an honourable father.

BENE.   If Signior Leonato be her father, she would not have his head on her shoulders for all Messina, as like him as she is.

BEAT.   I wonder that you will still be talking, Signior Benedick: nobody marks you.

---

6. *squarer*] braggart.

BENE. What, my dear Lady Disdain! are you yet living?

BEAT. Is it possible disdain should die while she hath such meet food to feed it, as Signior Benedick? Courtesy itself must convert to disdain, if you come in her presence.

BENE. Then is courtesy a turncoat. But it is certain I am loved of all ladies, only you excepted: and I would I could find in my heart that I had not a hard heart; for, truly, I love none.

BEAT. A dear happiness to women: they would else have been troubled with a pernicious suitor. I thank God and my cold blood, I am of your humour for that: I had rather hear my dog bark at a crow than a man swear he loves me.

BENE. God keep your ladyship still in that mind! so some gentleman or other shall 'scape a predestinate scratched face.

BEAT. Scratching could not make it worse, an 'twere such a face as yours were.

BENE. Well, you are a rare parrot-teacher.

BEAT. A bird of my tongue is better than a beast of yours.

BENE. I would my horse had the speed of your tongue, and so good a continuer. But keep your way, i' God's name; I have done.

BEAT. You always end with a jade's trick: I know you of old.

D. PEDRO. That is the sum of all, Leonato. Signior Claudio and Signior Benedick, my dear friend Leonato hath invited you all. I tell him we shall stay here at the least a month; and he heartily prays some occasion may detain us longer. I dare swear he is no hypocrite, but prays from his heart.

LEON. If you swear, my lord, you shall not be forsworn. [*To* DON JOHN] Let me bid you welcome, my lord: being reconciled to the prince your brother, I owe you all duty.

D. JOHN. I thank you: I am not of many words, but I thank you.

LEON. Please it your Grace lead on?

D. PEDRO. Your hand, Leonato; we will go together.

[*Exeunt all except* BENEDICK *and* CLAUDIO.]

CLAUD. Benedick, didst thou note the daughter of Signior Leonato?

BENE. I noted her not; but I looked on her.

CLAUD. Is she not a modest young lady?

BENE. Do you question me, as an honest man should do, for my simple true judgement? or would you have me speak after my custom, as being a professed tyrant to their sex?

CLAUD. No; I pray thee speak in sober judgement.

BENE. Why, i'faith, methinks she's too low for a high praise, too brown for a fair praise, and too little for a great praise: only this commendation I can afford her, that were she other than she is, she were unhandsome; and being no other but as she is, I do not like her.

CLAUD. Thou thinkest I am in sport: I pray thee tell me truly how thou likest her.

BENE. Would you buy her, that you inquire after her?

CLAUD. Can the world buy such a jewel?

BENE. Yea, and a case to put it into. But speak you this with a sad brow? or do you play the flouting Jack, to tell us Cupid is a good hare-finder,[7] and Vulcan a rare carpenter? Come, in what key shall a man take you, to go in the song?

CLAUD. In mine eye she is the sweetest lady that ever I looked on.

BENE. I can see yet without spectacles, and I see no such matter: there's her cousin, an she were not possessed with a fury, exceeds her as much in beauty as the first of May doth the last of December. But I hope you have no intent to turn husband, have you?

CLAUD. I would scarce trust myself, though I had sworn the contrary, if Hero would be my wife.

BENE. Is't come to this? In faith, hath not the world one man but he will wear his cap with suspicion? Shall I never see a bachelor of threescore again? Go to, i'faith; an thou wilt needs thrust thy neck into a yoke, wear the print of it, and sigh away Sundays. Look; Don Pedro is returned to seek you.

Re-enter DON PEDRO.

D. PEDRO. What secret hath held you here, that you followed not to Leonato's?

BENE. I would your Grace would constrain me to tell.

D. PEDRO. I charge thee on thy allegiance.

BENE. You hear, Count Claudio: I can be secret as a dumb man; I would have you think so; but, on my allegiance, mark you this, on my allegiance. He is in love. With who? now that is your Grace's part. Mark how short his answer is;—With Hero, Leonato's short daughter.

---

7. *hare-finder*] a directer of a hare hunt, chosen for his keen vision.

CLAUD. If this were so, so were it uttered.

BENE. Like the old tale, my lord: 'it is not so, nor 'twas not so, but, indeed, God forbid it should be so.'

CLAUD. If my passion change not shortly, God forbid it should be otherwise.

D. PEDRO. Amen, if you love her; for the lady is very well worthy.

CLAUD. You speak this to fetch me in, my lord.

D. PEDRO. By my troth, I speak my thought.

CLAUD. And, in faith, my lord, I spoke mine.

BENE. And, by my two faiths and troths, my lord, I spoke mine.

CLAUD. That I love her, I feel.

D. PEDRO. That she is worthy, I know.

BENE. That I neither feel how she should be loved, nor know how she should be worthy, is the opinion that fire cannot melt out of me: I will die in it at the stake.

D. PEDRO. Thou wast ever an obstinate heretic in the despite of beauty.

CLAUD. And never could maintain his part but in the force of his will.

BENE. That a woman conceived me, I thank her; that she brought me up, I likewise give her most humble thanks: but that I will have a recheat winded in my forehead,[8] or hang my bugle in an invisible baldrick,[9] all women shall pardon me. Because I will not do them the wrong to mistrust any, I will do myself the right to trust none; and the fine is, for the which I may go the finer, I will live a bachelor.

D. PEDRO. I shall see thee, ere I die, look pale with love.

BENE. With anger, with sickness, or with hunger, my lord; not with love: prove that ever I lose more blood with love than I will get again with drinking, pick out mine eyes with a ballad-maker's pen, and hang me up at the door of a brothel-house for the sign of blind Cupid.

D. PEDRO. Well, if ever thou dost fall from this faith, thou wilt prove a notable argument.

---

8. *a recheat . . . forehead*] to "wind a recheat" is to sound a note on the huntsman's bugle; Benedick refers to the popular notion that horns sprout from the forehead of a cuck-olded husband.

9. *baldrick*] the belt in which the huntsman's bugle is carried.

BENE.   If I do, hang me in a bottle like a cat, and shoot at me; and he that hits me, let him be clapped on the shoulder and called Adam.[10]

D. PEDRO.   Well, as time shall try:
'In time the savage bull doth bear the yoke.'

BENE.   The savage bull may; but if ever the sensible Benedick bear it, pluck off the bull's horns, and set them in my forehead: and let me be vilely painted; and in such great letters as they write 'Here is good horse to hire,' let them signify under my sign 'Here you may see Benedick the married man.'

CLAUD.   If this should ever happen, thou wouldst be horn-mad.

D. PEDRO.   Nay, if Cupid have not spent all his quiver in Venice, thou wilt quake for this shortly.

BENE.   I look for an earthquake too, then.

D. PEDRO.   Well, you will temporize with the hours. In the meantime, good Signior Benedick, repair to Leonato's: commend me to him, and tell him I will not fail him at supper; for indeed he hath made great preparation.

BENE.   I have almost matter enough in me for such an embassage; and so I commit you—

CLAUD.   To the tuition of God: From my house, if I had it,—

D. PEDRO.   The sixth of July:[11] Your loving friend, Benedick.

BENE.   Nay, mock not, mock not. The body of your discourse is sometime guarded with fragments, and the guards are but slightly basted on neither: ere you flout old ends any further, examine your conscience: and so I leave you.   [*Exit.*]

CLAUD.   My liege, your highness now may do me good.

D. PEDRO.   My love is thine to teach: teach it but how,
And thou shalt see how apt it is to learn
Any hard lesson that may do thee good.

CLAUD.   Hath Leonato any son, my lord?

D. PEDRO.   No child but Hero; she's his only heir.

---

10. *hang me ... Adam*] shooting at a cat enclosed in a wooden bottle or barrel was a favorite country sport; "Adam" may be a reference to Adam Bell, the outlaw of ballad tradition, held to be a champion archer.

11. *The sixth of July*] Midsummer-day according to older calculations; a fit date for midsummer madness.

      Dost thou affect her, Claudio?

CLAUD.   O, my lord,
     When you went onward on this ended action,
     I look'd upon her with a soldier's eye,
     That liked, but had a rougher task in hand
     Than to drive liking to the name of love:
     But now I am return'd and that war-thoughts
     Have left their places vacant, in their rooms
     Come thronging soft and delicate desires,
     All prompting me how fair young Hero is,
     Saying, I liked her ere I went to wars.

D. PEDRO.   Thou wilt be like a lover presently,
     And tire the hearer with a book of words.
     If thou dost love fair Hero, cherish it;
     And I will break[12] with her and with her father,
     And thou shalt have her. Was't not to this end
     That thou began'st to twist so fine a story?

CLAUD.   How sweetly you do minister to love,
     That know love's grief by his complexion!
     But lest my liking might too sudden seem,
     I would have salved it with a longer treatise.

D. PEDRO.   What need the bridge much broader than the flood?
     The fairest grant is the necessity.
     Look, what will serve is fit: 'tis once, thou lovest,
     And I will fit thee with the remedy.
     I know we shall have revelling to-night:
     I will assume thy part in some disguise,
     And tell fair Hero I am Claudio;
     And in her bosom I'll unclasp my heart,
     And take her hearing prisoner with the force
     And strong encounter of my amorous tale:
     Then after to her father will I break;
     And the conclusion is, she shall be thine.
     In practice let us put it presently.   [*Exeunt.*]

---

12. *break*] broach (the subject).

SCENE II. *A room in* LEONATO'S *house*.

Enter LEONATO *and* ANTONIO, *meeting*.

LEON.   How now, brother! Where is my cousin, your son? hath he
    provided this music?

ANT.   He is very busy about it. But, brother, I can tell you strange news,
    that you yet dreamt not of.

LEON.   Are they good?

ANT.   As the event stamps them: but they have a good cover; they show
    well outward. The prince and Count Claudio, walking in a thick-
    pleached[1] alley in mine orchard, were thus much overheard by a
    man of mine: the prince discovered[2] to Claudio that he loved my
    niece your daughter, and meant to acknowledge it this night in a
    dance; and if he found her accordant, he meant to take the present
    time by the top, and instantly break with you of it.

LEON.   Hath the fellow any wit that told you this?

ANT.   A good sharp fellow: I will send for him; and question him
    yourself.

LEON.   No, no; we will hold it as a dream till it appear itself: but I will
    acquaint my daughter withal, that she may be the better prepared
    for an answer, if peradventure this be true. Go you and tell her of it.
    [*Enter* Attendants.] Cousins, you know what you have to do. O, I
    cry you mercy, friend; go you with me, and I will use your skill.
    Good cousin, have a care this busy time.   [*Exeunt*.]

---

1. *thick-pleached*] with boughs thickly plaited or intertwined.
2. *discovered*] revealed.

SCENE III. *The same*.

Enter DON JOHN *and* CONRADE.

CON. What the good-year, my lord! why are you thus out of measure sad?

D. JOHN. There is no measure in the occasion that breeds; therefore the sadness is without limit.

CON. You should hear reason.

D. JOHN. And when I have heard it, what blessing brings it?

CON. If not a present remedy, at least a patient sufferance.

D. JOHN. I wonder that thou, being (as thou sayest thou art) born under Saturn,[1] goest about to apply a moral medicine to a mortifying mischief. I cannot hide what I am: I must be sad when I have cause, and smile at no man's jests; eat when I have stomach, and wait for no man's leisure; sleep when I am drowsy, and tend on no man's business; laugh when I am merry, and claw no man in his humour.

CON. Yea, but you must not make the full show of this till you may do it without controlment. You have of late stood out against your brother, and he hath ta'en you newly into his grace; where it is impossible you should take true root but by the fair weather that you make yourself: it is needful that you frame the season for your own harvest.

D. JOHN. I had rather be a canker in a hedge than a rose in his grace; and it better fits my blood to be disdained of all than to fashion a carriage to rob love from any: in this, though I cannot be said to be a flattering honest man, it must not be denied but I am a plain-dealing villain. I am trusted with a muzzle, and enfranchised with a clog;[2] therefore I have decreed not to sing in my cage. If I had my

---

1. *born under Saturn*] of Saturnine or melancholy temperament.
2. *enfranchised with a clog*] set at liberty, but with a "clog" (anything hung upon an animal to hinder motion).

mouth, I would bite; if I had my liberty, I would do my liking: in the meantime let me be that I am, and seek not to alter me.

CON.   Can you make no use of your discontent?

D. JOHN.   I make all use of it, for I use it only.
Who comes here?

Enter BORACHIO.

What news, Borachio?

BORA.   I came yonder from a great supper: the prince your brother is royally entertained by Leonato; and I can give you intelligence of an intended marriage.

D. JOHN.   Will it serve for any model to build mischief on? What is he for a fool that betroths himself to unquietness?

BORA.   Marry, it is your brother's right hand.

D. JOHN.   Who? the most exquisite Claudio?

BORA.   Even he. *verbal irony*

D. JOHN.   A proper squire! And who, and who? which way looks he?

BORA.   Marry, on Hero, the daughter and heir of Leonato.

D. JOHN.   A very forward March-chick! How came you to this?

BORA.   Being entertained for a perfumer,[3] as I was smoking a musty room, comes me the prince and Claudio, hand in hand, in sad conference: I whipt me behind the arras; and there heard it agreed upon, that the prince should woo Hero for himself, and having obtained her, give her to Count Claudio.

D. JOHN.   Come, come, let us thither: this may prove food to my displeasure. That young start-up hath all the glory of my overthrow: if I can cross him any way, I bless myself every way. You are both sure, and will assist me?

CON.   To the death, my lord.

D. JOHN.   Let us to the great supper: their cheer is the greater that I am subdued. Would the cook were of my mind! Shall we go prove what's to be done?

BORA.   We'll wait upon your lordship.   [*Exeunt.*]

---

3. *entertained . . . perfumer*] Borachio is mistaken for someone who perfumes rooms by smoking aromatic herbs in a censer.

ACT II.

SCENE I. *A hall in* LEONATO'S *house*.

Enter LEONATO, ANTONIO, HERO, BEATRICE, *and others*.

LEON. Was not Count John here at supper?

ANT. I saw him not.

BEAT. How tartly that gentleman looks! I never can see him but I am heart-burned an hour after.

HERO. He is of a very melancholy disposition.

BEAT. He were an excellent man that were made just in the midway between him and Benedick: the one is too like an image and says nothing, and the other too like my lady's eldest son, evermore tattling.

LEON. Then half Signior Benedick's tongue in Count John's mouth, and half Count John's melancholy in Signior Benedick's face,—

BEAT. With a good leg and a good foot, uncle, and money enough in his purse, such a man would win any woman in the world, if a' could get her good-will.

LEON. By my troth, niece, thou wilt never get thee a husband, if thou be so shrewd[1] of thy tongue.

ANT. In faith, she's too curst.

BEAT. Too curst is more than curst: I shall lessen God's sending that way; for it is said, 'God sends a curst cow short horns;' but to a cow too curst he sends none.

LEON. So, by being too curst, God will send you no horns.

BEAT. Just, if he send me no husband; for the which blessing I am at

---

1. *shrewd*] vicious, bad-tempered.

17

him upon my knees every morning and evening. Lord, I could not endure a husband with a beard on his face: I had rather lie in the woollen.[2]

LEON.   You may light on a husband that hath no beard.

BEAT.   What should I do with him? dress him in my apparel, and make him my waiting-gentlewoman? He that hath a beard is more than a youth; and he that hath no beard is less than a man: and he that is more than a youth is not for me; and he that is less than a man, I am not for him: therefore I will even take sixpence in earnest of the bear-ward, and lead his apes into hell.

LEON.   Well, then, go you into hell?

BEAT.   No, but to the gate; and there will the devil meet me, like an old cuckold, with horns on his head, and say 'Get you to heaven, Beatrice, get you to heaven; here's no place for you maids:' so deliver I up my apes, and away to Saint Peter for the heavens; he shows me where the bachelors sit, and there live we as merry as the day is long.

ANT.   [*To Hero*] Well, niece, I trust you will be ruled by your father.

BEAT.   Yes, faith; it is my cousin's duty to make courtesy, and say, 'Father, as it please you.' But yet for all that, cousin, let him be a handsome fellow, or else make another courtesy, and say, 'Father, as it please me.'

LEON.   Well, niece, I hope to see you one day fitted with a husband.

BEAT.   Not till God make men of some other metal than earth. Would it not grieve a woman to be overmastered with a piece of valiant dust? to make an account of her life to a clod of wayward marl? No, uncle, I'll none: Adam's sons are my brethren; and, truly, I hold it a sin to match in my kindred.

LEON.   Daughter, remember what I told you: if the prince do solicit you in that kind, you know your answer.

BEAT.   The fault will be in the music, cousin, if you be not wooed in good time: if the prince be too important, tell him there is measure in every thing, and so dance out the answer. For, hear me, Hero: wooing, wedding, and repenting, is as a Scotch jig, a measure, and

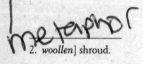

---

2. *woollen*] shroud.

a cinque pace:[3] the first suit is hot and hasty, like a Scotch jig, and full as fantastical; the wedding, mannerly-modest, as a measure, full of state and ancientry; and then comes repentance, and, with his bad legs, falls into the cinque pace faster and faster, till he sink into his grave.

LEON.   Cousin, you apprehend passing shrewdly.

BEAT.   I have a good eye, uncle; I can see a church by daylight.

LEON.   The revellers are entering, brother: make good room.

[All put on their masks.]

Enter DON PEDRO, CLAUDIO, BENEDICK, BALTHASAR, DON JOHN, BORACHIO, MARGARET, URSULA, *and others, masked.*

D. PEDRO.   Lady, will you walk about with your friend?

HERO.   So you walk softly, and look sweetly, and say nothing, I am yours for the walk; and especially when I walk away.

D. PEDRO.   With me in your company?

HERO.   I may say so, when I please.

D. PEDRO.   And when please you to say so?

HERO.   When I like your favour; for God defend the lute should be like the case!

D. PEDRO.   My visor is Philemon's roof; within the house is Jove.

HERO.   Why, then, your visor should be thatched.[4]

D. PEDRO.   Speak low, if you speak love.   *[Drawing her aside.]*

BALTH.   Well, I would you did like me.

MARG.   So would not I, for your own sake; for I have many ill qualities.

BALTH.   Which is one?

MARG.   I say my prayers aloud.

BALTH.   I love you the better: the hearers may cry, Amen.

MARG.   God match me with a good dancer!

BALTH.   Amen.

MARG.   And God keep him out of my sight when the dance is done! Answer, clerk.

---

3. *cinque pace*] the French dance called "cinq pas" or "galliard," of which each complete movement consisted of five steps; the pace quickened as the dance continued. The word is often written "sink-a-pace."

4. *Philemon's roof ... thatched*] In Ovid's *Metamorphoses* (VIII, 630), two peasants, Philemon and Baucis, unknowingly entertained Jove and Mercury in their rustic thatch-roofed cottage.

BALTH. No more words: the clerk is answered.

URS. I know you well enough; you are Signior Antonio.

ANT. At a word, I am not.

URS. I know you by the waggling of your head.

ANT. To tell you true, I counterfeit him.

URS. You could never do him so ill-well, unless you were the very man. Here's his dry hand up and down: you are he, you are he.

ANT. At a word, I am not.

URS. Come, come, do you think I do not know you by your excellent wit? can virtue hide itself? Go to, mum, you are he: graces will appear, and there's an end.

BEAT. Will you not tell me who told you so?

BENE. No, you shall pardon me.

BEAT. Nor will you not tell me who you are?

BENE. Not now.

BEAT. That I was disdainful, and that I had my good wit out of the 'Hundred Merry Tales':[5]—well, this was Signior Benedick that said so.

BENE. What's he?

BEAT. I am sure you know him well enough.

BENE. Not I, believe me.

BEAT. Did he never make you laugh?

BENE. I pray you, what is he?

BEAT. Why, he is the prince's jester: a very dull fool; only his gift is in devising impossible slanders: none but libertines delight in him; and the commendation is not in his wit, but in his villany; for he both pleases men and angers them, and then they laugh at him and beat him. I am sure he is in the fleet: I would he had boarded me.

BENE. When I know the gentleman, I'll tell him what you say.

BEAT. Do, do: he'll but break a comparison or two on me; which, peradventure not marked or not laughed at, strikes him into melancholy; and then there's a partridge wing saved, for the fool will eat no supper that night. [*Music.*] We must follow the leaders.

BENE. In every good thing.

BEAT. Nay, if they lead to any ill, I will leave them at the next turning.

---

5. *'Hundred Merry Tales'*] the title of a popular joke book, first published in 1526 and frequently reissued.

[*Dance. Then exeunt all except* DON JOHN, BORACHIO, *and* CLAUDIO.]

D. JOHN.   Sure my brother is amorous on Hero, and hath withdrawn
    her father to break with him about it. The ladies follow her, and but
    one visor remains.

BORA.   And that is Claudio: I know him by his bearing.

D. JOHN.   Are not you Signior Benedick?

CLAUD.   You know me well; I am he.

D. JOHN.   Signior, you are very near my brother in his love: he
    is enamoured on Hero; I pray you, dissuade him from her: she is
    no equal for his birth: you may do the part of an honest man
    in it.

CLAUD.   How know you he loves her?

D. JOHN.   I heard him swear his affection.

BORA.   So did I too; and he swore he would marry her to-night.

D. JOHN.   Come, let us to the banquet.

[Exeunt DON JOHN and BORACHIO.]

CLAUD.   Thus answer I in name of Benedick,
        But hear these ill news with the ears of Claudio.
        'Tis certain so; the prince wooes for himself.
        Friendship is constant in all other things
        Save in the office and affairs of love:
        Therefore all hearts in love use their own tongues;
        Let every eye negotiate for itself,
        And trust no agent; for beauty is a witch,
        Against whose charms faith melteth into blood.
        This is an accident of hourly proof,
        Which I mistrusted not. Farewell, therefore, Hero!

Re-enter BENEDICK.

BENE.   Count Claudio?

CLAUD.   Yea, the same.

BENE.   Come, will you go with me?

CLAUD.   Whither?

BENE.   Even to the next willow, about your own business, county.
    What fashion will you wear the garland of? about your neck, like an
    usurer's chain? or under your arm, like a lieutenant's scarf? You
    must wear it one way, for the prince hath got your Hero.

CLAUD.   I wish him joy of her.

BENE.   Why, that's spoken like an honest drovier;[6] so they sell bullocks. But did you think the prince would have served you thus?

CLAUD.   I pray you, leave me.

BENE.   Ho! now you strike like the blind man; 'twas the boy that stole your meat, and you'll beat the post.

CLAUD.   If it will not be, I'll leave you.   [*Exit.*]

BENE.   Alas, poor hurt fowl! now will he creep into sedges. But, that my Lady Beatrice should know me, and not know me! The prince's fool! Ha? It may be I go under that title because I am merry. Yea, but so I am apt to do myself wrong; I am not so reputed: it is the base, though bitter, disposition of Beatrice that puts the world into her person, and so gives me out. Well, I'll be revenged as I may.

Re-enter DON PEDRO.

D. PEDRO.   Now, signior, where's the count? did you see him?

BENE.   Troth, my lord, I have played the part of Lady Fame. I found him here as melancholy as a lodge in a warren:[7] I told him, and I think I told him true, that your grace had got the good will of this young lady; and I offered him my company to a willow-tree, either to make him a garland, as being forsaken, or to bind him up a rod, as being worthy to be whipped.

D. PEDRO.   To be whipped! What's his fault?

BENE.   The flat transgression of a school-boy, who, being overjoyed with finding a birds' nest, shows it his companion, and he steals it.

D. PEDRO.   Wilt thou make a trust a transgression? The transgression is in the stealer.

BENE.   Yet it had not been amiss the rod had been made, and the garland too; for the garland he might have worn himself, and the rod he might have bestowed on you, who, as I take it, have stolen his birds' nest.

D. PEDRO.   I will but teach them to sing, and restore them to the owner.

BENE.   If their singing answer your saying, by my faith, you say honestly.

---

6. *drovier*] cattle dealer.
7. *a lodge in a warren*] a keeper's hut, necessarily isolated in a game preserve.

D. PEDRO.   The Lady Beatrice hath a quarrel to you: the gentleman
       that danced with her told her she is much wronged by you.
BENE.   O, she misused me past the endurance of a block! an oak but
       with one green leaf on it would have answered her; my very visor
       began to assume life and scold with her. She told me, not thinking I
       had been myself, that I was the prince's jester, that I was duller than
       a great thaw; huddling jest upon jest, with such impossible convey-
       ance, upon me, that I stood like a man at a mark, with a whole army
       shooting at me. She speaks poniards, and every word stabs: if her
       breath were as terrible as her terminations,[8] there were no living
       near her; she would infect to the north star. I would not marry her,
       though she were endowed with all that Adam had left him before
       he transgressed: she would have made Hercules have turned spit,
       yea, and have cleft his club to make the fire too. Come, talk not of
       her: you shall find her the infernal Ate[9] in good apparel. I would to
       God some scholar would conjure[10] her; for certainly, while she is
       here, a man may live as quiet in hell as in a sanctuary; and people
       sin upon purpose, because they would go thither; so, indeed, all
       disquiet, horror, and perturbation follows her.
D. PEDRO.   Look, here she comes.

Re-enter CLAUDIO, BEATRICE, HERO, *and* LEONATO.

BENE.   Will your grace command me any service to the world's end? I
       will go on the slightest errand now to the Antipodes that you can
       devise to send me on; I will fetch you a toothpicker now from the
       furthest inch of Asia; bring you the length of Prester John's foot;
       fetch you a hair off the great Cham's beard; do you any embassage
       to the Pigmies;[11] rather than hold three words' conference with this
       harpy. You have no employment for me?
D. PEDRO.   None, but to desire your good company.

---

   8. *terminations*] terms, epithets.
   9. *Ate*] the spirit of discord in Homeric mythology.
  10. *conjure*] exorcise; exorcisms were performed in Latin, so the exorcist would have to be
       a scholar.
  11. *Prester John's foot . . . Cham's beard . . . Pigmies*] according to romances, Prester John
       was an Asian king of vast wealth; Cham was the supreme ruler of the Mongols; the
       Pigmies were a tribe in the northern mountains of India.

BENE. O God, sir, here's a dish I love not: I cannot endure my Lady
Tongue. [*Exit.*]

D. PEDRO. Come, lady, come; you have lost the heart of Signior
Benedick.

BEAT. Indeed, my lord, he lent it me awhile; and I gave him use for it,
a double heart for his single one: marry, once before he won it of
me with false dice, therefore your Grace may well say I have lost it.

D. PEDRO. You have put him down, lady, you have put him down.

BEAT. So I would not he should do me, my lord, lest I should prove the
mother of fools. I have brought Count Claudio, whom you sent me
to seek.

D. PEDRO. Why, how now, count! wherefore are you sad?

CLAUD. Not sad, my lord.

D. PEDRO. How then? sick?

CLAUD. Neither, my lord.

BEAT. The count is neither sad, nor sick, nor merry, nor well; but civil
count, civil as an orange, and something of that jealous complexion.

D. PEDRO. I' faith, lady, I think your blazon to be true; though, I'll be
sworn, if he be so, his conceit is false. Here, Claudio, I have wooed in
thy name, and fair Hero is won: I have broke with her father, and his
good will obtained: name the day of marriage, and God give thee joy!

LEON. Count, take of me my daughter, and with her my fortunes: his
Grace hath made the match, and all grace say Amen to it.

BEAT. Speak, count, 'tis your cue.

CLAUD. Silence is the perfectest herald of joy: I were but little happy,
if I could say how much. Lady, as you are mine, I am yours: I give
away myself for you, and dote upon the exchange.

BEAT. Speak, cousin; or, if you cannot, stop his mouth with a kiss, and
let not him speak neither.

D. PEDRO. In faith, lady, you have a merry heart.

BEAT. Yea, my lord; I thank it, poor fool, it keeps on the windy side of
care. My cousin tells him in his ear that he is in her heart.

CLAUD. And so she doth, cousin.

BEAT. Good Lord, for alliance! Thus goes every one to the world but I,
and I am sun-burnt;[12] I may sit in a corner, and cry heigh-ho for a
husband!

---

12. *sun-burnt*] neglected, exposed to the weather, homely, plain.

D. PEDRO.   Lady Beatrice, I will get you one.

BEAT.   I would rather have one of your father's getting. Hath your
Grace ne'er a brother like you? Your father got excellent husbands,
if a maid could come by them.

D. PEDRO.   Will you have me, lady?

BEAT.   No, my lord, unless I might have another for working-days: your
Grace is too costly to wear every day. But, I beseech your Grace,
pardon me: I was born to speak all mirth and no matter.

D. PEDRO.   Your silence most offends me, and to be merry best becomes you; for, out of question, you were born in a merry hour.

BEAT.   No, sure, my lord, my mother cried; but then there was a star
danced, and under that was I born. Cousins, God give you joy!

LEON.   Niece, will you look to those things I told you of?

BEAT.   I cry you mercy, uncle. By your Grace's pardon.   [Exit.]

D. PEDRO.   By my troth, a pleasant-spirited lady.

LEON.   There's little of the melancholy element in her, my lord: she is
never sad but when she sleeps; and not ever sad then; for I have
heard my daughter say, she hath often dreamed of unhappiness,
and waked herself with laughing.

D. PEDRO.   She cannot endure to hear tell of a husband.

LEON.   O, by no means: she mocks all her wooers out of suit.

D. PEDRO.   She were an excellent wife for Benedick.

LEON.   O Lord, my lord, if they were but a week married, they would
talk themselves mad.

D. PEDRO.   County Claudio, when mean you to go to church?

CLAUD.   To-morrow, my lord: time goes on crutches till love have all
his rites.

LEON.   Not till Monday, my dear son, which is hence a just seven-
night; and a time too brief, too, to have all things answer my mind.

D. PEDRO.   Come, you shake the head at so long a breathing: but, I
warrant thee, Claudio, the time shall not go dully by us. I will, in
the interim, undertake one of Hercules' labours; which is, to bring
Signior Benedick and the Lady Beatrice into a mountain of affection the one with the other. I would fain have it a match; and I
doubt not but to fashion it, if you three will but minister such
assistance as I shall give you direction.

LEON.   My lord, I am for you, though it cost me ten nights' watchings.

CLAUD.   And I, my lord.

D. PEDRO.   And you too, gentle Hero?

HERO. I will do any modest office, my lord, to help my cousin to a good husband.

D. PEDRO. And Benedick is not the unhopefullest husband that I know. Thus far can I praise him; he is of a noble strain, of approved valour, and confirmed honesty. I will teach you how to humour your cousin, that she shall fall in love with Benedick; and I, with your two helps, will so practise on Benedick, that, in despite of his quick wit and his queasy stomach, he shall fall in love with Beatrice. If we can do this, Cupid is no longer an archer: his glory shall be ours, for we are the only love-gods. Go in with me, and I will tell you my drift.   [*Exeunt.*]

SCENE II. *The same.*

Enter DON JOHN *and* BORACHIO.

D. JOHN. It is so; the Count Claudio shall marry the daughter of Leonato.

BORA. Yea, my lord; but I can cross it.

D. JOHN. Any bar, any cross, any impediment will be medicinable to me: I am sick in displeasure to him; and whatsoever comes athwart his affection ranges evenly with mine. How canst thou cross this marriage?

BORA. Not honestly, my lord; but so covertly that no dishonesty shall appear in me.

D. JOHN. Show me briefly how.

BORA. I think I told your lordship, a year since, how much I am in the favour of Margaret, the waiting gentlewoman to Hero.

D. JOHN. I remember.

BORA. I can, at any unseasonable instant of the night, appoint her to look out at her lady's chamber window.

D. JOHN. What life is in that, to be the death of this marriage?

BORA. The poison of that lies in you to temper. Go you to the prince your brother; spare not to tell him that he hath wronged his honour

in marrying the renowned Claudio—whose estimation do you
mightily hold up—to a contaminated stale, such a one as Hero.

D. JOHN.   What proof shall I make of that?

BORA.   Proof enough to misuse the prince, to vex Claudio, to undo
Hero, and kill Leonato. Look you for any other issue?

D. JOHN.   Only to despite them I will endeavour any thing.

BORA.   Go, then; find me a meet hour to draw Don Pedro and the
Count Claudio alone: tell them that you know that Hero loves me;
intend[1] a kind of zeal both to the prince and Claudio, as,—in love
of your brother's honour, who hath made this match, and his
friend's reputation, who is thus like to be cozened with the semblance of a maid,—that you have discovered thus. They will
scarcely believe this without trial: offer them instances; which shall
bear no less likelihood than to see me at her chamber-window;
hear me call Margaret, Hero; hear Margaret term me Claudio; and
bring them to see this the very night before the intended
wedding,—for in the meantime I will so fashion the matter that
Hero shall be absent,—and there shall appear such seeming truth
of Hero's disloyalty, that jealousy shall be called assurance and all
the preparation overthrown.

D. JOHN.   Grow this to what adverse issue it can, I will put it in
practice. Be cunning in the working this, and thy fee is a thousand
ducats.

BORA.   Be you constant in the accusation, and my cunning shall not
shame me.

D. JOHN.   I will presently go learn their day of marriage.

                                                       [Exeunt.]

---

1. *intend*] pretend.

SCENE III. LEONATO'S *orchard*.

Enter BENEDICK.

BENE.   Boy!

Enter Boy.

BOY.   Signior?

BENE.   In my chamber-window lies a book: bring it hither to me in the orchard.

BOY.   I am here already, sir.

BENE.   I know that; but I would have thee hence, and here again. [*Exit* Boy.] I do much wonder that one man, seeing how much another man is a fool when he dedicates his behaviours to love, will, after he hath laughed at such shallow follies in others, become the argument of his own scorn by falling in love: and such a man is Claudio. I have known when there was no music with him but the drum and the fife; and now had he rather hear the tabor and the pipe: I have known when he would have walked ten mile a-foot to see a good armour; and now will he lie ten nights awake, carving the fashion of a new doublet. He was wont to speak plain and to the purpose, like an honest man and a soldier; and now is he turned orthography; his words are a very fantastical banquet, — just so many strange dishes. May I be so converted, and see with these eyes? I cannot tell; I think not: I will not be sworn but love may transform me to an oyster; but I'll take my oath on it, till he have made an oyster of me, he shall never make me such a fool. One woman is fair, yet I am well; another is wise, yet I am well; another virtuous, yet I am well: but till all graces be in one woman, one woman shall not come in my grace. Rich she shall be, that's certain; wise, or I'll none; virtuous, or I'll never cheapen her; fair, or I'll never look on her; mild, or come not near me; noble, or not I for an angel; of good discourse, an excellent musician, and her hair shall be of what colour it please God. Ha! the prince and Monsieur Love! I will hide me in the arbour.   [*Withdraws.*]

Enter DON PEDRO, CLAUDIO, *and* LEONATO.

D. PEDRO.   Come, shall we hear this music?
CLAUD.   Yea, my good lord. How still the evening is,
    As hush'd on purpose to grace harmony!
D. PEDRO.   See you where Benedick hath hid himself?
CLAUD.   O, very well, my lord: the music ended,
    We'll fit the kid-fox with a pennyworth.

Enter BALTHASAR *with Music.*

D. PEDRO.   Come, Balthasar, we'll hear that song again.
BALTH.   O, good my lord, tax not so bad a voice
    To slander music any more than once.
D. PEDRO.   It is the witness still of excellency
    To put a strange face on his own perfection.
    I pray thee, sing, and let me woo no more.
BALTH.   Because you talk of wooing, I will sing;
    Since many a wooer doth commence his suit
    To her he thinks not worthy, yet he wooes,
    Yet will he swear he loves.
D. PEDRO.   Nay, pray thee, come;
    Or, if thou wilt hold longer argument,
    Do it in notes.
BALTH.   Note this before my notes;
    There's not a note of mine that's worth the noting.
D. PEDRO.   Why, these are very crotchets[1] that he speaks;
    Note, notes, forsooth, and nothing.   [*Air.*]
BENE.   Now, divine air! now is his soul ravished! Is it not strange that
    sheeps' guts should hale souls out of men's bodies? Well, a horn for
    my money, when all's done.

BALTH.   The Song.

        Sigh no more, ladies, sigh no more,
          Men were deceivers ever,
        One foot in sea and one on shore,
          To one thing constant never:

---

1. *crotchets*] perverse conceits; also, characters in music.

> Then sigh not so, but let them go,
>   And be you blithe and bonny,
> Converting all your sounds of woe
>   Into Hey nonny, nonny.
>
> Sing no more ditties, sing no moe,
>   Of dumps so dull and heavy;
> The fraud of men was ever so,
>   Since summer first was leavy:[2]
>   Then sigh not so, &c.

D. PEDRO.   By my troth, a good song.

BALTH.   And an ill singer, my lord.

D. PEDRO.   Ha, no, no, faith; thou singest well enough for a shift.

BENE.   An[3] he had been a dog that should have howled thus, they would have hanged him: and I pray God his bad voice bode no mischief. I had as lief have heard the night-raven, come what plague could have come after it.

D. PEDRO.   Yea, marry, dost thou hear, Balthasar? I pray thee, get us some excellent music; for to-morrow night we would have it at the Lady Hero's chamber-window.

BALTH.   The best I can, my lord.

D. PEDRO.   Do so: farewell. [*Exit* BALTHASAR.] Come hither, Leonato. What was it you told me of to-day, that your niece Beatrice was in love with Signior Benedick?

CLAUD.   O, ay: stalk on, stalk on; the fowl sits. I did never think that lady would have loved any man.

LEON.   No, nor I neither; but most wonderful that she should so dote on Signior Benedick, whom she hath in all outward behaviours seemed ever to abhor.

BENE.   Is't possible? Sits the wind in that corner?

LEON.   By my troth, my lord, I cannot tell what to think of it, but that she loves him with an enraged affection; it is past the infinite of thought.

D. PEDRO.   May be she doth but counterfeit.

CLAUD.   Faith, like enough.

---

2. *leavy*] full of leaves.
3. *An*] if.

LEON.   O God, counterfeit! There was never counterfeit of passion
    came so near the life of passion as she discovers it.

D. PEDRO.   Why, what effects of passion shows she?

CLAUD.   Bait the hook well; this fish will bite.

LEON.   What effects, my lord? She will sit you, you heard my daughter
    tell you how.

CLAUD.   She did, indeed.

D. PEDRO.   How, how, I pray you? You amaze me: I would have
    thought her spirit had been invincible against all assaults of affec-
    tion.

LEON.   I would have sworn it had, my lord; especially against Be-
    nedick.

BENE.   I should think this a gull,[4] but that the white-bearded fellow
    speaks it: knavery cannot, sure, hide himself in such reverence.

CLAUD.   He hath ta'en the infection: hold it up.

D. PEDRO.   Hath she made her affection known to Benedick?

LEON.   No; and swears she never will: that's her torment.

CLAUD.   'Tis true, indeed; so your daughter says: 'Shall I,' says she,
    'that have so oft encountered him with scorn, write to him that I
    love him?'

LEON.   This says she now when she is beginning to write to him; for
    she'll be up twenty times a night; and there will she sit in her smock
    till she have writ a sheet of paper: my daughter tells us all.

CLAUD.   Now you talk of a sheet of paper, I remember a pretty jest your
    daughter told us of.

LEON.   O, when she had writ it, and was reading it over, she found
    Benedick and Beatrice between the sheet?

CLAUD.   That.

LEON.   O, she tore the letter into a thousand halfpence; railed at her-
    self, that she should be so immodest to write to one that she knew
    would flout her; 'I measure him,' says she, 'by my own spirit; for I
    should flout him, if he writ to me; yea, though I love him, I should.'

CLAUD.   Then down upon her knees she falls, weeps, sobs, beats her
    heart, tears her hair, prays, curses; 'O sweet Benedick! God give me
    patience!'

---

4. *gull*] trick.

LEON.   She doth indeed; my daughter says so: and the ecstasy hath so much overborne her, that my daughter is sometime afeard she will do a desperate outrage to herself: it is very true.

D. PEDRO.   It were good that Benedick knew of it by some other, if she will not discover it.

CLAUD.   To what end? He would make but a sport of it, and torment the poor lady worse.

D. PEDRO.   An he should, it were an alms to hang him. She's an excellent sweet lady; and, out of all suspicion, she is virtuous.

CLAUD.   And she is exceeding wise.

D. PEDRO.   In every thing but in loving Benedick.

LEON.   O, my lord, wisdom and blood combating in so tender a body, we have ten proofs to one that blood hath the victory. I am sorry for her, as I have just cause, being her uncle and her guardian.

D. PEDRO.   I would she had bestowed this dotage on me: I would have daffed[5] all other respects, and made her half myself. I pray you, tell Benedick of it, and hear what a' will say.

LEON.   Were it good, think you?

CLAUD.   Hero thinks surely she will die; for she says she will die, if he love her not; and she will die, ere she make her love known; and she will die, if he woo her, rather than she will bate one breath of her accustomed crossness.

D. PEDRO.   She doth well: if she should make tender[6] of her love, 'tis very possible he'll scorn it; for the man, as you know all, hath a contemptible spirit.

CLAUD.   He is a very proper man.

D. PEDRO.   He hath indeed a good outward happiness.

CLAUD.   Before God! and in my mind, very wise.

D. PEDRO.   He doth indeed show some sparks that are like wit.

CLAUD.   And I take him to be valiant.

D. PEDRO.   As Hector, I assure you: and in the managing of quarrels you may say he is wise; for either he avoids them with great discretion, or undertakes them with a most Christian-like fear.

LEON.   If he do fear God, a' must necessarily keep peace: if he break the peace, he ought to enter into a quarrel with fear and trembling.

---

5. *daffed*] doffed, put aside.
6. *tender*] an offer for acceptance.

D. PEDRO.   And so will he do; for the man doth fear God, howsoever it
    seems not in him by some large jests he will make. Well, I am sorry
    for your niece. Shall we go seek Benedick, and tell him of her love?
CLAUD.   Never tell him, my lord: let her wear it out with good counsel.
LEON.   Nay, that's impossible: she may wear her heart out first.
D. PEDRO.   Well, we will hear further of it by your daughter: let it cool
    the while. I love Benedick well; and I could wish he would modestly
    examine himself, to see how much he is unworthy so good a lady.
LEON.   My lord, will you walk? dinner is ready.
CLAUD.   If he do not dote on her upon this, I will never trust my
    expectation.
D. PEDRO.   Let there be the same net spread for her; and that must
    your daughter and her gentlewomen carry. The sport will be, when
    they hold one an opinion of another's dotage, and no such matter:
    that's the scene that I would see, which will be merely a dumb-
    show. Let us send her to call him in to dinner.

                    [*Exeunt* DON PEDRO, CLAUDIO, *and* LEONATO.]

BENE.   [*Coming forward*] This can be no trick: the conference was sadly
    borne. They have the truth of this from Hero. They seem to pity the
    lady: it seems her affections have their full bent. Love me! why, it
    must be requited. I hear how I am censured: they say I will bear
    myself proudly, if I perceive the love come from her; they say too that
    she will rather die than give any sign of affection. I did never think to
    marry: I must not seem proud: happy are they that hear their detrac-
    tions, and can put them to mending. They say the lady is fair, — 'tis a
    truth, I can bear them witness; and virtuous, — 'tis so, I cannot re-
    prove it; and wise, but for loving me, — by my troth, it is no addition to
    her wit, nor no great argument of her folly, for I will be horribly in
    love with her. I may chance have some odd quirks and remnants of
    wit broken on me, because I have railed so long against marriage: but
    doth not the appetite alter? a man loves the meat in his youth that he
    cannot endure in his age. Shall quips and sentences and these paper
    bullets[7] of the brain awe a man from the career of his humour? No,
    the world must be peopled. When I said I would die a bachelor, I did
    not think I should live till I were married. Here comes Beatrice. By
    this day! she's a fair lady: I do spy some marks of love in her.

---

7. *paper bullets*] epigrams from books.

Enter BEATRICE.

BEAT.   Against my will I am sent to bid you come in to dinner.

BENE.   Fair Beatrice, I thank you for your pains.

BEAT.   I took no more pains for those thanks than you take pains to thank me: if it had been painful, I would not have come.

BENE.   You take pleasure, then, in the message?

BEAT.   Yea, just so much as you may take upon a knife's point, and choke a daw withal. You have no stomach, signior: fare you well.

[*Exit.*]

BENE.   Ha! 'Against my will I am sent to bid you come in to dinner;' there's a double meaning in that. 'I took no more pains for those thanks than you took pains to thank me;' that's as much as to say, Any pains that I take for you is as easy as thanks. If I do not take pity of her, I am a villain; if I do not love her, I am a Jew. I will go get her picture.

[*Exit.*]

ACT III.

Scene I. Leonato's *orchard*.

Enter Hero, Margaret, *and* Ursula.

Hero.   Good Margaret, run thee to the parlour;
  There shalt thou find my cousin Beatrice
  Proposing with the prince and Claudio:
  Whisper her ear, and tell her, I and Ursula
  Walk in the orchard, and our whole discourse
  Is all of her; say that thou overheard'st us;
  And bid her steal into the pleached bower,
  Where honeysuckles, ripen'd by the sun,
  Forbid the sun to enter; like favourites,
  Made proud by princes, that advance their pride
  Against that power that bred it: there will she hide her,
  To listen our propose. This is thy office;
  Bear thee well in it, and leave us alone.
Marg.   I'll make her come, I warrant you, presently.   [*Exit.*]
Hero.   Now, Ursula, when Beatrice doth come,
  As we do trace this alley up and down,
  Our talk must only be of Benedick.
  When I do name him, let it be thy part
  To praise him more than ever man did merit:
  My talk to thee must be, how Benedick
  Is sick in love with Beatrice. Of this matter
  Is little Cupid's crafty arrow made,
  That only wounds by hearsay.

Enter BEATRICE, *behind.*

                                   Now begin;
    For look where Beatrice, like a lapwing, runs
    Close by the ground, to hear our conference.
URS.   The pleasant'st angling is to see the fish
    Cut with her golden oars the silver stream,
    And greedily devour the treacherous bait:
    So angle we for Beatrice; who even now
    Is couched in the woodbine coverture.
    Fear you not my part of the dialogue.
HERO.   Then go we near her, that her ear lose nothing
    Of the false sweet bait that we lay for it.

                              [Approaching the bower.]

    No, truly, Ursula, she is too disdainful;
    I know her spirits are as coy and wild
    As haggerds[1] of the rock.
URS.   But are you sure
    That Benedick loves Beatrice so entirely?
HERO.   So says the prince and my new-trothed lord.
URS.   And did they bid you tell her of it, madam?
HERO.   They did entreat me to acquaint her of it;
    But I persuaded them, if they loved Benedick,
    To wish him wrestle with affection,
    And never to let Beatrice know of it.
URS.   Why did you so? Doth not the gentleman
    Deserve as full as fortunate a bed
    As ever Beatrice shall couch upon?
HERO.   O god of love! I know he doth deserve
    As much as may be yielded to a man:
    But Nature never framed a woman's heart
    Of prouder stuff than that of Beatrice;
    Disdain and scorn ride sparkling in her eyes,
    Misprising what they look on; and her wit
    Values itself so highly, that to her
    All matter else seems weak: she cannot love,

---

1. *haggerds*] haggards; wild, untrained hawks.

> Nor take no shape nor project of affection,
> She is so self-endeared.

URS.   Sure, I think so;
> And therefore certainly it were not good
> She knew his love, lest she make sport at it.

HERO.   Why, you speak truth. I never yet saw man,
> How wise, how noble, young, how rarely featured,
> But she would spell him backward: if fair-faced,
> She would swear the gentleman should be her sister;
> If black, why, Nature, drawing of an antique,
> Made a foul blot; if tall, a lance ill-headed;
> If low, an agate very vilely cut;
> If speaking, why, a vane blown with all winds;
> If silent, why, a block moved with none.
> So turns she every man the wrong side out;
> And never gives to truth and virtue that
> Which simpleness and merit purchaseth.

URS.   Sure, sure, such carping is not commendable.

HERO.   No, not to be so odd, and from all fashions,
> As Beatrice is, cannot be commendable:
> But who dare tell her so? If I should speak,
> She would mock me into air; O, she would laugh me
> Out of myself, press me to death with wit!
> Therefore let Benedick, like cover'd fire,
> Consume away in sighs, waste inwardly:
> It were a better death than die with mocks,
> Which is as bad as die with tickling.

URS.   Yet tell her of it: hear what she will say.

HERO.   No; rather I will go to Benedick,
> And counsel him to fight against his passion.
> And, truly, I'll devise some honest slanders
> To stain my cousin with: one doth not know
> How much an ill word may empoison liking.

URS.   O, do not do your cousin such a wrong!
> She cannot be so much without true judgement,—
> Having so swift and excellent a wit
> As she is prized to have,—as to refuse
> So rare a gentleman as Signior Benedick.

HERO.   He is the only man of Italy,

Always excepted my dear Claudio.

URS. I pray you, be not angry with me, madam,
Speaking my fancy: Signior Benedick,
For shape, for bearing, argument and valour,
Goes foremost in report through Italy.

HERO. Indeed, he hath an excellent good name.

URS. His excellence did earn it, ere he had it.
When are you married, madam?

HERO. Why, every day, to-morrow. Come, go in:
I'll show thee some attires; and have thy counsel
Which is the best to furnish me to-morrow.

URS. She's limed,[2] I warrant you: we have caught her, madam.

HERO. If it prove so, then loving goes by haps:
Some Cupid kills with arrows, some with traps.

[*Exeunt* HERO *and* URSULA.]

BEAT. [*Coming forward*] What fire is in mine ears? Can this be true?
Stand I condemn'd for pride and scorn so much?
Contempt, farewell! and maiden pride, adieu!
No glory lives behind the back of such.
And, Benedick, love on; I will requite thee,
Taming my wild heart to thy loving hand:
If thou dost love, my kindness shall incite thee
To bind our loves up in a holy band;
For others say thou dost deserve, and I
Believe it better than reportingly.

[*Exit.*]

SCENE II. *A room in* LEONATO'S *house.*

Enter DON PEDRO, CLAUDIO, BENEDICK, *and* LEONATO.

D. PEDRO. I do but stay till your marriage be consummate, and then
go I toward Arragon.

CLAUD. I'll bring you thither, my lord, if you'll vouchsafe me.

---

2. *limed*] trapped, ensnared as a bird with birdlime, a glutinous substance used to catch
birds.

D. PEDRO.   Nay, that would be as great a soil in the new gloss of your marriage, as to show a child his new coat and forbid him to wear it. I will only be bold with Benedick for his company; for, from the crown of his head to the sole of his foot, he is all mirth: he hath twice or thrice cut Cupid's bow-string, and the little hangman dare not shoot at him; he hath a heart as sound as a bell, and his tongue is the clapper, for what his heart thinks his tongue speaks.

BENE.   Gallants, I am not as I have been.

LEON.   So say I: methinks you are sadder.

CLAUD.   I hope he be in love.

D. PEDRO.   Hang him, truant! there's no true drop of blood in him, to be truly touched with love; if he be sad, he wants money.

BENE.   I have the toothache.

D. PEDRO.   Draw it.

BENE.   Hang it!

CLAUD.   You must hang it first, and draw it afterwards.[1]

D. PEDRO.   What! sigh for the toothache?

LEON.   Where is but a humour or a worm.

BENE.   Well, every one can master a grief but he that has it.

CLAUD.   Yet say I, he is in love.

D. PEDRO.   There is no appearance of fancy in him, unless it be a fancy that he hath to strange disguises; as, to be a Dutchman to-day, a Frenchman to-morrow; or in the shape of two countries at once, as, a German from the waist downward, all slops,[2] and a Spaniard from the hip upward, no doublet. Unless he have a fancy to this foolery, as it appears he hath, he is no fool for fancy, as you would have it appear he is.

CLAUD.   If he be not in love with some woman, there is no believing old signs: a' brushes his hat o' mornings; what should that bode?

D. PEDRO.   Hath any man seen him at the barber's?

CLAUD.   No, but the barber's man hath been seen with him; and the old ornament of his cheek hath already stuffed tennis-balls.

LEON.   Indeed, he looks younger than he did, by the loss of a beard.

---

1. *You must hang . . . afterwards*] an allusion to the punishment of "drawing," i.e., disembowelment, which followed hanging and preceded "quartering" (dividing the body into four parts) in convictions of treason.

2. *slops*] loose, ill-fitting trousers.

D. PEDRO. Nay, a' rubs himself with civet:[3] can you smell him out by that?

CLAUD. That's as much as to say, the sweet youth's in love.

D. PEDRO. The greatest note of it is his melancholy.

CLAUD. And when was he wont to wash his face?

D. PEDRO. Yea, or to paint himself? for the which, I hear what they say of him.

CLAUD. Nay, but his jesting spirit; which is now crept into a lute-string, and now governed by stops.[4]

D. PEDRO. Indeed, that tells a heavy tale for him: conclude, conclude he is in love.

CLAUD. Nay, but I know who loves him.

D. PEDRO. That would I know too: I warrant, one that knows him not.

CLAUD. Yes, and his ill conditions; and, in despite of all, dies for him.

D. PEDRO. She shall be buried with her face upwards.

BENE. Yet is this no charm for the toothache. Old signior, walk aside with me: I have studied eight or nine wise words to speak to you, which these hobby-horses must not hear.

> [*Exeunt* BENEDICK *and* LEONATO.]

D. PEDRO. For my life, to break with him about Beatrice.

CLAUD. 'Tis even so. Hero and Margaret have by this played their parts with Beatrice; and then the two bears will not bite one another when they meet.

Enter DON JOHN.

D. JOHN. My lord and brother, God save you!

D. PEDRO. Good den,[5] brother.

D. JOHN. If your leisure served, I would speak with you.

D. PEDRO. In private?

D. JOHN. If it please you: yet Count Claudio may hear; for what I would speak of concerns him.

D. PEDRO. What's the matter?

D. JOHN. [*To* CLAUDIO] Means your lordship to be married to-morrow?

---

3. *civet*] a perfume from the civet-cat.
4. *stops*] marks on the lute's fingerboard that indicate where the fingers should be pressed to produce various notes.
5. *den*] abbreviation for evening.

D. PEDRO.   You know he does.

D. JOHN.   I know not that, when he knows what I know.

CLAUD.   If there be any impediment, I pray you discover it.

D. JOHN.   You may think I love you not: let that appear hereafter, and aim better at me by that I now will manifest. For my brother, I think he holds you well, and in dearness of heart hath holp to effect your ensuing marriage,—surely suit ill spent and labour ill bestowed.

D. PEDRO.   Why, what's the matter?

D. JOHN.   I came hither to tell you; and, circumstances shortened, for she has been too long a talking of, the lady is disloyal.

CLAUD.   Who, Hero?

D. JOHN.   Even she; Leonato's Hero, your Hero, every man's Hero.

CLAUD.   Disloyal?

D. JOHN.   The word is too good to paint out her wickedness; I could say she were worse: think you of a worse title, and I will fit her to it. Wonder not till further warrant: go but with me to-night, you shall see her chamber-window entered, even the night before her wedding-day: if you love her then, to-morrow wed her; but it would better fit your honour to change your mind.

CLAUD.   May this be so?

D. PEDRO.   I will not think it.

D. JOHN.   If you dare not trust that you see, confess not that you know: if you will follow me, I will show you enough; and when you have seen more, and heard more, proceed accordingly.

CLAUD.   If I see any thing to-night why I should not marry her to-morrow, in the congregation, where I should wed, there will I shame her.

D. PEDRO.   And, as I wooed for thee to obtain her, I will join with thee to disgrace her.

D. JOHN.   I will disparage her no farther till you are my witnesses: bear it coldly but till midnight, and let the issue show itself.

D. PEDRO.   O day untowardly turned!

CLAUD.   O mischief strangely thwarting!

D. JOHN.   O plague right well prevented! so will you say when you have seen the sequel.   [*Exeunt.*]

SCENE III. *A street*.

Enter DOGBERRY *and* VERGES *with the* Watch.

DOG.   Are you good men and true?

VERG.   Yea, or else it were pity but they should suffer salvation, body and soul.

DOG.   Nay, that were a punishment too good for them, if they should have any allegiance in them, being chosen for the prince's watch.

VERG.   Well, give them their charge, neighbour Dogberry.

DOG.   First, who think you the most desartless man to be constable?

FIRST WATCH.   Hugh Otecake, sir, or George Seacole; for they can write and read.

DOG.   Come hither, neighbour Seacole. God hath blessed you with a good name: to be a well-favoured man is the gift of fortune; but to write and read comes by nature.

SEC. WATCH.   Both which, master constable,—

DOG.   You have: I knew it would be your answer. Well, for your favour, sir, why, give God thanks, and make no boast of it; and for your writing and reading, let that appear when there is no need of such vanity. You are thought here to be the most senseless[1] and fit man for the constable of the watch; therefore bear you the lantern. This is your charge: you shall comprehend[2] all vagrom[3] men; you are to bid any man stand, in the prince's name.

SEC. WATCH.   How if a' will not stand?

DOG.   Why, then, take no note of him, but let him go; and presently call the rest of the watch together, and thank God you are rid of a knave.

VERG. . If he will not stand when he is bidden, he is none of the prince's subjects.

---

1. *senseless*] i.e., sensible.
2. *comprehend*] i.e., apprehend.
3. *vagrom*] i.e., vagrant.

Dog. True, and they are to meddle with none but the prince's subjects. You shall also make no noise in the streets; for for the watch to
babble and to talk is most tolerable[4] and not to be endured.

Watch. We will rather sleep than talk: we know what belongs to a
watch.

Dog. Why, you speak like an ancient and most quiet watchman; for I
cannot see how sleeping should offend: only, have a care that your
bills[5] be not stolen. Well, you are to call at all the ale-houses, and
bid those that are drunk get them to bed.

Watch. How if they will not?

Dog. Why, then, let them alone till they are sober: if they make you
not then the better answer, you may say they are not the men you
took them for.

Watch. Well, sir.

Dog. If you meet a thief, you may suspect him, by virtue of your
office, to be no true man; and, for such kind of men, the less you
meddle or make with them, why, the more is for your honesty.

Watch. If we know him to be a thief, shall we not lay hands on him?

Dog. Truly, by your office, you may; but I think they that touch pitch
will be defiled: the most peaceable way for you, if you do take a thief,
is to let him show himself what he is, and steal out of your company.

Verg. You have been always called a merciful man, partner.

Dog. Truly, I would not hang a dog by my will, much more a man
who hath any honesty in him.

Verg. If you hear a child cry in the night, you must call to the nurse
and bid her still it.

Watch. How if the nurse be asleep and will not hear us?

Dog. Why, then, depart in peace, and let the child wake her with
crying; for the ewe that will not hear her lamb when it baes will
never answer a calf when he bleats.

Verg. 'Tis very true.

Dog. This is the end of the charge:—you, constable, are to present
the prince's own person: if you meet the prince in the night, you
may stay him.

---

4. *tolerable*] i.e., intolerable.
5. *bills*] a kind of pike or halbert.

VERG. Nay, by'r lady, that I think a' cannot.

DOG. Five shillings to one on't, with any man that knows the statues, he may stay him: marry, not without the prince be willing; for, indeed, the watch ought to offend no man; and it is an offence to stay a man against his will.

VERG. By'r lady, I think it be so.

DOG. Ha, ah, ha! Well, masters, good night: an there be any matter of weight chances, call up me: keep your fellows' counsels and your own; and good night. Come, neighbour.

WATCH. Well, masters, we hear our charge: let us go sit here upon the church-bench till two, and then all to bed.

DOG. One word more, honest neighbours. I pray you, watch about Signior Leonato's door; for the wedding being there to-morrow, there is a great coil to-night. Adieu: be vigitant,[6] I beseech you.

[*Exeunt* DOGBERRY *and* VERGES.]

Enter BORACHIO *and* CONRADE.

BORA. What, Conrade!

WATCH. [*Aside*] Peace! stir not.

BORA. Conrade, I say!

CON. Here, man; I am at thy elbow.

BORA. Mass, and my elbow itched; I thought there would a scab follow.

CON. I will owe thee an answer for that: and now forward with thy tale.

BORA. Stand thee close, then, under this pent-house, for it drizzles rain; and I will, like a true drunkard, utter all to thee.

WATCH. [*Aside*] Some treason, masters: yet stand close.

BORA. Therefore know I have earned of Don John a thousand ducats.

CON. Is it possible that any villany should be so dear?

BORA. Thou shouldst rather ask, if it were possible any villany should be so rich; for when rich villains have need of poor ones, poor ones may make what price they will.

CON. I wonder at it.

BORA. That shows thou art unconfirmed. Thou knowest that the fashion of a doublet, or a hat, or a cloak, is nothing to a man.

---

6. *vigitant*] i.e., vigilant.

CON. Yes, it is apparel.

BORA. I mean, the fashion.

CON. Yes, the fashion is the fashion.

BORA. Tush! I may as well say the fool's the fool. But seest thou not what a deformed thief this fashion is?

WATCH. [*Aside*] I know that Deformed; a' has been a vile thief this seven year; a' goes up and down like a gentleman: I remember his name.

BORA. Didst thou not hear somebody?

CON. No; 'twas the vane on the house.

BORA. Seest thou not, I say, what a deformed thief this fashion is? how giddily a' turns about all the hot bloods between fourteen and five-and-thirty? sometimes fashioning them like Pharaoh's soldiers in the reechy[7] painting, sometime like god Bel's priests in the old church-window, sometime like the shaven Hercules in the smirched worm-eaten tapestry, where his codpiece seems as massy as his club?

CON. All this I see; and I see that the fashion wears out more apparel than the man. But art not thou thyself giddy with the fashion too, that thou hast shifted out of thy tale into telling me of the fashion?

BORA. Not so, neither: but know that I have to-night wooed Margaret, the Lady Hero's gentlewoman, by the name of Hero: she leans me out at her mistress' chamber-window, bids me a thousand times good night, — I tell this tale vilely: — I should first tell thee how the prince, Claudio and my master, planted and placed and possessed by my master Don John, saw afar off in the orchard this amiable encounter.

CON. And thought they Margaret was Hero?

BORA. Two of them did, the prince and Claudio; but the devil my master knew she was Margaret; and partly by his oaths, which first possessed them, partly by the dark night, which did deceive them, but chiefly by my villany, which did confirm any slander that Don John had made, away went Claudio enraged; swore he would meet her, as he was appointed, next morning at the temple, and there, before the whole congregation, shame her with what he saw o'er night, and send her home again without a husband.

---

7. *reechy*] dirty, filthy.

FIRST WATCH. We charge you, in the prince's name, stand!

SEC. WATCH. Call up the right master constable. We have here recovered the most dangerous piece of lechery that ever was known in the commonwealth.

FIRST WATCH. And one Deformed is one of them: I know him; a' wears a lock.[8]

CON. Masters, masters,—

SEC. WATCH. You'll be made bring Deformed forth, I warrant you.

CON. Masters,—

FIRST WATCH. Never speak: we charge you let us obey you to go with us.

BORA. We are like to prove a goodly commodity, being taken up of these men's bills.

CON. A commodity in question, I warrant you. Come, we'll obey you.

[*Exeunt.*]

SCENE IV. HERO'S *apartment.*

Enter HERO, MARGARET, *and* URSULA.

HERO. Good Ursula, wake my cousin Beatrice, and desire her to rise.

URS. I will, lady.

HERO. And bid her come hither.

URS. Well. [*Exit.*]

MARG. Troth, I think your other rabato[1] were better.

HERO. No, pray thee, good Meg, I'll wear this.

MARG. By my troth's not so good; and I warrant your cousin will say so.

HERO. My cousin's a fool, and thou art another: I'll wear none but this.

---

8. *lock*] a "love-lock": a ringlet of hair tied with a ribbon worn near the left ear by young men about town.

1. *rabato*] the word is used both for a ruff (stiff collar) and for the wire-support of the ruff.

MARG.   I like the new tire[2] within excellently, if the hair were a thought browner; and your gown's a most rare fashion, i' faith. I saw the Duchess of Milan's gown that they praise so.

HERO.   O, that exceeds, they say.

MARG.   By my troth's but a night-gown in respect of yours,—cloth o' gold, and cuts, and laced with silver, set with pearls, down sleeves, side sleeves, and skirts, round underborne with a bluish tinsel: but for a fine, quaint, graceful and excellent fashion, yours is worth ten on't.

HERO.   God give me joy to wear it! for my heart is exceeding heavy.

MARG.   'Twill be heavier soon by the weight of a man.

HERO.   Fie upon thee! art not ashamed?

MARG.   Of what, lady? of speaking honourably? Is not marriage honourable in a beggar? Is not your lord honourable without marriage? I think you would have me say, 'saving your reverence, a husband:' an bad thinking do not wrest true speaking, I'll offend nobody: is there any harm in 'the heavier for a husband'? None, I think, an it be the right husband and the right wife; otherwise 'tis light, and not heavy: ask my Lady Beatrice else; here she comes.

Enter BEATRICE.

HERO.   Good morrow, coz.

BEAT.   Good morrow, sweet Hero.

HERO.   Why, how now? do you speak in the sick tune?

BEAT.   I am out of all other tune, methinks.

MARG.   Clap's into 'Light o' love;' that goes without a burden: do you sing it, and I'll dance it.

BEAT.   Ye light o' love, with your heels! then, if your husband have stables enough, you'll see he shall lack no barns.

MARG.   O illegitimate construction! I scorn that with my heels.

BEAT.   'Tis almost five o'clock, cousin; 'tis time you were ready. By my troth, I am exceeding ill: heigh-ho!

MARG.   For a hawk, a horse, or a husband?

BEAT.   For the letter that begins them all, H.

---

2. *tire*] headdress or cap to which false hair was attached.

MARG. Well, an you be not turned Turk, there's no more sailing by the star.

BEAT. What means the fool, trow?

MARG. Nothing I; but God send every one their heart's desire!

HERO. These gloves the count sent me; they are an excellent perfume.

BEAT. I am stuffed, cousin; I cannot smell.

MARG. A maid, and stuffed! there's goodly catching of cold.

BEAT. O, God help me! God help me! how long have you professed apprehension?

MARG. Ever since you left it. Doth not my wit become me rarely?

BEAT. It is not seen enough, you should wear it in your cap. By my troth, I am sick.

MARG. Get you some of this distilled Carduus Benedictus, and lay it to your heart: it is the only thing for a qualm.

HERO. There thou prickest her with a thistle.

BEAT. Benedictus! why Benedictus? you have some moral in this Benedictus.

MARG. Moral! no, by my troth, I have no moral meaning; I meant, plain holy-thistle. You may think perchance that I think you are in love: nay, by'r lady, I am not such a fool to think what I list; nor I list not to think what I can; nor, indeed, I cannot think, if I would think my heart out of thinking, that you are in love, or that you will be in love, or that you can be in love. Yet Benedick was such another, and now is he become a man: he swore he would never marry; and yet now, in despite of his heart, he eats his meat without grudging: and how you may be converted, I know not; but methinks you look with your eyes as other women do.

BEAT. What pace is this that thy tongue keeps?

MARG. Not a false gallop.

Re-enter URSULA.

URS. Madam, withdraw: the prince, the count, Signior Benedick, Don John, and all the gallants of the town, are come to fetch you to church.

HERO. Help to dress me, good coz, good Meg, good Ursula. [*Exeunt.*]

SCENE V. *Another room in* LEONATO'S *house.*

Enter LEONATO, *with* DOGBERRY *and* VERGES.

LEON.   What would you with me, honest neighbour?

DOG.   Marry, sir, I would have some confidence[1] with you that decerns[2] you nearly.

LEON.   Brief, I pray you; for you see it is a busy time with me.

DOG.   Marry, this it is, sir.

VERG.   Yes, in truth it is, sir.

LEON.   What is it, my good friends?

DOG.   Goodman Verges, sir, speaks a little off the matter: an old man,
sir, and his wits are not so blunt as, God help, I would desire they
were; but, in faith, honest as the skin between his brows.

VERG.   Yes, I thank God I am as honest as any man living that is an old
man and no honester than I.

DOG.   Comparisons are odorous:[3] palabras,[4] neighbour Verges.

LEON.   Neighbours, you are tedious.

DOG.   It pleases your worship to say so, but we are the poor duke's
officers; but truly, for mine own part, if I were as tedious as a king, I
could find in my heart to bestow it all of your worship.

LEON.   All thy tediousness on me, ah?

DOG.   Yea, an 'twere a thousand pound more than 'tis; for I hear as
good exclamation[5] on your worship as of any man in the city; and
though I be but a poor man, I am glad to hear it.

VERG.   And so am I.

LEON.   I would fain know what you have to say.

---

1. *confidence*] probably for "conference."
2. *decerns*] i.e., concerns.
3. *odorous*] i.e., odious.
4. *palabras*] *pocas palabras*, few words.
5. *exclamation*] possibly for "acclamation."

VERG.　Marry, sir, our watch to-night, excepting your worship's presence, ha' ta'en a couple of as arrant knaves as any in Messina.

DOG.　A good old man, sir; he will be talking: as they say, When the age is in, the wit is out: God help us! it is a world to see. Well said, i' faith, neighbour Verges: well, God's a good man; an two men ride of a horse, one must ride behind. An honest soul, i' faith, sir; by my troth he is, as ever broke bread; but God is to be worshipped; all men are not alike; alas, good neighbour!

LEON.　Indeed, neighbour, he comes too short of you.

DOG.　Gifts that God gives.

LEON.　I must leave you.

DOG.　One word, sir: our watch, sir, have indeed comprehended two aspicious[6] persons, and we would have them this morning examined before your worship.

LEON.　Take their examination yourself, and bring it me: I am now in great haste, as it may appear unto you.

DOG.　It shall be suffigance.[7]

LEON.　Drink some wine ere you go: fare you well.

Enter a Messenger.

MESS.　My lord, they stay for you to give your daughter to her husband.

LEON.　I'll wait upon them: I am ready.

[*Exeunt* LEONATO *and* MESSENGER.]

DOG.　Go, good partner, go, get you to Francis[8] Seacole; bid him bring his pen and inkhorn to the gaol: we are now to examination these men.

VERG.　And we must do it wisely.

DOG.　We will spare for no wit, I warrant you; here's that shall drive some of them to a noncome: only get the learned writer to set down our excommunication, and meet me at the gaol.　　　[*Exeunt.*]

---

6. *aspicious*] i.e., suspicious.
7. *suffigance*] i.e., sufficient.
8. *Francis*] earlier, Seacole's first name is given as George (Act III, scene iii).

ACT IV.

Scene I. *A church.*

Enter Don Pedro, Don John, Leonato, Friar Francis, Claudio, Benedick, Hero, Beatrice, *and* Attendants.

Leon. Come, Friar Francis, be brief; only to the plain form of marriage, and you shall recount their particular duties afterwards.

Friar. You come hither, my lord, to marry this lady.

Claud. No.

Leon. To be married to her: friar, you come to marry her.

Friar. Lady, you come hither to be married to this count.

Hero. I do.

Friar. If either of you know any inward impediment why you should not be conjoined, I charge you, on your souls, to utter it.

Claud. Know you any, Hero?

Hero. None, my lord.

Friar. Know you any, count?

Leon. I dare make his answer, none.

Claud. O, what men dare do! what men may do! what men daily do, not knowing what they do!

Bene. How now! interjections? Why, then, some be of laughing, as, ah, ha, he!

Claud. Stand thee by, friar. Father, by your leave:
  Will you with free and unconstrained soul
  Give me this maid, your daughter?

Leon. As freely, son, as God did give her me.

Claud. And what have I to give you back, whose worth
  May counterpoise this rich and precious gift?

51

D. PEDRO. Nothing, unless you render her again.
CLAUD. Sweet prince, you learn me noble thankfulness.
  There, Leonato, take her back again:
  Give not this rotten orange to your friend;
  She's but the sign and semblance of her honour.
  Behold how like a maid she blushes here!
  O, what authority and show of truth
  Can cunning sin cover itself withal!
  Comes not that blood as modest evidence
  To witness simple virtue? Would you not swear,
  All you that see her, that she were a maid,
  By these exterior shows? But she is none:
  She knows the heat of a luxurious bed;
  Her blush is guiltiness, not modesty.
LEON. What do you mean, my lord?
CLAUD.   Not to be married,
  Not to knit my soul to an approved wanton.
LEON. Dear my lord, if you, in your own proof,
  Have vanquish'd the resistance of her youth,
  And made defeat of her virginity,—
CLAUD. I know what you would say: if I have known her,
  You will say she did embrace me as a husband,
  And so extenuate the 'forehand sin:
  No, Leonato,
  I never tempted her with word too large;
  But, as a brother to his sister, show'd
  Bashful sincerity and comely love.
HERO. And seem'd I ever otherwise to you?
CLAUD. Out on thee! Seeming! I will write against it:
  You seem to me as Dian in her orb,
  As chaste as is the bud ere it be blown;
  But you are more intemperate in your blood
  Than Venus, or those pamper'd animals
  That rage in savage sensuality.
HERO. Is my lord well, that he doth speak so wide?
LEON. Sweet prince, why speak not you?
D. PEDRO.   What should I speak?
  I stand dishonour'd, that have gone about

To link my dear friend to a common stale.[1]
LEON.   Are these things spoken, or do I but dream?
D. JOHN.   Sir, they are spoken, and these things are true.
BENE.   This looks not like a nuptial.
HERO.   True! O God!
CLAUD.   Leonato, stand I here?
    Is this the prince? is this the prince's brother?
    Is this face Hero's? are our eyes our own?
LEON.   All this is so: but what of this, my lord?
CLAUD.   Let me but move one question to your daughter;
    And, by that fatherly and kindly power
    That you have in her, bid her answer truly.
LEON.   I charge thee do so, as thou art my child.
HERO.   O, God defend me! how am I beset!
    What kind of catechising call you this?
CLAUD.   To make you answer truly to your name.
HERO.   Is it not Hero? Who can blot that name
    With any just reproach?
CLAUD.   Marry, that can Hero;
    Hero itself can blot out Hero's virtue.
    What man was he talk'd with you yesternight
    Out at your window betwixt twelve and one?
    Now, if you are a maid, answer to this.
HERO.   I talk'd with no man at that hour, my lord.
D. PEDRO.   Why, then are you no maiden. Leonato,
    I am sorry you must hear: upon mine honour,
    Myself, my brother, and this grieved count
    Did see her, hear her, at that hour last night
    Talk with a ruffian at her chamber-window;
    Who hath indeed, most like a liberal villain,
    Confess'd the vile encounters they have had
    A thousand times in secret.
D. JOHN.   Fie, fie! they are not to be named, my lord,
    Not to be spoke of;

---

1. *stale*] something worn out by use; i.e., a prostitute.

    There is not chastity enough in language,
    Without offence to utter them. Thus, pretty lady,
    I am sorry for thy much misgovernment.
CLAUD.   O Hero, what a Hero hadst thou been,
    If half thy outward graces had been placed
    About thy thoughts and counsels of thy heart!
    But fare thee well, most foul, most fair! farewell,
    Thou pure impiety and impious purity!
    For thee I'll lock up all the gates of love,
    And on my eyelids shall conjecture hang,
    To turn all beauty into thoughts of harm,
    And never shall it more be gracious.
LEON.   Hath no man's dagger here a point for me?   [HERO *swoons.*]
BEAT.   Why, how now, cousin! wherefore sink you down?
D. JOHN.   Come, let us go. These things, come thus to light,
    Smother her spirits up.
                [Exeunt DON PEDRO, DON JOHN, *and* CLAUDIO.]
BENE.   How doth the lady?
BEAT.   Dead, I think. Help, uncle!
    Hero! why, Hero! Uncle! Signior Benedick! Friar!
LEON.   O Fate! take not away thy heavy hand.
    Death is the fairest cover for her shame
    That may be wish'd for.
BEAT.   How now, cousin Hero!
FRIAR.   Have comfort, lady.
LEON.   Dost thou look up?
FRIAR.   Yea, wherefore should she not?
LEON.   Wherefore! Why, doth not every earthly thing
    Cry shame upon her? Could she here deny
    The story that is printed in her blood?
    Do not live, Hero; do not ope thine eyes:
    For, did I think thou wouldst not quickly die,
    Thought I thy spirits were stronger than thy shames,
    Myself would, on the rearward of reproaches,
    Strike at thy life. Grieved I, I had but one?
    Chid I for that at frugal nature's frame?
    O, one too much by thee! Why had I one?
    Why ever wast thou lovely in my eyes?

Why had I not with charitable hand
Took up a beggar's issue at my gates,
Who smirched thus and mired with infamy,
I might have said, 'No part of it is mine;
This shame derives itself from unknown loins'?
But mine, and mine I loved, and mine I praised,
And mine that I was proud on, mine so much
That I myself was to myself not mine,
Valuing of her,—why, she, O, she is fallen
Into a pit of ink, that the wide sea
Hath drops too few to wash her clean again,
And salt too little which may season give
To her foul-tainted flesh!

BENE.   Sir, sir, be patient.
For my part, I am so attired in wonder,
I know not what to say.

BEAT.   O, on my soul, my cousin is belied!

BENE.   Lady, were you her bedfellow last night?

BEAT.   No, truly, not; although, until last night,
I have this twelvemonth been her bedfellow.

LEON.   Confirm'd, confirm'd! O, that is stronger made
Which was before barr'd up with ribs of iron!
Would the two princes lie, and Claudio lie,
Who loved her so, that, speaking of her foulness,
Wash'd it with tears? Hence from her! let her die.

FRIAR. Hear me a little;
For I have only been silent so long,
And given way unto this course of fortune,
By noting of the lady: I have mark'd
A thousand blushing apparitions
To start into her face; a thousand innocent shames
In angel whiteness beat away those blushes;
And in her eye there hath appear'd a fire,
To burn the errors that these princes hold
Against her maiden truth. Call me a fool;
Trust not my reading nor my observations,
Which with experimental seal doth warrant
The tenour of my book; trust not my age,

    My reverence, calling, nor divinity,
    If this sweet lady lie not guiltless here
    Under some biting error.
LEON.   Friar, it cannot be.
    Thou seest that all the grace that she hath left
    Is that she will not add to her damnation
    A sin of perjury; she not denies it:
    Why seek'st thou, then, to cover with excuse
    That which appears in proper nakedness?
FRIAR.   Lady, what man is he you are accused of?
HERO.   They know that do accuse me; I know none:
    If I know more of any man alive
    Than that which maiden modesty doth warrant,
    Let all my sins lack mercy! O my father,
    Prove you that any man with me conversed
    At hours unmeet, or that I yesternight
    Maintain'd the change of words with any creature,
    Refuse me, hate me, torture me to death!
FRIAR.   There is some strange misprision in the princes.
BENE.   Two of them have the very bent of honour;
    And if their wisdoms be misled in this,
    The practice of it lives in John the bastard,
    Whose spirits toil in frame of villanies.
LEON.   I know not. If they speak but truth of her,
    These hands shall tear her; if they wrong her honour,
    The proudest of them shall well hear of it.
    Time hath not yet so dried this blood of mine,
    Nor age so eat up my invention,
    Nor fortune made such havoc of my means,
    Nor my bad life reft me so much of friends,
    But they shall find, awaked in such a kind,
    Both strength of limb and policy of mind,
    Ability in means and choice of friends,
    To quit me of them thoroughly.
FRIAR.   Pause awhile,
    And let my counsel sway you in this case.
    Your daughter here the princes left for dead:
    Let her awhile be secretly kept in,

And publish it that she is dead indeed;
Maintain a mourning ostentation,
And on your family's old monument
Hang mournful epitaphs, and do all rites
That appertain unto a burial.

LEON. What shall become of this? what will this do?

FRIAR. Marry, this, well carried, shall on her behalf
Change slander to remorse; that is some good:
But not for that dream I on this strange course,
But on this travail look for greater birth.
She dying, as it must be so maintain'd,
Upon the instant that she was accused,
Shall be lamented, pitied, and excused
Of every hearer: for it so falls out,
That what we have we prize not to the worth
Whiles we enjoy it; but being lack'd and lost,
Why, then we rack the value, then we find
The virtue that possession would not show us
Whiles it was ours. So will it fare with Claudio:
When he shall hear she died upon his words,
The idea of her life shall sweetly creep
Into his study of imagination;
And every lovely organ of her life
Shall come apparell'd in more precious habit,
More moving-delicate and full of life,
Into the eye and prospect of his soul,
Than when she lived indeed; then shall he mourn,
If ever love had interest in his liver,
And wish he had not so accused her,
No, though he thought his accusation true.
Let this be so, and doubt not but success
Will fashion the event in better shape
Than I can lay it down in likelihood.
But if all aim but this be levell'd false,
The supposition of the lady's death
Will quench the wonder of her infamy:
And if it sort not well, you may conceal her,
As best befits her wounded reputation,

In some reclusive and religious life,
Out of all eyes, tongues, minds, and injuries.

BENE.   Signior Leonato, let the friar advise you:
And though you know my inwardness and love
Is very much unto the prince and Claudio,
Yet, by mine honour, I will deal in this
As secretly and justly as your soul
Should with your body.

LEON.   Being that I flow in grief,
The smallest twine may lead me.

FRIAR.   'Tis well consented: presently away;
For to strange sores strangely they strain the cure.
Come, lady, die to live: this wedding-day
Perhaps is but prolong'd: have patience and endure.

                        [*Exeunt all but* BENEDICK *and* BEATRICE.]

BENE.   Lady Beatrice, have you wept all this while?

BEAT.   Yea, and I will weep a while longer.

BENE.   I will not desire that.

BEAT.   You have no reason; I do it freely.

BENE.   Surely I do believe your fair cousin is wronged.

BEAT.   Ah, how much might the man deserve of me that would right
her!

BENE.   Is there any way to show such friendship?

BEAT.   A very even way, but no such friend.

BENE.   May a man do it?

BEAT.   It is a man's office, but not yours.

BENE.   I do love nothing in the world so well as you: is not that strange?

BEAT.   As strange as the thing I know not. It were as possible for me to
say I loved nothing so well as you: but believe me not; and yet I lie
not; I confess nothing, nor I deny nothing. I am sorry for my cousin.

BENE.   By my sword, Beatrice, thou lovest me.

BEAT.   Do not swear, and eat it.

BENE.   I will swear by it that you love me; and I will make him eat it
that says I love not you.

BEAT.   Will you not eat your word?

BENE.   With no sauce that can be devised to it. I protest I love thee.

BEAT.   Why, then, God forgive me!

BENE.   What offence, sweet Beatrice?

BEAT.   You have stayed me in a happy hour: I was about to protest I
        loved you.
BENE.   And do it with all thy heart.
BEAT.   I love you with so much of my heart, that none is left to protest.
BENE.   Come, bid me do any thing for thee.
BEAT.   Kill Claudio.
BENE.   Ha! not for the wide world.
BEAT.   You kill me to deny it. Farewell.
BENE.   Tarry, sweet Beatrice.
BEAT.   I am gone, though I am here: there is no love in you: nay, I pray
        you, let me go.
BENE.   Beatrice,—
BEAT.   In faith, I will go.
BENE.   We'll be friends first.
BEAT.   You dare easier be friends with me than fight with mine enemy.
BENE.   Is Claudio thine enemy?
BEAT.   Is he not approved in the height a villain, that hath slandered,
        scorned, dishonoured my kinswoman? O that I were a man! What,
        bear her in hand until they come to take hands; and then, with
        public accusation, uncovered slander, unmitigated rancour,—O
        God, that I were a man! I would eat his heart in the market-place.
BENE.   Hear me, Beatrice,—
BEAT.   Talk with a man out at a window! A proper saying!
BENE.   Nay, but, Beatrice,—
BEAT.   Sweet Hero! She is wronged, she is slandered, she is undone.
BENE.   Beat—
BEAT.   Princes and counties! Surely, a princely testimony, a goodly
        count, Count Comfect;[2] a sweet gallant, surely! O that I were a
        man for his sake! or that I had any friend would be a man for my
        sake! But manhood is melted into courtesies, valour into compli-
        ment, and men are only turned into tongue, and trim ones too: he
        is now as valiant as Hercules that only tells a lie, and swears it. I
        cannot be a man with wishing, therefore I will die a woman with
        grieving.
BENE.   Tarry, good Beatrice. By this hand, I love thee.

---

2. *Count Comfect*] a sugar-plum count; "comfect" is the same as "comfit," a sweetmeat.

BEAT. Use it for my love some other way than swearing by it.

BENE. Think you in your soul the Count Claudio hath wronged Hero?

BEAT. Yea, as sure as I have a thought or a soul.

BENE. Enough, I am engaged; I will challenge him. I will kiss your hand, and so I leave you. By this hand, Claudio shall render me a dear account. As you hear of me, so think of me. Go, comfort your cousin: I must say she is dead: and so, farewell. [*Exeunt.*]

SCENE II. A *prison*.

Enter DOGBERRY, VERGES, *and* Sexton, *in gowns; and the* Watch, *with* CONRADE *and* BORACHIO.

DOG. Is our whole dissembly[1] appeared?

VERG. O, a stool and a cushion for the sexton.

SEX. Which be the malefactors?

DOG. Marry, that am I and my partner.

VERG. Nay, that's certain; we have the exhibition to examine.

SEX. But which are the offenders that are to be examined? let them come before master constable.

DOG. Yea, marry, let them come before me. What is your name, friend?

BORA. Borachio.

DOG. Pray, write down, Borachio. Yours, sirrah?

CON. I am a gentleman, sir, and my name is Conrade.

DOG. Write down, master gentleman Conrade. Masters, do you serve God?

CON. ⎱
BORA. ⎰ Yea, sir, we hope.

---

1. *dissembly*] i.e., assembly.

DOG.   Write down, that they hope they serve God: and write God first; for God defend but God should go before such villains! Masters, it is proved already that you are little better than false knaves; and it will go near to be thought so shortly. How answer you for yourselves?

CON.   Marry, sir, we say we are none.

DOG.   A marvellous witty fellow, I assure you; but I will go about with him. Come you hither, sirrah; a word in your ear: sir, I say to you, it is thought you are false knaves.

BORA.   Sir, I say to you we are none.

DOG.   Well, stand aside. 'Fore God, they are both in a tale. Have you writ down, that they are none?

SEX.   Master constable, you go not the way to examine: you must call forth the watch that are their accusers.

DOG.   Yea, marry, that's the eftest[2] way. Let the watch come forth. Masters, I charge you, in the prince's name, accuse these men.

FIRST WATCH.   This man said, sir, that Don John, the prince's brother, was a villain.

DOG.   Write down, Prince John a villain. Why, this is flat perjury, to call a prince's brother villain.

BORA.   Master constable,—

DOG.   Pray thee, fellow, peace: I do not like thy look, I promise thee.

SEX.   What heard you him say else?

SEC. WATCH.   Marry, that he had received a thousand ducats of Don John for accusing the Lady Hero wrongfully.

DOG.   Flat burglary as ever was committed.

VERG.   Yea, by mass, that it is.

SEX.   What else, fellow?

FIRST WATCH.   And that Count Claudio did mean, upon his words, to disgrace Hero before the whole assembly, and not marry her.

DOG.   O villain! thou wilt be condemned into everlasting redemption[3] for this.

SEX.   What else?

WATCH.   This is all.

---

2. *eftest*] the meaning is uncertain; possibly Dogberry's word for easiest.
3. *redemption*] i.e., perdition.

SEX.   And this is more, masters, than you can deny. Prince John is this morning secretly stolen away; Hero was in this manner accused, in this very manner refused, and upon the grief of this suddenly died. Master constable, let these men be bound, and brought to Leonato's: I will go before and show him their examination. [*Exit.*]

DOG.   Come, let them be opinioned.[4]

VERG.   Let them be in the hands—

CON.   Off, coxcomb!

DOG.   God's my life, where's the sexton? let him write down, the prince's officer, coxcomb. Come, bind them. Thou naughty varlet!

CON.   Away! you are an ass, you are an ass.

DOG.   Dost thou not suspect[5] my place? dost thou not suspect my years? O that he were here to write me down an ass! But, masters, remember that I am an ass; though it be not written down, yet forget not that I am an ass. No, thou villain, thou art full of piety,[6] as shall be proved upon thee by good witness. I am a wise fellow; and, which is more, an officer; and, which is more, a householder; and, which is more, as pretty a piece of flesh as any is in Messina; and one that knows the law, go to; and a rich fellow enough, go to; and a fellow that hath had losses; and one that hath two gowns, and every thing handsome about him. Bring him away. O that I had been writ down an ass!   [*Exeunt.*]

---

4. *opinioned*] i.e., pinioned.
5. *suspect*] i.e., respect.
6. *piety*] i.e., impiety.

ACT V.

SCENE I. *Before* LEONATO'S *house*.

Enter LEONATO *and* ANTONIO.

ANT.   If you go on thus, you will kill yourself;
     And 'tis not wisdom thus to second grief
     Against yourself.
LEON.   I pray thee, cease thy counsel,
     Which falls into mine ears as profitless
     As water in a sieve: give not me counsel;
     Nor let no comforter delight mine ear
     But such a one whose wrongs do suit with mine.
     Bring me a father that so loved his child,
     Whose joy of her is overwhelm'd like mine,
     And bid him speak of patience;
     Measure his woe the length and breadth of mine,
     And let it answer every strain for strain,
     As thus for thus, and such a grief for such,
     In every lineament, branch, shape, and form:
     If such a one will smile, and stroke his beard,
     Bid sorrow wag, cry 'hem!' when he should groan,
     Patch grief with proverbs, make misfortune drunk
     With candle-wasters; bring him yet to me,
     And I of him will gather patience.
     But there is no such man: for, brother, men
     Can counsel and speak comfort to that grief
     Which they themselves not feel; but, tasting it,
     Their counsel turns to passion, which before
     Would give preceptial medicine to rage,

Fetter strong madness in a silken thread,
Charm ache with air, and agony with words:
No, no; 'tis all men's office to speak patience
To those that wring under the load of sorrow,
But no man's virtue nor sufficiency,
To be so moral when he shall endure
The like himself. Therefore give me no counsel:
My griefs cry louder than advertisement.

ANT.   Therein do men from children nothing differ.

LEON.   I pray thee, peace. I will be flesh and blood;
For there was never yet philosopher
That could endure the toothache patiently,
However they have writ the style of gods,
And made a push at chance and sufferance.

ANT.   Yet bend not all the harm upon yourself;
Make those that do offend you suffer too.

LEON.   There thou speak'st reason: nay, I will do so.
My soul doth tell me Hero is belied;
And that shall Claudio know; so shall the prince,
And all of them that thus dishonour her.

ANT.   Here comes the prince and Claudio hastily.

Enter DON PEDRO *and* CLAUDIO.

D. PEDRO.   Good den, good den.

CLAUD.   Good day to both of you.

LEON.   Hear you, my lords,—

D. PEDRO.   We have some haste, Leonato.

LEON.   Some haste, my lord! well, fare you well, my lord:
Are you so hasty now? well, all is one.

D. PEDRO.   Nay, do not quarrel with us, good old man.

ANT.   If he could right himself with quarrelling,
Some of us would lie low.

CLAUD.   Who wrongs him?

LEON.   Marry, thou dost wrong me, thou dissembler, thou:—
Nay, never lay thy hand upon thy sword;
I fear thee not.

CLAUD.   Marry, beshrew my hand,
If it should give your age such cause of fear:

In faith, my hand meant nothing to my sword.
LEON.   Tush, tush, man; never fleer and jest at me:
I speak not like a dotard nor a fool,
As, under privilege of age, to brag
What I have done being young, or what would do,
Were I not old. Know, Claudio, to thy head,
Thou hast so wrong'd mine innocent child and me,
That I am forced to lay my reverence by,
And, with grey hairs and bruise of many days,
Do challenge thee to trial of a man.
I say thou hast belied mine innocent child;
Thy slander hath gone through and through her heart,
And she lies buried with her ancestors;
O, in a tomb where never scandal slept,
Save this of hers, framed by thy villany!
CLAUD.   My villany?
LEON.   Thine, Claudio; thine, I say.
D. PEDRO.   You say not right, old man.
LEON.   My lord, my lord,
I'll prove it on his body, if he dare,
Despite his nice fence and his active practice,
His May of youth and bloom of lustihood.
CLAUD.   Away! I will not have to do with you.
LEON.   Canst thou so daff me? Thou hast kill'd my child:
If thou kill'st me, boy, thou shalt kill a man.
ANT.   He shall kill two of us, and men indeed:
But that's no matter; let him kill one first;
Win me and wear me; let him answer me.
Come, follow me, boy; come, sir boy, come, follow me:
Sir boy, I'll whip you from your foining[1] fence;
Nay, as I am a gentleman, I will.
LEON.   Brother,—
ANT.   Content yourself. God knows I loved my niece;
And she is dead, slander'd to death by villains,
That dare as well answer a man indeed

---

1. *foining*] thrusting.

As I dare take a serpent by the tongue:
Boys, apes, braggarts, Jacks, milksops!

LEON.   Brother Antony,—

ANT.   Hold you content. What, man! I know them, yea,
And what they weigh, even to the utmost scruple,—
Scambling, out-facing, fashion-monging boys,
That lie, and cog, and flout, deprave, and slander,
Go antiquely, and show outward hideousness,
And speak off half a dozen dangerous words,
How they might hurt their enemies, if they durst;
And this is all.

LEON.   But, brother Antony,—

ANT.   Come, 'tis no matter:
Do not you meddle; let me deal in this.

D. PEDRO.   Gentlemen both, we will not wake your patience.
My heart is sorry for your daughter's death:
But, on my honour, she was charged with nothing
But what was true, and very full of proof.

LEON.   My lord, my lord,—

D. PEDRO.   I will not hear you.

LEON.   No? Come, brother; away! I will be heard.

ANT.   And shall, or some of us will smart for it.

                        [*Exeunt* LEONATO *and* ANTONIO.]

D. PEDRO.   See, see; here comes the man we went to seek.

Enter BENEDICK.

CLAUD.   Now, signior, what news?

BENE.   Good day, my lord.

D. PEDRO.   Welcome, signior: you are almost come to part almost a
fray.

CLAUD.   We had like to have had our two noses snapped off with two
old men without teeth.

D. PEDRO.   Leonato and his brother. What thinkest thou? Had we
fought, I doubt we should have been too young for them.

BENE.   In a false quarrel there is no true valour. I came to seek you both.

CLAUD.   We have been up and down to seek thee; for we are high-
proof melancholy, and would fain have it beaten away. Wilt thou
use thy wit?

BENE.   It is in my scabbard: shall I draw it?

D. PEDRO.   Dost thou wear thy wit by thy side?

CLAUD.   Never any did so, though very many have been beside their wit.
I will bid thee draw, as we do the minstrels; draw, to pleasure us.

D. PEDRO.   As I am an honest man, he looks pale. Art thou sick, or
angry?

CLAUD.   What, courage, man! What though care killed a cat, thou hast
mettle enough in thee to kill care.

BENE.   Sir, I shall meet your wit in the career, an you charge it against
me. I pray you choose another subject.

CLAUD.   Nay, then, give him another staff: this last was broke cross.

D. PEDRO.   By this light, he changes more and more: I think he be
angry indeed.

CLAUD.   If he be, he knows how to turn his girdle.

BENE.   Shall I speak a word in your ear?

CLAUD.   God bless me from a challenge!

BENE.   [*Aside to* CLAUDIO] You are a villain; I jest not: I will make it
good how you dare, with what you dare, and when you dare. Do me
right, or I will protest your cowardice. You have killed a sweet lady,
and her death shall fall heavy on you. Let me hear from you.

CLAUD.   Well, I will meet you, so I may have good cheer.

D. PEDRO.   What, a feast, a feast?

CLAUD.   I'faith, I thank him; he hath bid me to a calf's-head and a
capon; the which if I do not carve most curiously, say my knife's
naught. Shall I not find a woodcock too?

BENE.   Sir, your wit ambles well; it goes easily.

D. PEDRO.   I'll tell thee how Beatrice praised thy wit the other day. I
said, thou hadst a fine wit: 'True,' said she, 'a fine little one.' 'No,'
said I, 'a great wit:' 'Right,' says she, 'a great gross one.' 'Nay,' said
I, 'a good wit:' 'Just,' said she, 'it hurts nobody.' 'Nay,' said I, 'the
gentleman is wise:' 'Certain,' said she, 'a wise gentleman.' 'Nay,'
said I, 'he hath the tongues:' 'That I believe,' said she, 'for he
swore a thing to me on Monday night, which he forswore on
Tuesday morning; there's a double tongue; there's two tongues.'
Thus did she, an hour together, trans-shape thy particular virtues:
yet at last she concluded with a sigh, thou wast the properest man
in Italy.

CLAUD.   For the which she wept heartily, and said she cared not.

D. PEDRO.   Yea, that she did; but yet, for all that, an if she did not hate him deadly, she would love him dearly: the old man's daughter told us all.

CLAUD.   All, all; and, moreover, God saw him when he was hid in the garden.

D. PEDRO.   But when shall we set the savage bull's horns on the sensible Benedick's head?

CLAUD.   Yea, and text underneath, 'Here dwells Benedick the married man'?

BENE.   Fare you well, boy: you know my mind. I will leave you now to your gossip-like humour: you break jests as braggarts do their blades, which, God be thanked, hurt not. My lord, for your many courtesies I thank you: I must discontinue your company: your brother the bastard is fled from Messina: you have among you killed a sweet and innocent lady. For my Lord Lackbeard there, he and I shall meet: and till then peace be with him.   [*Exit.*]

D. PEDRO.   He is in earnest.

CLAUD.   In most profound earnest; and, I'll warrant you, for the love of Beatrice.

D. PEDRO.   And hath challenged thee.

CLAUD.   Most sincerely.

D. PEDRO.   What a pretty thing man is when he goes in his doublet and hose, and leaves off his wit!

CLAUD.   He is then a giant to an ape: but then is an ape a doctor to such a man.

D. PEDRO.   But, soft you, let me be: pluck up, my heart, and be sad. Did he not say, my brother was fled?

Enter DOGBERRY, VERGES, *and the* Watch, *with* CONRADE *and* BO-RACHIO.

DOG.   Come, you, sir: if justice cannot tame you, she shall ne'er weigh more reasons in her balance: nay, an you be a cursing hypocrite once, you must be looked to.

D. PEDRO.   How now? two of my brother's men bound! Borachio one!

CLAUD.   Hearken after their offence, my lord.

D. PEDRO.   Officers, what offence have these men done?

DOG.   Marry, sir, they have committed false report; moreover, they have spoken untruths; secondarily, they are slanders; sixth and lastly, they have belied a lady; thirdly, they have verified unjust things; and, to conclude, they are lying knaves.

D. PEDRO.   First, I ask thee what they have done; thirdly, I ask thee what's their offence; sixth and lastly, why they are committed; and, to conclude, what you lay to their charge.

CLAUD.   Rightly reasoned, and in his own division; and, by my troth, there's one meaning well suited.

D. PEDRO.   Who have you offended, masters, that you are thus bound to your answer? this learned constable is too cunning to be understood: what's your offence?

BORA.   Sweet prince, let me go no farther to mine answer: do you hear me, and let this count kill me. I have deceived even your very eyes: what your wisdoms could not discover, these shallow fools have brought to light; who, in the night, overheard me confessing to this man, how Don John your brother incensed me to slander the Lady Hero; how you were brought into the orchard, and saw me court Margaret in Hero's garments: how you disgraced her, when you should marry her: my villany they have upon record; which I had rather seal with my death than repeat over to my shame. The lady is dead upon mine and my master's false accusation; and, briefly, I desire nothing but the reward of a villain.

D. PEDRO.   Runs not this speech like iron through your blood?

CLAUD.   I have drunk poison whiles he utter'd it.

D. PEDRO.   But did my brother set thee on to this?

BORA.   Yea, and paid me richly for the practice of it.

D. PEDRO.   He is composed and framed of treachery:
And fled he is upon this villany.

CLAUD.   Sweet Hero! now thy image doth appear
In the rare semblance that I loved it first.

DOG.   Come, bring away the plaintiffs: by this time our sexton hath reformed[2] Signior Leonato of the matter: and, masters, do not forget to specify, when time and place shall serve, that I am an ass.

VERG.   Here, here comes master Signior Leonato, and the sexton too.

---

2. *reformed*] i.e., informed.

Re-enter LEONATO *and* ANTONIO, *with the* Sexton.

LEON. Which is the villain? let me see his eyes,
        That, when I note another man like him,
        I may avoid him: which of these is he?
BORA. If you would know your wronger, look on me.
LEON. Art thou the slave that with thy breath hast kill'd
        Mine innocent child?
BORA.   Yea, even I alone.
LEON. No, not so, villain; thou beliest thyself:
        Here stand a pair of honourable men;
        A third is fled, that had a hand in it.
        I thank you, princes, for my daughter's death:
        Record it with your high and worthy deeds:
        'Twas bravely done, if you bethink you of it.
CLAUD. I know not how to pray your patience;
        Yet I must speak. Choose your revenge yourself;
        Impose me to what penance your invention
        Can lay upon my sin: yet sinn'd I not
        But in mistaking.
D. PEDRO.   By my soul, nor I:
        And yet, to satisfy this good old man,
        I would bend under any heavy weight
        That he'll enjoin me to.
LEON. I cannot bid you bid my daughter live;
        That were impossible: but, I pray you both,
        Possess[3] the people in Messina here
        How innocent she died; and if your love
        Can labour aught in sad invention,
        Hang her an epitaph upon her tomb,
        And sing it to her bones, sing it to-night:
        To-morrow morning come you to my house;
        And since you could not be my son-in-law,
        Be yet my nephew: my brother hath a daughter,
        Almost the copy of my child that's dead,

---

3. *Possess*] inform.

And she alone is heir to both of us:
Give her the right you should have given her cousin,
And so dies my revenge.

CLAUD.   O noble sir,
Your over-kindness doth wring tears from me!
I do embrace your offer; and dispose
For henceforth of poor Claudio.

LEON.   To-morrow, then, I will expect your coming;
To-night I take my leave. This naughty man
Shall face to face be brought to Margaret,
Who I believe was pack'd in all this wrong,
Hired to it by your brother.

BORA.   No, by my soul, she was not;
Nor knew not what she did when she spoke to me;
But always hath been just and virtuous
In any thing that I do know by her.

DOG.   Moreover, sir, which indeed is not under white and black, this
plaintiff here, the offender, did call me ass: I beseech you, let it be
remembered in his punishment. And also, the watch heard them
talk of one Deformed: they say he wears a key in his ear, and a lock
hanging by it; and borrows money in God's name, the which he
hath used so long and never paid, that now men grow hard-hearted,
and will lend nothing for God's sake: pray you, examine him upon
that point.

LEON.   I thank thee for thy care and honest pains.

DOG.   Your worship speaks like a most thankful and reverend youth;
and I praise God for you.

LEON.   There's for thy pains.

DOG.   God save the foundation!

LEON.   Go, I discharge thee of thy prisoner, and I thank thee.

DOG.   I leave an arrant knave with your worship; which I beseech your
worship to correct yourself, for the example of others. God keep
your worship! I wish your worship well; God restore you to health! I
humbly give you leave to depart; and if a merry meeting may be
wished, God prohibit it! Come, neighbour.

                         [*Exeunt* DOGBERRY *and* VERGES.]

LEON.   Until to-morrow morning, lords, farewell.

ANT.   Farewell, my lords: we look for you to-morrow.

D. PEDRO. We will not fail.

CLAUD.   To-night I'll mourn with Hero.

LEON. [*To the* Watch] Bring you these fellows on. We'll talk with Margaret,

  How her acquaintance grew with this lewd fellow.

                [*Exeunt, severally.*]

SCENE II. LEONATO'S *garden*.

Enter BENEDICK *and* MARGARET, *meeting*.

BENE. Pray thee, sweet Mistress Margaret, deserve well at my hands by helping me to the speech of Beatrice.

MARG. Will you, then, write me a sonnet in praise of my beauty?

BENE. In so high a style, Margaret, that no man living shall come over it; for, in most comely truth, thou deservest it.

MARG. To have no man come over me! why, shall I always keep below stairs?

BENE. Thy wit is as quick as the greyhound's mouth; it catches.

MARG. And yours as blunt as the fencer's foils, which hit, but hurt not.

BENE. A most manly wit, Margaret; it will not hurt a woman: and so, I pray thee, call Beatrice: I give thee the bucklers.

MARG. Give us the swords; we have bucklers of our own.

BENE. If you use them, Margaret, you must put in the pikes with a vice; and they are dangerous weapons for maids.

MARG. Well, I will call Beatrice to you, who I think hath legs.

BENE. And therefore will come.   [*Exit* MARGARET.]

 [*Sings*]   The god of love,
         That sits above,
      And knows me, and knows me,
        How pitiful I deserve,—

I mean in singing; but in loving, Leander the good swimmer,

Troilus the first employer of pandars, and a whole bookful of these quondam carpet-mongers, whose names yet run smoothly in the even road of a blank verse, why, they were never so truly turned over and over as my poor self in love. Marry, I cannot show it in rhyme; I have tried: I can find out no rhyme to 'lady' but 'baby,' an innocent rhyme; for 'scorn,' 'horn,' a hard rhyme; for 'school,' 'fool,' a babbling rhyme; very ominous endings: no, I was not born under a rhyming planet, nor I cannot woo in festival terms.

Enter BEATRICE.

Sweet Beatrice, wouldst thou come when I called thee?

BEAT.   Yea, signior, and depart when you bid me.

BENE.   O, stay but till then!

BEAT.   'Then' is spoken; fare you well now: and yet, ere I go, let me go with that I came; which is, with knowing what hath passed between you and Claudio.

BENE.   Only foul words; and thereupon I will kiss thee.

BEAT.   Foul words is but foul wind, and foul wind is but foul breath, and foul breath is noisome; therefore I will depart unkissed.

BENE.   Thou has frighted the word out of his right sense, so forcible is thy wit. But I must tell thee plainly, Claudio undergoes my challenge; and either I must shortly hear from him, or I will subscribe him a coward. And, I pray thee now, tell me for which of my bad parts didst thou first fall in love with me?

BEAT.   For them all together; which maintained so politic a state of evil, that they will not admit any good part to intermingle with them. But for which of my good parts did you first suffer love for me?

BENE.   Suffer love,—a good epithet! I do suffer love indeed, for I love thee against my will.

BEAT.   In spite of your heart, I think; alas, poor heart! If you spite it for my sake, I will spite it for yours; for I will never love that which my friend hates.

BENE.   Thou and I are too wise to woo peaceably.

BEAT.   It appears not in this confession: there's not one wise man among twenty that will praise himself.

BENE.   An old, an old instance, Beatrice, that lived in the time of good neighbours. If a man do not erect in this age his own tomb ere he dies, he shall live no longer in monument than the bell rings and the widow weeps.

BEAT.   And how long is that, think you?

BENE.   Question: why, an hour in clamour, and a quarter in rheum: therefore is it most expedient for the wise, if Don Worm, his conscience, find no impediment to the contrary, to be the trumpet of his own virtues, as I am to myself. So much for praising myself, who, I myself will bear witness, is praiseworthy: and now tell me, how doth your cousin?

BEAT.   Very ill.

BENE.   And how do you?

BEAT.   Very ill too.

BENE.   Serve God, love me, and mend. There will I leave you too, for here comes one in haste.

Enter URSULA.

URS.   Madam, you must come to your uncle. Yonder's old coil at home: it is proved my Lady Hero hath been falsely accused, the prince and Claudio mightily abused; and Don John is the author of all, who is fled and gone. Will you come presently?

BEAT.   Will you go hear this news, signior?

BENE.   I will live in thy heart, die in thy lap, and be buried in thy eyes; and moreover I will go with thee to thy uncle's.   [*Exeunt.*]

SCENE III. *A church*.

Enter DON PEDRO, CLAUDIO, *and three or four with tapers*.

CLAUD.   Is this the monument of Leonato?

A LORD.   It is, my lord.

CLAUD.   [*Reading out of a scroll*]

> Done to death by slanderous tongues
>   Was the Hero that here lies:
> Death, in guerdon[1] of her wrongs,
>   Gives her fame which never dies.
> So the life that died with shame
> Lives in death with glorious fame.

Hang thou there upon the tomb,
Praising her when I am dumb.
Now, music, sound, and sing your solemn hymn.

Song.

> Pardon, goddess of the night,
> Those that slew thy virgin knight;
> For the which, with songs of woe,
> Round about her tomb they go.
>   Midnight, assist our moan;
>   Help us to sigh and groan,
>   Heavily, heavily:
>   Graves, yawn, and yield your dead,
>   Till death be uttered,
>   Heavily, heavily.

CLAUD.   Now, unto thy bones good night!
          Yearly will I do this rite.
D. PEDRO.   Good morrow, masters; put your torches out:
      The wolves have prey'd; and look, the gentle day,
    Before the wheels of Phœbus, round about
      Dapples the drowsy east with spots of grey.
    Thanks to you all, and leave us: fare you well.
CLAUD.   Good morrow, masters: each his several way.
D. PEDRO.   Come, let us hence, and put on other weeds;
    And then to Leonato's we will go.
CLAUD.   And Hymen now with luckier issue speed's
    Than this for whom we render'd up this woe.   [*Exeunt.*]

---

[1] *guerdon*] reward, recompense.

SCENE IV. *A room in* LEONATO'S *house*.

Enter LEONATO, ANTONIO, BENEDICK, BEATRICE, MARGARET, UR-
SULA, FRIAR FRANCIS, *and* HERO.

FRIAR.   Did I not tell you she was innocent?
LEON.   So are the prince and Claudio, who accused her
  Upon the error that you heard debated:
  But Margaret was in some fault for this,
  Although against her will, as it appears
  In the true course of all the question.
ANT.   Well, I am glad that all things sort so well.
BENE.   And so am I, being else by faith enforced
  To call young Claudio to a reckoning for it.
LEON.   Well, daughter, and you gentlewomen all,
  Withdraw into a chamber by yourselves,
  And when I send for you, come hither mask'd.

              [*Exeunt* Ladies.]

  The prince and Claudio promised by this hour
  To visit me. You know your office, brother:
  You must be father to your brother's daughter,
  And give her to young Claudio.
ANT.   Which I will do with confirm'd countenance.
BENE.   Friar, I must entreat your pains, I think.
FRIAR.   To do what, signior?
BENE.   To bind me, or undo me; one of them.
  Signior Leonato, truth it is, good signior,
  Your niece regards me with an eye of favour.
LEON.   That eye my daughter lent her: 'tis most true.
BENE.   And I do with an eye of love requite her.
LEON.   The sight whereof I think you had from me,
  From Claudio, and the prince: but what's your will?
BENE.   Your answer, sir, is enigmatical:
  But, for my will, my will is, your good will

May stand with ours, this day to be conjoin'd
In the state of honourable marriage:
In which, good friar, I shall desire your help.
LEON.   My heart is with your liking.
FRIAR.   And my help.
Here comes the prince and Claudio.

Enter DON PEDRO *and* CLAUDIO, *and two or three others.*

D. PEDRO.   Good morrow to this fair assembly.
LEON.   Good morrow, prince; good morrow, Claudio:
We here attend you. Are you yet determined
To-day to marry with my brother's daughter?
CLAUD.   I'll hold my mind, were she an Ethiope.
LEON.   Call her forth, brother; here's the friar ready.
                                                [*Exit* ANTONIO.]
D. PEDRO.   Good morrow, Benedick. Why, what's the matter,
That you have such a February face,
So full of frost, of storm, and cloudiness?
CLAUD.   I think he thinks upon the savage bull.
Tush, fear not, man; we'll tip thy horns with gold,
And all Europa shall rejoice at thee;
As once Europa did at lusty Jove,
When he would play the noble beast in love.
BENE.   Bull Jove, sir, had an amiable low;
And some such strange bull leap'd your father's cow,
And got a calf in that same noble feat
Much like to you, for you have just his bleat.
CLAUD.   For this I owe you: here comes other reckonings.

Re-enter ANTONIO, *with the* Ladies *masked.*

Which is the lady I must seize upon?
ANT.   This same is she, and I do give you her.
CLAUD.   Why, then she's mine. Sweet, let me see your face.
LEON.   No, that you shall not, till you take her hand
Before this friar, and swear to marry her.
CLAUD.   Give me your hand: before this holy friar,
I am your husband, if you like of me.

HERO.   And when I lived, I was your other wife: [*Unmasking.*]
　　And when you loved, you were my other husband.
CLAUD.   Another Hero!
HERO.　　　　　　　Nothing certainer:
　　One Hero died defiled; but I do live,
　　And surely as I live, I am a maid.
D. PEDRO.   The former Hero! Hero that is dead!
LEON.   She died, my lord, but whiles her slander lived.
FRIAR.   All this amazement can I qualify;
　　When after that the holy rites are ended,
　　I'll tell you largely of fair Hero's death:
　　Meantime let wonder seem familiar,
　　And to the chapel let us presently.
BENE.   Soft and fair, friar. Which is Beatrice?
BEAT.   [*Unmasking*] I answer to that name. What is your will?
BENE.   Do not you love me?
BEAT.　　　　　　　Why, no; no more than reason.
BENE.   Why, then your uncle, and the prince, and Claudio
　　Have been deceived; they swore you did.
BEAT.   Do not you love me?
BENE.　　　　　　　Troth, no; no more than reason.
BEAT.   Why, then my cousin, Margaret, and Ursula
　　Are much deceived; for they did swear you did.
BENE.   They swore that you were almost sick for me.
BEAT.   They swore that you were well-nigh dead for me.
BENE.   'Tis no such matter. Then you do not love me?
BEAT.   No, truly, but in friendly recompence.
LEON.   Come, cousin, I am sure you love the gentleman.
CLAUD.   And I'll be sworn upon't that he loves her;
　　For here's a paper, written in his hand,
　　A halting sonnet of his own pure brain,
　　Fashion'd to Beatrice.
HERO.　　　　　　　And here's another,
　　Writ in my cousin's hand, stolen from her pocket,
　　Containing her affection unto Benedick.
BENE.   A miracle! here's our own hands against our hearts. Come, I
　　will have thee; but, by this light, I take thee for pity.
BEAT.   I would not deny you; but, by this good day, I yield upon great

persuasion; and partly to save your life, for I was told you were in a consumption.

BENE. Peace! I will stop your mouth.   [*Kissing her.*]

D. PEDRO.   How dost thou, Benedick, the married man?

BENE.   I'll tell thee what, prince; a college of wit-crackers cannot flout me out of my humour. Dost thou think I care for a satire or an epigram? No: if a man will be beaten with brains, a' shall wear nothing handsome about him. In brief, since I do purpose to marry, I will think nothing to any purpose that the world can say against it; and therefore never flout at me for what I have said against it; for man is a giddy thing, and this is my conclusion. For thy part, Claudio, I did think to have beaten thee; but in that thou art like to be my kinsman, live unbruised, and love my cousin.

CLAUD.   I had well hoped thou wouldst have denied Beatrice, that I might have cudgelled thee out of thy single life, to make thee a double-dealer; which, out of question, thou wilt be, if my cousin do not look exceeding narrowly to thee.

BENE. Come, come, we are friends: let's have a dance ere we are married, that we may lighten our own hearts, and our wives' heels.

LEON.   We'll have dancing afterward.

BENE.   First, of my word; therefore play, music. Prince, thou art sad; get thee a wife, get thee a wife: there is no staff more reverend than one tipped with horn.

Enter a Messenger.

MESS.   My lord, your brother John is ta'en in flight,
        And brought with armed men back to Messina.

BENE.   Think not on him till to-morrow: I'll devise thee brave punish-
        ments for him. Strike up, pipers.   [*Dance.*]
                                                            [*Exeunt.*]

Twelfth Night

Twelfth Night; or, What You Will

TWELFTH NIGHT (C. 1600–1601) is one of Shakespeare's most joyful plays, bringing together in a grand mixture many of the stock elements of comedy. Here may be found the maïden disguised as a man, the twins separated by mischance, the lovelorn suitor and the puritanical buffoon—all characters loaded with comic potential. The very choice of *Twelfth Night* as a title reveals the play's festive nature, alluding to the Feast of the Epiphany (January 6), the last day of the revelry-filled Christmas season. Traditionally a time when plays were performed, banquets and masques were held, and some release was to be had from rigid morality, it was also a time to celebrate joy and to lampoon those (such as the play's Malvolio) who would curb gaiety and dampen merriment. In keeping with this spirit, *Twelfth Night* closes amidst a carnival atmosphere, with all disguises cast off and all trickery revealed, with the siblings reunited and the killjoy brought down, and with the promise of three weddings to be celebrated.

The first recorded performance of the play was on February 2, 1602, although some scholars believe that it had already been staged on Twelfth Night of the year before (hence its name). In writing the play, Shakespeare was probably most influenced by one of the stories in Barnabe Riche's *Riche his Farewell to Militarie profession* (1581), which in turn took many of its plot elements from earlier French and Italian works. Whereas *Twelfth Night* casts a kind eye upon frivolity and abandon, however, Riche's story has a moralizing tone, blaming its characters' carnal appetites for the difficulties they encounter. It may well be that Shakespeare intended the disapproving Malvolio to be a parody of the censorious Riche, for the story of his comeuppance is unique to Shakespeare's version of the tale. It was a memorable addition, and popular: so much so that for many years the play was known solely by the title *Malvolio*.

CANDACE WARD

Dramatis Personæ

ORSINO, Duke of Illyria.
SEBASTIAN, brother to Viola.
ANTONIO, a sea captain, friend to Sebastian.
A Sea Captain, friend to Viola.
VALENTINE,
CURIO, } gentlemen attending on the Duke.
SIR TOBY BELCH, uncle to Olivia.
SIR ANDREW AGUECHEEK.
MALVOLIO, steward to Olivia.
FABIAN,
FESTE, a Clown, } servants to Olivia.

OLIVIA.
VIOLA.
MARIA, Olivia's woman.

Lords, Priests, Sailors, Officers, Musicians, and other Attendants.

SCENE: *A city in Illyria, and the sea-coast near it*

ACT I

Scene I. *An apartment in the* Duke's *palace.*

Enter Duke, Curio, *and other* Lords; Musicians *attending*

Duke.   If music be the food of love, play on;
  Give me excess of it, that, surfeiting,
  The appetite may sicken, and so die.
  That strain again! it had a dying fall:
  O, it came o'er my ear like the sweet sound,
  That breathes upon a bank of violets,
  Stealing and giving odour!
  Enough; no more:
  'T is not so sweet now as it was before.
  O spirit of love, how quick and fresh art thou!
  That, notwithstanding thy capacity
  Receiveth as the sea, nought enters there,
  Of what validity and pitch soe'er,
  But falls into abatement and low price,
  Even in a minute! so full of shapes is fancy,
  That it alone is high fantastical.
Cur.   Will you go hunt, my lord?
Duke.   What, Curio?
Cur.   The hart.
Duke.   Why, so I do, the noblest that I have:
  O, when mine eyes did see Olivia first,
  Methought she purged the air of pestilence!
  That instant was I turn'd into a hart;
  And my desires, like fell and cruel hounds,
  E'er since pursue me.

Enter Valentine

      How now! what news from her?

VAL.   So please my lord, I might not be admitted;
          But from her handmaid do return this answer:
          The element[1] itself, till seven years' heat,
          Shall not behold her face at ample view;
          But, like a cloistress, she will veiled walk
        . And water once a day her chamber round
          With eye-offending brine: all this to season
          A brother's dead love, which she would keep fresh
          And lasting in her sad remembrance.
DUKE. O, she that hath a heart of that fine frame
          To pay this debt of love but to a brother,
          How will she love, when the rich golden shaft
          Hath kill'd the flock of all affections else
          That live in her; when liver, brain and heart,
          These sovereign thrones, are all supplied, and fill'd
          Her sweet perfections with one self king!
          Away before me to sweet beds of flowers:
          Love-thoughts lie rich when canopied with bowers.   [*Exeunt.*

SCENE II. *The sea-coast.*

Enter VIOLA, *a* Captain, *and* Sailors

VIO.   What country, friends, is this?
CAP.   This is Illyria, lady.
VIO.   And what should I do in Illyria?
          My brother he is in Elysium.
          Perchance he is not drown'd: what think you, sailors?
CAP.   It is perchance that you yourself were saved.
VIO.   O my poor brother! and so perchance may he be.
CAP.   True, madam: and, to comfort you with chance,
          Assure yourself, after our ship did split,
          When you and those poor number saved with you
          Hung on our driving boat, I saw your brother,
          Most provident in peril, bind himself,

---

1. *element*] sky.

Courage and hope both teaching him the practice,
To a strong mast that lived upon the sea;
Where, like Arion on the dolphin's back,
I saw him hold acquaintance with the waves
So long as I could see.

VIO.   For saying so, there's gold:
Mine own escape unfoldeth to my hope,
Whereto thy speech serves for authority,
The like of him. Know'st thou this country?

CAP.   Ay, madam, well; for I was bred and born
Not three hours' travel from this very place.

VIO.   Who governs here?

CAP.   A noble Duke,[1] in nature as in name.

VIO.   What is his name?

CAP.   Orsino.

VIO.   Orsino! I have heard my father name him:
He was a bachelor then.

CAP.   And so is now, or was so very late;
For but a month ago I went from hence,
And then 't was fresh in murmur,—as, you know,
What great ones do the less will prattle of,—
That he did seek the love of fair Olivia.

VIO.   What's she?

CAP.   A virtuous maid, the daughter of a count
That died some twelvemonth since; then leaving her
In the protection of his son, her brother,
Who shortly also died: for whose dear love,
They say, she hath abjured the company
And sight of men.

VIO.   O that I served that lady,
And might not be delivered to the world,
Till I had made mine own occasion mellow,
What my estate is![2]

CAP.   That were hard to compass;
Because she will admit no kind of suit,
No, not the Duke's.

VIO.   There is a fair behaviour in thee, captain;

---

1. *Duke*] Orsino is subsequently spoken of merely as "Count."
2. O...is!] Viola wishes it were possible to keep her name and rank a secret until she chooses to make it known.

And though that nature with a beauteous wall
Doth oft close in pollution, yet of thee
I will believe thou hast a mind that suits
With this thy fair and outward character.
I prithee, and I 'll pay thee bounteously,
Conceal me what I am, and be my aid
For such disguise as haply shall become
The form of my intent. I 'll serve this Duke:
Thou shalt present me as an eunuch to him:
It may be worth thy pains; for I can sing,
And speak to him in many sorts of music,
That will allow me very worth his service.
What else may hap to time I will commit;
Only shape thou thy silence to my wit.

CAP. Be you his eunuch, and your mute I 'll be:
When my tongue blabs, then let mine eyes not see.

VIO. I thank thee: lead me on.   [*Exeunt.*]

SCENE III. OLIVIA'S *house.*

Enter SIR TOBY BELCH *and* MARIA

SIR TO. What a plague means my niece, to take the death of her
brother thus? I am sure care 's an enemy to life.

MAR. By my troth, Sir Toby, you must come in earlier o' nights: your
cousin, my lady, takes great exceptions to your ill hours.

SIR TO. Why, let her except, before excepted.

MAR. Ay, but you must confine yourself within the modest limits of
order.

SIR TO. Confine! I 'll confine myself no finer than I am: these clothes
are good enough to drink in; and so be these boots too: an they be
not, let them hang themselves in their own straps.

MAR. That quaffing and drinking will undoe you: I heard my lady
talk of it yesterday; and of a foolish knight that you brought in one
night here to be her wooer.

SIR TO. Who, Sir Andrew Aguecheek?

MAR. Ay, he.

SIR TO.   He 's as tall a man as any 's in Illyria.

MAR.   What 's that to the purpose?

SIR TO.   Why, he has three thousand ducats a year.

MAR.   Ay, but he 'll have but a year in all these ducats: he 's a very fool and a prodigal.

SIR TO.   Fie, that you 'll say so! he plays o' the viol-de-gamboys, and speaks three or four languages word for word without book, and hath all the good gifts of nature.

MAR.   He hath indeed, almost natural: for besides that he 's a fool, he 's a great quarreller; and but that he hath the gift of a coward to allay the gust he hath in quarrelling, 't is thought among the prudent he would quickly have the gift of a grave.

SIR TO.   By this hand, they are scoundrels and substractors that say so of him. Who are they?

MAR.   They that add, moreover, he 's drunk nightly in your company.

SIR TO.   With drinking healths to my niece: I 'll drink to her as long as there is a passage in my throat and drink in Illyria: he 's a coward and a coystrill[1] that will not drink to my niece till his brains turn o' the toe like a parish-top.[2] What, wench! Castiliano vulgo;[3] for here comes Sir Andrew Agueface.

Enter SIR ANDREW AGUECHEEK

SIR AND.   Sir Toby Belch! how now, Sir Toby Belch!

SIR TO.   Sweet Sir Andrew!

SIR AND.   Bless you, fair shrew.

MAR.   And you too, sir.

SIR TO.   Accost, Sir Andrew, accost.

SIR AND.   What 's that?

SIR TO.   My niece's chambermaid.

SIR AND.   Good Mistress Accost, I desire better acquaintance.

MAR.   My name is Mary, sir.

SIR AND.   Good Mistress Mary Accost,—

SIR TO.   You mistake, knight: "accost" is front her, board her, woo her, assail her.

SIR AND.   By my troth, I would not undertake her in this company. Is that the meaning of "accost"?

---

1. *coystrill*] a common term of contempt, meaning "a base fellow."
2. *parish-top*] A large top provided by the parochial authorities in Shakespeare's day for boys to play with.
3. *Castiliano vulgo*] literally, the Spanish for "Castilian people."

MAR. Fare you well, gentlemen.

SIR TO. An thou let part so, Sir Andrew, would thou mightst never draw sword again.

SIR AND. An you part so, mistress, I would I might never draw sword again. Fair lady, do you think you have fools in hand?

MAR. Sir, I have not you by the hand.

SIR AND. Marry, but you shall have; and here 's my hand.

MAR. Now, sir, "thought is free": I pray you, bring your hand to the buttery-bar[4] and let it drink.

SIR AND. Wherefore, sweet-heart? what 's your metaphor?

MAR. It 's dry,[5] sir.

SIR AND. Why, I think so: I am not such an ass but I can keep my hand dry. But what 's your jest?

MAR. A dry jest,[6] sir.

SIR AND. Are you full of them?

MAR. Ay, sir, I have them at my fingers' ends: marry, now I let go your hand, I am barren.[7] [*Exit.*]

SIR TO. O knight, thou lackest a cup of canary:[8] when did I see thee so put down?

SIR AND. Never in your life, I think; unless you see canary put me down. Methinks sometimes I have no more wit than a Christian or an ordinary man has: but I am a great eater of beef and I believe that does harm to my wit.

SIR TO. No question.

SIR AND. An I thought that, I 'ld forswear it. I 'll ride home to-morrow, Sir Toby.

SIR TO. Pourquoi, my dear knight?

SIR AND. What is "pourquoi"? do or not do? I would I had bestowed that time in the tongues[9] that I have in fencing, dancing and bear-baiting: O, had I but followed the arts!

SIR TO. Then had'st thou had an excellent head of hair.

SIR AND. Why, would that have mended my hair?

---

4. *buttery-bar*] a room where provisions are stored.

5. *It 's dry*] A dry hand was commonly held to be a sign of indifference to love, as well as of debility and old age. A moist hand was commonly taken to be the sign of an amorous disposition.

6. *A dry jest*] An insipid jest.

7. *barren*] dull, witless, tedious.

8. *canary*] a sweet wine from the Canary Islands.

9. *in the tongues*] studying languages; "tongues" was often written and commonly pronounced as "tongs," and Sir Toby's retort about Sir Andrew's "head of hair" obviously shows that a pun on "tongs" in the sense of curling irons was intended.

SIR TO.   Past question; for thou seest it will not curl by nature.

SIR AND.   But it becomes me well enough, does 't not?

SIR TO.   Excellent; it hangs like flax on a distaff; and I hope to see a housewife take thee between her legs and spin it off.

SIR AND.   Faith, I 'll home to-morrow, Sir Toby: your niece will not be seen; or if she be, it 's four to one she 'll none of me: the count himself here hard by woos her.

SIR TO.   She 'll none o' the count: she 'll not match above her degree, neither in estate, years, nor wit; I have heard her swear 't. Tut, there 's life in 't, man.

SIR AND.   I 'll stay a month longer. I am a fellow o' the strangest mind i' the world; I delight in masques and revels sometimes altogether.

SIR TO.   Art thou good at these kickshawses,[10] knight?

SIR AND.   As any man in Illyria, whatsoever he be, under the degree of my betters; and yet I will not compare with an old man.

SIR TO.   What is thy excellence in a galliard, knight?

SIR AND.   Faith, I can cut a caper.[11]

SIR TO.   And I can cut the mutton to 't.

SIR AND.   And I think I have the back-trick simply as strong as any man in Illyria.

SIR TO.   Wherefore are these things hid? wherefore have these gifts a curtain before 'em? are they like to take dust, like Mistress Mall's picture? why dost thou not go to church in a galliard and come home in a coranto?[12] My very walk should be a jig; I would not so much as make water but in a sink-a-pace.[13] What dost thou mean? Is it a world to hide virtues in? I did think, by the excellent constitution of thy leg, it was formed under the star of a galliard.

SIR AND.   Ay, 't is strong, and it does indifferent well in a flame-coloured stock. Shall we set about some revels?

SIR TO.   What shall we do else? were we not born under Taurus?

SIR AND.   Taurus! That 's sides and heart.

SIR TO.   No, sir; it is legs and thighs.[14] Let me see thee caper: ha! higher: ha, ha! excellent! –   [*Exeunt.*]

---

10. *kickshawses*] toys, trifles.

11. *galliard . . . caper*] lively dances.

12. *coranto*] another lively dance.

13. *sink-a-pace*] a phonetic spelling of "cinque pace," a lively dance.

14. *Taurus . . . thighs*] Astrology assumed that each part of the body was under the control of one or other signs of the zodiac. But both Sir Andrew and Sir Toby are in error in their reference to Taurus, who, according to the authorities, controls neither the "sides and hearts" nor the "legs and thighs," but the neck and throat.

SCENE IV. *The* DUKE'S *palace.*

Enter VALENTINE, *and* VIOLA *in man's attire*

VAL.   If the Duke continue these favours towards you, Cesario,[1] you
      are like to be much advanced: he hath known you but three days,
      and already you are no stranger.

VIO.   You either fear his humour or my negligence, that you call in
      question the continuance of his love: is he constant, sir, in his
      favours?

VAL.   No, believe me.

VIO.   I thank you. Here comes the count.[2]

Enter DUKE, CURIO, *and* Attendants

DUKE.   Who saw Cesario, ho?

VIO.   On your attendance, my lord; here.

DUKE.   Stand you a while aloof. Cesario,
      Thou know'st no less but all; I have unclasp'd
      To thee the book even of my secret soul:
      Therefore, good youth, address thy gait unto her;
      Be not denied access, stand at her doors,
      And tell them, there thy fixed foot shall grow
      Till thou have audience.

VIO.   Sure, my noble lord,
      If she be so abandon'd to her sorrow
      As it is spoke, she never will admit me.

DUKE.   Be clamorous and leap all civil bounds
      Rather than make unprofited return.

VIO.   Say I do speak with her, my lord, what then?

DUKE.   O, then unfold the passion of my love,
      Surprise her with discourse of my dear faith:
      It shall become thee well to act my woes;
      She will attend it better in thy youth
      Than in a nuncio's[3] of more grave aspect.

---

1. *Cesario*] Viola's male alias.
2. *the count*] In the stage directions throughout the play, Orsino is called "Duke," and is
    so spoken of at I, ii, 25. But everywhere else in the text he is referred to as "the count."
3. *nuncio's*] messenger's.

VIO.   I think not so, my lord.
DUKE.   Dear lad, believe it;
     For they shall yet belie thy happy years,
     That say thou art a man: Diana's lip
     Is not more smooth and rubious;[4] thy small pipe
     Is as the maiden's organ, shrill and sound;
     And all is semblative[5] a woman's part.
     I know thy constellation is right apt
     For this affair. Some four or five attend him;
     All, if you will; for I myself am best
     When least in company. Prosper well in this,
     And thou shalt live as freely as thy lord,
     To call his fortunes thine.
VIO.   I 'll do my best
     To woo your lady: [*Aside*] yet, a barful[6] strife!
     Whoe'er I woo, myself would be his wife.   [*Exeunt.*]

SCENE V. OLIVIA'S *house.*

Enter MARIA *and* Clown

MAR.   Nay, either tell me where thou hast been, or I will not open my
     lips so wide as a bristle may enter in way of thy excuse: my lady
     will hang thee for thy absence.
CLO.   Let her hang me: he that is well hanged in this world needs to
     fear no colours.[1]
MAR.   Make that good.
CLO.   He shall see none to fear.
MAR.   A good lenten[2] answer: I can tell thee where that saying was
     born, of "I fear no colours."
CLO.   Where, good Mistress Mary?

---

4. *rubious*] apparently a once-used word; formed from "ruby."
5. *semblative*] like or similar to.
6. *barful*] full of obstacles.

1. *fear no colours*] fear no enemies; "colours" were ensigns or standards, which would have
    been displayed during battles.
2. *lenten*] scanty, spare.

MAR.   In the wars; and that may you be bold to say in your foolery.

CLO.   Well, God give them wisdom that have it; and those that are fools, let them use their talents.

MAR.   Yet you will be hanged for being so long absent; or, to be turned away, is not that as good as a hanging to you?

CLO.   Many a good hanging prevents a bad marriage; and, for turning away, let summer bear it out.[3]

MAR.   You are resolute, then?

CLO.   Not so, neither; but I am resolved on two points.

MAR.   That if one break, the other will hold; or, if both break, your gaskins fall.[4]

CLO.   Apt, in good faith; very apt. Well, go thy way; if Sir Toby would leave drinking, thou wert as witty a piece of Eve's flesh as any in Illyria.

MAR.   Peace, you rogue, no more o' that. Here comes my lady: make your excuse wisely, you were best.   [*Exit.*]

CLO.   Wit, an 't be thy will, put me into good fooling! Those wits, that think they have thee, do very oft prove fools; and I, that am sure I lack thee, may pass for a wise man: for what says Quinapalus?[5] "Better a witty fool than a foolish wit."

Enter LADY OLIVIA *with* MALVOLIO

God bless thee, lady!

OLI.   Take the fool away.

CLO.   Do you not hear, fellows? Take away the lady.

OLI.   Go to, you 're a dry fool; I 'll no more of you: besides, you grow dishonest.

CLO.   Two faults, madonna, that drink and good counsel will amend: for give the dry fool drink, then is the fool not dry: bid the dishonest man mend himself; if he mend, he is no longer dishonest; if he cannot, let the botcher mend him. Any thing that 's mended is but patched: virtue that transgresses is but patched with sin; and sin that amends is but patched with virtue. If that this simple syllogism will serve, so; if it will not, what remedy? As there is no true cuckold but calamity, so beauty 's a flower. The lady bade take away the fool; therefore, I say again, take her away.

---

3. *for turning . . . out*] If I am threatened with dismissal, let us wait for next season,—next summer,—and see if the threat take effect, i.e., wait awhile and see.

4. *points . . . fall*] a "point" was a metal hook or tag, which attaches the gaskins, i.e., breeches or hose, to the doublet.

5. *Quinapalus*] An apocryphal philosopher invented for the occasion.

OLI.   Sir, I bade them take away you.

CLO.   Misprision[6] in the highest degree! Lady, cucullus non facit monachum;[7] that's as much to say as I wear not motley in my brain. Good madonna, give me leave to prove you a fool.

OLI.   Can you do it?

CLO.   Dexteriously,[8] good madonna.

OLI.   Make your proof.

CLO.   I must catechize you for it, madonna: good my mouse of virtue, answer me.

OLI.   Well, sir, for want of other idleness, I'll bide your proof.

CLO.   Good madonna, why mournest thou?

OLI.   Good fool, for my brother's death.

CLO.   I think his soul is in hell, madonna.

OLI.   I know his soul is in heaven, fool.

CLO.   The more fool, madonna, to mourn for your brother's soul being in heaven. Take away the fool, gentlemen.

OLI.   What think you of this fool, Malvolio? doth he not mend?

MAL.   Yes, and shall do till the pangs of death shake him: infirmity, that decays the wise, doth ever make the better fool.

CLO.   God send you, sir, a speedy infirmity, for the better increasing your folly! Sir Toby will be sworn that I am no fox; but he will not pass his word for two pence that you are no fool.

OLI.   How say you to that, Malvolio?

MAL.   I marvel your ladyship takes delight in such a barren rascal: I saw him put down the other day with an ordinary fool that has no more brain than a stone. Look you now, he's out of his guard already; unless you laugh and minister occasion to him, he is gagged. I protest, I take these wise men, that crow so at these set kind of fools, no better than the fools' zanies.[9]

OLI.   O, you are sick of self-love, Malvolio, and taste with a distempered appetite. To be generous, guiltless and of free disposition, is to take those things for bird-bolts[10] that you deem cannon-bullets: there is no slander in an allowed fool, though he do nothing but

---

6. *Misprision*] Legally the term "misprision," which literally means "contempt," was applied to evil speaking of the sovereign.

7. *cucullus . . . monachum*] "The cowl does not make the monk," a proverb in vogue throughout Europe.

8. *Dexteriously*] Dexterously.

9. *zanies*] a subordinate buffoon whose duty was to make awkward attempts at mimicking the tricks of the professional clown.

10. *bird-bolts*] short arrows with broad flat ends, used to kill birds without piercing them.

rail; nor no railing in a known discreet man, though he do nothing but reprove.

CLO.　Now Mercury endue thee with leasing,[11] for thou speakest well
of fools!

Re-enter MARIA

MAR.　Madam, there is at the gate a young gentleman much desires to
speak with you.

OLI.　From the Count Orsino, is it?

MAR.　I know not, madam: 't is a fair young man, and well attended.

OLI.　Who of my people hold him in delay?

MAR.　Sir Toby, madam, your kinsman.

OLI.　Fetch him off, I pray you; he speaks nothing but madman: fie on
him! [*Exit* MARIA.] Go you, Malvolio: if it be a suit from the
count, I am sick, or not at home; what you will, to dismiss it. [*Exit*
MALVOLIO.] Now you see, sir, how your fooling grows old, and
people dislike it.

CLO.　Thou hast spoke for us, madonna, as if thy eldest son should be
a fool; whose skull Jove cram with brains! for,—here he comes,—
one of thy kin has a most weak pia mater.[12]

Enter SIR TOBY

OLI.　By mine honour, half drunk. What is he at the gate, cousin?

SIR TO.　A gentleman.

OLI.　A gentleman! what gentleman?

SIR TO.　'T is a gentleman here—a plague o' these pickle-herring![13]
How now, sot!

CLO.　Good Sir Toby!

OLI.　Cousin, cousin, how have you come so early by this lethargy?

SIR TO.　Lechery! I defy lechery. There 's one at the gate.

OLI.　Ay, marry, what is he?

SIR TO.　Let him be the devil, an he will, I care not: give me faith, say
I. Well, it 's all one.　　　　　　　　　　　　　　　　[*Exit.*]

OLI.　What 's a drunken man like, fool?

CLO.　Like a drowned man, a fool and a mad man: one draught above

---

11. *Mercury . . . leasing*] May the god of cheats or liars endow thee, to thy profit, with the
gift of lying.

12. *pia mater*] the membrane that covers the brain; the term was used for the brain itself.

13. *pickle-herring*] the favourite relish for drunkards.

heat[14] makes him a fool; the second mads him; and a third drowns him.

OLI.   Go thou and seek the crowner,[15] and let him sit o' my coz; for he 's in the third degree of drink, he 's drowned: go look after him.

CLO.   He is but mad yet, madonna; and the fool shall look to the mad-man.   [Exit.]

Re-enter MALVOLIO

MAL.   Madam, yond young fellow swears he will speak with you. I told him you were sick; he takes on him to understand so much, and therefore comes to speak with you. I told him you were asleep; he seems to have a foreknowledge of that too, and therefore comes to speak with you. What is to be said to him, lady? he 's fortified against any denial.

OLI.   Tell him he shall not speak with me.

MAL.   Has been told so; and he says, he 'll stand at your door like a sheriff's post,[16] and be the supporter to a bench, but he 'll speak with you.

OLI.   What kind o' man is he?

MAL.   Why, of mankind.

OLI.   What manner of man?

MAL.   Of very ill manner; he 'll speak with you, will you or no.

OLI.   Of what personage and years is he?

MAL.   Not yet old enough for a man, nor young enough for a boy; as a squash is before 't is a peascod, or a codling[17] when 't is almost an apple: 't is with him in standing water,[18] between boy and man. He is very well-favoured and he speaks very shrewishly; one would think his mother's milk were scarce out of him.

OLI.   Let him approach: call in my gentlewoman.

MAL.   Gentlewoman, my lady calls.   [Exit.]

Re-enter MARIA

OLI.   Give me my veil: come, throw it o'er my face. We 'll once more hear Orsino's embassy.

---

14. *above heat*] above ordinary strength.

15. *crowner*] coroner.

16. *sheriff's post*] a post, often carved with elaborate ornament, which stood before the door of the house occupied by a city mayor and sheriff.

17. *squash . . . codling*] terms respectively for an unripe peascod and an unripe apple.

18. *in standing water*] just at the turn of the tide, in the condition of stationary water that neither ebbs nor flows.

Enter VIOLA, *and* Attendants

VIO.   The honourable lady of the house, which is she?

OLI.   Speak to me; I shall answer for her. Your will?

VIO.   Most radiant, exquisite and unmatchable beauty,—I pray you, tell me if this be the lady of the house, for I never saw her: I would be loath to cast away my speech, for besides that it is excellently well penned, I have taken great pains to con it. Good beauties, let me sustain no scorn; I am very comptible,[19] even to the least sinister usage.

OLI.   Whence came you, sir?

VIO.   I can say little more than I have studied, and that question 's out of my part. Good gentle one, give me modest assurance if you be the lady of the house, that I may proceed in my speech.

OLI.   Are you a comedian?

VIO.   No, my profound heart: and yet, by the very fangs of malice I swear, I am not that I play. Are you the lady of the house?

OLI.   If I do not usurp myself, I am.

VIO.   Most certain, if you are she, you do usurp yourself; for what is yours to bestow is not yours to reserve. But this is from my commission: I will on with my speech in your praise, and then show you the heart of my message.

OLI.   Come to what is important in 't: I forgive you the praise.

VIO.   Alas, I took great pains to study it, and 't is poetical.

OLI.   It is the more like to be feigned: I pray you, keep it in. I heard you were saucy at my gates, and allowed your approach rather to wonder at you than to hear you. If you be not mad, be gone; if you have reason, be brief: 't is not that time of moon with me to make one in so skipping a dialogue.[20]

MAR.   Will you hoist sail, sir? here lies your way.

VIO.   No, good swabber;[21] I am to hull[22] here a little longer. Some mollification for your giant,[23] sweet lady. Tell me your mind: I am a messenger.

---

19. *comptible*] sensitive.

20. *'t is . . . dialogue*] the waning and waxing of the moon served as images of change; the sense here is that Olivia is in no mood or humor to entertain any flighty or thoughtless (skipping) exchange with Viola/Cassio.

21. *swabber*] one who mops the ship's deck at sea.

22. *hull*] drift with the sails furled.

23. *giant*] an ironical reference to Maria, who, as implied elsewhere in the play, is small in size.

OLI.   Sure, you have some hideous matter to deliver, when the courtesy of it is so fearful. Speak your office.

VIO.   It alone concerns your ear. I bring no overture of war, no taxation of homage: I hold the olive in my hand; my words are as full
of peace as matter.

OLI.   Yet you began rudely. What are you? what would you?

VIO.   The rudeness that hath appeared in me have I learned from my
entertainment. What I am, and what I would, are as secret as
maidenhead; to your ears, divinity, to any other's, profanation.

OLI.   Give us the place alone: we will hear this divinity. [*Exeunt*
MARIA *and* Attendants.] Now, sir, what is your text?

VIO.   Most sweet lady,—

OLI.   A comfortable doctrine, and much may be said of it. Where lies
your text?

VIO.   In Orsino's bosom.

OLI.   In his bosom! In what chapter of his bosom?

VIO.   To answer by the method, in the first of his heart.

OLI.   O, I have read it: it is heresy. Have you no more to say?

VIO.   Good madam, let me see your face.

OLI.   Have you any commission from your lord to negotiate with my
face? You are now out of your text: but we will draw the curtain
and show you the picture. Look you, sir, such a one I was this present: is 't not well done?   [*Unveiling.*]

VIO.   Excellently done, if God did all.

OLI.   'T is in grain,[24] sir; 't will endure wind and weather.

VIO.   'T is beauty truly blent, whose red and white
Nature's own sweet and cunning hand laid on:
Lady, you are the cruell'st she alive,
If you will lead these graces to the grave
And leave the world no copy.

OLI.   O, sir, I will not be so hard-hearted; I will give out divers sched-
ules of my beauty: it shall be inventoried, and every particle and
utensil labelled to my will: as, item, two lips, indifferent red; item,
two grey eyes, with lids to them; item, one neck, one chin, and so
forth. Were you sent hither to praise me?

VIO.   I see you what you are, you are too proud;
But, if you were the devil, you are fair.
My lord and master loves you: O, such love
Could be but recompensed, though you were crown'd

---

24. *in grain*] of a fast dye that will not wash out.

             The nonpareil of beauty!
OLI.   How does he love me?
VIO.   With adorations, fertile tears,
       With groans that thunder love, with sighs of fire.
OLI.   Your lord does know my mind; I cannot love him:
       Yet I suppose him virtuous, know him noble,
       Of great estate, of fresh and stainless youth;
       In voices well divulged,[25] free, learn'd and valiant;
       And in dimension and the shape of nature
       A gracious person; but yet I cannot love him;
       He might have took his answer long ago.
VIO.   If I did love you in my master's flame,
       With such a suffering, such a deadly life,
       In your denial I would find no sense;
       I would not understand it.
OLI.   Why, what would you?
VIO.   Make me a willow cabin at your gate,
       And call upon my soul within the house;
       Write loyal cantons of contemned love
       And sing them loud even in the dead of night;
       Halloo your name to the reverberate hills,
       And make the babbling gossip of the air
       Cry out "Olivia!" O, you should not rest
       Between the elements of air and earth,
       But you should pity me!
OLI.   You might do much.
       What is your parentage?
VIO.   Above my fortunes, yet my state is well:
       I am a gentleman.
OLI.   Get you to your lord;
       I cannot love him: let him send no more;
       Unless, perchance, you come to me again,
       To tell me how he takes it. Fare you well:
       I thank you for your pains: spend this for me.
VIO.   I am no fee'd post,[26] lady; keep your purse:
       My master, not myself, lacks recompense.
       Love make his heart of flint that you shall love;
       And let your fervour, like my master's, be

---

25. *well divulged*] well spoken of by the world.
26. *fee'd post*] hired messenger.

       Placed in contempt! Farewell, fair cruelty.   [*Exit.*]
OLI.   "What is your parentage?"
       "Above my fortunes, yet my state is well:
       I am a gentleman." I 'll be sworn thou art;
       Thy tongue, thy face, thy limbs, actions, and spirit,
       Do give thee five-fold blazon:[27] not too fast: soft, soft!
       Unless the master were the man. How now!
       Even so quickly may one catch the plague?
       Methinks I feel this youth's perfections
       With an invisible and subtle stealth
       To creep in at mine eyes. Well, let it be.
       What ho, Malvolio!

Re-enter MALVOLIO

MAL.   Here, madam, at your service.
OLI.   Run after that same peevish messenger,
       The county's man: he left this ring behind him,
       Would I or not: tell him I 'll none of it.
       Desire him not to flatter with his lord,
       Nor hold him up with hopes; I am not for him:
       If that the youth will come this way to-morrow,
       I 'll give him reasons for 't: hie thee, Malvolio.
MAL.   Madam, I will.   [*Exit.*]
OLI.   I do I know not what, and fear to find
       Mine eye too great a flatterer for my mind.
       Fate, show thy force: ourselves we do not owe;
       What is decreed must be, and be this so.   [*Exit.*]

---

27. *blazon*] coat of arms.

ACT II

SCENE I. *The sea-coast.*

Enter ANTONIO *and* SEBASTIAN

ANT.　Will you stay no longer? nor will you not that I go with you?

SEB.　By your patience, no. My stars shine darkly over me: the malignancy of my fate might perhaps distemper yours; therefore I shall crave of you your leave that I may bear my evils alone: it were a bad recompense for your love, to lay any of them on you.

ANT.　Let me yet know of you whither you are bound.

SEB.　No, sooth, sir: my determinate voyage is mere extravagancy.[1] But I perceive in you so excellent a touch of modesty, that you will not extort from me what I am willing to keep in; therefore it charges me in manners the rather to express myself. You must know of me then, Antonio, my name is Sebastian, which I called Roderigo. My father was that Sebastian of Messaline, whom I know you have heard of. He left behind him myself and a sister, both born in an hour: if the heavens had been pleased, would we had so ended! but you, sir, altered that; for some hour before you took me from the breach of the sea was my sister drowned.

ANT.　Alas the day!

SEB.　A lady, sir, though it was said she much resembled me, was yet of many accounted beautiful: but, though I could not with such estimable wonder overfar believe that, yet thus far I will boldly publish her; she bore a mind that envy could not but call fair. She is drowned already, sir, with salt water, though I seem to drown her remembrance again with more.

ANT.　Pardon me, sir, your bad entertainment.

SEB.　O good Antonio, forgive me your trouble.

ANT.　If you will not murder me for my love, let me be your servant.

SEB.　If you will not undo what you have done, that is, kill him whom you have recovered, desire it not. Fare ye well at once: my bosom is full of kindness, and I am yet so near the manners of my moth-

---

1. *my determinate . . . extravagancy*] The voyage I have resolved upon is mere vagrancy, mere roaming.

er, that upon the least occasion more mine eyes will tell tales of me. I am bound to the Count Orsino's court: farewell.   [*Exit.*]

ANT.   The gentleness of all the gods go with thee!
I have many enemies in Orsino's court,
Else would I very shortly see thee there.
But, come what may, I do adore thee so,
That danger shall seem sport, and I will go.   [*Exit.*]

SCENE II. *A street.*

Enter VIOLA, MALVOLIO *following*

MAL.   Were not you even now with the Countess Olivia?

VIO.   Even now, sir; on a moderate pace I have since arrived but hither.

MAL.   She returns this ring to you, sir: you might have saved me my pains, to have taken it away yourself. She adds, moreover, that you should put your lord into a desperate assurance she will none of him: and one thing more, that you be never so hardy to come again in his affairs, unless it be to report your lord's taking of this. Receive it so.

VIO.   She took the ring of me: I 'll none of it.

MAL.   Come, sir, you peevishly threw it to her; and her will is, it should be so returned: if it be worth stooping for, there it lies in your eye; if not, be it his that finds it.   [*Exit.*]

VIO.   I left no ring with her: what means this lady?
Fortune forbid my outside have not charm'd her!
She made good view of me; indeed, so much,
That methought her eyes had lost her tongue,
For she did speak in starts distractedly.
She loves me, sure; the cunning of her passion
Invites me in this churlish messenger.
None of my lord's ring! why, he sent her none.
I am the man: if it be so, as 't is,
Poor lady, she were better love a dream.
Disguise, I see, thou art a wickedness,

Wherein the pregnant enemy[1] does much.
How easy is it for the proper-false
In women's waxen hearts to set their forms!
Alas, our frailty is the cause, not we!
For such as we are made of, such we be.
How will this fadge?[2] my master loves her dearly;
And I, poor monster, fond as much on him;
And she, mistaken, seems to dote on me.
What will become of this? As I am man,
My state is desperate for my master's love;
As I am woman,—now alas the day!—
What thriftless sighs shall poor Olivia breathe!
O time! thou must untangle this, not I;
It is too hard a knot for me to untie! [*Exit.*]

SCENE III. OLIVIA'S *house.*

Enter SIR TOBY *and* SIR ANDREW

SIR TO. Approach, Sir Andrew: not to be a-bed after midnight is to be up betimes; and "diluculo surgere,"[1] thou know'st,—

SIR AND. Nay, by my troth, I know not: but I know, to be up late is to be up late.

SIR TO. A false conclusion: I hate it as an unfilled can. To be up after midnight and to go to bed then, is early: so that to go to bed after midnight is to go to bed betimes. Does not our life consist of the four elements?

SIR AND. Faith, so they say; but I think it rather consists of eating and drinking.

SIR TO. Thou 'rt a scholar; let us therefore eat and drink. Marian, I say! a stoup of wine!

Enter Clown

---

1. *the pregnant enemy*] the alert enemy of mankind, i.e., the devil.
2. *fadge*] turn out.

---

1. *"diluculo surgere"*] sc. saluberrimum est, "To rise at dawn is very healthy."

SIR AND.   Here comes the fool, i' faith.

CLO.   How now, my hearts! did you never see the picture of "we three"?[2]

SIR TO.   Welcome, ass. Now let 's have a catch.[3]

SIR AND.   By my troth, the fool has an excellent breast. I had rather than forty shillings I had such a leg, and so sweet a breath to sing, as the fool has. In sooth, thou wast in very gracious fooling last night, when thou spokest of Pigrogromitus, of the Vapians passing the equinoctial of Queubus:[4] 't was very good, i' faith. I sent thee sixpence for thy leman:[5] hadst it?

CLO.   I did impeticos thy gratillity; for Malvolio's nose is no whip-stock: my lady has a white hand, and the Myrmidons are no bot-tle-ale houses.[6]

SIR AND.   Excellent! why, this is the best fooling, when all is done. Now, a song.

SIR TO.   Come on; there is sixpence for you: let 's have a song.

SIR AND.   There 's a testril[7] of me too: if one knight give a—

CLO.   Would you have a love-song, or a song of good life?

SIR TO.   A love-song, a love-song.

SIR AND.   Ay, ay: I care not for good life.

CLO.   [Sings]

> O mistress mine, where are you roaming?
> O, stay and hear; your true love's coming,
>   That can sing both high and low:
> Trip no further, pretty sweeting;
> Journeys end in lovers meeting,
>   Every wise man's son doth know.

SIR AND.   Excellent good, i' faith.

SIR TO.   Good, good.

---

2. *picture of "we three"*] a common ale-house sign on which was painted the heads of two fools, or two asses, with the legend "We three logger-heads be." The spectator makes up the trio.

3. *a catch*] a song sung in succession, i.e. a round.

4. *Pigrogromitus . . . Queubus*] proper names invented for the occasion.

5. *leman*] lover.

6. *I did impeticos . . . houses*] The clown talks nonsense to something of this effect: "I impocketed thy diminutive gratuity (or I gave it to my petticoat companion). Malvolio's inquisitive nose may smell out our sins, but cannot punish them. My sweetheart is a lady of refinement, and the myrmidons, the humbler retainers of a noble household, are not of the vulgar and coarse character attaching to pot-houses."

7. *testril*] sixpence.

CLO. [*Sings*]

> What is love? 't is not hereafter;
> Present mirth hath present laughter;
>   What 's to come is still unsure:
> In delay there lies no plenty;
> Then come kiss me, sweet and twenty,
>   Youth 's a stuff will not endure.

SIR AND.   A mellifluous voice, as I am true knight.

SIR TO.   A contagious breath.

SIR AND.   Very sweet and contagious, i' faith.

SIR TO.   To hear by the nose, it is dulcet in contagion. But shall we make the welkin dance indeed? shall we rouse the night-owl in a catch that will draw three souls out of one weaver?[8] shall we do that?

SIR AND.   An you love me, let 's do 't: I am dog at a catch.

CLO.   By 'r lady, sir, and some dogs will catch well.

SIR AND.   Most certain. Let our catch be, "Thou knave."

CLO.   "Hold thy peace, thou knave," knight? I shall be constrained in 't to call thee knave, knight.

SIR AND.   'T is not the first time I have constrained one to call me knave. Begin, fool: it begins "Hold thy peace."

CLO.   I shall never begin if I hold my peace.

SIR AND.   Good, i' faith. Come, begin.   [*Catch sung.*]

Enter MARIA

MAR.   What a caterwauling do you keep here! If my lady have not called up her steward Malvolio and bid him turn you out of doors, never trust me.

SIR TO.   My lady 's a Cataian,[9] we are politicians, Malvolio 's a Peg-a-Ramsey, and "Three merry men be we."[10] Am not I consanguineous? am I not of her blood? Tillyvally. Lady! [*Sings*] "There dwelt a man in Babylon, lady, lady!"

CLO.   Beshrew me, the knight 's in admirable fooling.

SIR AND.   Ay, he does well enough if he be disposed, and so do I too: he does it with a better grace, but I do it more natural.

SIR TO.   [*Sings*] "O, the twelfth day of December," —

---

8. *catch . . . weaver*] Weavers were commonly held to be good singers. The "catch that will draw three souls out of one weaver" must have rare powers of enchantment.

9. *a Cataian*] a Chinese person (used as a term of reproach).

10. *Peg-a-Ramsey. . . be we*"] songs.

MAR.   For the love o' God, peace!

Enter MALVOLIO

MAL.   My masters, are you mad? or what are you? Have you no wit, manners, nor honesty, but to gabble like tinkers at this time of night? Do ye make an ale-house of my lady's house, that ye squeak out your coziers'[11] catches without any mitigation or remorse of voice? Is there no respect of place, persons, nor time in you?

SIR TO.   We did keep time, sir, in our catches. Sneck up!

MAL.   Sir Toby, I must be round with you. My lady bade me tell you, that, though she harbours you as her kinsman, she 's nothing allied to your disorders. If you can separate yourself and your misdemeanours, you are welcome to the house; if not, an it would please you to take leave of her, she is very willing to bid you farewell.

SIR TO.   "Farewell, dear heart, since I must needs be gone."

MAR.   Nay, good Sir Toby.

CLO.   "His eyes do show his days are almost done."

MAL.   Is 't even so?

SIR TO.   "But I will never die."

CLO.   Sir Toby, there you lie.

MAL.   This is much credit to you.

SIR TO.   "Shall I bid him go?"

CLO.   "What an if you do?"

SIR TO.   "Shall I bid him go, and spare not?"

CLO.   "O no, no, no, no, you dare not."

SIR TO.   Out o' tune, sir: ye lie. Art any more than a steward? Dost thou think, because thou art virtuous, there shall be no more cakes and ale?

CLO.   Yes, by Saint Anne, and ginger shall be hot i' the mouth too.

SIR TO.   Thou 'rt i' the right. Go, sir, rub your chain[12] with crums. A stoup of wine, Maria!

MAL.   Mistress Mary, if you prized my lady's favour at any thing more than contempt, you would not give means for this uncivil rule: she shall know of it, by this hand.   [*Exit.*]

MAR.   Go shake your ears.

SIR AND.   'T were as good a deed as to drink when a man 's a-hungry,

---

11. *coziers'*] cobblers'.
12. *rub your chain*] Stewards wore gold chains round their necks in right of their office.

to challenge him the field, and then to break promise with him and make a fool of him.

SIR TO.　Do 't, knight: I 'll write thee a challenge; or I 'll deliver thy indignation to him by word of mouth.

MAR.　Sweet Sir Toby, be patient for to-night: since the youth of the count's was to-day with my lady, she is much out of quiet. For Monsieur Malvolio, let me alone with him: if I do not gull him into a nayword,[13] and make him a common recreation, do not think I have wit enough to lie straight in my bed: I know I can do it.

SIR TO.　Possess us, possess us; tell us something of him.

MAR.　Marry, sir, sometimes he is a kind of puritan.

SIR AND.　O, if I thought that, I 'ld beat him like a dog!

SIR TO.　What, for being a puritan? thy exquisite reason, dear knight?

SIR AND.　I have no exquisite reason for 't, but I have reason good enough.

MAR.　The devil a puritan that he is, or any thing constantly, but a time-pleaser; an affectioned ass, that cons state without book and utters it by great swarths:[14] the best persuaded of himself, so crammed, as he thinks, with excellencies, that it is his grounds of faith that all that look on him love him; and on that vice in him will my revenge find notable cause to work.

SIR TO.　What wilt thou do?

MAR.　I will drop in his way some obscure epistles of love; wherein, by the colour of his beard, the shape of his leg, the manner of his gait, the expressure[15] of his eye, forehead, and complexion, he shall find himself most feelingly personated. I can write very like my lady your niece: on a forgotten matter we can hardly make distinction of our hands.

SIR TO.　Excellent! I smell a device.

SIR AND.　I have 't in my nose too.

SIR TO.　He shall think, by the letters that thou wilt drop, that they come from my niece, and that she 's in love with him.

MAR.　My purpose is, indeed, a horse of that colour.

SIR AND.　And your horse now would make him an ass.

MAR.　Ass, I doubt not.

SIR AND.　O, 't will be admirable!

---

13. *gull him . . . nayword*] trick him so that he becomes a byword or laughing-stock.
14. *cons . . . swarths*] learns by heart gossip of state affairs and spouts it in great lengths or masses.
15. *expressure*] accurate description.

MAR.   Sport royal, I warrant you: I know my physic will work with
      him. I will plant you two, and let the fool make a third, where he
      shall find the letter: observe his construction of it. For this night,
      to bed, and dream on the event. Farewell.   [*Exit.*]
SIR TO.   Good night, Penthesilea.[16]
SIR AND.   Before me, she 's a good wench.
SIR TO.   She 's a beagle, true-bred, and one that adores me: what o'
      that?
SIR AND.   I was adored once too.
SIR TO.   Let 's to bed, knight. Thou hadst need send for more money.
SIR AND.   If I cannot recover your niece, I am a foul way out.
SIR TO.   Send for money, knight: if thou hast her not i' the end, call
      me cut.[17]
SIR AND.   If I do not, never trust me, take it how you will.
SIR TO.   Come, come, I 'll go burn some sack; 't is too late to go to
      bed now: come, knight; come, knight.   [*Exeunt.*]

SCENE IV. *The* DUKE'S *palace.*

Enter DUKE, VIOLA, CURIO, *and others*

DUKE.   Give me some music. Now, good morrow, friends.
      Now, good Cesario, but that piece of song,
      That old and antique song we heard last night:
      Methought it did relieve my passion much,
      More than light airs and recollected terms[1]
      Of these most brisk and giddy-paced times:
      Come, but one verse.
CUR.   He is not here, so please your lordship, that should sing it.
DUKE.   Who was it?
CUR.   Feste, the jester, my lord; a fool that the lady Olivia's father took
      much delight in. He is about the house.
DUKE.   Seek him out, and play the tune the while.

---

16. *Penthesilea*] Queen of the Amazons (another ironic reference to Maria's small size).
17. *cut*] a common expression of contempt, "cut" meaning a bobtailed horse.

---

1. *recollected terms*] studied or stilted expressions; phrases lacking spontaneity.

                            [*Exit* CURIO. *Music plays.*]

    Come hither, boy: if ever thou shalt love,
    In the sweet pangs of it remember me;
    For such as I am all true lovers are,
    Unstaid and skittish in all motions else,
    Save in the constant image of the creature
    That is beloved. How dost thou like this tune?

VIO.   It gives a very echo to the seat
    Where Love is throned.

DUKE.   Thou dost speak masterly:
    My life upon 't, young though thou art, thine eye
    Hath stay'd upon some favour that it loves:
    Hath it not, boy?

VIO.   A little, by your favour.

DUKE.   What kind of woman is 't?

VIO.   Of your complexion.

DUKE.   She is not worth thee, then. What years, i' faith?

VIO.   About your years, my lord.

DUKE.   Too old, by heaven: let still the woman take
    An elder than herself; so wears she to him,
    So sways she level in her husband's heart:
    For, boy, however we do praise ourselves,
    Our fancies are more giddy and unfirm,
    More longing, wavering, sooner lost and worn,
    Than women's are.

VIO.   I think it well, my lord.

DUKE.   Then let thy love be younger than thyself,
    Or thy affection cannot hold the bent;
    For women are as roses, whose fair flower
    Being once display'd, doth fall that very hour.

VIO.   And so they are: alas, that they are so;
    To die, even when they to perfection grow!

Re-enter CURIO *and* Clown

DUKE.   O, fellow, come, the song we had last night.
    Mark it, Cesario, it is old and plain;
    The spinsters and the knitters in the sun
    And the free maids that weave their thread with bones
    Do use to chant it: it is silly sooth,
    And dallies with the innocence of love,

Like the old age.[2]

CLO.   Are you ready, sir?

DUKE.   Ay; prithee, sing.   [*Music.*]

SONG

CLO.   Come away, come away, death,
          And in sad cypress[3] let me be laid;
        Fly away, fly away, breath;
          I am slain by a fair cruel maid.
        My shroud of white, stuck all with yew,
                  O, prepare it!
        My part of death, no one so true
                  Did share it.

        Not a flower, not a flower sweet,
          On my black coffin let there be strown;
        Not a friend, not a friend greet
          My poor corpse, where my bones shall be thrown:
        A thousand thousand sighs to save,
                  Lay me, O, where
        Sad true lover never find my grave,
                  To weep there!

DUKE.   There 's for thy pains.

CLO.   No pains, sir; I take pleasure in singing, sir.

DUKE.   I 'll pay thy pleasure then.

CLO.   Truly, sir, and pleasure will be paid, one time or another.

DUKE.   Give me now leave to leave thee.

CLO.   Now, the melancholy god protect thee; and the tailor make thy
        doublet of changeable taffeta, for thy mind is a very opal. I would
        have men of such constancy put to sea, that their business might
        be every thing and their intent every where; for that 's it that always
        makes a good voyage of nothing. Farewell.   [*Exit.*]

DUKE.   Let all the rest give place.   [CURIO *and* Attendants *retire.*]
                          Once more, Cesario,
        Get thee to yond same sovereign cruelty:
        Tell her, my love, more noble than the world,
        Prizes not quantity of dirty lands;
        The parts that fortune hath bestow'd upon her,
        Tell her, I hold as giddily as fortune;

---

2. *the old age*] times past.
3. *cypress*] coffin of cypress wood.

But 't is that miracle and queen of gems
That nature pranks her in attracts my soul.

VIO.   But if she cannot love you, sir?

DUKE.   I cannot be so answer'd.

VIO.   Sooth, but you must.
Say that some lady, as perhaps there is,
Hath for your love as great a pang of heart
As you have for Olivia: you cannot love her;
You tell her so; must she not then be answer'd?

DUKE.   There is no woman's sides
Can bide the beating of so strong a passion
As love doth give my heart; no woman's heart
So big, to hold so much; they lack retention.[4]
Alas, their love may be call'd appetite,—
No motion of the liver, but the palate,—
That suffer surfeit, cloyment[5] and revolt;
But mine is all as hungry as the sea,
And can digest as much: make no compare
Between that love a woman can bear me
And that I owe Olivia.

VIO.   Ay, but I know,—

DUKE.   What dost thou know?

VIO.   Too well what love women to men may owe:
In faith, they are as true of heart as we.
My father had a daughter loved a man,
As it might be, perhaps, were I a woman,
I should your lordship.

DUKE.   And what 's her history?

VIO.   A blank, my lord. She never told her love,
But let concealment, like a worm i' the bud,
Feed on her damask cheek: she pined in thought;
And with a green and yellow melancholy
She sat like patience on a monument,
Smiling at grief. Was not this love indeed?
We men may say more, swear more: but indeed
Our shows are more than will; for still we prove
Much in our vows, but little in our love.

DUKE.   But died thy sister of her love, my boy?

---

4. *retention*] power of retaining.
5. *cloyment*] satiety.

Vio.   I am all the daughters of my father's house,
    And all the brothers too: and yet I know not.
    Sir, shall I to this lady?
Duke.   Ay, that 's the theme.
    To her in haste; give her this jewel; say,
    My love can give no place, bide no denay.   *[Exeunt.]*

Scene V. Olivia's *garden.*

Enter Sir Toby, Sir Andrew, *and* Fabian

Sir To.   Come thy ways, Signior Fabian.
Fab.   Nay, I 'll come: if I lose a scruple of this sport, let me be boiled
    to death with melancholy.
Sir To.   Wouldst thou not be glad to have the niggardly rascally
    sheep-biter[1] come by some notable shame?
Fab.   I would exult, man: you know, he brought me out o' favour with
    my lady about a bear-baiting here.
Sir To.   To anger him we 'll have the bear again; and we will fool him
    black and blue: shall we not, Sir Andrew?
Sir And.   An we do not, it is pity of our lives.
Sir To.   Here comes the little villain.

Enter Maria

    How now, my metal of India![2]
Mar.   Get ye all three into the box-tree: Malvolio's coming down this
    walk: he has been yonder i' the sun practising behaviour to his
    own shadow this half hour: observe him, for the love of mockery;
    for I know this letter will make a contemplative idiot of him.
    Close, in the name of jesting! Lie thou there [*throws down a let-*
    ter]; for here comes the trout that must be caught with tickling.
                                          [Exit.]

Enter Malvolio

---

1. *sheep-biter*] A contemptuous term derived from a dog that worries sheep by biting.
2. *my metal of India*] my treasure of gold.

MAL. 'T is but fortune; all is fortune. Maria once told me she[3] did affect me: and I have heard herself come thus near, that, should she fancy, it should be one of my complexion. Besides, she uses me with a more exalted respect than any one else that follows her. What should I think on 't?

SIR TO. Here's an overweening rogue!

FAB. O, peace! Contemplation makes a rare turkey-cock of him: how he jets under his advanced plumes!

SIR AND. 'Slight, I could so beat the rogue!

SIR TO. Peace, I say.

MAL. To be Count Malvolio!

SIR TO. Ah, rogue!

SIR AND. Pistol him, pistol him.

SIR TO. Peace, peace!

MAL. There is example for 't; the lady of the Strachy married the yeoman of the wardrobe.

SIR AND. Fie on him Jezebel!

FAB. O, peace! now he 's deeply in: look how imagination blows him.

MAL. Having been three months married to her, sitting in my state,—

SIR TO. O, for a stone-bow,[4] to hit him in the eye!

MAL. Calling my officers about me, in my branched velvet[5] gown; having come from a day-bed, where I have left Olivia sleeping,—

SIR TO. Fire and brimstone!

FAB. O, peace, peace!

MAL. And then to have the humour of state; and after a demure travel of regard, telling them I know my place as I would they should do theirs, to ask for my kinsman Toby,—

SIR TO. Bolts and shackles!

FAB. O, peace, peace, peace! now, now.

MAL. Seven of my people, with an obedient start, make out for him: I frown the while; and perchance wind up my watch, or play with my—some rich jewel. Toby approaches; courtesies there to me,—

SIR TO. Shall this fellow live?

FAB. Though our silence be drawn from us with cars,[6] yet peace.

MAL. I extend my hand to him thus, quenching my familiar smile with an austere regard of control,—

---

3. *she*] i. e., Olivia, Maria's mistress.
4. *stone-bow*] a cross-bow from which stones were shot.
5. *branched velvet*] velvet ornamented with patterns of leaves and flowers.
6. *cars*] as in teams of horses.

SIR TO.   And does not Toby take you a blow o' the lips then?

MAL.   Saying, "Cousin Toby, my fortunes having cast me on your niece give me this prerogative of speech,"—

SIR TO.   What, what?

MAL.   "You must amend your drunkenness."

SIR TO.   Out, scab!

FAB.   Nay, patience, or we break the sinews of our plot.

MAL.   "Besides, you waste the treasure of your time with a foolish knight,"—

SIR AND.   That's me, I warrant you.

MAL.   "One Sir Andrew,"—

SIR AND.   I knew 't was I; for many do call me fool.

MAL.   What employment[7] have we here?   [*Taking up the letter.*]

FAB.   Now is the woodcock near the gin.[8]

SIR TO.   O, peace! and the spirit of humours intimate reading aloud to him!

MAL.   By my life, this is my lady's hand: these be her very C's, her U's, and her T's; and thus makes she her great P's. It is, in contempt of question, her hand.

SIR AND.   Her C's, her U's and her T's: why that?

MAL.   [*Reads*]   To the unknown beloved, this, and my good wishes:—her very phrases! By your leave, wax. Soft! and the impressure her Lucrece,[9] with which she uses to seal: 't is my lady. To whom should this be?

FAB.   This wins him, liver and all.

MAL. [*Reads*]
>Jove knows I love:
>   But who?
>Lips, do not move;
>No man must know.

"No man must know." What follows? the numbers altered! "No man must know:" if this should be thee, Malvolio?

SIR TO.   Marry, hang thee, brock![10]

---

7. *employment*] work, business.

8. *gin*] snare.

9. *impressure her Lucrece*] the impression on the letter's sealing wax was made by a seal bearing the figure of the Roman matron Lucrece.

10. *brock*] badger.

MAL. [*Reads*]   I may command where I adore;
                But silence, like a Lucrece knife,
                With bloodless stroke my heart doth gore:
                M, O, A, I, doth sway my life.

FAB.   A fustian riddle!

SIR TO.   Excellent wench, say I.

MAL.   "M, O, A, I, doth sway my life." Nay, but first, let me see, let me see, let me see.

FAB.   What dish o' poison has she dressed him!

SIR TO.   And with what wing the staniel checks[11] at it!

MAL.   "I may command where I adore." Why, she may command me: I serve her; she is my lady. Why, this is evident to any formal capacity;[12] there is no obstruction in this: and the end,—what should that alphabetical position portend? If I could make that resemble something in me,—Softly! M, O, A, I,—

SIR TO.   O, ay, make up that: he is now at a cold scent.

FAB.   Sowter will cry upon 't for all this, though it be as rank as a fox.[13]

MAL.   M,—Malvolio; M,—why, that begins my name.

FAB.   Did not I say he would work it out? the cur is excellent at faults.

MAL.   M,—but then there is no consonancy in the sequel; that suffers under probation: A should follow, but O does.

FAB.   And O shall end, I hope.

SIR TO.   Ay, or I 'll cudgel him, and make him cry O!

MAL.   And then I comes behind.

FAB.   Ay, an you had any eye behind you, you might see more detraction at your heels than fortunes before you.

MAL.   M, O, A, I; this simulation is not as the former: and yet, to crush this a little, it would bow to me, for every one of these letters are in my name. Soft! here follows prose.

[*Reads*]   If this fall into thy hand, revolve. In my stars I am above thee; but be not afraid of greatness: some are born great, some achieve greatness, and some have greatness thrust upon 'em. Thy Fates open their hands; let thy blood and spirit embrace them; and, to inure thyself to what thou art like to be, cast thy humble slough and appear fresh. Be

---

11. *staniel checks*] staniel is a kind of hawk, and the verb "check" is a technical term in falconry, applied to the hawk's sudden swoop in flight when she catches sight of winged prey.

12. *formal capacity*] well-regulated mind.

13. *Sowter . . . fox*] "Sowter" (i. e., botcher, cobbler) is used as the name of a bad, dull hound. So poor a cur, although capable of any amount of bungling, must take this scent.

opposite with a kinsman, surly with servants; let thy tongue tang[14] arguments of state; put thyself into the trick of singularity: she thus advises thee that sighs for thee. Remember who commended thy yellow stockings, and wished to see thee ever cross-gartered:[15] I say, remember. Go to, thou art made, if thou desirest to be so; if not, let me see thee a steward still, the fellow of servants, and not worthy to touch Fortune's fingers. Farewell. She that would alter services with thee,

THE FORTUNATE-UNHAPPY.

Daylight and champain[16] discovers not more: this is open. I will be proud, I will read politic authors, I will baffle Sir Toby, I will wash off gross acquaintance, I will be point-devise[17] the very man. I do not now fool myself, to let imagination jade me; for every reason excites to this, that my lady loves me. She did commend my yellow stockings of late, she did praise my leg being cross-gartered; and in this she manifests herself to my love, and with a kind of injunction drives me to these habits of her liking. I thank my stars I am happy. I will be strange, stout, in yellow stockings, and cross-gartered, even with the swiftness of putting on. Jove and my stars be praised! Here is yet a postscript.

[*Reads*]   Thou canst not choose but know who I am. If thou entertainest my love, let it appear in thy smiling; thy smiles become thee well; therefore in my presence still smile, dear my sweet, I prithee.

Jove, I thank thee: I will smile; I will do every thing that thou wilt have me.   [*Exit.*]

FAB.   I will not give my part of this sport for a pension of thousands to be paid from the Sophy.[18]

SIR TO.   I could marry this wench for this device,—

SIR AND.   So could I too.

SIR TO.   And ask no other dowry with her but such another jest.

SIR AND.   Nor I neither.

FAB.   Here comes my noble gull-catcher.[19]

Re-enter MARIA

---

14. *tang*] ring or sound loud with.
15. *yellow stockings and . . . cross-gartered*] Yellow was at the time a popular colour of stockings; men of fashion were in the habit of wearing their garters crossed both above and below the knee, with the ends fastened together behind the knee.
16. *champain*] open country.
17. *point-devise*] exactly (point-by-point) as the letter describes.
18. *the Sophy*] the Shah of Persia.
19. *gull-catcher*] fool-catcher.

SIR TO.   Wilt thou set thy foot o' my neck?

SIR AND.   Or o' mine either?

SIR TO.   Shall I play my freedom at tray-trip,[20] and become thy bond-slave?

SIR AND.   I' faith, or I either?

SIR TO.   Why, thou has put him in such a dream, that when the image of it leaves him he must run mad.

MAR.   Nay, but say true; does it work upon him?

SIR TO.   Like aqua-vitæ[21] with a midwife.

MAR.   If you will then see the fruits of the sport, mark his first approach before my lady: he will come to her in yellow stockings, and 't is a colour she abhors, and cross-gartered, a fashion she detests; and he will smile upon her, which will now be so unsuitable to her disposition, being addicted to a melancholy as she is, that it cannot but turn him into a notable contempt. If you will see it, follow me.

SIR TO.   To the gates of Tartar,[22] thou most excellent devil of wit!

SIR AND.   I 'll make one too.   [*Exeunt.*]

ACT III.

SCENE I. OLIVIA'S *garden.*

Enter VIOLA, *and* Clown *with a tabor*

VIO.   Save thee, friend, and thy music: dost thou live by thy tabor?

CLO.   No, sir, I live by the church.

VIO.   Art thou a churchman?

CLO.   No such matter, sir: I do live by the church; for I do live at my house, and my house doth stand by the church.

VIO.   So thou mayst say, the king lies by a beggar, if a beggar dwell near him; or, the church stands by the tabor, if thy tabor stand by the church.

---

20. *tray-trip*] a game of dice in which rolling a three ("tray") was desirable.
21. *aqua-vitæ*] strong spirits.
22. *Tartar*] Hell.

CLO.   You have said, sir. To see this age! A sentence[1] is but a cheveril[2] glove to a good wit: how quickly the wrong side may be turned outward!

VIO.   Nay, that 's certain; they that dally nicely with words may quickly make them wanton.

CLO.   I would, therefore, my sister had had no name, sir.

VIO.   Why, man?

CLO.   Why, sir, her name 's a word; and to dally with that word might make my sister wanton. But indeed words are very rascals since bonds disgraced them.

VIO.   Thy reason, man?

CLO.   Troth, sir, I can yield you none without words; and words are grown so false, I am loath to prove reason with them.

VIO.   I warrant thou art a merry fellow and carest for nothing.

CLO.   Not so, sir, I do care for something; but in my conscience, sir, I do not care for you: if that be to care for nothing, sir, I would it would make you invisible.

VIO.   Art not thou the Lady Olivia's fool?

CLO.   No, indeed, sir; the Lady Olivia has no folly: she will keep no fool, sir, till she be married; and fools are as like husbands as pilchards[3] are to herrings; the husband 's the bigger: I am indeed not her fool, but her corrupter of words.

VIO.   I saw thee late at the Count Orsino's.

CLO.   Foolery, sir, does walk about the orb like the sun, it shines every where. I would be sorry, sir, but the fool should be as oft with your master as with my mistress: I think I saw your wisdom there.

VIO.   Nay, an thou pass upon me,[4] I 'll no more with thee. Hold, there 's expenses for thee.

CLO.   Now Jove, in his next commodity of hair, send thee a beard!

VIO.   By my troth, I 'll tell thee, I am almost sick for one; [Aside] though I would not have it grow on my chin. Is thy lady within?

CLO.   Would not a pair of these have bred, sir?[5]

VIO.   Yes, being kept together and put to use.

CLO.   I would play Lord Pandarus of Phrygia, sir, to bring a Cressida to this Troilus.

---

1. *sentence*] maxim.
2. *cheveril*] very flexible leather from roebuck.
3. *pilchards*] or pilchers; fish resembling herrings.
4. *an . . . me*] if you make jokes at my expense.
5. *Would . . . bred*] Viola has given the clown two coins, and he wonders that they did not multiply (i.e., that his tip was not bigger).

VIO.   I understand you, sir; 't is well begged.
CLO.   The matter, I hope, is not great, sir, begging but a beggar:
    Cressida was a beggar. My lady is within, sir. I will construe to
    them whence you come; who you are and what you would are out
    of my welkin,[6] I might say "element," but the word is over-worn.

[*Exit.*]

VIO.   This fellow is wise enough to play the fool;
    And to do that well craves a kind of wit:
    He must observe their mood on whom he jests,
    The quality of persons, and the time,
    And, like the haggard, check at every feather[7]
    That comes before his eye. This is a practice
    As full of labour as a wise man's art:
    For folly that he wisely shows is fit;
    But wise men, folly-fall'n, quite taint their wit.

Enter SIR TOBY, *and* SIR ANDREW

SIR TO.   Save you, gentleman.
VIO.   And you, sir.
SIR AND.   Dieu vous garde, monsieur.
VIO.   Et vous aussi; votre serviteur.[8]
SIR AND.   I hope, sir, you are; and I am yours.
SIR TO.   Will you encounter[9] the house? my niece is desirous you
    should enter, if your trade be to her.
VIO.   I am bound to your niece, sir; I mean, she is the list[10] of my voy-
    age.
SIR TO.   Taste[11] your legs, sir; put them to motion.
VIO.   My legs do better understand me, sir, than I understand what
    you mean by bidding me taste my legs.
SIR TO.   I mean, to go, sir, to enter.
VIO.   I will answer you with gait and entrance. But we are prevented.

Enter OLIVIA *and* MARIA

    Most excellent accomplished lady, the heavens rain odours on you!

---

6. *welkin*] sky.
7. *like . . . feather*] see note 11 on page 32; a haggard is a wild, untrained hawk.
8. *Dieu . . . serviteur*] (Sir Andrew): God keep you, sir.
                    (Viola): And you, too; [I am] your servant.
9. *encounter*] enter.
10. *list*] bound, limit.
11. *Taste*] Try.

SIR AND.   That youth 's a rare courtier: "Rain odours"; well.

VIO.   My matter hath no voice, lady, but to your own most pregnant
and vouchsafed ear.

SIR AND.   "Odours," "pregnant," and "vouchsafed": I 'll get 'em all
three all ready.

OLI.   Let the garden door be shut, and leave me to my hearing.
[*Exeunt* SIR TOBY, SIR ANDREW, *and* MARIA.] Give me your hand,
sir.

VIO.   My duty, madam, and most humble service.

OLI.   What is your name?

VIO.   Cesario is your servant's name, fair princess.

OLI.   My servant, sir! 'T was never merry world
Since lowly feigning was call'd compliment:
You 're servant to the Count Orsino, youth.

VIO.   And he is yours, and his must needs be yours:
Your servant's servant is your servant, madam.

OLI.   For him, I think not on him: for his thoughts,
Would they were blanks, rather than fill'd with me!

VIO.   Madam, I come to whet your gentle thoughts
On his behalf.

OLI.   O, by your leave, I pray you;
I bade you never speak again of him:
But, would you undertake another suit,
I had rather hear you to solicit that
Than music from the spheres.

VIO.   Dear lady,—

OLI.   Give me leave, beseech you. I did send,
After the last enchantment you did here,
A ring in chase of you: so did I abuse
Myself, my servant and, I fear me, you:
Under your hard construction must I sit,
To force that on you, in a shameful cunning,
Which you knew none of yours: what might you think?
Have you not set mine honour at the stake
And baited it with all the unmuzzled thoughts
That tyrannous heart can think? To one of your receiving
Enough is shown: a cypress,[12] not a bosom,
Hides my heart. So, let me hear you speak.

---

12. *cypress*] mourning garments.

VIO. I pity you.

OLI.   That 's a degree to love.

VIO.   No, not a grize;[13] for 't is a vulgar proof,
     That very oft we pity enemies.

OLI.   Why, then, methinks, 't is time to smile again.
     O world, how apt the poor are to be proud!
     If one should be a prey, how much the better
     To fall before the lion than the wolf!   [*Clock strikes.*]
     The clock upbraids me with the waste of time.
     Be not afraid, good youth, I will not have you:
     And yet, when wit and youth is come to harvest,
     Your wife is like to reap a proper man:
     There lies your way, due west.

VIO.   Then westward-ho!
     Grace and good disposition attend your ladyship!
     You 'll nothing, madam, to my lord by me?

OLI.   Stay:
     I prithee, tell me what thou think'st of me.

VIO.   That you do think you are not what you are.

OLI.   If I think so, I think the same of you.

VIO.   Then think you right: I am not what I am.

OLI.   I would you were as I would have you be!

VIO.   Would it be better, madam, than I am?
     I wish it might, for now I am your fool.

OLI.   O, what a deal of scorn looks beautiful
     In the contempt and anger of his lip!
     A murderous guilt shows not itself more soon
     Than love that would seem hid: love's night is noon.
     Cesario, by the roses of the spring,
     By maidenhood, honour, truth and every thing,
     I love thee so, that, maugre[14] all thy pride,
     Nor wit nor reason can my passion hide.
     Do not extort thy reasons from this clause,
     For that I woo, thou therefore hast no cause;
     But rather reason thus with reason fetter,
     Love sought is good, but given unsought is better.

VIO.   By innocence I swear, and by my youth,
     I have one heart, one bosom and one truth,

---

13. *grize*] step.
14. *maugre*] in spite of.

And that no woman has; nor never none
Shall mistress be of it, save I alone.
And so adieu, good madam: never more
Will I my master's tears to you deplore.

OLI.   Yet come again; for thou perhaps mayst move
That heart, which now abhors, to like his love.   [*Exeunt.*]

SCENE II. OLIVIA'S *house.*

Enter SIR TOBY, SIR ANDREW, *and* FABIAN

SIR AND.   No, faith, I 'll not stay a jot longer.

SIR TO.   Thy reason, dear venom, give thy reason.

FAB.   You must needs yield your reason, Sir Andrew.

SIR AND.   Marry, I saw your niece do more favours to the count's serving-man than ever she bestowed upon me; I saw 't i' the orchard.

SIR TO.   Did she see thee the while, old boy? tell me that.

SIR AND.   As plain as I see you now.

FAB.   This was a great argument of love in her toward you.

SIR AND.   'Slight, will you make an ass o' me?

FAB.   I will prove it legitimate, sir, upon the oaths of judgement and
reason.

SIR TO.   And they have been grand-jurymen since before Noah was a
sailor.

FAB.   She did show favour to the youth in your sight only to exasperate
you, to awake your dormouse valour, to put fire in your heart, and
brimstone in your liver. You should then have accosted her; and
with some excellent jests, fire-new from the mint, you should have
banged the youth into dumbness. This was looked for at your hand,
and this was balked: the double gilt of this opportunity you let time
wash off, and you are now sailed into the north of my lady's opinion; where you will hang like an icicle on a Dutchman's beard,[1]

---

1. *like an icicle . . . beard*] This simile seems to have been suggested by an English translation of a Dutch account of the discovery by a Dutchman, Willem Barents, in 1596,
of Nova Zembla, and of the explorer's sufferings from extremity of cold. The translation seems to have been first published in 1598, though no copy earlier than 1609 has
been met with.

unless you do redeem it by some laudable attempt either of valour or policy.

SIR AND. An 't be any way, it must be with valour; for policy I hate: I had as lief be a Brownist[2] as a politician.

SIR TO. Why, then, build me thy fortunes upon the basis of valour. Challenge me the count's youth to fight with him; hurt him in eleven places: my niece shall take note of it; and assure thyself, there is no love-broker in the world can more prevail in man's commendation with woman than report of valour.

FAB. There is no way but this, Sir Andrew.

SIR AND. Will either of you bear me a challenge to him?

SIR TO. Go, write it in a martial hand; be curst[3] and brief; it is no matter how witty, so it be eloquent and full of invention: taunt him with the license of ink: if thou thou'st[4] him some thrice, it shall not be amiss; and as many lies as will lie in thy sheet of paper, although the sheet were big enough for the bed of Ware[5] in England, set 'em down: go, about it. Let there be gall enough in thy ink, though thou write with a goose-pen, no matter: about it.

SIR AND. Where shall I find you?

SIR TO. We 'll call thee at the cubiculo:[6] go.   [*Exit* SIR ANDREW.]

FAB. This is a dear manakin to you, Sir Toby.

SIR TO. I have been dear to him, lad, some two thousand strong, or so.

FAB. We shall have a rare letter from him: but you 'll not deliver 't?

SIR TO. Never trust me, then; and by all means stir on the youth to an answer. I think oxen and wainropes[7] cannot hale[8] them together. For Andrew, if he were opened, and you find so much blood in his liver as will clog the foot of a flea, I 'll eat the rest of the anatomy.

FAB. And his opposite, the youth, bears in his visage no great presage of cruelty.

Enter MARIA

---

2. *Brownist*] a member of the religious sect of Puritan separatists or independents, which was founded by Robert Brown about 1580, and rapidly spread in secret, despite efforts made to suppress it.

3. *curst*] waspish, bellicose.

4. *thou thou'st*] To address a person as "thou" was held to be insulting.

5. *bed of Ware*] A giant bed, capable of holding twelve persons, long gave notoriety to an inn at Ware, a village in Hertfordshire.

6. *the cubiculo*] Sir Toby's bombastic periphrasis for Sir Andrew's lodging or bedroom.

7. *wainropes*] cart ropes.

8. *hale*] pull, drag.

SIR TO.   Look, where the youngest wren of nine comes.[9]

MAR.   If you desire the spleen, and will laugh yourselves into stitches, follow me. Yond gull[10] Malvolio is turned heathen, a very renegado; for there is no Christian, that means to be saved by believing rightly, can ever believe such impossible passages of grossness.[11] He 's in yellow stockings.

SIR TO.   And cross-gartered?

MAR.   Most villanously; like a pedant that keeps a school i' the church. I have dogged him, like his murderer. He does obey every point of the letter that I dropped to betray him: he does smile his face into more lines than is in the new map with the augmentation of the Indies:[12] you have not seen such a thing as 't is. I can hardly forbear hurling things at him. I know my lady will strike him: if she do, he 'll smile and take 't for a great favour.

SIR TO.   Come, bring us, bring us where he is.   [*Exeunt.*]

SCENE III. *A street.*

Enter SEBASTIAN *and* ANTONIO

SEB.   I would not by my will have troubled you;
     But, since you make your pleasure of your pains,
     I will no further chide you.

ANT.   I could not stay behind you: my desire,
     More sharp than filed steel, did spur me forth;
     And not all love to see you, though so much
     As might have drawn one to a longer voyage,
     But jealousy what might befall your travel,
     Being skilless in these parts; which to a stranger,
     Unguided and unfriended, often prove

---

9. *wren of nine*] The allusion is to Maria's diminutive stature. The wren lays at a time nine or ten eggs, usually of descending size.

10. *gull*] fool; someone easily tricked.

11. *passages of grossness*] acts of absurdity.

12. *new map . . . Indies*] A new map of the world was made in 1599 by Emmerie Mollineux. It is multilineal, and plainly marks recent exploration in both the East and the West hemispheres.

Rough and unhospitable: my willing love,
The rather by these arguments of fear,
Set forth in your pursuit.

SEB.   My kind Antonio,
I can no other answer make but thanks,
And thanks; and ever. . . . oft good turns
Are shuffled off with such uncurrent pay:
But, were my worth as is my conscience firm,
You should find better dealing. What 's to do?
Shall we go see the reliques of this town?

ANT.   To-morrow, sir: best first go see your lodging.

SEB.   I am not weary, and 't is long to night:
I pray you, let us satisfy our eyes
With the memorials and the things of fame
That do renown this city.

ANT.   Would you 'ld pardon me;
I do not without danger walk these streets:
Once, in a sea-fight, 'gainst the count his galleys
I did some service; of such note indeed,
That were I ta'en here it would scarce be answer'd.

SEB.   Belike you slew great number of his people.

ANT.   The offence is not of such a bloody nature;
Albeit the quality of the time and quarrel
Might well have given us bloody argument.
It might have since been answer'd in repaying
What we took from them; which, for traffic's sake,
Most of our city did: only myself stood out;
For which, if I be lapsed[1] in this place,
I shall pay dear.

SEB.   Do not then walk too open.

ANT.   It doth not fit me. Hold, sir, here 's my purse.
In the south suburbs, at the Elephant,[2]
Is best to lodge: I will bespeak our diet,
Whiles you beguile the time and feed your knowledge
With viewing of the town: there shall you have me.

SEB.   Why I your purse?

ANT.   Haply your eye shall light upon some toy
You have desire to purchase; and your store,

---

1. *lapsed*] caught, surprised.
2. *Elephant*] an inn.

    I think, is not for idle markets, sir.
SEB.   I 'll be your purse-bearer and leave you
    For an hour.
ANT.   To the Elephant.
SEB.   I do remember.   [*Exeunt.*]

SCENE IV. OLIVIA'S *garden.*

Enter OLIVIA *and* MARIA

OLI.   I have sent after him: he[1] says he 'll come;
    How shall I feast him? what bestow of him?
    For youth is bought more oft than begg'd or borrow'd.
    I speak too loud.
    Where is Malvolio? he is sad and civil,
    And suits well for a servant with my fortunes:
    Where is Malvolio?
MAR.   He 's coming, madam; but in very strange manner. He is, sure,
    possessed, madam.
OLI.   Why, what 's the matter? does he rave?
MAR.   No, madam, he does nothing but smile: your ladyship were
    best to have some guard about you, if he come; for, sure, the man
    is tainted in 's wits.
OLI.   Go call him hither. [*Exit* MARIA.] I am as mad as he,
    If sad and merry madness equal be.

Re-enter MARIA, *with* MALVOLIO

    How now, Malvolio!
MAL.   Sweet lady, ho, ho.
OLI.   Smilest thou?
    I sent for thee upon a sad occasion.
MAL.   Sad, lady? I could be sad: this does make some obstruction in
    the blood, this cross-gartering; but what of that? if it please the eye
    of one, it is with me as the very true sonnet is, "Please one, and
    please all."

---

1. *he*] Cesario (i.e., Viola).

OLI. Why, how dost thou, man? what is the matter with thee?

MAL. Not black in my mind, though yellow in my legs. It did come to his hands, and commands shall be executed: I think we do know the sweet Roman hand.

OLI. Wilt thou go to bed, Malvolio?

MAL. To bed! ay, sweet-heart, and I 'll come to thee.

OLI. God comfort thee! Why dost thou smile so and kiss thy hand so oft?

MAR. How do you, Malvolio?

MAL. At your request! yes; nightingales answer daws.

MAR. Why appear you with this ridiculous boldness before my lady?

MAL. "Be not afraid of greatness": 't was well writ.

OLI. What meanest thou by that, Malvolio?

MAL. "Some are born great,"—

OLI. Ha!

MAL. "Some achieve greatness,"—

OLI. What sayest thou?

MAL. "And some have greatness thrust upon them."

OLI. Heaven restore thee!

MAL. "Remember who commended thy yellow stockings,"—

OLI. Thy yellow stockings!

MAL. "And wished to see thee cross-gartered."

OLI. Cross-gartered!

MAL. "Go to, thou art made, if thou desirest to be so";—

OLI. Am I made?

MAL. "If not, let me see thee a servant still."

OLI. Why, this is very midsummer madness.

Enter Servant

SER. Madam, the young gentleman of the Count Orsino's is returned: I could hardly entreat him back: he attends your ladyship's pleasure.

OLI. I 'll come to him. [*Exit* Servant.] Good Maria, let this fellow be looked to. Where 's my cousin Toby? Let some of my people have a special care of him: I would not have him miscarry for the half of my dowry. [*Exeunt* OLIVIA *and* MARIA.]

MAL. O, ho! do you come near² me now? no worse man than Sir Toby to look to me! This concurs directly with the letter: she sends

---

2. *come near*] understand.

him on purpose, that I may appear stubborn to him; for she incites
me to that in the letter. "Cast thy humble slough," says she; "be
opposite with a kinsman, surly with servants; let thy tongue tang
with arguments of state; put thyself into the trick of singularity";
and consequently sets down the manner how; as, a sad face, a reverend carriage, a slow tongue, in the habit of some sir of note, and
so forth. I have limed[3] her; but it is Jove's doing, and Jove make me
thankful! And when she went away now, "Let this fellow be looked
to": fellow! not Malvolio, nor after my degree, but fellow. Why,
every thing adheres together, that no dram of a scruple, no scruple of a scruple, no obstacle, no incredulous or unsafe circumstance— What can be said? Nothing that can be can come
between me and the full prospect of my hopes. Well, Jove, not I,
is the doer of this, and he is to be thanked.

Re-enter MARIA, *with* SIR TOBY *and* FABIAN

SIR TO.   Which way is he, in the name of sanctity? If all the devils of
      hell be drawn in little, and Legion[4] himself possessed him, yet I 'll
      speak to him.
FAB.   Here he is, here he is. How is 't with you, sir? how is 't with you,
      man?
MAL.   Go off; I discard you: let me enjoy my private: go off.
MAR.   Lo, how hollow the fiend speaks within him! did not I tell you?
      Sir Toby, my lady prays you to have a care of him.
MAL.   Ah, ha! does she so?
SIR TO.   Go to, go to; peace, peace; we must deal gently with him: let
      me alone. How do you, Malvolio? how is 't with you? What, man!
      defy the devil: consider, he 's an enemy to mankind.
MAL.   Do you know what you say?
MAR.   La you, an you speak ill of the devil, how he takes it at heart!
      Pray God, he be not bewitched!
FAB.   Carry his water to the wise woman.
MAR.   Marry, and it shall be done to-morrow morning, if I live. My
      lady would not lose him for more than I 'll say.
MAL.   How now, mistress!
MAR.   O Lord!

---

3. *limed*] caught, ensnared.
4. *Legion*] in the New Testament Christ exorcises a demon who calls himself "Legion: for
   we are many" (Mark 5:9).

SIR TO.   Prithee, hold thy peace; this is not the way: do you not see
     you move him? let me alone with him.
FAB.   No way but gentleness; gently, gently: the fiend is rough, and
     will not be roughly used.
SIR TO.   Why, how now, my bawcock! how dost thou, chuck?
MAL.   Sir!
SIR TO.   Ay, Biddy,[5] come with me. What, man! 't is not for gravity to
     play at cherry-pit with Satan: hang him, foul collier![6]
MAR.   Get him to say his prayers, good Sir Toby, get him to pray.
MAL.   My prayers, minx!
MAR.   No, I warrant you, he will not hear of godliness.
MAL.   Go, hang yourselves all! you are idle shallow things: I am not of
     your element: you shall know more hereafter.   [*Exit.*]
SIR TO.   Is 't possible?
FAB.   If this were played upon a stage now, I could condemn it as an
     improbable fiction.
SIR TO.   His very genius hath taken the infection of the device, man.
MAR.   Nay, pursue him now, lest the device take air and taint.
FAB.   Why, we shall make him mad indeed.
MAR.   The house will be the quieter.
SIR TO.   Come, we 'll have him in a dark room and bound. My niece
     is already in the belief that he 's mad: we may carry it thus, for our
     pleasure and his penance, till our very pastime, tired out of breath,
     prompt us to have mercy on him: at which time we will bring the
     device to the bar and crown thee for a finder of madmen.[7] But see,
     but see.

Enter SIR ANDREW

FAB.   More matter for a May morning.[8]
SIR AND.   Here 's the challenge, read it: I warrant there 's vinegar and
     pepper in 't.
FAB.   Is 't so saucy?
SIR AND.   Ay, is 't, I warrant him: do but read.

---

5. *Biddy*] term used to call chickens.
6. *play . . . collier!*] cherry-pit was a children's game played by throwing cherry pits into a
   little hole; the references to Satan and the collier allude to the proverb "Like will to
   like, as the devil with the collier," a digger or seller of coals.
7. *finder of madmen*] those appointed to report on persons suspected of madness.
8. *More . . . morning*] On May Day it was the custom to perform comic interludes or fan-
   tastic dances.

SIR TO.   Give me. [*Reads*] Youth, whatsoever thou art, thou art but a
    scurvy fellow.

FAB.   Good, and valiant.

SIR TO.   [*Reads*] Wonder not, nor admire not in thy mind, why I do call
    thee so, for I will show thee no reason for 't.

FAB.   A good note; that keeps you from the blow of the law.

SIR TO.   [*Reads*] Thou comest to the lady Olivia, and in my sight she uses
    thee kindly: but thou liest in thy throat; that is not the matter I challenge
    thee for.

FAB.   Very brief, and to exceeding good sense—less.

SIR TO.   [*Reads*] I will waylay thee going home; where if it be thy chance
    to kill me,—

FAB.   Good.

SIR TO.   [*Reads*] Thou killest me like a rogue and a villain.

FAB.   Still you keep o' the windy side of the law: good.

SIR TO.   [*Reads*] Fare thee well; and God have mercy upon one of our
    souls! He may have mercy upon mine; but my hope is better, and so look
    to thyself. Thy friend, as thou usest him, and thy sworn enemy,

                                        ANDREW AGUECHEEK.

    If this letter move him not, his legs cannot: I'll give 't him.

MAR.   You may have very fit occasion for 't: he is now in some com-
    merce with my lady, and will by and by depart.

SIR TO.   Go, Sir Andrew; scout me for him at the corner of the
    orchard like a bum-baily:[9] so soon as ever thou seest him, draw;
    and, as thou drawest, swear horrible; for it comes to pass oft that a
    terrible oath, with a swaggering accent sharply twanged off, gives
    manhood more approbation than ever proof itself would have
    earned him. Away!

SIR AND.   Nay, let me alone for swearing.   [*Exit.*]

SIR TO.   Now will not I deliver his letter: for the behaviour of the
    young gentleman gives him out to be of good capacity and breed-
    ing; his employment between his lord and my niece confirms no
    less: therefore this letter, being so excellently ignorant, will breed
    no terror in the youth: he will find it comes from a clodpole. But,
    sir, I will deliver his challenge by word of mouth; set upon
    Aguecheek a notable report of valour; and drive the gentleman, as
    I know his youth will aptly receive it, into a most hideous opinion

---

9. *bum-baily*] junior officer employed in making arrests.

of his rage, skill, fury, and impetuosity. This will so fright them both, that they will kill one another by the look, like cockatrices.[10]

Re-enter OLIVIA, *with* VIOLA

FAB.   Here he comes with your niece: give them way till he take leave, and presently after him.

SIR TO.   I will meditate the while upon some horrid message for a challenge.   [*Exeunt* SIR TOBY, FABIAN, *and* MARIA.]

OLI.   I have said too much unto a heart of stone,
And laid mine honour too unchary out:
There 's something in me that reproves my fault;
But such a headstrong potent fault it is,
That it but mocks reproof.

VIO.   With the same 'haviour that your passion bears
Goes on my master's grief.

OLI.   Here, wear this jewel for me, 't is my picture;
Refuse it not; it hath no tongue to vex you;
And I beseech you come again to-morrow.
What shall you ask of me that I 'll deny,
That honour saved may upon asking give?

VIO.   Nothing but this;—your true love for my master.

OLI.   How with mine honour may I give him that
Which I have given to you?

VIO.   I will acquit you.

OLI.   Well, come again to-morrow: fare thee well:
A fiend like thee might bear my soul to hell.   [*Exit.*]

Re-enter SIR TOBY *and* FABIAN

SIR TO.   Gentleman, God save thee.

VIO.   And you, sir.

SIR TO.   That defence thou hast, betake thee to 't: of what nature the wrongs are thou hast done him, I know not; but thy intercepter, full of despite, bloody as the hunter, attends thee at the orchard-end: dismount thy tuck,[11] be yare[12] in thy preparation, for thy assailant is quick, skilful and deadly.

VIO.   You mistake, sir; I am sure no man hath any quarrel to me: my

---

10. *cockatrices*] imaginary birds, supposed to be hatched from cocks' eggs, and that could kill with a look.
11. *dismount thy tuck*] draw thy sword or rapier.
12. *yare*] ready, brisk.

remembrance is very free and clear from any image of offence done to any man.

SIR TO.   You 'll find it otherwise, I assure you: therefore, if you hold your life at any price, betake you to your guard; for your opposite hath in him what youth, strength, skill and wrath can furnish man withal.

VIO.   I pray you, sir, what is he?

SIR TO.   He is knight, dubbed with unhatched rapier and on carpet consideration;[13] but he is a devil in private brawl: souls and bodies hath he divorced three; and his incensement at this moment is so implacable, that satisfaction can be none but by pangs of death and sepulchre. Hob, nob,[14] is his word; give 't or take 't.

VIO.   I will return again into the house and desire some conduct of the lady. I am no fighter. I have heard of some kind of men that put quarrels purposely on others, to taste their valour: belike this is a man of that quirk.

SIR TO.   Sir, no; his indignation derives itself out of a very competent injury: therefore, get you on and give him his desire. Back you shall not to the house, unless you undertake that with me which with as much safety you might answer him: therefore, on, or strip your sword stark naked; for meddle you must, that 's certain, or forswear to wear iron about you.

VIO.   This is as uncivil as strange. I beseech you, do me this courteous office, as to know of the knight what my offence to him is: it is something of my negligence, nothing of my purpose.

SIR TO.   I will do so. Signior Fabian, stay you by this gentleman till my return.   [Exit.]

VIO.   Pray you, sir, do you know of this matter?

FAB.   I know the knight is incensed against you, even to a mortal arbitrement;[15] but nothing of the circumstance more.

VIO.   I beseech you, what manner of man is he?

FAB.   Nothing of that wonderful promise, to read him by his form, as you are like to find him in the proof of his valour. He is, indeed, sir, the most skilful, bloody and fatal opposite that you could pos-

---

13. *knight . . . on carpet consideration*] a carpet knight was one whose title was not derived from military service; an "unhatched rapier" is a rapier that has not been used in military combat.

14. *Hob, nob*] "Hob" is a corruption of "have," and the expression here means "have or have not," "hit or miss."

15. *arbitrement*] decision.

sibly have found in any part of Illyria. Will you walk towards him?
I will make your peace with him if I can.

VIO.   I shall be much bound to you for 't: I am one that had rather go
with sir priest than sir knight: I care not who knows so much of my
mettle.   [*Exeunt.*]

Re-enter SIR TOBY, *with* SIR ANDREW

SIR TO.   Why, man, he 's a very devil; I have not seen such a firago.[16]
I had a pass with him, rapier, scabbard and all, and he gives me
the stuck in[17] with such a mortal motion, that it is inevitable; and
on the answer, he pays you as surely as your feet hit the ground
they step on. They say he has been fencer to the Sophy.

SIR AND.   Pox on 't, I 'll not meddle with him.

SIR TO.   Ay, but he will not now be pacified: Fabian can scarce hold
him yonder.

SIR AND.   Plague on 't, an I thought he had been valiant and so cunning in fence, I 'ld have seen him damned ere I 'ld have challenged him. Let him let the matter slip, and I 'll give him my
horse, grey Capilet.[18]

SIR TO.   I 'll make the motion: stand here, make a good show on 't:
this shall end without the perdition of souls. [*Aside*] Marry, I 'll
ride your horse as well as I ride you.

Re-enter FABIAN *and* VIOLA

[*To* FAB.] I have his horse to take up the quarrel: I have persuaded him
the youth 's a devil.

FAB.   He is as horribly conceited of him; and pants and looks pale, as
if a bear were at his heels.

SIR TO.   [*To* VIO.] There's no remedy, sir; he will fight with you for 's
oath sake: marry, he hath better bethought him of his quarrel, and
he finds that now scarce to be worth talking of: therefore draw, for
the supportance of his vow; he protests he will not hurt you.

VIO.   [*Aside*] Pray God defend me! A little thing would make me tell
them how much I lack of a man.

FAB.   Give ground, if you see him furious.

SIR TO.   Come, Sir Andrew, there 's no remedy; the gentleman will,
for his honour's sake, have one bout with you; he cannot by the

---

16. *firago*] virago.
17. *stuck in*] Sir Toby's corruption of the Italian fencing term for thrust, "stoccata."
18. *Capilet*] apparently a diminutive, formed from "capul" or "caple," a north-country
word for a horse.

    duello[19] avoid it: but he has promised me, as he is a gentleman and
    a soldier, he will not hurt you. Come on; to 't.

SIR AND.   Pray God, he keep his oath!

VIO.   I do assure you, 't is against my will.   *[They draw.]*

Enter Antonio

ANT.   Put up your sword. If this young gentleman
        Have done offence, I take the fault on me:
        If you offend him, I for him defy you.

SIR TO.   You, sir! why, what are you?

ANT.   One, sir, that for his love dares yet do more
        Than you have heard him brag to you he will.

SIR TO.   Nay, if you be an undertaker,[20] I am for you.   *[They draw.]*

Enter Officers

FAB.   O good Sir Toby, hold! here comes the officers.

SIR TO.   I 'll be with you anon.

VIO.   Pray, sir, put your sword up, if you please.

SIR AND.   Marry, will I, sir; and, for that I promised you, I 'll be as
    good as my word: he will bear you easily and reins well.[21]

FIRST OFF.   This is the man; do thy office.

SEC. OFF.   Antonio, I arrest thee at the suit of Count Orsino.

ANT.   You do mistake me, sir.

FIRST OFF.   No, sir, no jot; I know your favour well,
        Though now you have no sea-cap on your head.
        Take him away: he knows I know him well.

ANT.   I must obey. *[To* VIO.*]* This comes with seeking you:
        But there 's no remedy; I shall answer it.
        What will you do, now my necessity
        Makes me to ask you for my purse? It grieves me
        Much more for what I cannot do for you
        Than what befalls myself. You stand amazed;
        But be of comfort.

SEC. OFF.   Come, sir, away.

ANT.   I must entreat of you some of that money.

VIO.   What money, sir?
        For the fair kindness you have show'd me here,

---

19. *duello*] the code of the duel.
20. *undertaker*] an intermedler.
21. *he . . . well*] Sir Andrew refers to his horse.

And, part, being prompted by your present trouble,
Out of my lean and low ability
I 'll lend you something: my having[22] is not much;
I 'll make division of my present[23] with you:
Hold, there 's half my coffer.

ANT.   Will you deny me now?
Is 't possible that my deserts to you
Can lack persuasion? Do not tempt my misery,
Lest that it make me so unsound a man
As to upbraid you with those kindnesses
That I have done for you.

VIO.   I know of none;
Nor know I you by voice or any feature:
I hate ingratitude more in a man
Than lying vainness,[24] babbling drunkenness,
Or any taint of vice whose strong corruption
Inhabits our frail blood.

ANT.   O heavens themselves!
SEC. OFF.   Come, sir, I pray you, go.
ANT.   Let me speak a little. This youth that you see here
I snatch'd one half out of the jaws of death;
Relieved him with such sanctity of love;
And to his image, which methought did promise
Most venerable worth, did I devotion.
FIRST OFF.   What 's that to us? The time goes by: away!
ANT.   But O how vile an idol proves his god!
Thou hast, Sebastian, done good feature shame.
In nature there 's no blemish but the mind;
None can be call'd deform'd but the unkind:
Virtue is beauty; but the beauteous evil
Are empty trunks, o'erflourish'd by the devil.
FIRST OFF.   The man grows mad: away with him! Come, come, sir.
ANT.   Lead me on.   [*Exit with* Officers.]
VIO.   Methinks his words do from such passion fly,
That he believes himself: so do not I.
Prove true, imagination, O prove true,
That I, dear brother, be now ta'en for you!

---

22. *having*] property, fortune.
23. *my present*] my present store.
24. *lying vainness*] lying boastfulness.

SIR TO. Come hither, knight; come hither, Fabian: we 'll whisper
    o'er a couplet or two of most sage saws.
VIO.   He named Sebastian: I my brother know
    Yet living in my glass; even such and so
    In favour was my brother, and he went
    Still in this fashion, colour, ornament,
    For him I imitate: O, if it prove,
    Tempests are kind and salt waves fresh in love!   [*Exit.*]
SIR TO.   A very dishonest paltry boy, and more a coward than a hare:
    his dishonesty appears in leaving his friend here in necessity and
    denying him; and for his cowardship, ask Fabian.
FAB.   A coward, a most devout coward, religious in it.
SIR AND.   'Slid,[25] I 'll after him again and beat him.
SIR TO.   Do; cuff him soundly, but never draw thy sword.
SIR AND.   An I do not,—   [*Exit.*]
FAB.   Come, let 's see the event.
SIR TO.   I dare lay any money 't will be nothing yet.   [*Exeunt.*]

ACT IV

SCENE I. *Before* OLIVIA'S *house*.

Enter SEBASTIAN *and* Clown

CLO.   Will you make me believe that I am not sent for you?
SEB.   Go to, go to, thou art a foolish fellow:
    Let me be clear of thee.
CLO.   Well held out, i' faith! No, I do not know you; nor I am not sent
    to you by my lady, to bid you come speak with her; nor your name
    is not Master Cesario; nor this is not my nose neither. Nothing
    that is so is so.
SEB.   I prithee, vent thy folly somewhere else:
    Thou know'st not me.
CLO.   Vent my folly! he has heard that word of some great man and
    now applies it to a fool. Vent my folly! I am afraid this great lub-

---

25. *'Slid*] an oath, from "God's [eye]lid."

ber, the world, will prove a cockney.[1] I prithee now, ungird thy
strangeness and tell me what I shall vent to my lady: shall I vent to
her that thou art coming?

SEB. I prithee, foolish Greek,[2] depart from me:
There 's money for thee: if you tarry longer,
I shall give worse payment.

CLO. By my troth, thou hast an open hand. These wise men that give
fools money get themselves a good report—after fourteen years'
purchase.

Enter SIR ANDREW, SIR TOBY, *and* FABIAN

SIR AND. Now, sir, have I met you again? there 's for you.

SEB. Why, there 's for thee, and there, and there.
Are all the people mad?

SIR TO. Hold, sir, or I 'll throw your dagger o'er the house.

CLO. This will I tell my lady straight: I would not be in some of your
coats for two pence.   [*Exit.*]

SIR TO. Come on, sir; hold.

SIR AND. Nay, let him alone: I 'll go another way to work with him;
I 'll have an action of battery against him, if there be any law in
Illyria: though I struck him first, yet it 's no matter for that.

SEB. Let go thy hand.

SIR TO. Come, sir, I will not let you go. Come, my young soldier, put
up your iron: you are well fleshed; come on.

SEB. I will be free from thee. What wouldst thou now?
If thou darest tempt me further, draw thy sword.

SIR TO. What, what? Nay, then I must have an ounce or two of this
malapert blood from you.

Enter OLIVIA

OLI. Hold, Toby; on thy life, I charge thee, hold!

SIR TO. Madam!

OLI. Will it be ever thus? Ungracious wretch,
Fit for the mountains and the barbarous caves,
Where manners ne'er were preach'd! out of my sight!
Be not offended, dear Cesario.
Rudesby,[3] be gone! [*Exeunt* SIR TOBY, SIR ANDREW, *and* FABIAN.]
I prithee, gentle friend,

---

1. *cockney*] an effeminate fellow.
2. *Greek*] colloquial term for "fellow" or "companion."
3. *Rudesby*] boor.

Let thy fair wisdom, not thy passion, sway
In this uncivil and unjust extent
Against thy peace. Go with me to my house;
And hear thou there how many fruitless pranks
This ruffian hath botch'd up, that thou thereby
Mayst smile at this: thou shalt not choose but go:
Do not deny. Beshrew his soul for me,
He started one poor heart of mine in thee.

SEB.   What relish is in this? how runs the stream?
Or I am mad, or else this is a dream:
Let fancy still my sense in Lethe steep;
If it be thus to dream, still let me sleep!

OLI.   Nay, come, I prithee: would thou 'ldst be ruled by me!

SEB.   Madam, I will.

OLI.   O, say so, and so be!   [*Exeunt.*]

SCENE II. OLIVIA'S *house*.

Enter MARIA *and* Clown

MAR.   Nay, I prithee, put on this gown and this beard; make him
believe thou art Sir Topas the curate: do it quickly; I 'll call Sir
Toby the whilst.   [*Exit.*]

CLO.   Well, I 'll put it on, and I will dissemble myself in 't; and I
would I were the first that ever dissembled in such a gown. I am
not tall enough to become the function well, nor lean enough to
be thought a good student; but to be said an honest man and a
good housekeeper goes as fairly as to say a careful man and a great
scholar. The competitors enter.

Enter SIR TOBY *and* MARIA

SIR TO.   Jove bless thee, master Parson.

CLO.   Bonos dies, Sir Toby: for, as the old hermit of Prague, that never
saw pen and ink, very wittily said to a niece of King Gorboduc,[1]
"That that is is"; so I, being master Parson, am master Parson; for,
what is "that" but "that," and "is" but "is"?

---

1. *Gorboduc*] a king of ancient Britain..

SIR TO. To him, Sir Topas.

CLO. What, ho, I say! peace in this prison!

SIR TO. The knave counterfeits well; a good knave.

MAL. [*within*] Who calls there?

CLO. Sir Topas the curate, who comes to visit Malvolio the lunatic.

MAL. Sir Topas, Sir Topas, good Sir Topas, go to my lady.

CLO. Out, hyperbolical fiend! how vexest thou this man! talkest thou nothing but of ladies?

SIR TO. Well said, master Parson.

MAL. Sir Topas, never was man thus wronged: good Sir Topas, do not think I am mad: they have laid me here in hideous darkness.

CLO. Fie, thou dishonest Satan! I call thee by the most modest terms; for I am one of those gentle ones that will use the devil himself with courtesy: sayest thou that house is dark?

MAL. As hell, Sir Topas.

CLO. Why, it hath bay windows transparent as barricadoes, and the clearstories[2] toward the south north are as lustrous as ebony; and yet complainest thou of obstruction?

MAL. I am not mad, Sir Topas: I say to you, this house is dark.

CLO. Madman, thou errest: I say, there is no darkness but ignorance; in which thou art more puzzled than the Egyptians in their fog.[3]

MAL. I say, this house is as dark as ignorance, though ignorance were as dark as hell; and I say, there was never man thus abused. I am no more mad than you are: make the trial of it any constant question.

CLO. What is the opinion of Pythagoras concerning wild fowl?

MAL. That the soul of our grandam might haply inhabit a bird.

CLO. What thinkest thou of his opinion?

MAL. I think nobly of the soul, and no way approve his opinion.

CLO. Fare thee well. Remain thou still in darkness: thou shalt hold the opinion of Pythagoras ere I will allow of thy wits; and fear to kill a woodcock, lest thou dispossess the soul of thy grandam. Fare thee well.

MAL. Sir Topas, Sir Topas!

SIR TO. My most exquisite Sir Topas!

CLO. Nay, I am for all waters.

MAR. Thou mightst have done this without thy beard and gown: he sees thee not.

---

2. *clearstories*] according to some sources, the upper row of windows on a house or church.

3. *Egyptians . . . fog*] One of the seven plagues inflicted upon the Egyptians as God's punishment of the Pharaoh for refusing to free the Hebrew slaves (see Exodus 10:21–23).

SIR TO.   To him in thine own voice, and bring me word how thou
   findest him: I would we were well rid of this knavery. If he may be
   conveniently delivered, I would he were; for I am now so far in
   offence with my niece, that I cannot pursue with any safety this
   sport to the upshot. Come by and by to my chamber.

                                        [*Exeunt* SIR TOBY *and* MARIA.]

CLO.   [*Singing*] Hey, Robin, jolly Robin,
                   Tell me how thy lady does.
MAL.   Fool,—
CLO.   My lady is unkind, perdy.[4]
MAL.   Fool,—
CLO.   Alas, why is she so?
MAL.   Fool, I say,—
CLO.·   She loves another—Who calls, ha?
MAL.   Good fool, as ever thou wilt deserve well at my hand, help me
   to a candle, and pen, ink and paper: as I am a gentleman, I will
   live to be thankful to thee for 't.
CLO.   Master Malvolio!
MAL.   Ay, good fool.
CLO.   Alas, sir, how fell you besides your five wits?[5]
MAL.   Fool, there was never man so notoriously abused: I am as well
   in my wits, fool, as thou art.
CLO.   But as well? then you are mad indeed, if you be no better in
   your wits than a fool.
MAL.   They have here propertied me;[6] keep me in darkness, send min-
   isters to me, asses, and do all they can to face me out of my wits.
CLO.   Advise you what you say; the minister is here. Malvolio,
   Malvolio, thy wits the heavens restore! endeavour thyself to sleep,
   and leave thy vain bibble babble.
MAL.   Sir Topas,—
CLO.   Maintain no words with him, good fellow. Who, I, sir? not I, sir.
   God be wi' you, good Sir Topas. Marry, amen. I will, sir, I will.
MAL.   Fool, fool, fool, I say,—
CLO.   Alas, sir, be patient. What say you, sir? I am shent[7] for speaking
   to you.

---

4. *perdy*] "by God" (from "par Dieu").
5. *five wits*] The "five wits" were common wit or intellectual power, imagination, fancy,
   estimation and memory.
6. *propertied*] as a verb, to make property of, to make a tool, prop of.
7. *shent*] blamed, reproached.

MAL.   Good fool, help me to some light and some paper: I tell thee, I
   am as well in my wits as any man in Illyria.

CLO.   Well-a-day that you were, sir!

MAL.   By this hand, I am. Good fool, some ink, paper and light; and
   convey what I will set down to my lady: it shall advantage thee
   more than ever the bearing of letter did.

CLO.   I will help you to 't. But tell me true, are you not mad indeed?
   or do you but counterfeit?

MAL.   Believe me, I am not; I tell thee true.

CLO.   Nay, I 'll ne'er believe a madman till I see his brains. I will fetch
   you light and paper and ink.

MAL.   Fool, I 'll requite it in the highest degree: I prithee, be gone.

CLO.   [*Singing*] I am gone, sir,
                And anon, sir,
          I 'll be with you again,
                In a trice,
                Like to the old vice,
          Your need to sustain;
          Who, with dagger of lath,[8]
          In his rage and his wrath,
                Cries, ah, ha! to the devil:
          Like a mad lad,
          Pare thy nails, dad;
                Adieu, goodman devil.   [*Exit.*]

SCENE III. OLIVIA'S *garden.*

Enter SEBASTIAN

SEB.   This is the air; that is the glorious sun;
   This pearl she gave me, I do feel 't and see 't;
   And though 't is wonder that enwraps me thus,
   Yet 't is not madness. Where 's Antonio, then?
   I could not find him at the Elephant:
   Yet there he was; and there I found this credit,[1]

---

8. *lath*] a piece of wood.

1. *credit*] belief or opinion.

That he did range the town to seek me out.
His counsel now might do me golden service;
For though my soul disputes well with my sense,
That this may be some error, but no madness,
Yet doth this accident and flood of fortune
So far exceed all instance, all discourse,
That I am ready to distrust mine eyes
And wrangle with my reason, that persuades me
To any other trust but that I am mad,
Or else the lady 's mad; yet, if 't were so,
She could not sway her house, command her followers,
Take and give back affairs and their dispatch
With such a smooth, discreet, and stable bearing
As I perceive she does: there 's something in 't
That is deceivable. But here the lady comes.

Enter OLIVIA *and* Priest

OLI.   Blame not this haste of mine. If you mean well,
     Now go with me and with this holy man
     Into the chantry by: there, before him,
     And underneath that consecrated roof,
     Plight me the full assurance of your faith;
     That my most jealous and too doubtful soul
     May live at peace. He shall conceal it
     Whiles you are willing it shall come to note,
     What time we will our celebration keep
     According to my birth. What do you say?
SEB.   I 'll follow this good man, and go with you;
     And, having sworn truth, ever will be true.
OLI.   Then lead the way, good father; and heavens so shine,
     That they may fairly note this act of mine!   [*Exeunt.*]

ACT V

Scene I. *Before* Olivia's *house*.

Enter Clown *and* Fabian

Fab. Now, as thou lovest me, let me see his letter.

Clo. Good Master Fabian, grant me another request.

Fab. Any thing.

Clo. Do not desire to see this letter.

Fab. This is, to give a dog, and in recompense desire my dog again.

Enter Duke, Viola, Curio, *and* Lords

Duke. Belong you to the Lady Olivia, friends?

Clo. Ay, sir; we are some of her trappings.

Duke. I know thee well: how dost thou, my good fellow?

Clo. Truly, sir, the better for my foes and the worse for my friends.

Duke. Just the contrary; the better for thy friends.

Clo. No, sir, the worse.

Duke. How can that be?

Clo. Marry, sir, they praise me and make an ass of me; now my foes tell me plainly I am an ass: so that by my foes, sir, I profit in the knowledge of myself; and by my friends I am abused: so that, conclusions to be as kisses, if your four negatives make your two affirmatives, why then, the worse for my friends, and the better for my foes.

Duke. Why, this is excellent.

Clo. By my troth, sir, no; though it please you to be one of my friends.

Duke. Thou shalt not be the worse for me: there 's gold.

Clo. But that it would be double-dealing, sir, I would you could make it another.

Duke. O, you give me ill counsel.

Clo. Put your grace in your pocket, sir, for this once, and let your flesh and blood obey it.

Duke. Well, I will be so much a sinner, to be a double-dealer: there's another.

Clo. Primo, secundo, tertio, is a good play; and the old saying is, the

144

third pays for all: the triplex, sir, is a good tripping measure; or the
bells of Saint Bennet,[1] sir, may put you in mind; one, two, three.

DUKE.   You can fool no more money out of me at this throw: if you
will let your lady know I am here to speak with her, and bring her
along with you, it may awake my bounty further.

CLO.   Marry, sir, lullaby to your bounty till I come again. I go, sir; but
I would not have you to think that my desire of having is the sin
of covetousness: but, as you say, sir, let your bounty take a nap, I
will awake it anon.   [*Exit.*]

VIO.   Here comes the man, sir, that did rescue me.

Enter ANTONIO *and* Officers

DUKE.   That face of his I do remember well;
Yet, when I saw it last, it was besmear'd
As black as Vulcan[2] in the smoke of war:
A bawbling[3] vessel was he captain of,
For shallow draught and bulk unprizable;[4]
With which such scathful grapple did he make
With the most noble bottom of our fleet,
That very envy and the tongue of loss
Cried fame and honour on him.[5] What 's the matter?

FIRST OFF.   Orsino, this is that Antonio
That took the Phœnix and her fraught[6] from Candy;[7]
And this is he that did the Tiger board,
When your young nephew Titus lost his leg:
Here in the streets, desperate of shame and state,[8]
In private brabble did we apprehend him.

VIO.   He did me kindness, sir, drew on my side;
But in conclusion put strange speech upon me:
I know not what 't was but distraction.

---

1. *bells of Saint Bennet*] a reference to the chimes sounded by the bells of St. Bennet's
Church on Paul's Wharf, which was destroyed in the great fire of London.
2. *Vulcan*] the Roman god of fire and metalsmithing, usually portrayed with skin black-
ened from the smoke of his forge
3. *bawbling*] trifling, of small value.
4. *unprizable*] without value as a prize of war.
5. *scathful grapple . . . on him*] He grappled with such destructive violence with the finest
ship of our fleet that those who had best right to hate him and loudly lamented their
loss, extolled him.
6. *fraught*] freight, cargo.
7. *Candy*] the island of Crete, at that time called Candia.
8. *desperate . . . state*] reckless of disgrace and oblivious of his rank.

DUKE.   Notable pirate! thou salt-water thief!
    What foolish boldness brought thee to their mercies,
    Whom thou, in terms so bloody and so dear,
    Hast made thine enemies?

ANT.   Orsino, noble sir,
    Be pleased that I shake off these names you give me:
    Antonio never yet was thief or pirate,
    Though I confess, on base and ground enough,
    Orsino's enemy. A witchcraft drew me hither:
    That most ingrateful boy there by your side,
    From the rude sea's enraged and foamy mouth
    Did I redeem; a wreck past hope he was:
    His life I gave him and did thereto add
    My love, without retention or restraint,
    All his in dedication; for his sake
    Did I expose myself, pure[9] for his love,
    Into the danger of this adverse town;
    Drew to defend him when he was beset:
    Where being apprehended, his false cunning,
    Not meaning to partake with me in danger,
    Taught him to face me out of his acquaintance,[10]
    And grew a twenty years removed thing
    While one would wink; denied me mine own purse,
    Which I had recommended to his use
    Not half an hour before.

VIO.   How can this be?

DUKE.   When came he to this town?

ANT.   To-day, my lord; and for three months before,
    No interim, not a minute's vacancy,
    Both day and night did we keep company.

Enter OLIVIA *and* Attendants

DUKE.   Here comes the countess: now heaven walks on earth.
    But for thee, fellow; fellow, thy words are madness:
    Three months this youth hath tended upon me;
    But more of that anon. Take him aside.

OLI.   What would my lord, but that he may not have,
    Wherein Olivia may seem serviceable?

---

9. *pure*] the adjective used adverbially, "purely," "solely."
10. *face me . . . acquaintance*] brazenly deny knowledge of me.

<blockquote>
Cesario, you do not keep promise with me.
</blockquote>

VIO.   Madam!

DUKE.   Gracious Olivia,—

OLI.   What do you say, Cesario? Good my lord,—

VIO.   My lord would speak; my duty hushes me.

OLI.   If it be aught to the old tune, my lord,
    It is as fat and fulsome[11] to mine ear
    As howling after music.

DUKE.   Still so cruel?

OLI.   Still so constant, lord.

DUKE.   What, to perverseness? you uncivil lady,
    To whose ingrate and unauspicious altars
    My soul the faithfull'st offerings hath breathed out
    That e'er devotion tender'd! What shall I do?

OLI.   Even what it please my lord, that shall become him.

DUKE.   Why should I not, had I the heart to do it,
    Like to the Egyptian thief at point of death,
    Kill what I love?—[12]a savage jealousy
    That sometimes savours nobly. But hear me this:
    Since you to non-regardance cast my faith,
    And that I partly know the instrument
    That screws me from my true place in your favour,
    Live you the marble-breasted tyrant still;
    But this your minion, whom I know you love,
    And whom, by heaven I swear, I tender dearly,
    Him will I tear out of that cruel eye,
    Where he sits crowned in his master's spite.
    Come, boy, with me; my thoughts are ripe in mischief:
    I 'll sacrifice the lamb that I do love,
    To spite a raven's heart within a dove.

VIO.   And I, most jocund, apt and willing,
    To do you rest, a thousand deaths would die.

OLI.   Where goes Cesario?

VIO.   After him I love
    More than I love these eyes, more than my life,
    More, by all mores, than e'er I shall love wife.

---

11. *fat and fulsome*] nauseous and cloying.

12. *the Egyptian thief . . . love?*] A reference to the story of Theagenes and Chariclea in Heliodorus, *Æthiopica* (translated by Thomas Underdowne, 1569), where Thyamis, an Egyptian thief, slays a captive whom he mistakes for the object of his affection, in the fear that he is about to be robbed of her.

     If I do feign, you witnesses above
     Punish my life for tainting of my love!
OLI.   Ay me, detested! how am I beguiled!
VIO.   Who does beguile you? who does do you wrong?
OLI.   Hast thou forgot thyself? is it so long?
     Call forth the holy father.
DUKE.   Come, away!
OLI.   Whither, my lord? Cesario, husband, stay.
DUKE.   Husband!
OLI.   Ay, husband: can he that deny?
DUKE.   Her husband, sirrah!
VIO.   No, my lord, not I.
OLI.   Alas, it is the baseness of thy fear
     That makes thee strangle thy propriety:[13]
     Fear not, Cesario; take thy fortunes up;
     Be that thou know'st thou art, and then thou art
     As great as that thou fear'st.

Enter Priest

                        O, welcome, father!
     Father, I charge thee, by thy reverence,
     Here to unfold, though lately we intended
     To keep in darkness what occasion now
     Reveals before 't is ripe, what thou dost know
     Hath newly pass'd between this youth and me.
PRIEST.   A contract of eternal bond of love,[14]
     Confirm'd by mutual joinder of your hands,
     Attested by the holy close of lips,
     Strengthen'd by interchangement of your rings;
     And all the ceremony of this compact
     Seal'd in my function,[15] by my testimony:
     Since when, my watch hath told me, toward my grave
     I have travell'd but two hours.
DUKE.   O thou dissembling cub! what wilt thou be
     When time hath sow'd a grizzle on thy case?[16]
     Or will not else thy craft so quickly grow,

---

13. *propriety*] identity or individuality.
14. *A contract . . . love*] the ordinary ceremony of a betrothal, which preceeded the marriage rite.
15. *function*] office as chaplain to Olivia.
16. *a grizzle on thy case*] a touch of grey on thy skin.

That thine own trip shall be thine overthrow?
Farewell, and take her; but direct thy feet
Where thou and I henceforth may never meet.

VIO.   My lord, I do protest—
OLI.   O, do not swear!
Hold little faith, though thou hast too much fear.

Enter SIR ANDREW

SIR AND.   For the love of God, a surgeon! Send one presently to Sir
Toby.
OLI.   What 's the matter?
SIR AND.   He has broke my head across and has given Sir Toby a
bloody coxcomb too: for the love of God, your help! I had rather
than forty pound I were at home.
OLI.   Who has done this, Sir Andrew?
SIR AND.   The count's gentleman, one Cesario: we took him for a
coward, but he 's the very devil incardinate.
DUKE.   My gentleman, Cesario?
SIR AND.   'Od's lifelings, here he is! You broke my head for nothing;
and that that I did, I was set on to do 't by Sir Toby.
VIO.   Why do you speak to me? I never hurt you:
You drew your sword upon me without cause;
But I bespake you fair, and hurt you not.
SIR AND.   If a bloody coxcomb be a hurt, you have hurt me: I think
you set nothing by a bloody coxcomb.

Enter SIR TOBY *and* Clown

Here comes Sir Toby halting; you shall hear more: but if he had
not been in drink, he would have tickled you othergates[17] than he
did.
DUKE.   How now, gentleman! how is 't with you?
SIR TO.   That 's all one: has hurt me, and there 's the end on 't. Sot,
didst see Dick surgeon, sot?
CLO.   O, he 's drunk, Sir Toby, an hour agone; his eyes were set at
eight i' the morning.
SIR TO.   Then he 's a rogue, and a passy measures pavin:[18] I hate a
drunken rogue.

---

17. *othergates*] Sir Andrew's word for otherwise, in another manner.
18. *passy measures pavin*] "Pavin" is the name of a stately dance, and "passy measures" is
a corruption of "passamezzo," a slow and solemn step which formed chief part of the
"pavin."

OLI. Away with him! Who hath made this havoc with them?

SIR AND. I 'll help you, Sir Toby, because we 'll be dressed together.

SIR TO. Will you help? an ass-head and a coxcomb and a knave, a
    thin-faced knave, a gull!

OLI. Get him to bed, and let his hurt be look'd to.

            [*Exeunt* Clown, FABIAN, SIR TOBY, *and* SIR ANDREW.]

Enter SEBASTIAN

SEB. I am sorry, madam, I have hurt your kinsman;
    But, had it been the brother of my blood,
    I must have done no less with wit and safety.
    You throw a strange regard[19] upon me, and by that
    I do perceive it hath offended you:
    Pardon me, sweet one, even for the vows
    We made each other but so late ago.

DUKE. One face, one voice, one habit, and two persons,
    A natural perspective,[20] that is and is not!

SEB. Antonio, O my dear Antonio!
    How have the hours rack'd and tortured me,
    Since I have lost thee!

ANT. Sebastian are you?

SEB.   Fear'st thou that, Antonio?

ANT. How have you made division of yourself?
    An apple, cleft in two, is not more twin
    Than these two creatures. Which is Sebastian?

OLI. Most wonderful!

SEB. Do I stand there? I never had a brother;
    Nor can there be that deity in my nature,
    Of here and every where. I had a sister,
    Whom the blind waves and surges have devour'd.
    Of charity, what kin are you to me?
    What countryman? what name? what parentage?

VIO. Of Messaline: Sebastian was my father;
    Such a Sebastian was my brother too,
    So went he suited[21] to his watery tomb:
    If spirits can assume both form and suit,
    You come to fright us.

---

19. *regard*] look.

20. *perspective*] an ingeniously contrived glass, which was capable of producing the opti-
    cal delusion of making one person look like two.

21. *suited*] in such a suit of clothes.

SEB.   A spirit I am indeed;
    But am in that dimension grossly clad
    Which from the womb I did participate.
    Were you a woman, as the rest goes even,
    I should my tears let fall upon your cheek,
    And say, "Thrice-welcome, drowned Viola!"
VIO.   My father had a mole upon his brow.
SEB. And so had mine.
VIO.   And died that day when Viola from her birth
    Had number'd thirteen years.
SEB.   O, that record is lively in my soul!
    He finished indeed his mortal act
    That day that made my sister thirteen years.
VIO.   If nothing lets[22] to make us happy both
    But this my masculine usurp'd attire,
    Do not embrace me till each circumstance
    Of place, time, fortune, do cohere and jump
    That I am Viola: which to confirm,
    I 'll bring you to a captain in this town,
    Where lie my maiden weeds; by whose gentle help
    I was preserved to serve this noble count.
    All the occurrence of my fortune since
    Hath been between this lady and this lord.
SEB.   [*To* OLIVIA] So comes it, lady, you have been mistook:
    But nature to her bias drew in that.
    You would have been contracted to a maid;
    Nor are you therein, by my life, deceived,
    You are betroth'd both to a maid and man.
DUKE.   Be not amazed; right noble is his blood.
    If this be so, as yet the glass seems true,
    I shall have share in this most happy wreck.
    [*To* VIOLA] Boy, thou hast said to me a thousand times
    Thou never shouldst love woman like to me.
VIO.   And all those sayings will I over-swear;
    And all those swearings keep as true in soul
    As doth that orbed continent the fire
    That severs day from night.
DUKE.   Give me thy hand;
    And let me see thee in thy woman's weeds.

---

22. *lets*] prevents.

VIO.   The captain that did bring me first on shore
  Hath my maid's garments: he upon some action
  Is now in durance, at Malvolio's suit,
  A gentleman, and follower of my lady's.

OLI.   He shall enlarge him: fetch Malvolio hither:
  And yet, alas, now I remember me,
  They say, poor gentleman, he 's much distract.

Re-enter Clown *with a letter, and* FABIAN

  A most extracting frenzy of mine own
  From my remembrance clearly banish'd his.
  How does he, sirrah?

CLO.   Truly, madam, he holds Belzebub at the stave's end as well as a
man in his case may do: has here writ a letter to you; I should have
given 't you to-day morning, but as a madman's epistles are no
gospels, so it skills not much when they are delivered.

OLI.   Open 't, and read it.

CLO.   Look then to be well edified when the fool delivers the madman. [*Reads*] By the Lord, madam,—

OLI.   How now! art thou mad?

CLO.   No, madam, I do but read madness: an your ladyship will have
it as it ought to be, you must allow Vox.[23]

OLI.   Prithee, read i' thy right wits.

CLO.   So I do, madonna; but to read his right wits is to read thus:
therefore perpend,[24] my princess, and give ear.

OLI.   Read it you, sirrah.   [*To* FABIAN.]

FAB.   [*Reads*] By the Lord, madam, you wrong me, and the world shall know
it: though you have put me into darkness and given your drunken cousin
rule over me, yet have I the benefit of my senses as well as your ladyship.
I have your own letter that induced me to the semblance I put on; with
the which I doubt not but to do myself much right, or you much shame.
Think of me as you please. I leave my duty a little unthought of, and
speak out of my injury.

          THE MADLY-USED MALVOLIO.

OLI.   Did he write this?

CLO.   Ay, madam.

DUKE.   This savours not much of distraction.

OLI.   See him deliver'd, Fabian; bring him hither.   [*Exit* FABIAN.]
  My lord, so please you, these things further thought on,

---

23. *allow Vox*] allow me the use of my voice.
24. *perpend*] consider.

To think me as well a sister as a wife,
One day shall crown the alliance on 't, so please you,
Here at my house and at my proper cost.

DUKE.   Madam, I am most apt to embrace your offer.
[*To* VIOLA] Your master quits you; and for your service done him,
So much against the mettle of your sex,
So far beneath your soft and tender breeding,
And since you call'd me master for so long,
Here is my hand: you shall from this time be
Your master's mistress.

OLI.   A sister! you are she.

Re-enter FABIAN, *with* MALVOLIO

DUKE.   Is this the madman?

OLI.   Ay, my lord, this same:
How now, Malvolio!

MAL.   Madam, you have done me wrong,
Notorious wrong.

OLI.   Have I, Malvolio? no.

MAL.   Lady, you have. Pray you, peruse that letter.
You must not now deny it is your hand:
Write from it,[25] if you can, in hand or phrase;
Or say 't is not your seal, not your invention:
You can say none of this: well, grant it then
And tell me, in the modesty of honour,
Why you have given me such clear lights of favour,
Bade me come smiling and cross-garter'd to you,
To put on yellow stockings and to frown
Upon Sir Toby and the lighter people;
And, acting this in an obedient hope,
Why have you suffer'd me to be imprison'd,
Kept in a dark house, visited by the priest,
And made the most notorious geck[26] and gull
That e'er invention play'd on? tell my why.

OLI.   Alas, Malvolio, this is not my writing,
Though, I confess, much like the character:
But out of question 't is Maria's hand.
And now I do bethink me, it was she

---

25. *Write from it*] Write differently from it.
26. *geck*] dupe.

First told me thou wast mad; then camest in smiling,
And in such forms which here were presupposed
Upon thee in the letter. Prithee, be content:
This practice hath most shrewdly pass'd upon thee;
But when we know the grounds and authors of it,
Thou shalt be both the plaintiff and the judge
Of thine own cause.

FAB.   Good madam, hear me speak,
And let no quarrel nor no brawl to come
Taint the condition of this present hour,
Which I have wonder'd at. In hope it shall not,
Most freely I confess, myself and Toby
Set this device against Malvolio here,
Upon some stubborn and uncourteous parts
We had conceived against him: Maria writ
The letter at Sir Toby's great importance;[27]
In recompense whereof he hath married her.
How with a sportful malice it was follow'd
May rather pluck on laughter than revenge;
If that the injuries be justly weigh'd
That have on both sides pass'd.

OLI.   Alas, poor fool, how have they baffled thee!

CLO.   Why, "some are born great, some achieve greatness, and some
have greatness thrown upon them." I was one, sir, in this interlude; one Sir Topas, sir; but that's all one. "By the Lord, fool, I am
not mad." But do you remember? "Madam, why laugh you at such
a barren rascal? an you smile not, he's gagged": and thus the
whirligig of time brings in his revenges.

MAL.   I'll be revenged on the whole pack of you.   [*Exit.*]

OLI.   He hath been most notoriously abused.

DUKE.   Pursue him, and entreat him to a peace:
He hath not told us of the captain yet:
When that is known, and golden time convents,[28]
A solemn combination shall be made
Of our dear souls. Meantime, sweet sister,
We will not part from hence. Cesario, come;
For so you shall be, while you are a man;
But when in other habits you are seen,

---

27. *importance*] insistent request.
28. *convents*] suits.

Orsino's mistress and his fancy's queen.

[*Exeunt all, except* Clown.]

CLO. [*Sings*]

> When that I was and a little tiny boy,
>   With hey, ho, the wind and the rain,
> A foolish thing was but a toy,
>   For the rain it raineth every day.
>
> But when I came to man's estate,
>   With hey, ho, &c.
> 'Gainst knaves and thieves men shut their gate,
>   For the rain, &c.
>
> But when I came, alas! to wive,
>   With hey, ho, &c.
> By swaggering could I never thrive,
>   For the rain, &c.
>
> But when I came unto my beds,
>   With hey, ho, &c.
> With toss-pots still had drunken heads,
>   For the rain, &c.
>
> A great while ago the world begun,
>   With hey, ho, &c.
> But that's all one, our play is done,
>   And we 'll strive to please you every day.   [*Exit.*]

A Midsummer Night's Dream

A Midsummer Night's Dream

SHAKESPEARE probably wrote *A Midsummer Night's Dream* between 1594 and 1595. In several respects the play heralds a movement away from the conventionality of the early toward the subtleties and ambiguities of the mature comedies. It demonstrates both Shakespeare's great facility for a wide range of verse forms and rhyme schemes and his ability to bring together in a single work plots and characters derived from diverse literary sources. The story of the marriage of Theseus, Duke of Athens, and Hippolyta, Queen of the Amazons, was available to Shakespeare in two forms: in Chaucer's *Knight's Tale* and in Thomas North's *Lives of the noble Grecians and Romanes* (1579), a translation of Plutarch. The story of the crossed lovers Lysander, Hermia, and Demetrius is also in Chaucer's work, though Shakespeare complicates things by introducing a second woman, Helena, and by playing on the vagaries of love. Bottom and his troupe of Athenian laborers provide an often hilarious depiction of the theatrical world of Elizabethan England. Their play-within-the-play, *Pyramus and Thisbe,* is derived from Arthur Golding's translation of Ovid's *Metamorphoses.* As for Bottom's transformation into an ass, Shakespeare's most likely source was Apuleius's *Golden Ass,* translated by William Adlington in 1566. English folklore and popular literature contained ample material on the "puck," Robin Goodfellow, whereas Oberon and Titania, King and Queen of the Fairies, appear in various literary works, both English and French. Of course, in *A Midsummer Night's Dream* these preexisting literary creations take on a new, inimitably Shakespearean, life.

The play is in part about the potentially tragic conflict between social order and the freedom of the imagination embodied in the young lovers. The experience of love unfolds as a journey away from the city, and the parental and political authority that governs there, into a sylvan realm of fantasy, dream, and delusion. Marriage comes to symbolize the reconciliation of forces that in another context would remain in tragic opposition to one another. But, in a typical Shakespearean manner, the play turns upon the metaphor of the theater itself, questioning, sometimes mockingly, sometimes reverently, the nature of art and imagination, and their relationship to the world they reflect and transform.

SHANE WELLER

Dramatis Personae

THESEUS, Duke of Athens.
EGEUS, father to Hermia.
LYSANDER, }
DEMETRIUS, } in love with Hermia.
PHILOSTRATE, master of the revels to Theseus.
QUINCE, a carpenter.
SNUG, a joiner.
BOTTOM, a weaver.
FLUTE, a bellows-mender.
SNOUT, a tinker.
STARVELING, a tailor.

HIPPOLYTA, Queen of the Amazons, betrothed to Theseus.
HERMIA, daughter to Egeus, in love with Lysander.
HELENA, in love with Demetrius.

OBERON, King of the Fairies.
TITANIA, Queen of the Fairies.
PUCK, or Robin Goodfellow.
PEASEBLOSSOM, }
COBWEB, }
MOTH, } fairies.
MUSTARDSEED, }

Other fairies attending their King and Queen. Attendants on
Theseus and Hippolyta.

SCENE—*Athens, and a wood near it*

Act I—Scene I—Athens

THE PALACE OF THESEUS

Enter THESEUS, HIPPOLYTA, PHILOSTRATE, *and* Attendants.

THE.   Now, fair Hippolyta, our nuptial hour
      Draws on apace; four happy days bring in
      Another moon: but, O, methinks, how slow
      This old moon wanes! she lingers[1] my desires,
      Like to a step-dame, or a dowager,
      Long withering out a young man's revenue.
HIP.   Four days will quickly steep themselves in night;
      Four nights will quickly dream away the time;
      And then the moon, like to a silver bow
      New-bent in heaven, shall behold the night
      Of our solemnities.[2]
THE.   Go, Philostrate,
      Stir up the Athenian youth to merriments;
      Awake the pert[3] and nimble spirit of mirth:
      Turn melancholy forth to funerals;
      The pale companion is not for our pomp. [*Exit* PHILOSTRATE.
      Hippolyta, I woo'd thee with my sword,
      And won thy love, doing thee injuries;
      But I will wed thee in another key,
      With pomp, with triumph[4] and with revelling.

Enter EGEUS, HERMIA, LYSANDER, *and* DEMETRIUS.

[1] *lingers*] prolongs.
[2] *solemnities*] celebration (of the wedding).
[3] *pert*] lively.
[4] *triumph*] public festivity.

EGE.   Happy be Theseus, our renowned duke!

THE.   Thanks, good Egeus: what's the news with thee?

EGE.   Full of vexation come I, with complaint
    Against my child, my daughter Hermia.
    Stand forth, Demetrius. My noble lord,
    This man hath my consent to marry her.
    Stand forth, Lysander: and, my gracious duke,
    This man hath bewitch'd the bosom[5] of my child:
    Thou, thou, Lysander, thou hast given her rhymes,
    And interchanged love-tokens with my child:
    Thou hast by moonlight at her window sung,
    With feigning[6] voice, verses of feigning love;
    And stolen the impression of her fantasy[7]
    With bracelets of thy hair, rings, gawds, conceits,[8]
    Knacks,[9] trifles, nosegays, sweetmeats, messengers
    Of strong prevailment[10] in unharden'd[11] youth:
    With cunning hast thou filch'd my daughter's heart;
    Turn'd her obedience, which is due to me,
    To stubborn harshness: and, my gracious duke,
    Be it so she will not here before your Grace
    Consent to marry with Demetrius,
    I beg the ancient privilege of Athens,
    As she is mine, I may dispose of her:
    Which shall be either to this gentleman
    Or to her death, according to our law
    Immediately[12] provided in that case.

THE.   What say you, Hermia? be advised, fair maid:
    To you your father should be as a god;
    One that composed your beauties; yea, and one
    To whom you are but as a form in wax
    By him imprinted and within his power
    To leave the figure or disfigure it.
    Demetrius is a worthy gentleman.

HER.   So is Lysander.

---

[5] *bosom*] heart.

[6] *feigning*] soft.

[7] *stolen . . . fantasy*] captured her imagination and love.

[8] *gawds, conceits*] baubles, fanciful presents.

[9] *Knacks*] knickknacks.

[10] *prevailment*] influence.

[11] *unharden'd*] impressionable.

[12] *Immediately*] expressly.

THE.   In himself he is;
            But in this kind, wanting your father's voice,[13]
            The other must be held the worthier.
HER.   I would my father look'd but with my eyes.
THE.   Rather your eyes must with his judgement look.
HER.   I do entreat your Grace to pardon me.
            I know not by what power I am made bold,
            Nor how it may concern[14] my modesty,
            In such a presence here to plead my thoughts;
            But I beseech your Grace that I may know
            The worst that may befall me in this case,
            If I refuse to wed Demetrius.
THE.   Either to die the death, or to abjure
            For ever the society of men.
            Therefore, fair Hermia, question your desires;
            Know of your youth, examine well your blood,
            Whether, if you yield not to your father's choice,
            You can endure the livery of a nun;
            For aye[15] to be in shady cloister mew'd,[16]
            To live a barren sister all your life,
            Chanting faint hymns to the cold fruitless moon.
            Thrice-blessed they that master so their blood,
            To undergo such maiden pilgrimage;
            But earthlier happy is the rose distill'd,[17]
            Than that which, withering on the virgin thorn,
            Grows, lives, and dies in single blessedness.
HER.   So will I grow, so live, so die, my lord,
            Ere I will yield my virgin patent[18] up
            Unto his lordship, whose unwished yoke
            My soul consents not to give sovereignty.
THE.   Take time to pause; and, by the next new moon,—
            The sealing-day betwixt my love and me,
            For everlasting bond of fellowship,—
            Upon that day either prepare to die
            For disobedience to your father's will,

---

[13] *in this kind . . . voice*] in business of this nature, lacking your father's approval.
[14] *concern*] befit.
[15] *aye*] ever.
[16] *mew'd*] confined.
[17] *earthlier . . . distill'd*] i.e., happier on earth is the one who will live on after death
    through his or her child.
[18] *virgin patent*] privilege of remaining a virgin.

        Or else to wed Demetrius, as he would;
        Or on Diana's altar to protest[19]
        For aye austerity and single life.

DEM.   Relent, sweet Hermia: and, Lysander, yield
        Thy crazed title[20] to my certain right.

LYS.   You have her father's love, Demetrius;
        Let me have Hermia's: do you marry him.

EGE.   Scornful Lysander! true, he hath my love,
        And what is mine my love shall render him.
        And she is mine, and all my right of her
        I do estate unto Demetrius.

LYS.   I am, my lord, as well derived[21] as he,
        As well possess'd;[22] my love is more than his;
        My fortunes every way as fairly rank'd,
        If not with vantage,[23] as Demetrius';
        And, which is more than all these boasts can be,
        I am beloved of beauteous Hermia:
        Why should not I then prosecute my right?
        Demetrius, I'll avouch it to his head,[24]
        Made love to Nedar's daughter, Helena,
        And won her soul; and she, sweet lady, dotes,
        Devoutly dotes, dotes in idolatry,
        Upon this spotted[25] and inconstant man.

THE.   I must confess that I have heard so much,
        And with Demetrius thought to have spoke thereof;
        But, being over-full of self-affairs,
        My mind did lose it. But, Demetrius, come;
        And come, Egeus; you shall go with me,
        I have some private schooling[26] for you both.
        For you, fair Hermia, look you arm yourself
        To fit your fancies[27] to your father's will;
        Or else the law of Athens yields you up,—
        Which by no means we may extenuate,—[28]

[19] *protest*] vow.
[20] *crazed title*] invalid claim.
[21] *well derived*] nobly born.
[22] *well possess'd*] wealthy.
[23] *vantage*] superiority.
[24] *avouch it to his head*] declare it in his presence.
[25] *spotted*] guilty.
[26] *schooling*] admonition.
[27] *fancies*] thoughts of love.
[28] *extenuate*] mitigate.

To death, or to a vow of single life.
Come, my Hippolyta: what cheer, my love?
Demetrius and Egeus, go along:
I must employ you in some business
Against[29] our nuptial, and confer with you
Of something nearly that concerns yourselves.

EGE. With duty and desire we follow you.

                              [*Exeunt all but* LYSANDER *and* HERMIA.

LYS. How now, my love! why is your cheek so pale?
How chance the roses there do fade so fast?

HER. Belike for want of rain, which I could well
Beteem[30] them from the tempest of my eyes.

LYS. Ay me! for aught that I could ever read,
Could ever hear by tale or history,
The course of true love never did run smooth;
But, either it was different in blood,—

HER. O cross![31] too high to be enthrall'd to low.

LYS. Or else misgraffed in respect of years,—

HER. O spite! too old to be engaged to young.

LYS. Or else it stood upon the choice of friends,—

HER. O hell! to choose love by another's eyes.

LYS. Or, if there were a sympathy in choice,
War, death, or sickness did lay siege to it,
Making it momentany as a sound,
Swift as a shadow, short as any dream;
Brief as the lightning in the collied[32] night,
That, in a spleen,[33] unfolds both heaven and earth,
And ere a man hath power to say "Behold!"
The jaws of darkness do devour it up:
So quick bright things come to confusion.[34]

HER. If then true lovers have been ever cross'd,[35]
It stands as an edict in destiny:
Then let us teach our trial patience,
Because it is a customary cross,

[29] *against*] in preparation for.
[30] *Beteem*] grant.
[31] *cross*] The cross symbolizes here that which thwarts or hinders.
[32] *collied*] dark.
[33] *spleen*] fit of passion.
[34] *confusion*] ruin.
[35] *ever cross'd*] always thwarted.

As due to love as thoughts and dreams and sighs,
Wishes and tears, poor fancy's followers.

LYS. A good persuasion:[36] therefore, hear me, Hermia.
I have a widow aunt, a dowager
Of great revenue, and she hath no child:
From Athens is her house remote seven leagues;
And she respects me as[37] her only son.
There, gentle Hermia, may I marry thee;
And to that place the sharp Athenian law
Cannot pursue us. If thou lovest me, then,
Steal forth thy father's house to-morrow night;
And in the wood, a league without the town,
Where I did meet thee once with Helena,
To do observance to a morn of May,[38]
There will I stay for thee.

HER.   My good Lysander!
I swear to thee, by Cupid's strongest bow,
By his best arrow with the golden head,
By the simplicity of Venus' doves,
By that which knitteth souls and prospers loves,
And by that fire which burn'd the Carthage queen,
When the false Troyan[39] under sail was seen,
By all the vows that ever men have broke,
In number more than ever women spoke,
In that same place thou hast appointed me,
To-morrow truly will I meet with thee.

LYS. Keep promise, love. Look, here comes Helena.

Enter HELENA.

HER. God speed fair Helena! whither away?
HEL. Call you me fair? that fair again unsay.
Demetrius loves your fair: O happy fair!
Your eyes are lode-stars;[40] and your tongue's sweet air
More tuneable[41] than lark to shepherd's ear,
When wheat is green, when hawthorn buds appear.
Sickness is catching: O, were favour so,

---

[36] *persuasion*] opinion.
[37] *respects me as*] thinks of me as.
[38] *do observance to a morn of May*] celebrate May Day.
[39] *false Troyan*] Aeneas, who abandoned his lover Dido, Queen of Carthage.
[40] *lode-stars*] stars that guide and attract.
[41] *tuneable*] harmonious.

Yours would I catch, fair Hermia, ere I go;
My ear should catch your voice, my eye your eye,
My tongue should catch your tongue's sweet melody.
Were the world mine, Demetrius being bated,[42]
The rest I'd give to be to you translated.[43]
O, teach me how you look; and with what art
You sway the motion[44] of Demetrius' heart!

HER.   I frown upon him, yet he loves me still.

HEL.   O that your frowns would teach my smiles such skill!

HER.   I give him curses, yet he gives me love.

HEL.   O that my prayers could such affection move![45]

HER.   The more I hate, the more he follows me.

HEL.   The more I love, the more he hateth me.

HER.   His folly, Helena, is no fault of mine.

HEL.   None, but your beauty: would that fault were mine!

HER.   Take comfort: he no more shall see my face;
Lysander and myself will fly this place.
Before the time I did Lysander see,
Seem'd Athens as a paradise to me:
O, then, what graces in my love do dwell,
That he hath turn'd a heaven unto a hell!

LYS.   Helen, to you our minds we will unfold:
To-morrow night, when Phoebe[46] doth behold
Her silver visage in the watery glass,[47]
Decking with liquid pearl the bladed grass,
A time that lovers' flights doth still conceal,
Through Athens' gates have we devised to steal.

HER.   And in the wood, where often you and I
Upon faint[48] primrose-beds were wont to lie,
Emptying our bosoms of their counsel sweet,
There my Lysander and myself shall meet;
And thence from Athens turn away our eyes,
To seek new friends and stranger companies.
Farewell, sweet playfellow: pray thou for us;
And good luck grant thee thy Demetrius!

[42] *bated*] excepted.
[43] *to you translated*] transformed into you.
[44] *sway the motion*] control the impulse.
[45] *such affection move*] arouse such passion.
[46] *Phoebe*] the goddess of the moon.
[47] *glass*] mirror.
[48] *faint*] pale.

Keep word, Lysander: we must starve our sight
From lovers' food till morrow deep midnight.

LYS. I will, my Hermia. [*Exit* HERMIA.

Helena, adieu:
As you on him, Demetrius dote on you! [*Exit.*

HEL. How happy some o'er other some can be!
Through Athens I am thought as fair as she.
But what of that? Demetrius thinks not so;
He will not know what all but he do know:
And as he errs, doting on Hermia's eyes,
So I, admiring of his qualities:
Things base and vile, holding no quantity,[49]
Love can transpose to form and dignity:
Love looks not with the eyes, but with the mind;
And therefore is wing'd Cupid painted blind:
Nor hath Love's mind of any judgement taste;
Wings, and no eyes, figure[50] unheedy haste:
And therefore is Love said to be a child,
Because in choice he is so oft beguiled.
As waggish boys in game themselves forswear,
So the boy Love is perjured everywhere:
For ere Demetrius look'd on Hermia's eyne,[51]
He hail'd down oaths that he was only mine;
And when this hail some heat from Hermia felt,
So he dissolved, and showers of oaths did melt.
I will go tell him of fair Hermia's flight:
Then to the wood will he to-morrow night
Pursue her; and for this intelligence
If I have thanks, it is a dear expense:
But herein mean I to enrich my pain,
To have his sight thither and back again. [*Exit.*

[49] *holding no quantity*] not having the value given them.
[50] *figure*] symbolize.
[51] *eyne*] eyes.

Scene II—The same

QUINCE'S HOUSE

Enter QUINCE, SNUG, BOTTOM, FLUTE, SNOUT, *and* STARVELING.

QUIN. Is all our company here?

BOT. You were best to call them generally,[1] man by man, according to the scrip.[2]

QUIN. Here is the scroll of every man's name, which is thought fit, through all Athens, to play in our interlude[3] before the duke and the duchess, on his wedding-day at night.

BOT. First, good Peter Quince, say what the play treats on; then read the names of the actors; and so grow to a point.[4]

QUIN. Marry, our play is, The most lamentable comedy, and most cruel death of Pyramus and Thisbe.

BOT. A very good piece of work, I assure you, and a merry. Now, good Peter Quince, call forth your actors by the scroll. Masters, spread yourselves.

QUIN. Answer as I call you. Nick Bottom, the weaver.

BOT. Ready. Name what part I am for, and proceed.

QUIN. You, Nick Bottom, are set down for Pyramus.

BOT. What is Pyramus? a lover, or a tyrant?

QUIN. A lover, that kills himself most gallant for love.

BOT. That will ask some tears in the true performing of it: if I do it, let the audience look to their eyes; I will move storms, I will condole[5] in some measure. To the rest: yet my chief humour[6] is for a tyrant: I could play Ercles[7] rarely, or a part to tear a cat in, to make all split.[8]

> The raging rocks
> And shivering shocks
> Shall break the locks
> Of prison-gates;

[1] *generally*] Bottom's malapropism for "severally" (one by one).
[2] *scrip*] written list.
[3] *interlude*] short play.
[4] *grow to a point*] get to the end.
[5] *condole*] show signs of lamentation.
[6] *humour*] inclination.
[7] *Ercles*] Hercules.
[8] *a part . . . split*] a dramatic role that allows for ranting and extravagant gestures.

> And Phibbus' car[9]
> Shall shine from far,
> And make and mar
> The foolish Fates.

This was lofty! Now name the rest of the players. This is Ercles' vein, a tyrant's vein; a lover is more condoling.

QUIN. Francis Flute, the bellows-mender.

FLU. Here, Peter Quince.

QUIN. Flute, you must take Thisbe on you.

FLU. What is Thisbe? a wandering knight?[10]

QUIN. It is the lady that Pyramus must love.

FLU. Nay, faith, let not me play a woman; I have a beard coming.

QUIN. That's all one: you shall play it in a mask, and you may speak as small[11] as you will.

BOT. An[12] I may hide my face, let me play Thisbe too, I'll speak in a monstrous little voice, "Thisne, Thisne;" "Ah Pyramus, my lover dear! thy Thisbe dear, and lady dear!"

QUIN. No, no; you must play Pyramus: and, Flute, you Thisbe.

BOT. Well, proceed.

QUIN. Robin Starveling, the tailor.

STAR. Here, Peter Quince.

QUIN. Robin Starveling, you must play Thisbe's mother. Tom Snout, the tinker.

SNOUT. Here, Peter Quince.

QUIN. You, Pyramus' father: myself, Thisbe's father: Snug, the joiner; you, the lion's part: and, I hope, here is a play fitted.

SNUG. Have you the lion's part written? pray you, if it be, give it me, for I am slow of study.

QUIN. You may do it extempore, for it is nothing but roaring.

BOT. Let me play the lion too: I will roar, that I will do any man's heart good to hear me; I will roar, that I will make the duke say, "Let him roar again, let him roar again."

QUIN. An you should do it too terribly, you would fright the duchess and the ladies, that they would shriek; and that were enough to hang us all.

ALL. That would hang us, every mother's son.

---

[9] *Phibbus' car*] Phoebus Apollo's chariot, the sun.

[10] *wandering knight*] knight-errant.

[11] *as small*] in as clear and high-pitched a voice.

[12] *An*] if.

BOT.   I grant you, friends, if you should fright the ladies out of their wits, they would have no more discretion but to hang us: but I will aggravate[13] my voice so, that I will roar you as gently as any sucking dove; I will roar you an't were any nightingale.

QUIN. You can play no part but Pyramus; for Pyramus is a sweet-faced man; a proper[14] man, as one shall see in a summer's day; a most lovely, gentleman-like man: therefore you must needs play Pyramus.

BOT.   Well, I will undertake it. What beard were I best to play it in?

QUIN. Why, what you will.

BOT.   I will discharge[15] it in either your straw colour beard, your orange-tawny beard, your purple-in-grain[16] beard, or your French crown[17] colour beard, your perfect yellow.

QUIN. Some of your French crowns[18] have no hair at all, and then you will play barefaced. But, masters, here are your parts: and I am to entreat you, request you, and desire you, to con[19] them by tomorrow night; and meet me in the palace wood, a mile without the town, by moonlight; there will we rehearse, for if we meet in the city, we shall be dogged with company, and our devices known. In the mean time I will draw a bill of properties, such as our play wants. I pray you, fail me not.

BOT.   We will meet; and there we may rehearse most obscenely[20] and courageously. Take pains; be perfect:[21] adieu.

QUIN. At the duke's oak we meet.

BOT.   Enough; hold or cut bow-strings.[22]

[*Exeunt.*

---

[13] *aggravate*] Bottom's malapropism for "diminish" (tone down).
[14] *proper*] handsome.
[15] *discharge*] perform.
[16] *purple-in-grain*] scarlet or crimson.
[17] *crown*] coin.
[18] *crowns*] heads, bald as a result of syphilis.
[19] *con*] memorize.
[20] *obscenely*] Bottom's error for "seemly."
[21] *perfect*] word-perfect.
[22] *hold . . . bow-strings*] i.e., be there or give up the play altogether.

Act II—Scene I—A wood near Athens

Enter, from opposite sides, a FAIRY *and* PUCK.

PUCK. How now, spirit! whither wander you?

FAI. Over hill, over dale,
　　　　Thorough[1] bush, thorough brier,
　　Over park, over pale,
　　　　Thorough flood, thorough fire,
　　I do wander every where,
　　Swifter than the moon's sphere;
　　And I serve the fairy queen,
　　To dew her orbs upon the green.[2]
　　The cowslips tall her pensioners[3] be:
　　In their gold coats spots you see;
　　Those be rubies, fairy favours,
　　In those freckles live their savours:[4]
　　I must go seek some dewdrops here,
　　And hang a pearl in every cowslip's ear.
　　Farewell, thou lob of[5] spirits; I'll be gone:
　　Our queen and all her elves come here anon.

PUCK. The king doth keep his revels here to-night:
　　Take heed the queen come not within his sight;
　　For Oberon is passing fell and wrath,[6]
　　Because that she as her attendant hath

---

[1] *Thorough*] through.

[2] *To dew her orbs upon the green*] to sprinkle with dew the fairy rings on the village green.

[3] *pensioners*] bodyguards.

[4] *their savours*] the cowslips' fragrance.

[5] *lob of*] country bumpkin among.

[6] *passing fell and wrath*] exceedingly fierce and angry.

A lovely boy, stolen from an Indian king;
She never had so sweet a changeling:[7]
And jealous Oberon would have the child
Knight of his train, to trace[8] the forests wild;
But she perforce[9] withholds the loved boy,
Crowns him with flowers, and makes him all her joy:
And now they never meet in grove or green,
By fountain clear, or spangled starlight sheen,
But they do square,[10] that all their elves for fear
Creep into acorn cups and hide them there.

FAI.   Either I mistake your shape and making quite,
Or else you are that shrewd[11] and knavish sprite
Call'd Robin Goodfellow:[12] are not you he
That frights the maidens of the villagery;
Skim milk, and sometimes labour in the quern,[13]
And bootless[14] make the breathless housewife churn;
And sometime make the drink to bear no barm;[15]
Mislead night-wanderers, laughing at their harm?
Those that Hobgoblin call you, and sweet Puck,
You do their work, and they shall have good luck:
Are not you he?

PUCK.   Thou speak'st aright;
I am that merry wanderer of the night.
I jest to Oberon, and make him smile,
When I a fat and bean-fed horse beguile,
Neighing in likeness of a filly foal:
And sometimes lurk I in a gossip's bowl,[16]
In very likeness of a roasted crab;[17]
And when she drinks, against her lips I bob
And on her withered dewlap[18] pour the ale.

---

[7] *changeling*] "Changeling" is normally the name for the frail fairy child left in place of a stolen child. In this instance, however, the changeling is the stolen child.

[8] *trace*] range.

[9] *perforce*] by means of force.

[10] *square*] quarrel.

[11] *shrewd*] mischievous.

[12] *Robin Goodfellow*] a mischievous sprite in English folklore.

[13] *quern*] hand mill for grinding grain.

[14] *bootless*] in vain.

[15] *barm*] yeast or froth.

[16] *a gossip's bowl*] a gossiping old woman's drink of spiced ale with crab apples.

[17] *crab*] crab apple.

[18] *dewlap*] wrinkled skin on the neck.

The wisest aunt,[19] telling the saddest tale,
Sometime for three-foot stool mistaketh me;
Then slip I from her bum, down topples she,
And "tailor" cries, and falls into a cough;
And then the whole quire[20] hold their hips and laugh;
And waxen in their mirth, and neeze,[21] and swear
A merrier hour was never wasted there.
But, room, fairy! here comes Oberon.

FAI.   And here my mistress. Would that he were gone!

Enter, from one side, OBERON, *with his train; from the other,* TITANIA,
   with hers.

OBE.   Ill met by moonlight, proud Titania.

TITA.   What, jealous Oberon! Fairies, skip hence:
I have forsworn his bed and company.

OBE.   Tarry, rash wanton: am not I thy lord?

TITA.   Then I must be thy lady: but I know
When thou hast stolen away from fairy land,
And in the shape of Corin sat all day,
Playing on pipes of corn, and versing love
To amorous Phillida.[22] Why art thou here,
Come from the farthest steep of India?
But that, forsooth, the bouncing Amazon,
Your buskin'd[23] mistress and your warrior love,
To Theseus must be wedded, and you come
To give their bed joy and prosperity.

OBE.   How canst thou thus for shame, Titania,
Glance at[24] my credit with Hippolyta,
Knowing I know thy love to Theseus?
Didst thou not lead him through the glimmering night
From Perigenia, whom he ravished?
And make him with fair Aegle break his faith,
With Ariadne and Antiopa?

TITA.   These are the forgeries of jealousy:
And never, since the middle summer's spring,[25]

---

[19] *aunt*] old gossip.
[20] *quire*] company.
[21] *neeze*] sneeze.
[22] *Corin . . . Phillida*] traditional names for pastoral lovers.
[23] *buskin'd*] wearing buskins (laced boots reaching halfway to the knee).
[24] *Glance at*] hint at, censure.
[25] *middle summer's spring*] beginning of midsummer.

Met we on hill, in dale, forest, or mead,
By paved fountain or by rushy brook,
Or in[26] the beached margent[27] of the sea,
To dance our ringlets[28] to the whistling wind,
But with thy brawls thou hast disturb'd our sport.
Therefore the winds, piping to us in vain,
As in revenge, have suck'd up from the sea
Contagious fogs; which, falling in the land,
Have every pelting[29] river made so proud,
That they have overborne their continents:[30]
The ox hath therefore stretch'd his yoke in vain,
The ploughman lost his sweat; and the green corn
Hath rotted ere his youth attain'd a beard:
The fold stands empty in the drowned field,
And crows are fatted with the murrion[31] flock;
The nine men's morris[32] is fill'd up with mud;
And the quaint mazes in the wanton green,[33]
For lack of tread, are undistinguishable:
The human mortals want their winter here;[34]
No night is now with hymn or carol blest:
Therefore the moon, the governess of floods,
Pale in her anger, washes all the air,
That rheumatic diseases do abound:
And thorough this distemperature we see
The seasons alter: hoary-headed frosts
Fall in the fresh lap of the crimson rose;
And on old Hiems'[35] thin and icy crown
An odorous chaplet[36] of sweet summer buds
Is, as in mockery, set: the spring, the summer,
The childing[37] autumn, angry winter, change

[26] *in*] on.
[27] *margent*] edge.
[28] *ringlets*] circular dances.
[29] *pelting*] paltry.
[30] *continents*] banks.
[31] *murrion*] diseased.
[32] *nine men's morris*] a game played with nine counters on the village green.
[33] *quaint mazes in the wanton green*] labyrinthine figures made on the lush village green.
[34] *want . . . here*] lack their usual winter mood.
[35] *Hiems'*] Hiems is the personification of winter.
[36] *chaplet*] garland.
[37] *childing*] fruitful.

   Their wonted liveries; and the mazed[38] world,
   By their increase, now knows not which is which:
   And this same progeny of evils comes
   From our debate, from our dissension;
   We are their parents and original.[39]

OBE. Do you amend it, then; it lies in you:
   Why should Titania cross her Oberon?
   I do but beg a little changeling boy,
   To be my henchman.[40]

TITA.   Set your heart at rest:
   The fairy land buys not the child of me.
   His mother was a votaress of my order:
   And, in the spiced Indian air, by night,
   Full often hath she gossip'd by my side;
   And sat with me on Neptune's yellow sands,
   Marking the embarked traders on the flood;
   When we have laugh'd to see the sails conceive
   And grow big-bellied with the wanton wind;
   Which she, with pretty and with swimming gait[41]
   Following,—her womb then rich with my young squire,—
   Would imitate, and sail upon the land,
   To fetch me trifles, and return again,
   As from a voyage, rich with merchandise.
   But she, being mortal, of that boy did die;
   And for her sake do I rear up her boy;
   And for her sake I will not part with him.

OBE. How long within this wood intend you stay?

TITA. Perchance till after Theseus' wedding-day.
   If you will patiently dance in our round,
   And see our moonlight revels, go with us;
   If not, shun me, and I will spare your haunts.

OBE. Give me that boy, and I will go with thee.

TITA. Not for thy fairy kingdom. Fairies, away!
   We shall chide downright, if I longer stay.

           [*Exit* TITANIA *with her train.*

OBE. Well, go thy way: thou shalt not from this grove
   Till I torment thee for this injury.

---

[38] *mazed*] perplexed.
[39] *original*] source.
[40] *henchman*] page boy.
[41] *swimming gait*] gliding step.

My gentle Puck, come hither. Thou rememberest
Since once I sat upon a promontory,
And heard a mermaid, on a dolphin's back,
Uttering such dulcet and harmonious breath,[42]
That the rude sea grew civil at her song,
And certain stars shot madly from their spheres,
To hear the sea-maid's music.

PUCK.   I remember.

OBE.   That very time I saw, but thou couldst not,
Flying between the cold moon and the earth,
Cupid all arm'd: a certain aim he took
At a fair vestal throned by the west,
And loosed his love-shaft smartly from his bow,
As it should pierce a hundred thousand hearts:
But I might see young Cupid's fiery shaft
Quench'd in the chaste beams of the watery moon,
And the imperial votaress passed on,
In maiden meditation, fancy-free.[43]
Yet mark'd I where the bolt of Cupid fell:
It fell upon a little western flower,
Before milk-white, now purple with love's wound,
And maidens call it love-in-idleness.[44]
Fetch me that flower; the herb I shew'd thee once:
The juice of it on sleeping eye-lids laid
Will make or man or woman madly dote
Upon the next live creature that it sees.
Fetch me this herb; and be thou here again
Ere the leviathan[45] can swim a league.

PUCK.   I'll put a girdle round about the earth
In forty minutes.   [Exit.

OBE.   Having once this juice,
I'll watch Titania when she is asleep,
And drop the liquor of it in her eyes.
The next thing then she waking looks upon,
Be it on lion, bear, or wolf, or bull,
On meddling monkey, or on busy ape,
She shall pursue it with the soul of love:

---

[42] *breath*] notes, words.
[43] *fancy-free*] free from love.
[44] *love-in-idleness*] a popular name for the pansy.
[45] *leviathan*] sea monster.

And ere I take this charm from off her sight,
As I can take it with another herb,
I'll make her render up her page to me.
But who comes here? I am invisible;
And I will overhear their conference.

Enter DEMETRIUS, HELENA *following him.*

DEM. I love thee not, therefore pursue me not.
Where is Lysander and fair Hermia?
The one I'll slay, the other slayeth me.
Thou told'st me they were stolen unto this wood;
And here am I, and wode[46] within this wood;
Because I cannot meet my Hermia.
Hence, get thee gone, and follow me no more.

HEL. You draw me, you hard-hearted adamant;[47]
But yet you draw not iron, for my heart
Is true as steel: leave you[48] your power to draw,
And I shall have no power to follow you.

DEM. Do I entice you? do I speak you fair?[49]
Or, rather, do I not in plainest truth
Tell you, I do not nor I cannot love you?

HEL. And even for that do I love you the more.
I am your spaniel; and, Demetrius,
The more you beat me, I will fawn on you:
Use me but as your spaniel, spurn me, strike me,
Neglect me, lose me; only give me leave,
Unworthy as I am, to follow you.
What worser place can I beg in your love,—
And yet a place of high respect with me,—
Than to be used as you use your dog?

DEM. Tempt not too much the hatred of my spirit;
For I am sick when I do look on thee.

HEL. And I am sick when I look not on you.

DEM. You do impeach your modesty too much,
To leave the city, and commit yourself
Into the hands of one that loves you not;
To trust the opportunity of night

---

[46] *wode*] mad, frantic. The normal Shakespearean form of "wode" is "wood."
[47] *adamant*] lodestone.
[48] *leave you*] abandon.
[49] *fair*] kindly.

And the ill counsel of a desert place
With the rich worth of your virginity.

HEL.   Your virtue is my privilege:[50] for that[51]
     It is not night when I do see your face,
     Therefore I think I am not in the night;
     Nor doth this wood lack worlds of company,
     For you in my respect[52] are all the world:
     Then how can it be said I am alone,
     When all the world is here to look on me?

DEM.   I'll run from thee and hide me in the brakes,[53]
     And leave thee to the mercy of wild beasts.

HEL.   The wildest hath not such a heart as you.
     Run when you will, the story shall be changed:
     Apollo flies, and Daphne holds the chase;[54]
     The dove pursues the griffin;[55] the mild hind
     Makes speed to catch the tiger; bootless speed,
     When cowardice pursues, and valour flies.

DEM.   I will not stay thy questions;[56] let me go:
     Or, if thou follow me, do not believe
     But I shall do thee mischief in the wood.

HEL.   Ay, in the temple, in the town, the field,
     You do me mischief. Fie, Demetrius!
     Your wrongs do set a scandal on my sex:
     We cannot fight for love, as men may do;
     We should be woo'd, and were not made to woo. [Exit DEM.
     I'll follow thee, and make a heaven of hell,
     To die upon[57] the hand I love so well.   [Exit.

OBE.   Fare thee well, nymph: ere he do leave this grove,
     Thou shalt fly him, and he shall seek thy love.

Re-enter PUCK.

     Hast thou the flower there? Welcome, wanderer.

PUCK. Ay, there it is.

---

50 *privilege*] safeguard.
51 *for that*] since.
52 *in my respect*] in my opinion.
53 *brakes*] thickets.
54 *Apollo . . . chase*] an allusion to the myth in which the amorous god Apollo pursues
   Daphne.
55 *griffin*] a mythical beast with the head of an eagle and the body of a lion.
56 *stay thy questions*] wait around for your arguments.
57 *upon*] by.

OBE.   I pray thee, give it me.
    I know a bank where the wild thyme blows,
    Where oxlips and the nodding violet grows;
    Quite over-canopied with luscious woodbine,
    With sweet musk-roses, and with eglantine:
    There sleeps Titania sometime of the night,
    Lull'd in these flowers with dances and delight;
    And there the snake throws her enamell'd skin,
    Weed[58] wide enough to wrap a fairy in:
    And with the juice of this I'll streak[59] her eyes,
    And make her full of hateful fantasies.
    Take thou some of it, and seek through this grove:
    A sweet Athenian lady is in love
    With a disdainful youth: anoint his eyes;
    But do it when the next thing he espies
    May be the lady: thou shalt know the man
    By the Athenian garments he hath on.
    Effect it with some care that he may prove
    More fond on her than she upon her love:
    And look thou meet me ere the first cock crow.

PUCK. Fear not, my lord, your servant shall do so.   [*Exeunt.*

Scene II—Another part of the wood

Enter TITANIA, *with her train.*

TITA. Come, now a roundel[1] and a fairy song;
    Then, for the third part of a minute, hence;
    Some to kill cankers[2] in the musk-rose buds;
    Some war with rere-mice[3] for their leathern wings,
    To make my small elves coats; and some keep back
    The clamorous owl, that nightly hoots and wonders
    At our quaint spirits. Sing me now asleep;
    Then to your offices, and let me rest.

[58] *Weed*] garment.
[59] *streak*] anoint.

[1] *roundel*] dance in a circle.
[2] *cankers*] caterpillars.
[3] *rere-mice*] bats.

SONG

FIRST FAI.   You spotted snakes with double tongue,
   Thorny hedgehogs, be not seen;
 Newts[4] and blind-worms, do no wrong,
   Come not near our fairy queen.

CHORUS

 Philomel,[5] with melody
 Sing in our sweet lullaby;
Lulla, lulla, lullaby, lulla, lulla, lullaby:
  Never harm,
  Nor spell, nor charm,
 Come our lovely lady nigh;
 So, good night, with lullaby.

FIRST FAI.   Weaving spiders, come not here;
   Hence, you long-legg'd spinners, hence!
 Beetles black, approach not near;
   Worm nor snail, do no offence.

CHORUS

 Philomel, with melody, &c.

SEC. FAI.   Hence, away! now all is well:
  One aloof stand sentinel.   [*Exeunt* Fairies. TITANIA *sleeps.*

Enter OBERON, *and squeezes the flower on* TITANIA'S *eyelids.*

OBE.   What thou seest when thou dost wake,
 Do it for thy true-love take;
 Love and languish for his sake:
 Be it ounce,[6] or cat, or bear,
 Pard,[7] or boar with bristled hair,
 In thy eye that shall appear
 When thou wakest, it is thy dear:
 Wake when some vile thing is near.   [*Exit.*

Enter LYSANDER *and* HERMIA.

 [4] *Newts*] small lizards.
 [5] *Philomel*] nightingale.
 [6] *ounce*] lynx.
 [7] *Pard*] leopard.

LYS.   Fair love, you faint with wandering in the wood;
             And to speak troth,[8] I have forgot our way:
            We'll rest us, Hermia, if you think it good,
             And tarry for the comfort of the day.

HER.   Be it so, Lysander: find you out a bed;
             For I upon this bank will rest my head.

LYS.   One turf shall serve as pillow for us both;
             One heart, one bed, two bosoms, and one troth.

HER.   Nay, good Lysander; for my sake, my dear,
             Lie further off yet, do not lie so near.

LYS.   O, take the sense,[9] sweet, of my innocence!
             Love takes the meaning in love's conference.
             I mean, that my heart unto yours is knit,
             So that but one heart we can make of it:
             Two bosoms interchained with an oath;
             So then two bosoms and a single troth.
             Then by your side no bed-room me deny;
             For lying so, Hermia, I do not lie.

HER.   Lysander riddles very prettily:
             Now much beshrew[10] my manners and my pride,
             If Hermia meant to say Lysander lied.
             But, gentle friend, for love and courtesy
             Lie further off; in human[11] modesty,
             Such separation as may well be said
             Becomes a virtuous bachelor and a maid,
             So far be distant; and, good night, sweet friend:
             Thy love ne'er alter till thy sweet life end!

LYS.   Amen, amen, to that fair prayer, say I;
             And then end life when I end loyalty!
             Here is my bed: sleep give thee all his rest!

HER.   With half that wish the wisher's eyes be press'd!   [*They sleep.*

Enter PUCK.

PUCK.   Through the forest have I gone,
              But Athenian found I none,
              On whose eyes I might approve[12]
              This flower's force in stirring love.

---

[8] *troth*] truth.
[9] *take the sense*] consider the significance.
[10] *much beshrew*] a curse on.
[11] *human*] benevolent.
[12] *approve*] test.

Night and silence.—Who is here?
Weeds of Athens he doth wear:
This is he, my master said,
Despised the Athenian maid;
And here the maiden, sleeping sound,
On the dank and dirty ground.
Pretty soul! she durst not lie
Near this lack-love, this kill-courtesy.
Churl, upon thy eyes I throw
All the power this charm doth owe.[13]
When thou wakest, let love forbid
Sleep his seat on thy eyelid:
So awake when I am gone;
For I must now to Oberon.   [Exit.

Enter DEMETRIUS *and* HELENA, *running.*

HEL. Stay, though thou kill me, sweet Demetrius.
DEM. I charge thee, hence, and do not haunt me thus.
HEL. O, wilt thou darkling[14] leave me? do not so.
DEM. Stay, on thy peril: I alone will go.   [Exit.
HEL. O, I am out of breath in this fond[15] chase!
      The more my prayer, the lesser is my grace.[16]
      Happy is Hermia, wheresoe'er she lies;
      For she hath blessed and attractive eyes.
      How came her eyes so bright? Not with salt tears:
      If so, my eyes are oftener wash'd than hers.
      No, no, I am as ugly as a bear;
      For beasts that meet me run away for fear:
      Therefore no marvel though Demetrius
      Do, as a monster, fly my presence thus.
      What wicked and dissembling glass[17] of mine
      Made me compare with Hermia's sphery eyne?[18]
      But who is here? Lysander! on the ground!
      Dead? or asleep? I see no blood, no wound.
      Lysander, if you live, good sir, awake.

[13] *owe*] possess.
[14] *darkling*] in the dark.
[15] *fond*] both doting and foolish.
[16] *my grace*] the favor I receive.
[17] *glass*] mirror.
[18] *sphery eyne*] starlike eyes.

LYS.   [*Awaking*] And run through fire I will for thy sweet sake.
      Transparent Helena! Nature shews art,
      That through thy bosom makes me see thy heart.
      Where is Demetrius? O, how fit a word
      Is that vile name to perish on my sword!

HEL.   Do not say so, Lysander; say not so.
      What though he love your Hermia? Lord, what though?
      Yet Hermia still loves you: then be content.

LYS.   Content with Hermia! No; I do repent
      The tedious minutes I with her have spent.
      Not Hermia but Helena I love:
      Who will not change a raven for a dove?
      The will of man is by his reason sway'd
      And reason says you are the worthier maid.
      Things growing are not ripe until their season:
      So I, being young, till now ripe not to reason;
      And touching now the point of human skill,
      Reason becomes the marshal to my will,
      And leads me to your eyes; where I o'erlook
      Love's stories, written in love's richest book.

HEL.   Wherefore was I to this keen[19] mockery born?
      When at your hands did I deserve this scorn?
      Is't not enough, is't not enough, young man,
      That I did never, no, nor never can,
      Deserve a sweet look from Demetrius' eye,
      But you must flout my insufficiency?
      Good troth, you do me wrong, good sooth, you do,
      In such disdainful manner me to woo.
      But fare you well: perforce I must confess
      I thought you lord of more true gentleness.
      O, that a lady, of[20] one man refused,
      Should of another therefore be abused!   [*Exit.*

LYS.   She sees not Hermia. Hermia, sleep thou there:
      And never mayst thou come Lysander near!
      For as a surfeit of the sweetest things
      The deepest loathing to the stomach brings,
      Or as the heresies that men do leave
      Are hated most of those they did deceive,
      So thou, my surfeit and my heresy,

[19] *keen*] bitter.
[20] *of*] by.

Of all be hated, but the most of me!
And, all my powers, address[21] your love and might
To honour Helen and to be her knight!   [*Exit.*

HER.   [*Awaking*] Help me, Lysander, help me! do thy best
To pluck this crawling serpent from my breast!
Ay me, for pity! what a dream was here!
Lysander, look how I do quake with fear:
Methought a serpent eat my heart away,
And you sat smiling at his cruel prey.[22]
Lysander! what, removed? Lysander! lord!
What, out of hearing? gone? no sound, no word?
Alack, where are you? speak, an if you hear:
Speak, of all loves![23] I swoon almost with fear.
No? then I well perceive you are not nigh:
Either death or you I'll find immediately.   [*Exit.*

[21] *address*] direct.
[22] *prey*] act of preying.
[23] *of all loves*] in the the name of all loves.

Act III—Scene I—The wood

TITANIA LYING ASLEEP

Enter QUINCE, SNUG, BOTTOM, FLUTE, SNOUT, *and* STARVELING.

BOT.   Are we all met?

QUIN.   Pat, pat; and here's a marvellous convenient place for our rehearsal. This green plot shall be our stage, this hawthorn-brake our tiring-house;[1] and we will do it in action as we will do it before the duke.

BOT.   Peter Quince,—

QUIN.   What sayest thou, bully[2] Bottom?

BOT.   There are things in this comedy of Pyramus and Thisbe that will never please. First, Pyramus must draw a sword to kill himself; which the ladies cannot abide. How answer you that?

SNOUT.   By'r lakin,[3] a parlous[4] fear.

STAR.   I believe we must leave the killing out, when all is done.

BOT.   Not a whit: I have a device to make all well. Write me a prologue; and let the prologue seem to say, we will do no harm with our swords, and that Pyramus is not killed indeed; and, for the more better assurance, tell them that I Pyramus am not Pyramus, but Bottom the weaver: this will put them out of fear.

QUIN.   Well, we will have such a prologue; and it shall be written in eight and six.[5]

BOT.   No, make it two more; let it be written in eight and eight.

SNOUT.   Will not the ladies be afeard of the lion?

---

[1] *tiring-house*] dressing room.
[2] *bully*] good fellow.
[3] *By'r lakin*] by our ladykin (the Virgin Mary).
[4] *parlous*] perilous.
[5] *eight and six*] alternate lines of eight and six syllables, a common ballad meter.

188

STAR. I fear it, I promise you.

BOT.   Masters, you ought to consider with yourselves: to bring in,—
God shield us!—a lion among ladies, is a most dreadful thing; for
there is not a more fearful[6] wild-fowl than your lion living: and we
ought to look to't.

SNOUT.   Therefore another prologue must tell he is not a lion.

BOT.   Nay, you must name his name, and half his face must be seen
through the lion's neck; and he himself must speak through, saying
thus, or to the same defect,[7]—"Ladies,"—or, "Fair ladies,—I
would wish you," —or, "I would request you,"—or, "I would
entreat you,—not to fear, not to tremble: my life for yours. If you
think I come hither as a lion, it were pity of my life: no, I am no such
thing; I am a man as other men are:" and there indeed let him name
his name, and tell them plainly, he is Snug the joiner.

QUIN. Well, it shall be so. But there is two hard things; that is, to bring
the moonlight into a chamber; for, you know, Pyramus and Thisbe
meet by moonlight.

SNOUT.   Doth the moon shine that night we play our play?

BOT.   A calendar, a calendar! look in the almanac; find out moonshine,
find out moonshine.

QUIN. Yes, it doth shine that night.

BOT.   Why, then may you leave a casement of the great chamber
window, where we play, open, and the moon may shine in at the
casement.

QUIN. Ay; or else one must come in with a bush of thorns[8] and a
lantern, and say he comes to disfigure,[9] or to present,[10] the person
of moonshine. Then, there is another thing: we must have a wall in
the great chamber; for Pyramus and Thisbe, says the story, did talk
through the chink of a wall.

SNOUT.   You can never bring in a wall. What say you, Bottom?

BOT.   Some man or other must present Wall: and let him have some
plaster, or some loam, or some rough-cast[11] about him, to signify
"wall"; and let him hold his fingers thus, and through that cranny
shall Pyramus and Thisbe whisper.

QUIN. If that may be, then all is well. Come, sit down, every mother's

---

[6] *fearful*] terrifying.

[7] *defect*] Bottom's malapropism for "effect."

[8] *bush of thorns*] The man in the moon was said to have been exiled there for collecting
firewood on Sundays.

[9] *disfigure*] Quince's malapropism for "figure."

[10] *present*] represent.

[11] *rough-cast*] plaster mixed with pebbles.

son, and rehearse your parts. Pyramus, you begin: when you have
spoken your speech, enter into that brake: and so every one
according to his cue.

Enter PUCK *behind.*

PUCK.   What hempen home-spuns[12] have we swaggering here,
        So near the cradle of the fairy queen?
        What, a play toward![13] I'll be an auditor;
        An actor too perhaps, if I see cause.
QUIN.   Speak, Pyramus. Thisbe, stand forth.
BOT.   Thisbe, the flowers of odious savours sweet,—
QUIN.   Odours, odours.
BOT.   ——odours savours sweet:
            So hath thy breath, my dearest Thisbe dear.
            But hark, a voice! stay thou but here awhile,
            And by and by I will to thee appear.   [*Exit.*
PUCK.   A stranger Pyramus than e'er play'd here.   [*Exit.*
FLU.   Must I speak now?
QUIN.   Ay, marry, must you; for you must understand he goes but to see a
        noise that he heard, and is to come again.
FLU.   Most radiant Pyramus, most lily-white of hue,
                Of colour like the red rose on triumphant brier,
            Most brisky juvenal,[14] and eke most lovely Jew,[15]
                As true as truest horse, that yet would never tire,
            I'll meet thee, Pyramus, at Ninny's[16] tomb.
QUIN.   "Ninus' tomb," man: why, you must not speak that yet; that you
        answer to Pyramus: you speak all your part at once, cues and all.
        Pyramus enter: your cue is past; it is, "never tire."
FLU.   O,—As true as truest horse, that yet would never tire.

Re-enter PUCK, *and* BOTTOM *with an ass's head.*

BOT.   If I were fair, Thisbe, I were only thine.
QUIN.   O monstrous! O strange! we are haunted. Pray, masters! fly,
        masters! Help!

                [*Exeunt* QUINCE, SNUG, FLUTE, SNOUT, *and* STARVELING.

PUCK.   I'll follow you, I'll lead you about a round,
            Through bog, through bush, through brake, through brier:

---

12 *hempen home-spuns*] rustics, wearing homespun clothes of hemp.
13 *toward*] in rehearsal.
14 *brisky juvenal*] nimble youth.
15 *Jew*] youth (a play on the first syllable of "juvenal").
16 *Ninny's*] Ninus, the legendary founder of Babylon.

      Sometime a horse I'll be, sometime a hound,
         A hog, a headless bear, sometime a fire;
      And neigh, and bark, and grunt, and roar, and burn,
      Like horse, hound, hog, bear, fire, at every turn.   [*Exit.*

BOT.   Why do they run away? this is a knavery of them to make me
afeard.

Re-enter SNOUT.

SNOUT.   O Bottom, thou art changed! what do I see on thee?
BOT.   What do you see? you see an ass-head of your own, do you?
                                                  [*Exit* SNOUT.

Re-enter QUINCE.

QUIN.   Bless thee, Bottom! bless thee! thou art translated.[17]   [*Exit.*
BOT.   I see their knavery: this is to make an ass of me; to fright me, if
they could. But I will not stir from this place, do what they can: I
will walk up and down here, and I will sing, that they shall hear I am
not afraid.   [*Sings.*

            The ousel[18] cock so black of hue,
               With orange-tawny bill,
            The throstle[19] with his note so true,
               The wren with little quill;[20]

TITA.   [*Awaking*] What angel wakes me from my flowery bed?
BOT.   [*Sings*]

            The finch, the sparrow, and the lark,
               The plain-song cuckoo gray,
            Whose note full many a man doth mark,
             And dares not answer nay;—

for, indeed, who would set his wit to[21] so foolish a bird? who would
give a bird the lie, though he cry "cuckoo" never so?
TITA.   I pray thee, gentle mortal, sing again:
      Mine ear is much enamour'd of thy note;
      So is mine eye enthralled to thy shape;
      And thy fair virtue's force perforce doth move me

[17] *translated*] transformed.
[18] *ousel*] blackbird.
[19] *throstle*] thrush.
[20] *quill*] musical pipe.
[21] *set his wit to*] match his wit against.

       On the first view to say, to swear, I love thee.

BOT.   Methinks, mistress, you should have little reason for that: and yet, to say the truth, reason and love keep little company together now-a-days; the more the pity, that some honest neighbours will not make them friends. Nay, I can gleek[22] upon occasion.

TITA.   Thou art as wise as thou art beautiful.

BOT.   Not so, neither: but if I had wit enough to get out of this wood, I have enough to serve mine own turn.

TITA.   Out of this wood do not desire to go:
       Thou shalt remain here, whether thou wilt or no.
       I am a spirit of no common rate:[23]
       The summer still doth tend[24] upon my state;
       And I do love thee: therefore, go with me;
       I'll give thee fairies to attend on thee;
       And they shall fetch thee jewels from the deep,
       And sing, while thou on pressed flowers dost sleep:
       And I will purge thy mortal grossness so,
       That thou shalt like an airy spirit go.
       Peaseblossom! Cobweb! Moth! and Mustardseed!

Enter PEASEBLOSSOM, COBWEB, MOTH, *and* MUSTARDSEED.

FIRST FAI.   Ready.
SEC. FAI.   And I.
THIRD FAI.   And I.
FOURTH FAI.   And I.
ALL.   Where shall we go?
TITA.   Be kind and courteous to this gentleman;
       Hop in his walks, and gambol in his eyes;
       Feed him with apricocks and dewberries,
       With purple grapes, green figs, and mulberries;
       The honey-bags steal from the humble-bees,
       And for night-tapers crop their waxen thighs,
       And light them at the fiery glow-worm's eyes,
       To have my love to bed and to arise;
       And pluck the wings from painted butterflies,
       To fan the moonbeams from his sleeping eyes:
       Nod to him, elves, and do him courtesies.

FIRST FAI.   Hail, mortal!
SEC. FAI.   Hail!

---

[22] *gleek*] joke, scoff.
[23] *rate*] rank.
[24] *still doth tend*] always attends.

THIRD FAI.   Hail!
FOURTH FAI.   Hail!
BOT.   I cry your worships mercy, heartily: I beseech your worship's
　　name.
COB.   Cobweb.
BOT.   I shall desire you of more acquaintance, good Master Cobweb: if
　　I cut my finger, I shall make bold with you. Your name, honest
　　gentleman?
PEAS.   Peaseblossom.
BOT.   I pray you, commend me to Mistress Squash,[26] your mother, and
　　to Master Peascod, your father. Good Master Peaseblossom, I shall
　　desire you of more acquaintance too. Your name, I beseech you, sir?
MUS.   Mustardseed.
BOT.   Good Master Mustardseed, I know your patience[27] well: that
　　same cowardly, giant-like ox-beef hath devoured many a gentleman
　　of your house: I promise you your kindred hath made my eyes water
　　ere now. I desire your more acquaintance, good Master Mus-
　　tardseed.
TITA.   Come, wait upon him; lead him to my bower.
　　　　The moon methinks looks with a watery eye;
　　And when she weeps, weeps every little flower,
　　　　Lamenting some enforced[28] chastity.
　　Tie up my love's tongue, bring him silently.   [Exeunt.

Scene II—Another part of the wood

Enter OBERON.

OBE.   I wonder if Titania be awaked;
　　　　Then, what it was that next came in her eye,
　　　　Which she must dote on in extremity.

Enter PUCK.

　　　　Here comes my messenger.
　　　　　　　　　　　　How now, mad spirit!
　　　　What night-rule[1] now about this haunted grove?
PUCK.   My mistress with a monster is in love.
　　　　Near to her close and consecrated bower,

---

　[26] *Squash*] unripe pea pod.
　[27] *patience*] endurance in adversity.
　[28] *enforced*] violated.

---

　[1] *night-rule*] nighttime revelry.

While she was in her dull and sleeping hour,
A crew of patches, rude mechanicals, [2]
That work for bread upon Athenian stalls,
Were met together to rehearse a play,
Intended for great Theseus' nuptial-day.
The shallowest thick-skin of that barren sort, [3]
Who Pyramus presented, in their sport
Forsook his scene, and enter'd in a brake:
When I did him at this advantage take,
An ass's nole [4] I fixed on his head:
Anon his Thisbe must be answered,
And forth my mimic [5] comes. When they him spy,
As wild geese that the creeping fowler eye,
Or russet-pated choughs, [6] many in sort,
Rising and cawing at the gun's report,
Sever themselves and madly sweep the sky,
So, at his sight, away his fellows fly;
And, at our stamp, [7] here o'er and o'er one falls;
He murder cries, and help from Athens calls.
Their sense thus weak, lost with their fears thus strong,
Made senseless things begin to do them wrong;
For briers and thorns at their apparel snatch;
Some sleeves, some hats, from yielders all things catch.
I led them on in this distracted fear,
And left sweet Pyramus translated there:
When in that moment, so it came to pass,
Titania waked, and straightway loved an ass.

OBE. This falls out better than I could devise.
But hast thou yet latch'd [8] the Athenian's eyes
With the love-juice, as I did bid thee do?

PUCK. I took him sleeping,—that is finish'd too,—
And the Athenian woman by his side;
That, when he waked, of force [9] she must be eyed.

Enter HERMIA *and* DEMETRIUS.

---

[2] *patches, rude mechanicals*] clowns, uncivilized workingmen.
[3] *The shallowest . . . sort*] the stupidest blockhead of that brainless company.
[4] *nole*] head.
[5] *mimic*] actor.
[6] *russet-pated choughs*] red-headed jackdaws.
[7] *at our stamp*] on hearing our footsteps.
[8] *latch'd*] moistened.
[9] *of force*] necessarily.

OBE. Stand close: this is the same Athenian.

PUCK. This is the woman, but not this the man.

DEM. Oh, why rebuke you him that loves you so?
    Lay breath so bitter on your bitter foe.

HER. Now I but chide; but I should use[10] thee worse,
    For thou, I fear, hast given me cause to curse.
    If thou hast slain Lysander in his sleep,
    Being o'er shoes in blood, plunge in the deep,
    And kill me too.
    The sun was not so true unto the day
    As he to me: would he have stolen away
    From sleeping Hermia? I'll believe as soon
    This whole earth may be bored, and that the moon
    May through the centre creep, and so displease
    Her brother's noontide with the Antipodes.
    It cannot be but thou hast murder'd him;
    So should a murderer look, so dead,[11] so grim.

DEM. So should the murder'd look; and so should I,
    Pierced through the heart with your stern cruelty:
    Yet you, the murderer, look as bright, as clear,
    As yonder Venus in her glimmering sphere.

HER. What's this to my Lysander? where is he?
    Ah, good Demetrius, wilt thou give him me?

DEM. I had rather give his carcass to my hounds.

HER. Out, dog! out, cur! thou drivest me past the bounds
    Of maiden's patience. Hast thou slain him, then?
    Henceforth be never number'd among men!
    O, once tell true, tell true, even for my sake!
    Durst thou have look'd upon him being awake,
    And hast thou kill'd him sleeping? O brave touch!
    Could not a worm,[12] an adder, do so much?
    An adder did it; for with doubler[13] tongue
    Than thine, thou serpent, never adder stung.

DEM. You spend your passion on a misprised mood:[14]
    I am not guilty of Lysander's blood;
    Nor is he dead, for aught that I can tell.

---

[10] *use*] treat.

[11] *dead*] deadly.

[12] *worm*] serpent.

[13] *doubler*] more forked and more deceitful.

[14] *a misprised mood*] a fit of anger caused by a mistake.

HER. I pray thee, tell me then that he is well.
DEM. An if I could, what should I get therefore?
HER. A privilege, never to see me more.
    And from thy hated presence part I so:
    See me no more, whether he be dead or no.   *[Exit.*
DEM. There is no following her in this fierce vein:
    Here therefore for a while I will remain.
    So sorrow's heaviness doth heavier grow
    For debt that bankrupt sleep doth sorrow owe;
    Which now in some slight measure it will pay,
    If for his tender[15] here I make some stay. *[Lies down and sleeps.*
OBE. What hast thou done? thou hast mistaken quite,
    And laid the love-juice on some true-love's sight:
    Of thy misprision must perforce ensue
    Some true love turn'd, and not a false turn'd true.
PUCK. Then fate o'er-rules, that, one man holding troth,
    A million fail, confounding oath on oath.[16]
OBE. About the wood go swifter than the wind,
    And Helena of Athens look thou find:
    All fancy-sick[17] she is and pale of cheer,[18]
    With sighs of love, that costs the fresh blood dear:
    By some illusion see thou bring her here:
    I'll charm his eyes against[19] she do appear.
PUCK. I go, I go; look how I go,
    Swifter than arrow from the Tartar's bow.   *[Exit.*
OBE.   Flower of this purple dye,
    Hit with Cupid's archery,
    Sink in apple of his eye.
    When his love he doth espy,
    Let her shine as gloriously
    As the Venus of the sky.
    When thou wakest, if she be by,
    Beg of her for remedy.

Re-enter PUCK.

PUCK.   Captain of our fairy band,
    Helena is here at hand;

---

[15] *his tender*] sleep's offering of itself.
[16] *confounding oath on oath*] subverting one oath by another.
[17] *fancy-sick*] lovesick.
[18] *cheer*] countenance.
[19] *against*] in provision for the time when.

And the youth, mistook by me,
Pleading for a lover's fee.
Shall we their fond pageant[20] see?
Lord, what fools these mortals be!

OBE.   Stand aside: the noise they make
Will cause Demetrius to awake.

PUCK.   Then will two at once woo one;
That must needs be sport alone;
And those things do best please me
That befal preposterously.[21]

Enter LYSANDER *and* HELENA.

LYS.   Why should you think that I should woo in scorn?
Scorn and derision never come in tears:
Look, when I vow, I weep; and vows so born,
In their nativity all truth appears.
How can these things in me seem scorn to you,
Bearing the badge of faith, to prove them true?

HEL.   You do advance your cunning more and more.
When truth kills truth, O devilish-holy fray!
These vows are Hermia's: will you give her o'er?
Weigh oath with oath, and you will nothing weigh:
Your vows to her and me, put in two scales,
Will even weigh; and both as light as tales.

LYS.   I had no judgement when to her I swore.

HEL.   Nor none, in my mind,[22] now you give her o'er.

LYS.   Demetrius loves her, and he loves not you.

DEM.   [*Awaking*] O Helen, goddess, nymph, perfect, divine!
To what, my love, shall I compare thine eyne?
Crystal is muddy. O, how ripe in show
Thy lips, those kissing cherries, tempting grow!
That pure congealed white, high Taurus'[23] snow,
Fann'd with the eastern wind, turns to a crow
When thou hold'st up thy hand: O, let me kiss
This princess of pure white, this seal of bliss!

HEL.   O spite! O hell! I see you all are bent
To set against me for your merriment:
If you were civil and knew courtesy,

---

[20] *fond pageant*] foolish spectacle.
[21] *preposterously*] contrary to the natural order of things.
[22] *mind*] opinion.
[23] *Taurus'*] Taurus is a mountain range in southern Turkey.

You would not do me thus much injury.
Can you not hate me, as I know you do,
But you must join in souls to mock me too?
If you were men, as men you are in show,
You would not use a gentle lady so;
To vow, and swear, and superpraise my parts, [24]
When I am sure you hate me with your hearts.
You both are rivals, and love Hermia;
And now both rivals, to mock Helena:
A trim[25] exploit, a manly enterprise,
To conjure tears up in a poor maid's eyes
With your derision! none of noble sort
Would so offend a virgin, and extort
A poor soul's patience, all to make you sport.

LYS.   You are unkind, Demetrius; be not so;
For you love Hermia; this you know I know:
And here, with all good will, with all my heart,
In Hermia's love I yield you up my part;
And yours of Helena to me bequeath,
Whom I do love, and will do till my death.

HEL.   Never did mockers waste more idle breath.

DEM.   Lysander, keep thy Hermia; I will none:[26]
If e'er I loved her, all that love is gone.
My heart to her but as guest-wise sojourn'd,
And now to Helen is it home return'd,
There to remain.

LYS.   Helen, it is not so.

DEM.   Disparage not the faith thou dost not know,
Lest, to thy peril, thou aby[27] it dear.
Look, where thy love comes; yonder is thy dear.

Re-enter HERMIA.

HER.   Dark night, that from the eye his function takes,
The ear more quick of apprehension makes;
Wherein it doth impair the seeing sense,
It pays the hearing double recompense.
Thou art not by mine eye, Lysander, found;

---

[24] *superpraise my parts*] overpraise my qualities.
[25] *trim*] fine.
[26] *I will none*] I want nothing to do with her.
[27] *aby*] pay for.

Mine ear, I thank it, brought me to thy sound.
But why unkindly didst thou leave me so?

LYS.   Why should he stay, whom love doth press to go?

HER.   What love could press Lysander from my side?

LYS.   Lysander's love, that would not let him bide,
Fair Helena, who more engilds the night
Than all yon fiery oes[28] and eyes of light.
Why seek'st thou me? could not this make thee know,
The hate I bare thee made me leave thee so?

HER.   You speak not as you think: it cannot be.

HEL.   Lo, she is one of this confederacy!
Now I perceive they have conjoin'd all three
To fashion this false sport, in spite of[29] me.
Injurious Hermia! most ungrateful maid!
Have you conspired, have you with these contrived
To bait me with this foul derision?
Is all the counsel that we two have shared,
The sisters' vows, the hours that we have spent,
When we have chid[30] the hasty-footed time
For parting us,—O, is all forgot?
All school-days' friendship, childhood innocence?
We, Hermia, like two artificial[31] gods,
Have with our needles created both one flower,
Both on one sampler, sitting on one cushion,
Both warbling of one song, both in one key;
As if our hands, our sides, voices, and minds,
Had been incorporate.[32] So we grew together,
Like to a double cherry, seeming parted,
But yet an union in partition;
Two lovely berries moulded on one stem;
So, with two seeming bodies, but one heart;
Two of the first, like coats in heraldry,
Due but to one, and crowned with one crest.[33]
And will you rent[34] our ancient love asunder,

---

[28] *fiery oes*] circles of fire, stars.

[29] *in spite of*] out of spite for.

[30] *chid*] scolded.

[31] *artificial*] artistically creative.

[32] *incorporate*] of one body.

[33] *Two of the first, . . . crest*] Our two bodies resemble two coats of arms in heraldry,
which belong to a single person, and are surrounded by a single crest.

[34] *rent*] rend, tear.

To join with men in scorning your poor friend?
It is not friendly, 't is not maidenly:
Our sex, as well as I, may chide you for it,
Though I alone do feel the injury.

HER. I am amazed at your passionate words.
I scorn you not: it seems that you scorn me.

HEL. Have you not set Lysander, as in scorn,
To follow me and praise my eyes and face?
And made your other love, Demetrius,
Who even but now did spurn me with his foot,
To call me goddess, nymph, divine and rare,
Precious, celestial? Wherefore speaks he this
To her he hates? and wherefore doth Lysander
Deny your love, so rich within his soul,
And tender[35] me, forsooth, affection,
But by your setting on,[36] by your consent?
What though I be not so in grace as you,
So hung upon with love, so fortunate,
But miserable most, to love unloved?
This you should pity rather than despise.

HER. I understand not what you mean by this.

HEL. Ay, do, persever,[37] counterfeit sad[38] looks,
Make mouths upon[39] me when I turn my back;
Wink each at other; hold the sweet jest up:
This sport, well carried, shall be chronicled.
If you have any pity, grace, or manners,
You would not make me such an argument.[40]
But fare ye well: 't is partly my own fault;
Which death or absence soon shall remedy.

LYS. Stay, gentle Helena; hear my excuse:
My love, my life, my soul, fair Helena!

HEL. O excellent!

HER. Sweet, do not scorn her so.

DEM. If she cannot entreat, I can compel.

LYS. Thou canst compel no more than she entreat:
Thy threats have no more strength than her weak prayers.

---

[35] *tender*] offer.
[36] *setting on*] instigation.
[37] *persever*] persevere.
[38] *sad*] serious.
[39] *Make mouths upon*] make faces at.
[40] *make me such an argument*] ridicule me so.

Helen, I love thee; by my life, I do:
I swear by that which I will lose for thee,
To prove him false that says I love thee not.

DEM. I say I love thee more than he can do.

LYS. If thou say so, withdraw, and prove it too.

DEM. Quick, come!

HER.   Lysander, whereto tends all this?

LYS. Away, you Ethiope![41]

DEM.   No, no; he'll . . .[42]
Seem to break loose; take on as you would follow,
But yet come not: you are a tame man, go!

LYS. Hang off,[43] thou cat, thou burr![44] vile thing, let loose,
Or I will shake thee from me like a serpent!

HER. Why are you grown so rude? what change is this?
Sweet love,—

LYS. Thy love! out, tawny Tartar, out!
Out, loathed medicine! hated potion, hence!

HER. Do you not jest?

HEL.   Yes, sooth; and so do you.

LYS. Demetrius, I will keep my word with thee.

DEM. I would I had your bond, for I perceive
A weak bond holds you: I'll not trust your word.

LYS. What, should I hurt her, strike her, kill her dead?
Although I hate her, I'll not harm her so.

HER. What, can you do me greater harm than hate?
Hate me! wherefore? O me! what news,[45] my love!
Am not I Hermia? are not you Lysander?
I am as fair now as I was erewhile.[46]
Since night you loved me; yet since night you left me:
Why, then you left me,—O, the gods forbid!—
In earnest, shall I say?

LYS.   Ay, by my life;
And never did desire to see thee more.
Therefore be out of hope, of question, of doubt;
Be certain, nothing truer; 't is no jest
That I do hate thee, and love Helena.

---

[41] *Ethiope*] sneering allusion to Hermia's brunette complexion.

[42] *No, no; he'll . . .*] The text seems to be corrupt here.

[43] *Hang off*] let go.

[44] *burr*] the prickly envelope of the fruit on a burdock.

[45] *what news*] What is the matter?

[46] *erewhile*] up to this time.

HER.   O me! you juggler! you canker-blossom!
       You thief of love! what, have you come by night
       And stolen my love's heart from him?

HEL.   Fine, i' faith!
       Have you no modesty, no maiden shame,
       No touch of bashfulness? What, will you tear
       Impatient answers from my gentle tongue?
       Fie, fie! you counterfeit, you puppet,[47] you!

HER.   Puppet? why so? ay, that way goes the game.
       Now I perceive that she hath made compare
       Between our statures; she hath urged[48] her height;
       And with her personage, her tall personage,
       Her height, forsooth, she hath prevail'd with him.
       And are you grown so high in his esteem,
       Because I am so dwarfish and so low?
       How low am I, thou painted maypole? speak;
       How low am I? I am not yet so low
       But that my nails can reach unto thine eyes.

HEL.   I pray you, though you mock me, gentlemen,
       Let her not hurt me: I was never curst;[49]
       I have no gift at all in shrewishness;
       I am a right[50] maid for my cowardice:
       Let her not strike me. You perhaps may think,
       Because she is something lower[51] than myself,
       That I can match her.

HER.   Lower! hark, again.

HEL.   Good Hermia, do not be so bitter with me.
       I evermore did love you, Hermia,
       Did ever keep your counsels, never wrong'd you;
       Save that, in love unto Demetrius,
       I told him of your stealth[52] unto this wood.
       He follow'd you; for love I follow'd him;
       But he hath chid me hence, and threaten'd me
       To strike me, spurn me, nay, to kill me too:
       And now, so[53] you will let me quiet go,

---

[47] *puppet*] someone of short stature.
[48] *urged*] asserted.
[49] *curst*] shrewish.
[50] *right*] proper.
[51] *something lower*] somewhat shorter.
[52] *stealth*] secret flight.
[53] *so*] if.

	To Athens will I bear my folly back,
	And follow you no further: let me go:
	You see how simple and how fond[54] I am.
HER.	Why, get you gone: who is't that hinders you?
HEL.	A foolish heart, that I leave here behind.
HER.	What, with Lysander?
HEL.	With Demetrius.
LYS.	Be not afraid; she shall not harm thee, Helena.
DEM.	No, sir, she shall not, though you take her part.
HEL.	O, when she's angry, she is keen and shrewd!
	She was a vixen when she went to school;
	And though she be but little, she is fierce.
HER.	Little again! nothing but low and little!
	Why will you suffer her to flout me thus?
	Let me come to her.
LYS.	Get you gone, you dwarf;
	You minimus,[55] of hindering knot-grass[56] made;
	You bead, you acorn.
DEM.	You are too officious
	In her behalf that scorns your services.
	Let her alone: speak not of Helena;
	Take not her part; for, if thou dost intend
	Never so little show of love to her,
	Thou shalt aby it.
LYS.	Now she holds me not;
	Now follow, if thou darest, to try whose right,
	Of thine or mine, is most in Helena.
DEM.	Follow! nay, I'll go with thee, cheek by jole.[57]

[*Exeunt* LYSANDER *and* DEMETRIUS.

HER.	You, mistress, all this coil is 'long of you:[58]
	Nay, go not back.
HEL.	I will not trust you, I,
	Nor longer stay in your curst company.
	Your hands than mine are quicker for a fray,
	My legs are longer though, to run away. [*Exit*.
HER.	I am amazed, and know not what to say. [*Exit*.
OBE.	This is thy negligence: still thou mistakest,

[54] *fond*] foolish.
[55] *minimus*] tiny creature.
[56] *knot-grass*] a weed that, when eaten by a child, was thought to impede growth.
[57] *cheek by jole*] cheek to cheek.
[58] *this coil is 'long of you*] this confusion is on account of you.

Or else committ'st thy knaveries wilfully.

PUCK. Believe me, king of shadows, I mistook.
Did not you tell me I should know the man
By the Athenian garments he had on?
And so far blameless proves my enterprise,
That I have 'nointed an Athenian's eyes;
And so far am I glad it so did sort,[59]
As this their jangling I esteem a sport.

OBE. Thou see'st these lovers seek a place to fight:
Hie therefore, Robin, overcast the night;
The starry welkin[60] cover thou anon
With drooping fog, as black as Acheron;[61]
And lead these testy rivals so astray,
As one come not within another's way.
Like to Lysander sometime frame thy tongue,
Then stir Demetrius up with bitter wrong;
And sometime rail thou like Demetrius;
And from each other look thou lead them thus,
Till o'er their brows death-counterfeiting sleep
With leaden legs and batty wings doth creep:
Then crush this herb into Lysander's eye;
Whose liquor hath this virtuous property,
To take from thence all error with his might,
And make his eyeballs roll with wonted[62] sight.
When they next wake, all this derision
Shall seem a dream and fruitless vision;
And back to Athens shall the lovers wend,
With league whose date[63] till death shall never end.
Whiles I in this affair do thee employ,
I'll to my queen and beg her Indian boy;
And then I will her charmed eye release
From monster's view, and all things shall be peace.

PUCK. My fairy lord, this must be done with haste,
For night's swift dragons[64] cut the clouds full fast,
And yonder shines Aurora's harbinger;[65]

---

[59] *sort*] turn out.
[60] *welkin*] sky.
[61] *Acheron*] a river in Hades, the water of which was black.
[62] *wonted*] normal.
[63] *date*] duration.
[64] *dragons*] the dragons drawing the chariot of night.
[65] *Aurora's harbinger*] Venus, the morning star.

>   At whose approach, ghosts, wandering here and there,
>   Troop home to churchyards: damned spirits all,
>   That in crossways and floods have burial,[66]
>   Already to their wormy beds are gone;
>   For fear lest day should look their shames upon,
>   They wilfully themselves exile from light,
>   And must for aye consort with black-brow'd night.

OBE.   But we are spirits of another sort:
>   I with the morning's love[67] have oft made sport;
>   And, like a forester, the groves may tread,
>   Even till the eastern gate, all fiery-red,
>   Opening on Neptune with fair blessed beams,
>   Turns into yellow gold his salt green streams.
>   But, notwithstanding, haste; make no delay:
>   We may effect this business yet ere day.   [*Exit.*

PUCK.   Up and down, up and down,
>   I will lead them up and down:
>   I am fear'd in field and town:
>   Goblin, lead them up and down.
>   Here comes one.

Re-enter LYSANDER.

LYS.   Where art thou, proud Demetrius? speak thou now.
PUCK.   Here, villain; drawn[68] and ready. Where art thou?
LYS.   I will be with thee straight.[69]
PUCK.   Follow me, then,
>   To plainer ground.   [*Exit* LYSANDER, *as following the voice.*

Re-enter DEMETRIUS.

DEM.   Lysander! speak again:
>   Thou runaway, thou coward, art thou fled?
>   Speak! In some bush? Where dost thou hide thy head?
PUCK.   Thou coward, art thou bragging to the stars,
>   Telling the bushes that thou look'st for wars,
>   And wilt not come? Come, recreant;[70] come, thou child;
>   I'll whip thee with a rod: he is defiled
>   That draws a sword on thee.

---

[66] *That . . . burial*] those who have committed suicide or have drowned.
[67] *the morning's love*] Cephalus, a youthful huntsman loved by Aurora, goddess of the morning.
[68] *drawn*] sword drawn.
[69] *straight*] immediately.
[70] *recreant*] coward, deserter.

DEM.   Yea, art thou there?
PUCK. Follow my voice: we'll try no manhood here.   [*Exeunt.*

Re-enter LYSANDER.

LYS.   He goes before me and still dares me on:
        When I come where he calls, then he is gone.
        The villain is much lighter-heel'd than I:
        I follow'd fast, but faster he did fly;
        That fallen am I in dark uneven way,
        And here will rest me. [*Lies down.*] Come, thou gentle day!
        For if but once thou show me thy grey light,
        I'll find Demetrius, and revenge this spite.   [*Sleeps.*

Re-enter PUCK *and* DEMETRIUS.

PUCK. Ho, ho, ho! Coward, why comest thou not?
DEM.   Abide me, if thou darest; for well I wot[71]
        Thou runn'st before me, shifting every place,
        And darest not stand, nor look me in the face.
        Where art thou now?
PUCK.   Come hither: I am here.
DEM.   Nay, then, thou mock'st me. Thou shalt buy this dear,
        If ever I thy face by daylight see:
        Now, go thy way. Faintness constraineth me
        To measure out my length on this cold bed.
        By day's approach look to be visited.   [*Lies down and sleeps.*

Re-enter HELENA.

HEL.   O weary night, O long and tedious night,
           Abate[72] thy hours! Shine comforts from the east,
        That I may back to Athens by daylight,
           From these that my poor company detest:
        And sleep, that sometimes shuts up sorrow's eye,
        Steal me awhile from mine own company.
                                 [*Lies down and sleeps.*

PUCK.   Yet but three? Come one more;
        Two of both kinds makes up four.
        Here she comes, curst and sad:
        Cupid is a knavish lad,
        Thus to make poor females mad.

---

[71] *wot*] know.
[72] *Abate*] shorten.

Re-enter HERMIA.

HER.   Never so weary, never so in woe;
       Bedabbled with the dew, and torn with briers;
   I can no further crawl, no further go;
     My legs can keep no pace with my desires.
   Here will I rest me till the break of day.
   Heavens shield Lysander, if they mean a fray!

                                 [*Lies down and sleeps.*

PUCK.   On the ground
                   Sleep sound:
                   I'll apply
                   To your eye,
             Gentle lover, remedy.

                     [*Squeezing the juice on* LYSANDER'*s eye.*
                   When thou wakest
                   Thou takest
                   True delight
                   In the sight
        Of thy former lady's eye:
        And the country proverb known,
        That every man should take his own,
        In your waking shall be shown:
                Jack shall have Jill;
                Nought shall go ill;
   The man shall have his mare again, and all shall be well. [*Exit.*

Act IV—Scene I—The same

LYSANDER, DEMETRIUS, HELENA,
AND HERMIA, LYING ASLEEP

Enter TITANIA *and* BOTTOM; PEASEBLOSSOM, COBWEB, MOTH, MUSTARDSEED, *and other* Fairies *attending*; OBERON *behind unseen.*

TITA. Come, sit thee down upon this flowery bed,
   While I thy amiable cheeks do coy,[1]
   And stick musk-roses in thy sleek smooth head,
   And kiss thy fair large ears, my gentle joy.

BOT. Where's Peaseblossom?

PEAS. Ready.

BOT. Scratch my head, Peaseblossom. Where's Mounsieur Cobweb?

COB. Ready.

BOT. Mounsieur Cobweb, good mounsieur, get you your weapons in your hand, and kill me a red-hipped humble-bee on the top of a thistle; and, good mounsieur, bring me the honey-bag. Do not fret yourself too much in the action, mounsieur; and, good mounsieur, have a care the honey-bag break not; I would be loth to have you overflown with a honey-bag, signior. Where's Mounsieur Mustard-seed?

MUS. Ready.

BOT. Give me your neaf,[2] Mounsieur Mustardseed. Pray you, leave your courtesy, good mounsieur.

MUS. What's your will?

BOT. Nothing, good mounsieur, but to help Cavalery[3] Cobweb to scratch. I must to the barber's, mounsieur; for methinks I am

---

[1] *amiable cheeks do coy*] caress your lovely cheeks.

[2] *neaf*] fist.

[3] *Cavalery*] gentleman.

    marvellous hairy about the face; and I am such a tender ass, if my
    hair do but tickle me, I must scratch.

TITA.   What, wilt thou hear some music, my sweet love?

BOT.   I have a reasonable good ear in music. Let's have the tongs and the
    bones.[4]

TITA.   Or say, sweet love, what thou desirest to eat.

BOT.   Truly, a peck of provender: I could munch your good dry oats.
    Methinks I have a great desire to a bottle[5] of hay: good hay, sweet
    hay, hath no fellow.[6]

TITA.   I have a venturous fairy that shall seek
    The squirrel's hoard, and fetch thee new nuts.

BOT.   I had rather have a handful or two of dried peas. But, I pray you,
    let none of your people stir me: I have an exposition[7] of sleep come
    upon me.

TITA.   Sleep thou, and I will wind thee in my arms.
    Fairies, be gone, and be all ways away.[8]   *[Exeunt Fairies.*
    So doth the woodbine the sweet honeysuckle
    Gently entwist; the female ivy so
    Enrings the barky fingers of the elm.
    O, how I love thee! how I dote on thee!   *[They sleep.*

Enter PUCK.

OBE.   *[Advancing]*   Welcome, good Robin. See'st thou this sweet sight?
    Her dotage now I do begin to pity:
    For, meeting her of late behind the wood,
    Seeking sweet favours for this hateful fool,
    I did upbraid her, and fall out with her;
    For she his hairy temples then had rounded
    With coronet of fresh and fragrant flowers;
    And that same dew, which sometime on the buds
    Was wont to swell, like round and orient[9] pearls,
    Stood now within the pretty flowerets' eyes,
    Like tears, that did their own disgrace bewail.
    When I had at my pleasure taunted her,
    And she in mild terms begg'd my patience,

---

[4] *the tongs and the bones*] rustic musical instruments.
[5] *bottle*] bundle.
[6] *fellow*] equal.
[7] *exposition*] Bottom's malapropism for "disposition."
[8] *be all ways away*] disperse in all directions.
[9] *orient*] from the East and, thereby, of the finest quality.

I then did ask of her her changeling child;
Which straight she gave me, and her fairy sent
To bear him to my bower in fairy land.
And now I have the boy, I will undo
This hateful imperfection of her eyes:
And, gentle Puck, take this transformed scalp
From off the head of this Athenian swain;[10]
That, he awaking when the other[11] do,
May all to Athens back again repair,
And think no more of this night's accidents
But as the fierce vexation of a dream.
But first I will release the fairy queen.
　　　　　Be as thou wast wont to be;
　　　　　See as thou wast wont to see:
　　　　　Dian's bud[12] o'er Cupid's flower[13]
　　　　　Hath such force and blessed power.
Now, my Titania; wake you, my sweet queen.

TITA. My Oberon! what visions have I seen!
　　　Methought I was enamour'd of an ass.
OBE. There lies your love.
TITA. 　　　　　　　　How came these things to pass?
　　　O, how mine eyes do loathe his visage now!
OBE. Silence awhile. Robin, take off this head.
　　　Titania, music call; and strike more dead
　　　Than common sleep of all these five the sense.
TITA. Music, ho! music, such as charmeth sleep! 　　[*Music, still.*
PUCK. Now, when thou wakest, with thine own fool's eyes peep.
OBE. Sound, music! Come, my queen, take hands with me,
　　　And rock the ground whereon these sleepers be.
　　　Now thou and I are new in amity,
　　　And will to-morrow midnight solemnly
　　　Dance in Duke Theseus' house triumphantly,
　　　And bless it to all fair prosperity:
　　　There shall the pairs of faithful lovers be
　　　Wedded, with Theseus, all in jollity.
PUCK. 　　Fairy king, attend, and mark:
　　　　　I do hear the morning lark.

---

[10] *swain*] peasant.
[11] *other*] others.
[12] *Dian's bud*] *Agnus castus* (or the chaste tree).
[13] *Cupid's flower*] the pansy.

OBE.   Then, my queen, in silence sad,[14]
        Trip we after night's shade:
        We the globe can compass soon,
        Swifter than the wandering moon.
TITA.   Come, my lord; and in our flight,
    .   Tell me how it came this night,
        That I sleeping here was found
        With these mortals on the ground.   [*Exeunt.*
                                    [*Horns winded within.*

Enter THESEUS, HIPPOLYTA, EGEUS, *and train.*

THE.   Go, one of you, find out the forester;
        For now our observation[15] is perform'd;
        And since we have the vaward[16] of the day,
        My love shall hear the music of my hounds.
        Uncouple in the western valley; let them go:
        Dispatch, I say, and find the forester.   [*Exit an attendant.*
        We will, fair queen, up to the mountain's top,
        And mark the musical confusion
        Of hounds and echo in conjunction.
HIP.   I was with Hercules and Cadmus once,
        When in a wood of Crete they bay'd[17] the bear
        With hounds of Sparta: never did I hear
        Such gallant chiding; for, besides the groves,
        The skies, the fountains, every region near
        Seem'd all one mutual cry: I never heard
        So musical a discord, such sweet thunder.
THE.   My hounds are bred out of the Spartan kind,
        So flew'd,[18] so sanded;[19] and their heads are hung
        With ears that sweep away the morning dew;
        Crook-knee'd, and dew-lapp'd like Thessalian bulls;
        Slow in pursuit, but match'd in mouth[20] like bells,
        Each under each.[21] A cry[22] more tuneable

---

[14] *sad*] serious, solemn.
[15] *observation*] celebration (of the rites of May Day).
[16] *vaward*] vanguard, earliest part.
[17] *bay'd*] pursued with barking dogs.
[18] *flew'd*] with large, hanging chaps.
[19] *sanded*] sandy in color.
[20] *mouth*] voice.
[21] *Each under each*] in various notes.
[22] *cry*] pack of hounds.

	Was never holla'd to, nor cheer'd with horn,
	In Crete, in Sparta, nor in Thessaly:
	Judge when you hear. But, soft! what nymphs are these?

EGE. My lord, this is my daughter here asleep;
And this, Lysander; this Demetrius is;
This Helena, old Nedar's Helena:
I wonder of their being here together.

THE. No doubt they rose up early to observe
The rite of May; and, hearing our intent,
Came here in grace of our solemnity.[23]
But speak, Egeus; is not this the day
That Hermia should give answer of her choice?

EGE. It is, my lord.

THE. Go, bid the huntsmen wake them with their horns.

                    [*Horns and shout within.* LYS., DEM., HEL., *and*
                                  HER., *wake and start up.*

Good morrow, friends. Saint Valentine[24] is past:
Begin these wood-birds but to couple now?

LYS. Pardon, my lord.

THE.   I pray you all, stand up.
I know you two are rival enemies:
How comes this gentle concord in the world,
That hatred is so far from jealousy,
To sleep by hate, and fear no enmity?

LYS. My lord, I shall reply amazedly,
Half sleep, half waking: but as yet, I swear,
I cannot truly say how I came here;
But, as I think,—for truly would I speak,
And now I do bethink me, so it is,—
I came with Hermia hither: our intent
Was to be gone from Athens, where[25] we might,
Without[26] the peril of the Athenian law.

EGE. Enough, enough, my lord; you have enough:
I beg the law, the law, upon his head.
They would have stolen away; they would, Demetrius,
Thereby to have defeated you and me,
You of your wife and me of my consent,
Of my consent that she should be your wife.

[23] *in grace of our solemnity*] in honor of our marriage.
[24] *Saint Valentine*] Birds were said to choose their mates on St. Valentine's Day.
[25] *where*] wherever.
[26] *Without*] beyond.

DEM. My lord, fair Helen told me of their stealth,
      Of this their purpose hither to this wood;
      And I in fury hither follow'd them,
      Fair Helena in fancy[27] following me.
      But, my good lord, I wot not by what power,—
      But by some power it is,—my love to Hermia,
      Melted as the snow, seems to me now
      As the remembrance of an idle gaud,[28]
      Which in my childhood I did dote upon;
      And all the faith, the virtue of my heart,
      The object and the pleasure of mine eye,
      Is only Helena. To her, my lord,
      Was I betroth'd ere I saw Hermia:
      But, like in sickness, did I loathe this food;
      But, as in health, come to my natural taste,
      Now I do wish it, love it, long for it,
      And will for evermore be true to it.
THE. Fair lovers, you are fortunately met:
      Of this discourse we more will hear anon.
      Egeus, I will overbear[29] your will;
      For in the temple, by and by, with us
      These couples shall eternally be knit:
      And, for the morning now is something[30] worn,
      Our purposed hunting shall be set aside.
      Away with us to Athens! three and three,
      We'll hold a feast in great solemnity.
      Come, Hippolyta.   [*Exeunt* THE., HIP., EGE., *and train.*
DEM. These things seem small and undistinguishable,
      Like far-off mountains turned into clouds.
HER. Methinks I see these things with parted eye,[31]
      When every thing seems double.
HEL.   So methinks:
      And I have found Demetrius like a jewel,[32]
      Mine own, and not mine own.
DEM.   Are you sure
      That we are awake? It seems to me

---

[27] *fancy*] love.
[28] *idle gaud*] useless bauble.
[29] *overbear*] overrule.
[30] *something*] somewhat.
[31] *with parted eye*] with eye out of focus.
[32] *like a jewel*] just like one who finds and possesses a jewel not his own.

That yet we sleep, we dream. Do not you think
The Duke was here, and bid us follow him?

HER. Yea; and my father.

HEL.   And Hippolyta.

LYS. And he did bid us follow to the temple.

DEM. Why, then, we are awake: let's follow him;
And by[33] the way let us recount our dreams.   [*Exeunt.*

BOT. [*Awaking*] When my cue comes, call me, and I will answer: my next is, "Most fair Pyramus." Heigh-ho! Peter Quince! Flute, the bellows-mender! Snout, the tinker! Starveling! God's my life, stolen hence, and left me asleep! I have had a most rare vision. I have had a dream, past the wit of man to say what dream it was: man is but an ass, if he go about to expound this dream. Methought I was—there is no man can tell what. Methought I was,—and methought I had,—but man is but a patched[34] fool, if he will offer to say what methought I had. The eye of man hath not heard, the ear of man hath not seen, man's hand is not able to taste, his tongue to conceive, nor his heart to report, what my dream was. I will get Peter Quince to write a ballad of this dream: it shall be called Bottom's Dream, because it hath no bottom; and I will sing it in the latter end of a play, before the Duke: peradventure, to make it the more gracious, I shall sing it at her death.[35]   [*Exit.*

Scene II—Athens

QUINCE'S HOUSE

Enter QUINCE, FLUTE, SNOUT, *and* STARVELING.

QUIN. Have you sent to Bottom's house? is he come home yet?

STAR. He cannot be heard of. Out of doubt he is transported.[1]

FLU. If he come not, then the play is marred: it goes not forward, doth it?

---

[33] *by*] along.

[34] *patched*] dressed in motley.

[35] *her death*] Thisbe's death in the play.

---

[1] *transported*] carried off or transformed.

QUIN. It is not possible: you have not a man in all Athens able to discharge[2] Pyramus but he.

FLU.   No, he hath simply the best wit of any handicraft man in Athens.

QUIN. Yea, and the best person too; and he is a very paramour for a sweet voice.

FLU.   You must say "paragon": a paramour is, God bless us, a thing of naught.[3]

Enter SNUG.

SNUG. Masters, the Duke is coming from the temple, and there is two or three lords and ladies more married: if our sport had gone forward, we had all been made men.

FLU.   O sweet bully Bottom! Thus hath he lost sixpence a day[4] during his life; he could not have scaped sixpence a day: an the Duke had not given him sixpence a day for playing Pyramus, I'll be hanged; he would have deserved it: sixpence a day in Pyramus, or nothing.

Enter BOTTOM.

BOT.   Where are these lads? where are these hearts?

QUIN. Bottom! O most courageous day! O most happy hour!

BOT.   Masters, I am to discourse wonders: but ask me not what; for if I tell you, I am no true Athenian. I will tell you every thing, right as it fell out.

QUIN. Let us hear, sweet Bottom.

BOT.   Not a word of me. All that I will tell you is, that the Duke hath dined. Get your apparel together, good strings to your beards, new ribbons to your pumps;[5] meet presently at the palace; every man look o'er his part; for the short and the long is, our play is preferred.[6] In any case, let Thisbe have clean linen; and let not him that plays the lion pare his nails, for they shall hang out for the lion's claws. And, most dear actors, eat no onions nor garlic, for we are to utter sweet breath; and I do not doubt but to hear them say, it is a sweet comedy. No more words: away! go, away!   [*Exeunt.*

---

[2] *discharge*] play the part of.
[3] *a thing of naught*] something shameful, wicked.
[4] *sixpence a day*] i.e., a royal pension.
[5] *pumps*] light shoes.
[6] *preferred*] chosen for consideration.

Act V—Scene I—Athens

THE PALACE OF THESEUS

Enter THESEUS, HIPPOLYTA, PHILOSTRATE, Lords, *and* Attendants.

HIP.   'T is strange, my Theseus, that these lovers speak of.

THE.   More strange than true: I never may believe
These antique[1] fables, nor these fairy toys.[2]
Lovers and madmen have such seething brains,
Such shaping fantasies, that apprehend
More than cool reason ever comprehends.
The lunatic, the lover and the poet
Are of imagination all compact:[3]
One sees more devils than vast hell can hold,
That is, the madman: the lover, all as frantic,
Sees Helen's beauty in a brow of Egypt:[4]
The poet's eye, in a fine frenzy rolling,
Doth glance from heaven to earth, from earth to heaven;
And as imagination bodies forth
The forms of things unknown, the poet's pen
Turns them to shapes, and gives to airy nothing
A local habitation and a name.
Such tricks hath strong imagination,
That, if it would but apprehend some joy,
It comprehends some bringer of that joy;
Or in the night, imagining some fear,[5]
How easy is a bush supposed a bear!

[1] *antique*] strange.
[2] *toys*] trifles.
[3] *all compact*] entirely constituted.
[4] *Sees . . . Egypt*] sees Helen of Troy's beauty in the face of a Gypsy.
[5] *some fear*] something inducing fear.

HIP.   But all the story of the night told over,
        And all their minds transfigured so together,
        More witnesseth than fancy's images,
        And grows to something of great constancy;[6]
        But, howsoever, strange and admirable.
THE.   Here come the lovers, full of joy and mirth.

Enter LYSANDER, DEMETRIUS, HERMIA, *and* HELENA.

        Joy, gentle friends! joy and fresh days of love
        Accompany your hearts!
LYS.   More than to us
        Wait in your royal walks, your board, your bed!
THE.   Come now; what masques, what dances shall we have,
        To wear away this long age of three hours
        Between our after-supper and bed-time?
        Where is our usual manager of mirth?
        What revels are in hand? Is there no play,
        To ease the anguish of a torturing hour?
        Call Philostrate.
PHIL.   Here, mighty Theseus.
THE.   Say, what abridgement[7] have you for this evening?
        What masque? what music? How shall we beguile
        The lazy time, if not with some delight?
PHIL.   There is a brief how many sports are ripe:[8]
        Make choice of which your highness will see first.
                                            [*Giving a paper.*
THE.   [*reads*]   The battle with the Centaurs, to be sung
        By an Athenian eunuch to the harp.
        We'll none of that: that have I told my love,
        In glory of my kinsman Hercules.
        [*Reads*]   The riot of the tipsy Bacchanals,
        Tearing the Thracian singer[9] in their rage.
        That is an old device;[10] and it was play'd
        When I from Thebes came last a conqueror.
        [*Reads*]   The thrice three Muses mourning for the death
        Of Learning, late deceased in beggary.

        [6] *constancy*] consistency.
        [7] *abridgement*] pastime, entertainment.
        [8] *a brief . . . ripe*] a written statement of how many entertainments are ready to be
        performed.
        [9] *the Thracian singer*] Orpheus, the legendary poet.
        [10] *device*] dramatic piece.

That is some satire, keen and critical,
Not sorting with[11] a nuptial ceremony.
[*Reads*]   A tedious brief scene of young Pyramus
And his love Thisbe; very tragical mirth.
Merry and tragical! tedious and brief!
That is, hot ice and wondrous strange snow.
How shall we find the concord of this discord?

PHIL. A play there is, my lord, some ten words long,
Which is as brief as I have known a play;
But by ten words, my lord, it is too long,
Which makes it tedious; for in all the play
There is not one word apt, one player fitted:
And tragical, my noble lord, it is;
For Pyramus therein doth kill himself.
Which, when I saw rehearsed, I must confess,
Made mine eyes water; but more merry tears
The passion of loud laughter never shed.

THE. What are they that do play it?

PHIL. Hard-handed men, that work in Athens here,
Which never labour'd in their minds till now;
And now have toil'd their unbreathed[12] memories
With this same play, against[13] your nuptial.

THE. And we will hear it.

PHIL.   No, my noble lord;
It is not for you: I have heard it over,
And it is nothing, nothing in the world;
Unless you can find sport in their intents,
Extremely stretch'd and conn'd with cruel pain,
To do you service.

THE.   I will hear that play;
For never any thing can be amiss,
When simpleness and duty tender it.
Go, bring them in: and take your places, ladies.

                                   [*Exit* PHILOSTRATE.

HIP. I love not to see wretchedness o'ercharged,
And duty in his service perishing.

THE. Why, gentle sweet, you shall see no such thing.

HIP. He says they can do nothing in this kind.

---

[11] *sorting with*] befitting.
[12] *unbreathed*] unexercised.
[13] *against*] in expectation of.

THE.   The kinder we, to give them thanks for nothing.
        Our sport shall be to take what they mistake:
        And what poor duty cannot do, noble respect
        Takes it in might, not merit.[14]
        Where I have come, great clerks[15] have purposed
        To greet me with premeditated welcomes;
        Where I have seen them shiver and look pale,
        Make periods in the midst of sentences,
        Throttle their practised accent in their fears,
        And, in conclusion, dumbly have broke off,
        Not paying me a welcome. Trust me, sweet,
        Out of this silence yet I picked a welcome;
        And in the modesty of fearful duty
        I read as much as from the rattling tongue
        Of saucy and audacious eloquence.
        Love, therefore, and tongue-tied simplicity
        In least speak most, to my capacity.[16]

Re-enter PHILOSTRATE.

PHIL.   So please your Grace, the Prologue is address'd.[17]
THE.   Let him approach.   [*Flourish of trumpets.*

Enter QUINCE *for the* Prologue.

PRO.   If we offend, it is with our good will.
                That you should think, we come not to offend,
         But with good will. To show our simple skill,
                That is the true beginning of our end.
         Consider, then, we come but in despite.
                We do not come, as minding to content you,
         Our true intent is. All for your delight,
                We are not here. That you should here repent you,
         The actors are at hand; and, by their show,
         You shall know all, that you are like to know.[18]
THE.   This fellow doth not stand upon points.[19]
LYS.   He hath rid his prologue like a rough colt; he knows not the stop.

---

[14] *Takes . . . merit*] values it for the intention rather than for its intrinsic merit.
[15] *clerks*] scholars.
[16] *to my capacity*] as I understand it.
[17] *the Prologue is address'd*] the actor who will speak the Prologue is ready.
[18] *If . . . to know*] The mispunctuation of the Prologue reverses its intended meaning.
[19] *does not stand upon points*] (1) is not respectful; (2) does not follow the correct punctuation.

     A good moral, my lord: it is not enough to speak, but to speak true.

HIP.   Indeed he hath played on his prologue like a child on a recorder; a sound, but not in government. [20]

THE.   His speech was like a tangled chain; nothing impaired, but all disordered. Who is next?

Enter PYRAMUS *and* THISBE, WALL, MOONSHINE, *and* LION.

PRO.   Gentles, perchance you wonder at this show;
              But wonder on, till truth make all things plain.
       This man is Pyramus, if you would know;
              This beauteous lady Thisbe is certain.
       This man, with lime and rough-cast, doth present
              Wall, that vile Wall which did these lovers sunder;
       And through Wall's chink, poor souls, they are content
              To whisper. At the which let no man wonder.
       This man, with lanthorn, dog, and bush of thorn,
              Presenteth Moonshine; for, if you will know,
       By moonshine did these lovers think no scorn
              To meet at Ninus' tomb, there, there to woo.
       This grisly beast, which Lion hight[21] by name,
              The trusty Thisbe, coming first by night,
              Did scare away, or rather did affright;
       And, as she fled, her mantle she did fall,[22]
              Which Lion vile with bloody mouth did stain.
       Anon comes Pyramus, sweet youth and tall,[23]
              And finds his trusty Thisbe's mantle slain:
       Whereat, with blade, with bloody blameful blade,
              He bravely broach'd his boiling bloody breast;
       And Thisbe, tarrying in mulberry shade,
              His dagger drew, and died. For all the rest,
       Let Lion, Moonshine, Wall, and lovers twain
       At large[24] discourse, while here they do remain.

      [*Exeunt* Prologue, PYRAMUS, THISBE, LION, *and* MOONSHINE.

THE.   I wonder if the lion be to speak.

DEM.   No wonder, my lord: one lion may, when many asses do.

---

[20] *in government*] controlled.
[21] *hight*] is called.
[22] *did fall*] dropped.
[23] *tall*] spirited.
[24] *At large*] in detail.

WALL.   In this same interlude it doth befall
              That I, one Snout by name, present a wall;
              And such a wall, as I would have you think,
              That had in it a crannied hole or chink,
              Through which the lovers, Pyramus and Thisbe,
              Did whisper often very secretly.
              This loam, this rough-cast, and this stone, doth show
              That I am that same wall; the truth is so:
              And this the cranny is, right and sinister,[25]
              Through which the fearful lovers are to whisper.

THE.   Would you desire lime and hair to speak better?

DEM.   It is the wittiest partition that ever I heard discourse, my lord.

THE.   Pyramus draws near the wall: silence!

Re-enter PYRAMUS.

PYR.   O grim-look'd night! O night with hue so black!
                  O night, which ever art when day is not!
              O night, O night! alack, alack, alack,
                  I fear my Thisbe's promise is forgot!
              And thou, O wall, O sweet, O lovely wall,
                  That stand'st between her father's ground and mine!
              Thou wall, O wall, O sweet and lovely wall,
                  Show me thy chink, to blink through with mine eyne!
                                            [WALL *holds up his fingers.*
              Thanks, courteous wall: Jove shield thee well for this!
                  But what see I? No Thisbe do I see.
              O wicked wall, through whom I see no bliss!
                  Cursed be thy stones for thus deceiving me!

THE.   The wall, methinks, being sensible,[26] should curse again.

PYR.   No, in truth, sir, he should not. "Deceiving me" is Thisbe's cue:
         she is to enter now, and I am to spy her through the wall. You shall
         see, it will fall pat as I told you. Yonder she comes.

Re-enter THISBE.

THIS.   O wall, full often hast thou heard my moans,
                  For parting my fair Pyramus and me!
              My cherry lips have often kiss'd thy stones,
                  Thy stones with lime and hair knit up in thee.

[25] *sinister*] left.
[26] *sensible*] endowed with feeling.

PYR. I see a voice: now will I to the chink,
    To spy an I can hear my Thisbe's face.
    Thisbe!
THIS. My love thou art, my love I think.
PYR.   Think what thou wilt, I am thy lover's grace;
    And, like Limander, am I trusty still.
THIS. And I like Helen,[27] till the Fates me kill.
PYR. Not Shafalus to Procrus[28] was so true.
THIS. As Shafalus to Procrus, I to you.
PYR. O, kiss me through the hole of this vile wall!
THIS. I kiss the wall's hole, not your lips at all.
PYR. Wilt thou at Ninny's tomb meet me straightway?
THIS. 'Tide life, 'tide death,[29] I come without delay.

                        [Exeunt PYRAMUS *and* THISBE.

WALL. Thus have I, wall, my part discharged so;
    And, being done, thus wall away doth go.
THE. Now is the mural down between the two neighbours.
DEM. No remedy, my lord, when walls are so wilful to hear without warning.
HIP. This is the silliest stuff that ever I heard.
THE. The best in this kind are but shadows;[30] and the worst are no worse, if imagination amend them.
HIP. It must be your imagination then, and not theirs.
THE. If we imagine no worse of them than they of themselves, they may pass for excellent men. Here come two noble beasts in, a man and a lion.

Re-enter LION *and* MOONSHINE.

LION. You, ladies, you, whose gentle hearts do fear
    The smallest monstrous mouse that creeps on floor,
    May now perchance both quake and tremble here,
    When lion rough in wildest rage doth roar.
    Then know that I, one Snug the joiner, am
    A lion-fell,[31] nor else no lion's dam;
    For, if I should as lion come in strife
    Into this place, 't were pity on my life.
THE. A very gentle beast, and of a good conscience.

[27]*Limander ... Helen*] the actors' blunders for "Leander" and "Hero," two legendary doomed lovers.
[28] *Shafalus to Procrus*] a blunder for Cephalus and Procris, two legendary lovers.
[29] *'Tide life, 'tide death*] whether I live or die.
[30] *shadows*] images, representations.
[31] A *lion-fell*] both a fierce lion and merely a lion's skin.

DEM. The very best at a beast, my lord, that e'er I saw.

LYS. This lion is a very fox for his valour.

THE. True; and a goose for his discretion.[32]

DEM. Not so, my lord; for his valour cannot carry his discretion; and
the fox carries the goose.

THE. His discretion, I am sure, cannot carry his valour; for the goose
carries not the fox. It is well: leave it to his discretion, and let us
listen to the moon.

MOON. This lanthorn doth the horned moon present;—

DEM. He should have worn the horns on his head.[33]

THE. He is no crescent, and his horns are invisible within the
circumference.

MOON. This lanthorn doth the horned moon present;
               Myself the man i' the moon do seem to be.

THE. This is the greatest error of all the rest: the man should be put into
the lantern. How is it else the man i' the moon?

DEM. He dares not come there for the candle; for, you see, it is already
in snuff.[34]

HIP. I am aweary of this moon: would he would change!

THE. It appears, by his small light of discretion, that he is in the wane;
but yet, in courtesy, in all reason, we must stay the time.

LYS. Proceed, Moon.

MOON. All that I have to say, is, to tell you that the lanthorn is
the moon; I, the man i' the moon; this thorn-bush, my thorn-bush;
and this dog, my dog.

DEM. Why, all these should be in the lantern; for all these are in the
moon. But, silence! here comes Thisbe.

Re-enter THISBE.

THIS.   This is old Ninny's tomb. Where is my love?

LION.   [*Roaring*] Oh————   [THISBE *runs off*.

DEM. Well roared, Lion.

THE. Well run, Thisbe.

HIP. Well shone, Moon. Truly, the moon shines with a good grace.
                              [*The* LION *shakes* THISBE's *mantle, and exit*.

THE. Well moused, Lion.

DEM. And then came Pyramus.

LYS. And so the lion vanished.

Re-enter PYRAMUS.

[32] *discretion*] good sense.
[33] *horns on his head*] i.e., as the sign of a cuckold.
[34] *in snuff*] (1) needing to be snuffed; (2) offended.

PYR.   Sweet Moon, I thank thee for thy sunny beams;
              I thank thee, Moon, for shining now so bright;
          For, by thy gracious, golden, glittering gleams,
              I trust to take of truest Thisbe sight.
                  But stay, O spite!
                  But mark, poor knight,
              What dreadful dole[35] is here!
                    Eyes, do you see?
                    How can it be?
              O dainty duck! O dear!
                    Thy mantle good,
                    What, stain'd with blood!
              Approach, ye Furies fell!
                    O Fates, come, come,
                    Cut thread and thrum;[36]
              Quail,[37] crush, conclude, and quell![38]

THE.   This passion, and the death of a dear friend, would go near to
    make a man look sad.

HIP.   Beshrew my heart, but I pity the man.

PYR.   O wherefore, Nature, didst thou lions frame?[39]
              Since lion vile hath here deflower'd my dear:
          Which is—no, no—which was the fairest dame
               That lived, that loved, that liked, that look'd with cheer.[40]
                  Come, tears, confound;
                  Out, sword, and wound
              The pap[41] of Pyramus;
                  Ay, that left pap,
                  Where heart doth hop: *[Stabs himself.*
              Thus die I, thus, thus, thus.
                  Now am I dead,
                  Now am I fled;
              My soul is in the sky:
                  Tongue, lose thy light;
                  Moon, take thy flight: *[Exit* MOONSHINE.
              Now die, die, die, die, die.   *[Dies.*

DEM.   No die, but an ace,[42] for him; for he is but one.

---

[35] *dole*] grief.
[36] *thrum*] the tufted end of weavers' thread.
[37] *Quail*] overpower.
[38] *quell*] destroy.
[39] *frame*] form, produce.
[40] *cheer*] face.
[41] *pap*] breast.
[42] *No die, but an ace*] a play on die-casting terms. The "ace" is the side of a die showing only one spot. In Shakespearean London, "ace" was pronounced so as to be scarcely distinguishable from "ass" (idiot).

LYS. Less than an ace, man; for he is dead; he is nothing.

THE. With the help of a surgeon he might yet recover, and prove an ass.

HIP. How chance Moonshine is gone before Thisbe comes back and finds her lover?

THE. She will find him by starlight. Here she comes; and her passion ends the play.

Re-enter THISBE.

HIP. Methinks she should not use a long one for such a Pyramus: I hope she will be brief.

DEM. A mote will turn the balance, which Pyramus, which Thisbe, is the better; he for a man, God warrant us; she for a woman, God bless us.

LYS. She hath spied him already with those sweet eyes.

DEM. And thus she means,[43] videlicet:—

THIS.   Asleep, my love?
               What, dead, my dove?
            O Pyramus, arise!
               Speak, speak. Quite dumb?
               Dead, dead? A tomb
            Must cover thy sweet eyes.
               These lily lips,
               This cherry nose,
            These yellow cowslip cheeks,
               Are gone, are gone:
               Lovers, make moan:
            His eyes were green as leeks.
               O Sisters Three,[44]
               Come, come to me,
            With hands as pale as milk:
               Lay them in gore,
               Since you have shore[45]
            With shears his thread of silk.[46]
               Tongue, not a word:
               Come, trusty sword;
            Come, blade, my breast imbrue:[47]   [*Stabs herself.*

---

[43] *means*] laments.

[44] *Sisters Three*] the three beings in Greek mythology who determine human and divine fate.

[45] *shore*] shorn.

[46] *thread of silk*] the thread symbolizing his life.

[47] *imbrue*] shed the blood of.

And, farewell, friends;
Thus Thisbe ends:
Adieu, adieu, adieu.   [*Dies.*

THE.   Moonshine and Lion are left to bury the dead.

DEM.   Ay, and Wall too.

BOT.   [*Starting up*]   No, I assure you; the wall is down that parted their
fathers. Will it please you to see the epilogue, or to hear a Bergomask
dance[48] between two of our company?

THE.   No epilogue, I pray you; for your play needs no excuse. Never
excuse; for when the players are all dead, there need none to be
blamed. Marry, if he that writ it had played Pyramus and hanged
himself in Thisbe's garter, it would have been a fine tragedy: and so
it is, truly; and very notably discharged. But, come, your
Bergomask: let your epilogue alone.   [*A dance.*

The iron tongue of midnight hath told[49] twelve:
Lovers, to bed; 't is almost fairy time.
I fear we shall out-sleep the coming morn,
As much as we this night have overwatch'd.
This palpable-gross[50] play hath well beguiled
The heavy gait of night. Sweet friends, to bed.
A fortnight hold we this solemnity,
In nightly revels and new jollity.   [*Exeunt.*

Enter PUCK.

PUCK.   Now the hungry lion roars,
        And the wolf behowls the moon;
Whilst the heavy ploughman snores,
        All with weary task fordone.[51]
Now the wasted brands do glow,
        Whilst the screech-owl, screeching loud,
Puts the wretch that lies in woe
        In remembrance of a shroud.
Now it is the time of night,
        That the graves, all gaping wide,
Every one lets forth his sprite,
        In the church-way paths to glide:

---

[48] *Bergomask dance*] a dance named after the Italian commune of Bergamo, noted for
the rusticity of its populace.
[49] *told*] counted.
[50] *palpable-gross*] palpably·stupid.
[51] *fordone*] exhausted.

And we fairies, that do run
    By the triple Hecate's[52] team,
From the presence of the sun,
    Following darkness like a dream,
Now are frolic:[53] not a mouse
Shall disturb this hallow'd house:
I am sent with broom before,
To sweep the dust behind the door.

Enter OBERON *and* TITANIA *with their train.*

OBE.   Through the house give glimmering light,
            By the dead and drowsy fire:
        Every elf and fairy sprite
            Hop as light as bird from brier;
        And this ditty, after me,
        Sing, and dance it trippingly.[54]
TITA.   First, rehearse your song by rote,
        To each word a warbling note:
        Hand in hand, with fairy grace,
        Will we sing, and bless this place.   [*Song and dance.*
OBE.   Now, until the break of day,
        Through this house each fairy stray.
        To the best bride-bed will we,
        Which by us shall blessed be;
        And the issue there create[55]
        Ever shall be fortunate.
        So shall all the couples three
        Ever true in loving be;
        And the blots of Nature's hand
        Shall not in their issue stand;
        Never mole, hare lip, nor scar,
        Nor mark prodigious,[56] such as are
        Despised in nativity,
        Shall upon their children be.

---

[52] *triple Hecate's*] The goddess Hecate has three roles in classical mythology: as Luna in
    heaven, as Diana on earth and as Proserpina in hell. Her chariot was drawn by a
    "triple . . . team" of dragons.
[53] *frolic*] merry.
[54] *trippingly*] nimbly.
[55] *create*] created.
[56] *prodigious*] portentous.

With this field-dew consecrate,[57]
Every fairy take his gait;[58]
And each several[59] chamber bless,
Through this palace, with sweet peace,
Ever shall in safety rest,
And the owner of it blest.
Trip away; make no stay;
Meet me all by break of day.

                                        [*Exeunt* OBERON, TITANIA, *and train.*

PUCK. If we shadows have offended,
Think but this, and all is mended,
That you have but slumber'd here,
While these visions did appear.
And this weak and idle theme,
No more yielding but a dream,
Gentles, do not reprehend:
If you pardon, we will mend.
And, as I am an honest Puck,
If we have unearned luck
Now to scape the serpent's tongue,[60]
We will make amends ere long;
Else the Puck a liar call:
So, good night unto you all.
Give me your hands,[61] if we be friends,
And Robin shall restore amends.

                                                          [*Exit.*

---

[57] *consecrate*] consecrated.
[58] *take his gait*] make his way.
[59] *several*] separate.
[60] *the serpent's tongue*] hissing (of the audience).
[61] *hands*] applause.

As You Like It

As You Like It

As You Like It, one of Shakespeare's great comedies, was first published in 1623 in the collected edition of Shakespeare's plays known as the First Folio. Written sometime between 1599 and 1600, the play is based on *Rosalynde* (1590), a pastoral romance by Thomas Lodge. Shakespeare changed Lodge's euphuistic story into a satire involving disguises, mistaken identity, and love. With the addition of several new characters, such as Jaques, William, Touchstone, and Audrey, Shakespeare imbues the story with realism and humor. Similar in style to his earlier play, *Love's Labour's Lost* (1598), *As You Like It* focuses on the dramatic elements of characterization and dialogue. The play's woodland setting is established almost at once, allowing the audience to appreciate the charms of nature and the outdoors.

SUSAN RATTINER

Dramatis Personæ[1]

DUKE, living in banishment.

FREDERICK, his brother, and usurper of his dominions.

AMIENS,
JAQUES, } lords attending on the banished Duke.

LE BEAU, a courtier attending upon Frederick.

CHARLES, wrestler to Frederick.

OLIVER,
JAQUES, } sons of Sir Rowland de Boys.
ORLANDO,

ADAM,
DENNIS, } servants to Oliver.

TOUCHSTONE, a clown.

SIR OLIVER MARTEXT, a vicar.

CORIN,
SYLVIUS, } shepherds.

WILLIAM, a country fellow, in love with Audrey.

A person representing Hymen.

ROSALIND, daughter to the banished Duke.

CELIA, daughter to Frederick.

PHEBE, a shepherdess.

AUDREY, a country wench.

Lords, pages, and attendants; &c.

SCENE—*Oliver's house; Duke Frederick's court; and the Forest of Arden*

---

[1]This play, which was first printed in the First Folio in 1623, is there divided into acts and scenes. There is no list of *Dramatis Personæ*. This was supplied for the first time in Rowe's edition of 1709.

ACT I.

Scene I. *Orchard of Oliver's House.*

Enter ORLANDO *and* ADAM

ORLANDO. As I remember, Adam, it was upon this fashion: bequeathed me[1] by will but poor a thousand crowns, and, as thou
sayest, charged my brother, on his blessing, to breed me well: and
there begins my sadness. My brother Jaques[2] he keeps at school,
and report speaks goldenly of his profit: for my part, he keeps me
rustically at home, or, to speak more properly, stays me here at
home unkept; for call you that keeping for a gentleman of my
birth, that differs not from the stalling of an ox? His horses are bred
better; for, besides that they are fair with their feeding, they are
taught their manage, and to that end riders dearly hired: but I, his
brother, gain nothing under him but growth; for the which his animals on his dunghills are as much bound to him as I. Besides this
nothing that he so plentifully gives me, the something that nature
gave me his countenance[3] seems to take from me: he lets me feed
with his hinds, bars me the place of a brother, and, as much as in

---

[1]*bequeathed me, etc.*] This sentence lacks a subject. It is possible that "he" was omitted
before "bequeathed" by a typographical error. It is so obvious that Orlando is talking
of his father's bequest that a corrector of the press could not be severely blamed for the
accidental elision.

[2]*My brother Jaques*] This character, Sir Rowland de Boys' second son, only plays a small
part at the end of the last act, where the folio editions call him "second brother" and
Rowe and later editors "Jaques de Boys." In Lodge's story of *Rosalynd*, on which
Shakespeare based his play, the character is called Ferdinand. That Shakespeare
should have bestowed the same name on a far more important personage of his own
creation, the banished Duke's cynical companion, is proof of hasty composition and of
defective revision. Cf. note on I, ii, 74, *infra*.

[3]*countenance*] Cf. Selden's *Table Talk* (Art. "Fines"): "If you will come unto my house,
I will show you the best *countenance* I can," *i.e.* not the best face, but the best
entertainment.

him lies, mines my gentility with my education.[4] This is it, Adam, that grieves me; and the spirit of my father, which I think is within me, begins to mutiny against this servitude: I will no longer endure it, though yet I know no wise remedy how to avoid it.

ADAM. Yonder comes my master, your brother.

ORL. Go apart, Adam, and thou shalt hear how he will shake me up.

Enter OLIVER

OLI. Now, sir! what make you here?

ORL. Nothing: I am not taught to make any thing.

OLI. What mar you then, sir?

ORL. Marry, sir, I am helping you to mar that which God made, a poor unworthy brother of yours, with idleness.

OLI. Marry, sir, be better employed, and be naught awhile.[5]

ORL. Shall I keep your hogs and eat husks with them? What prodigal portion have I spent, that I should come to such penury?

OLI. Know you where you are, sir?

ORL. O, sir, very well; here in your orchard.

OLI. Know you before whom, sir?

ORL. Ay, better than him I am before knows me. I know you are my eldest brother; and, in the gentle condition of blood, you should so know me. The courtesy of nations allows you my better, in that you are the firstborn; but the same tradition takes not away my blood, were there twenty brothers betwixt us: I have as much of my father in me as you; albeit, I confess, your coming before me is nearer to his reverence.[6]

OLI. What, boy!

ORL. Come, come, elder brother, you are too young in this.[7]

OLI. Wilt thou lay hands on me, villain?

ORL. I am no villain; I am the youngest son of Sir Rowland de Boys; he was my father, and he is thrice a villain that says such a father begot villains. Wert thou not my brother, I would not take this hand from thy throat till this other had pulled out thy tongue for saying so: thou hast railed on thyself.

---

[4] *mines . . . education*] undermines or destroys the gentleness of my birth and nature, by means of my bringing up.

[5] *be naught awhile*] a colloquial form of imprecation, "be hanged to you."

[6] *your coming . . . reverence*] your priority of birth more closely associates you with the respect which was his due. The chief share of the father's reputation descends to his eldest born.

[7] *Come, come . . . young in this*] Cf. the elder brother's remark in Lodge's story of *Rosalynd,* "Though I am *eldest* by birth, yet never having attempted any deeds of arms, I am *youngest* to perform any martial exploits."

ADAM.   Sweet masters, be patient: for your father's remembrance, be at accord.

OLI.   Let me go, I say.

ORL.   I will not, till I please: you shall hear me. My father charged you in his will to give me good education: you have trained me like a peasant, obscuring and hiding from me all gentleman-like qualities. The spirit of my father grows strong in me, and I will no longer endure it: therefore allow me such exercises as may become a gentleman, or give me the poor allottery my father left me by testament; with that I will go buy my fortunes.

OLI.   And what wilt thou do? beg, when that is spent? Well, sir, get you in: I will not long be troubled with you; you shall have some part of your will: I pray you, leave me.

ORL.   I will no further offend you than becomes me for my good.

OLI.   Get you with him, you old dog.

ADAM.   Is "old dog" my reward?? Most true, I have lost my teeth in your service. God be with my old master! he would not have spoke such a word.

[Exeunt ORLANDO *and* ADAM.

OLI.   Is it even so? begin you to grow upon me? I will physic your rankness, and yet give no thousand crowns neither. Holla, Dennis!

Enter DENNIS

DEN.   Calls your worship?

OLI.   Was not Charles, the Duke's wrestler, here to speak with me?

DEN.   So please you, he is here at the door and importunes access to you.

OLI.   Call him in. *[Exit* DENNIS.] 'T will be a good way; and tomorrow the wrestling is.

Enter CHARLES

CHA.   Good morrow to your worship.

OLI.   Good Monsieur Charles, what's the new news at the new court?

CHA.   There's no news at the court, sir, but the old news: that is, the old Duke is banished by his younger brother the new Duke; and three or four loving lords have put themselves into voluntary exile with him, whose lands and revenues enrich the new Duke; therefore he gives them good leave to wander.

OLI.   Can you tell if Rosalind, the Duke's daughter, be banished with her father?

CHA.   O, no; for the Duke's daughter, her cousin, so loves her, being ever from their cradles bred together, that she would have followed her exile, or have died to stay behind her. She is at the court, and no less beloved of her uncle than his own daughter; and never two ladies loved as they do.

OLI. Where will the old Duke live?

CHA. They say he is already in the forest of Arden,[8] and a many merry men with him; and there they live like the old Robin Hood of England: they say many young gentlemen flock to him every day, and fleet the time carelessly, as they did in the golden world.

OLI. What, you wrestle to-morrow before the new Duke?

CHA. Marry, do I, sir; and I came to acquaint you with a matter. I am given, sir, secretly to understand that your younger brother, Orlando, hath a disposition to come in disguised against me to try a fall. To-morrow, sir, I wrestle for my credit; and he that escapes me without some broken limb shall acquit him well. Your brother is but young and tender; and, for your love, I would be loath to foil him, as I must, for my own honour, if he come in: therefore, out of my love to you, I came hither to acquaint you withal; that either you might stay him from his intendment, or brook such disgrace well as he shall run into; in that it is a thing of his own search, and altogether against my will.

OLI. Charles, I thank thee for thy love to me, which thou shalt find I will most kindly requite. I had myself notice of my brother's purpose herein, and have by underhand means laboured to dissuade him from it, but he is resolute. I'll tell thee, Charles:—it is the stubbornest young fellow of France; full of ambition, an envious emulator of every man's good parts, a secret and villanous contriver against me his natural brother: therefore use thy discretion; I had as lief thou didst break his neck as his finger. And thou wert best look to 't; for if thou dost him any slight disgrace, or if he do not mightily grace himself on thee,[9] he will practise against thee by poison, entrap thee by some treacherous device, and never leave thee till he hath ta'en thy life by some indirect means or other; for, I assure thee, and almost with tears I speak it, there is not one so young and so villanous this day living. I speak but brotherly of him; but should I anatomize him to thee as he is, I must blush and weep, and thou must look pale and wonder.

CHA. I am heartily glad I came hither to you. If he come to-morrow, I'll give him his payment: if ever he go alone again, I'll never wrestle for prize more: and so, God keep your worship!

---

[8]*forest of Arden*] Lodge, like Shakespeare, makes the scene of his story "the forest of *Ardennes*," in Flanders (now Belgium). But the dramatist's familiarity with the English forest of *Arden* in Warwickshire, near his native town of Stratford-on-Avon, probably coloured his allusions to woodland scenery in the play.

[9]*grace himself on thee*] get grace or honour at your expense.

OLI.   Farewell, good Charles. [*Exit* CHARLES.] Now will I stir this gamester: I hope I shall see an end of him; for my soul, yet I know not why, hates nothing more than he. Yet he's gentle; never schooled, and yet learned; full of noble device;[10] of all sorts enchantingly beloved; and indeed so much in the heart of the world, and especially of my own people, who best know him, that I am altogether misprised: but it shall not be so long; this wrestler shall clear all: nothing remains but that I kindle the boy thither; which now I'll go about.   [*Exit.*

SCENE II. *Lawn Before the Duke's Palace.*

Enter ROSALIND *and* CELIA

CEL.   I pray thee, Rosalind, sweet my coz, be merry.

ROS.   Dear Celia, I show more mirth than I am mistress of; and would you yet I were merrier? Unless you could teach me to forget a banished father, you must not learn me how to remember any extraordinary pleasure.

CEL.   Herein I see thou lovest me not with the full weight that I love thee. If my uncle, thy banished father, had banished thy uncle, the Duke my father, so thou hadst been still with me, I could have taught my love to take thy father for mine: so wouldst thou, if the truth of thy love to me were so righteously tempered as mine is to thee.

ROS.   Well, I will forget the condition of my estate, to rejoice in yours.

CEL.   You know my father hath no child but I, nor none is like to have: and, truly, when he dies, thou shalt be his heir; for what he hath taken away from thy father perforce, I will render thee again in affection; by mine honour, I will; and when I break that oath, let me turn monster: therefore, my sweet Rose, my dear Rose, be merry.

ROS.   From henceforth I will, coz, and devise sports. Let me see; what think you of falling in love?

CEL.   Marry, I prithee, do, to make sport withal: but love no man in good earnest; nor no further in sport neither, than with safety of a pure blush thou mayst in honour come off again.

ROS.   What shall be our sport, then?

---

[10]*noble device*] noble conceptions and aims.

CEL.   Let us sit and mock the good housewife Fortune from her wheel,[1] that her gifts may henceforth be bestowed equally.

ROS.   I would we could do so; for her benefits are mightily misplaced; and the bountiful blind woman doth most mistake in her gifts to women.

CEL.   'T is true; for those that she makes fair she scarce makes honest; and those that she makes honest she makes very ill-favouredly.

ROS.   Nay, now thou goest from Fortune's office to Nature's: Fortune reigns in gifts of the world, not in the lineaments of Nature.

Enter TOUCHSTONE

CEL.   No? when Nature hath made a fair creature, may she not by Fortune fall into the fire? Though Nature hath given us wit to flout at Fortune, hath not Fortune sent in this fool to cut off the argument?

ROS.   Indeed, there is Fortune too hard for Nature, when Fortune makes Nature's natural the cutter-off of Nature's wit.

CEL.   Peradventure this is not Fortune's work neither, but Nature's; who perceiveth our natural wits too dull to reason of[2] such goddesses, and hath sent this natural for our whetstone; for always the dulness of the fool is the whetstone of the wits. How now, wit! whither wander you?[3]

TOUCH.   Mistress, you must come away to your father.

CEL.   Were you made the messenger?

TOUCH.   No, by mine honour, but I was bid to come for you.

ROS.   Where learned you that oath, fool?

TOUCH.   Of a certain knight that swore by his honour they were good pancakes, and swore by his honour the mustard was naught; now I'll stand to it, the pancakes were naught and the mustard was good, and yet was not the knight forsworn.

CEL.   How prove you that, in the great heap of your knowledge?

ROS.   Ay, marry, now unmuzzle your wisdom.

TOUCH.   Stand you both forth now: stroke your chins, and swear by your beards that I am a knave.

CEL.   By our beards, if we had them, thou art.

TOUCH.   By my knavery, if I had it, then I were; but if you swear by that that is not, you are not forsworn: no more was this knight, swearing by his honour, for he never had any; or if he had, he had sworn it away before ever he saw those pancakes or that mustard.

---

[1] *Fortune . . . wheel*] Cf. *Hen. V*, III, vi, 32–34: "*Fortune* is painted . . . with a *wheel*, to signify to you, which is the moral of it, that she is turning, and inconstant, and mutability, and variation."

[2] *reason of*] discuss about. Cf. *Merch. of Ven.*, I, iii, 54, "I am debating *of* my present store," and *ibid.* II, viii, 27, "I *reasoned with* a Frenchman yesterday."

[3] *wit! whither wander you?*] a proverbial phrase serving as a check on too abundant a flow of conversation. The cognate form IV, i, 149, *infra*, "Wit! whither wilt?" is more frequently met with. Malone conjectured that the words formed part of some lost madrigal.

CEL.   Prithee, who is 't that thou meanest?

TOUCH.   One that old Frederick, your father,[4] loves.

CEL.   My father's love is enough to honour him: enough! speak no
more of him; you'll be whipped for taxation one of these days.

TOUCH.   The more pity, that fools may not speak wisely what wise
men do foolishly.

CEL.   By my troth, thou sayest true; for since the little wit that fools
have was silenced, the little foolery that wise men have makes a
great show.[5] Here comes Monsieur Le Beau.

ROS.   With his mouth full of news.

CEL.   Which he will put on us, as pigeons feed their young.

ROS.   Then shall we be news-crammed.

CEL.   All the better; we shall be the more marketable.

Enter LE BEAU

Bon jour, Monsieur Le Beau: what's the news?

LE BEAU.   Fair princess, you have lost much good sport.

CEL.   Sport! of what colour?[6]

LE BEAU.   What colour, madam! how shall I answer you?

ROS.   As wit and fortune will.

TOUCH.   Or as the Destinies decrees.

CEL.   Well said: that was laid on with a trowel.

TOUCH.   Nay, if I keep not my rank,—

ROS.   Thou losest thy old smell.[7]

LE BEAU.   You amaze me, ladies: I would have told you of good
wrestling, which you have lost the sight of.

ROS.   Yet tell us the manner of the wrestling.

LE BEAU.   I will tell you the beginning; and, if it please your ladyships,

---

[4] *old Frederick, your father*] The reference here must be to Celia's father, the usurping
Duke, who at line 213 of the present scene and at V, iv, 148, *infra*, is also called
Frederick. Yet the Folios give the succeeding speech to *Rosalind*, and thereby imply that
Touchstone refers here to Rosalind's father, the banished Duke, who is designated
throughout the play as "Duke, senior," without any Christian name; it is clear that his
name could not have been Frederick, like that of his brother. Capell, who accepted the
Folios' assignment of the next speech to Rosalind, substituted Ferdinand for Frederick.
But it is best to adopt Theobald's emendation, which is followed above, and assign the
next speech to Celia.

[5] *since . . . great show*] There may be a reference here to some topical event, either to
an unidentified inhibition of players, or to the notorious suppression of satirical and li-
centious books, which took place in 1599.

[6] *colour*] kind or nature. Cf. *Lear*, II, ii, 133, where the Quartos read "a fellow of the self-
same *nature*," and the Folio, "a fellow of the self-same *colour*."

[7] *rank . . . smell*] This punning comment on the word "rank," which Touchstone uses in
its sense of "quality" or "place," and Rosalind in that of "rancidity," is precisely paral-
leled in *Cymb.*, II, i, 15–16: "CLO. Would he had been one of my *rank*! SEC. LORD
[*Aside*]. To have *smelt* like a fool."

you may see the end; for the best is yet to do; and here, where you are, they are coming to perform it.

CEL. Well, the beginning, that is dead and buried.

LE BEAU. There comes an old man and his three sons,—

CEL. I could match this beginning with an old tale.

LE BEAU. Three proper young men, of excellent growth and presence.

ROS. With bills on their necks,[8] "Be it known unto all men by these presents."

LE BEAU. The eldest of the three wrestled with Charles, the Duke's wrestler; which Charles in a moment threw him, and broke three of his ribs, that there is little hope of life in him: so he served the second, and so the third. Yonder they lie; the poor old man, their father, making such pitiful dole over them that all the beholders take his part with weeping.

ROS. Alas!

TOUCH. But what is the sport, monsieur, that the ladies have lost?

LE BEAU. Why, this that I speak of.

TOUCH. Thus men may grow wiser every day: it is the first time that ever I heard breaking of ribs was sport for ladies.

CEL. Or I, I promise thee.

ROS. But is there any else longs to see this broken music[9] in his sides? is there yet another dotes upon rib-breaking? Shall we see this wrestling, cousin?

LE BEAU. You must, if you stay here; for here is the place appointed for the wrestling, and they are ready to perform it.

CEL. Yonder, sure, they are coming: let us now stay and see it.

Flourish. Enter DUKE FREDERICK, LORDS, ORLANDO, CHARLES, *and* Attendants

DUKE F. Come on: since the youth will not be entreated, his own peril on his forwardness.

ROS. Is yonder the man?

LE BEAU. Even he, madam.

CEL. Alas, he is too young! yet he looks successfully.

DUKE F. How now, daughter and cousin! are you crept hither to see the wrestling?

---

[8]*Ros. With bills on their necks*] Thus the Folios. Farmer transferred these words to Le Beau's preceding speech, and interpreted them as meaning "with halberds, or weapons of war, on their shoulders." Lodge in the novel writes of his hero "with his forest *bill on his neck.*" In any case Rosalind puns on the word "bills" [*i.e.* halberds] in the sense of placards or proclamations.

[9]*broken music*] A quibbling use of a technical musical term for a musical performance, in which the instruments employed did not keep tune, according to strict rules of harmony. There is no connection between broken music and broken ribs, save the verbal identity of the epithet.

Ros.   Ay, my liege, so please you give us leave.

Duke F.   You will take little delight in it, I can tell you, there is such odds in the man.[10] In pity of the challenger's youth I would fain dissuade him, but he will not be entreated. Speak to him, ladies; see if you can move him.

Cel.   Call him hither, good Monsieur Le Beau.

Duke F.   Do so: I'll not be by.

Le Beau.   Monsieur the challenger, the princess calls[11] for you.

Orl.   I attend them with all respect and duty.

Ros.   Young man, have you challenged Charles the wrestler?

Orl.   No, fair princess; he is the general challenger: I come but in, as others do, to try with him the strength of my youth.

Cel.   Young gentleman, your spirits are too bold for your years. You have seen cruel proof of this man's strength: if you saw yourself with your eyes, or knew yourself with your judgement,[12] the fear of your adventure would counsel you to a more equal enterprise. We pray you, for your own sake, to embrace your own safety, and give over this attempt.

Ros.   Do, young sir; your reputation shall not therefore be misprised: we will make it our suit to the Duke that the wrestling might not go forward.

Orl.   I beseech you, punish me not with your hard thoughts; wherein I confess me much guilty, to deny so fair and excellent ladies any thing. But let your fair eyes and gentle wishes go with me to my trial: wherein if I be foiled, there is but one shamed that was never gracious; if killed, but one dead that is willing to be so: I shall do my friends no wrong, for I have none to lament me; the world no injury, for in it I have nothing: only in the world I fill up a place, which may be better supplied when I have made it empty.

Ros.   The little strength that I have, I would it were with you.

Cel.   And mine, to eke out hers.

Ros.   Fare you well: pray heaven I be deceived in you!

Cel.   Your heart's desires be with you!

Cha.   Come, where is this young gallant that is so desirous to lie with his mother earth?

Orl.   Ready, sir; but his will hath in it a more modest working.

Duke F.   You shall try but one fall.

Cha.   No, I warrant your Grace, you shall not entreat him to a second, that have so mightily persuaded him from a first.

---

[10]*odds in the man*] advantage on the side of the wrestler Charles.

[11]*princess calls*] Theobald reads *princesses call*, which Orlando's reference to *them* seems to justify.

[12]*saw . . . judgement*] exerted all your powers of vision and judgment.

ORL. You mean to mock me after; you should not have mocked me
　　before: but come your ways.

ROS. Now Hercules be thy speed, young man!

CEL. I would I were invisible, to catch the strong fellow by the leg.

　　　　　　　　　　　　　　　　　　　　　　　[*They wrestle.*

ROS. O excellent young man!

CEL. If I had a thunderbolt in mine eye, I can tell who should down.

　　　　　　　　　　　　　　　　　[*Shout. Charles is thrown.*

DUKE F. No more, no more.

ORL. Yes, I beseech your Grace: I am not yet well breathed.[13]

DUKE F. How dost thou, Charles?

LE BEAU. He cannot speak, my lord.

DUKE F. Bear him away. What is thy name, young man?

ORL. Orlando, my liege; the youngest son of Sir Rowland de Boys.

DUKE F. I would thou hadst been son to some man else:
　　The world esteem'd thy father honourable,
　　But I did find him still mine enemy:
　　Thou shouldst have better pleased me with this deed,
　　Hadst thou descended from another house.
　　But fare thee well; thou art a gallant youth:
　　I would thou hadst told me of another father.

　　　　　　　　　　[*Exeunt* DUKE FRED., *train, and* LE BEAU.

CEL. Were I my father, coz, would I do this?

ORL. I am more proud to be Sir Rowland's son,
　　His youngest son; and would not change that calling,[14]
　　To be adopted heir to Frederick.

ROS. My father loved Sir Rowland as his soul,
　　And all the world was of my father's mind:
　　Had I before known this young man his son,
　　I should have given him tears unto entreaties,[15]
　　Ere he should thus have ventured.

CEL. 　　　　　　　　　　　　　　Gentle cousin,
　　Let us go thank him and encourage him:
　　My father's rough and envious disposition
　　Sticks me at heart. Sir, you have well deserved:
　　If you do keep your promises in love
　　But justly, as you have exceeded all promise,
　　Your mistress shall be happy.

---

[13]*not yet well breathed*] not yet in thorough practice, in full career. Cf. *Ant. and Cleop.*,
　　III, xiii, 178: "I will be treble-sinewed, hearted, *breathed.*"

[14]*calling*] name, or appellation. This usage is rare. The word is more common in
　　Shakespeare in the modern sense of "vocation" or "profession," especially of an ec-
　　clesiastical kind.

[15]*tears unto entreaties*] tears in addition to entreaties.

ROS.   Gentleman,
                         [*Giving him a chain from her neck.*
        Wear this for me, one out of suits with fortune,[16]
        That could give more, but that her hand lacks means.
        Shall we go, coz?
CEL.   Ay. Fare you well, fair gentleman.
ORL.   Can I not say, I thank you? My better parts
        Are all thrown down, and that which here stands up
        Is but a quintain, a mere lifeless block.
ROS.   He calls us back: my pride fell with my fortunes;
        I'll ask him what he would. Did you call, sir?
        Sir, you have wrestled well and overthrown
        More than your enemies.
CEL.   Will you go, coz?
ROS.   Have with you. Fare you well.   [*Exeunt* ROSALIND *and* CELIA.
ORL.   What passion hangs these weights upon my tongue?
        I cannot speak to her, yet she urged conference.
        O poor Orlando, thou art overthrown!
        Or Charles or something weaker masters thee.

Re-enter LE BEAU

LE BEAU.   Good sir, I do in friendship counsel you
        To leave this place. Albeit you have deserved
        High commendation, true applause, and love,
        Yet such is now the Duke's condition,[17]
        That he misconstrues all that you have done.
        The Duke is humorous: what he is, indeed,
        More suits you to conceive than I to speak of.
ORL.   I thank you, sir: and, pray you, tell me this,
        Which of the two was daughter of the Duke,
        That here was at the wrestling?
LE BEAU.   Neither his daughter, if we judge by manners;
        But yet, indeed, the taller[18] is his daughter:
        The other is daughter to the banish'd Duke,
        And here detain'd by her usurping uncle,

---

[16]*out of suits with fortune*] out of fortune's service, deprived of her livery. Cf. I, iii, 24,
    infra: "turning these jests *out of service.*"
[17]*condition*] temperament. Cf. *Merch. of Ven.*, I, ii, 143: "*the condition* [*i.e.* tempera-
    ment or disposition] of a saint."
[18]*taller*] This is the reading of the Folios. Rowe and almost all subsequent editors read
    here *shorter* (or *smaller*). A change of the kind seems necessary. Rosalind, in the next
    scene, line 110, gives as a reason for her assuming a man's disguise when fleeing with
    Celia that she is "more than common tall," and at IV, iii, 86–87, Celia is described
    as "low and browner" than Rosalind.

To keep his daughter company; whose loves
Are dearer than the natural bond of sisters.
But I can tell you that of late this Duke
Hath ta'en displeasure 'gainst his gentle niece,
Grounded upon no other argument
But that the people praise her for her virtues,
And pity her for her good father's sake;
And, on my life, his malice 'gainst the lady
Will suddenly break forth. Sir, fare you well.
Hereafter, in a better world than this,
I shall desire more love and knowledge of you.

ORL.   I rest much bounden to you: fare you well.   [*Exit* LE BEAU.
Thus must I from the smoke into the smother;[19]
From tyrant Duke unto a tyrant brother:
But heavenly Rosalind!   [*Exit.*

SCENE III. *A Room in the Palace.*

Enter CELIA *and* ROSALIND

CEL.   Why, cousin! why, Rosalind! Cupid have mercy! not a word?
ROS.   Not one to throw at a dog.
CEL.   No, thy words are too precious to be cast away upon curs; throw
some of them at me; come, lame me with reasons.
ROS.   Then there were two cousins laid up; when the one should be
lamed with reasons and the other mad without any.
CEL.   But is all this for your father?
ROS.   No, some of it is for my child's father.[1] O, how full of briers is
this working-day world!
CEL.   They are but burs, cousin, thrown upon thee in holiday foolery: if
we walk not in the trodden paths, our very petticoats will catch them.
ROS.   I could shake them off my coat: these burs are in my heart.
CEL.   Hem[2] them away.

---

[19]*from the smoke . . . smother*] from bad to worse. "Smother" is the thick stifling smoke
of a smouldering fire.

[1]*my child's father*] this would mean "my husband." Thus the Folios. Numerous modern
editors substitute *my father's child, i.e.* myself.
[2]*Hem*] an onomatopœic word implying the act of coughing slightly. "Hem them away"
is remove them by a small effort of the throat.

Ros.   I would try, if I could cry hem and have him.[3]
CEL.   Come, come, wrestle with thy affections.
Ros.   O, they take the part of a better wrestler than myself!
CEL.   O, a good wish upon you! you will try in time, in despite of a
       fall. But, turning these jests out of service, let us talk in good
       earnest: is it possible, on such a sudden, you should fall into so
       strong a liking with old Sir Rowland's youngest son?
Ros.   The Duke my father loved his father dearly.
CEL.   Doth it therefore ensue that you should love his son dearly? By
       this kind of chase, I should hate him, for my father hated his fa-
       ther dearly;[4] yet I hate not Orlando.
Ros.   No, faith, hate him not, for my sake.
CEL.   Why should I not? doth he not deserve well?
Ros.   Let me love him for that, and do you love him because I do.
       Look, here comes the Duke.
CEL.   With his eyes full of anger.

Enter DUKE FREDERICK, *with* Lords

DUKE F.   Mistress, dispatch you with your safest[5] haste
          And get you from our court.
Ros.   Me, uncle?
DUKE F.   You, cousin:
          Within these ten days if that thou be'st found
          So near our public court as twenty miles,
          Thou diest for it.
Ros.   I do beseech your Grace,
          Let me the knowledge of my fault bear with me:
          If with myself I hold intelligence,
          Or have acquaintance with mine own desires;
          If that I do not dream, or be not frantic,—
          As I do trust I am not,—then, dear uncle,
          Never so much as in a thought unborn
          Did I offend your Highness.
DUKE F.   Thus do all traitors:
          If their purgation did consist in words,
          They are as innocent as grace itself:
          Let it suffice thee that I trust thee not.
Ros.   Yet your mistrust cannot make me a traitor:
          Tell me whereon the likelihood depends.
DUKE F.   Thou art thy father's daughter; there's enough.

[3]*cry hem and have him*] have for the asking; a proverbial expression.
[4]*dearly*] greatly, extremely. Cf. *Hamlet*, I, ii, 182: "my *dearest* foe."
[5]*safest*] surest, least exposed to doubt or delay.

Ros. So was I when your Highness took his dukedom;
   So was I when your Highness banish'd him:
   Treason is not inherited, my lord;
   Or, if we did derive it from our friends,
   What's that to me? my father was no traitor:
   Then, good my liege, mistake me not so much
   To think my poverty is treacherous.
Cel. Dear sovereign, hear me speak.
Duke F. Ay, Celia; we stay'd her for your sake,
   Else had she with her father ranged along.
Cel. I did not then entreat to have her stay;
   It was your pleasure and your own remorse:
   I was too young that time to value her;
   But now I know her: if she be a traitor,
   Why so am I; we still have slept together,
   Rose at an instant, learn'd, play'd, eat together,
   And wheresoe'er we went, like Juno's swans,[6]
   Still we went coupled and inseparable.
Duke F. She is too subtle for thee; and her smoothness,
   Her very silence and her patience
   Speak to the people, and they pity her.
   Thou art a fool: she robs thee of thy name;
   And thou wilt show more bright and seem more virtuous
   When she is gone. Then open not thy lips:
   Firm and irrevocable is my doom
   Which I have pass'd upon her; she is banish'd.
Cel. Pronounce that sentence then on me, my liege:
   I cannot live out of her company.
Duke F. You are a fool. You, niece, provide yourself:
   If you outstay the time, upon mine honour,
   And in the greatness of my word, you die.

                       [*Exeunt* Duke Frederick *and* Lords.

Cel. O my poor Rosalind, whither wilt thou go?
   Wilt thou change fathers? I will give thee mine.
   I charge thee, be not thou more grieved than I am.
Ros. I have more cause.
Cel.   Thou hast not, cousin;
   Prithee, be cheerful: know'st thou not, the Duke
   Hath banish'd me, his daughter?

---

[6]*like Juno's swans*] There is nothing in classical mythology to justify this simile, which seems due to an error of memory. Ovid associates *Venus* and *not Juno* with swans. Cf. *Met.*, X, 708 *seq.* Shakespeare mentions "Venus' doves" seven times in the course of his works, but he ignores her swans.

Ros.   That he hath not.
CEL.   No, hath not? Rosalind lacks then the love
     Which teacheth thee that thou and I am one:
     Shall we be sunder'd? shall we part, sweet girl?
     No: let my father seek another heir.
     Therefore devise with me how we may fly,
     Whither to go and what to bear with us;
     And do not seek to take your change[7] upon you,
     To bear your griefs yourself and leave me out;
     For, by this heaven, now at our sorrows pale,
     Say what thou canst, I'll go along with thee.
Ros.   Why, whither shall we go?
CEL.   To seek my uncle in the forest of Arden.
Ros.   Alas, what danger will it be to us,
     Maids as we are, to travel forth so far!
     Beauty provoketh thieves sooner than gold.
CEL.   I'll put myself in poor and mean attire
     And with a kind of umber smirch my face;
     The like do you: so shall we pass along
     And never stir assailants.
Ros.   Were it not better,
     Because that I am more than common tall,
     That I did suit me all points like a man?
     A gallant curtle-axe upon my thigh,
     A boar-spear in my hand; and—in my heart
     Lie there what hidden woman's fear there will—
     We'll have a swashing and a martial outside,
     As many other mannish cowards have
     That do outface it with their semblances.
CEL.   What shall I call thee when thou art a man?
Ros.   I'll have no worse a name than Jove's own page;
     And therefore look you call me Ganymede.
     But what will you be call'd?
CEL.   Something that hath a reference to my state;
     No longer Celia, but Aliena.
Ros.   But, cousin, what if we assay'd to steal
     The clownish fool out of your father's court?
     Would he not be a comfort to our travel?
CEL.   He'll go along o'er the wide world with me;
     Leave me alone to woo him. Let's away,

---

[7] *your change*] For this reading of the First Folio the Second and later Folios substituted
   your charge, which seems to improve the sense. But the original reading *change, i.e.*
   "reverse of fortune," may be right.

And get our jewels and our wealth together;
Devise the fittest time and safest way
To hide us from pursuit that will be made
After my flight. Now go we in content
To liberty and not to banishment.   [*Exeunt.*

ACT II.

Scene I. *The Forest of Arden.*

Enter Duke Senior, Amiens, *and two or three* Lords, *like foresters*

Duke S.   Now, my co-mates and brothers in exile,
    Hath not old custom made this life more sweet
    Than that of painted pomp?
    Are not these woods
    More free from peril than the envious court?
    Here feel we but the penalty of Adam,
    The seasons' difference; as the icy fang
    And churlish chiding of the winter's wind,
    Which, when it bites and blows upon my body,
    Even till I shrink with cold, I smile and say
    "This is no flattery: these are counsellors
    That feelingly persuade me what I am."
    Sweet are the uses of adversity;
    Which, like the toad, ugly and venomous,
    Wears yet a precious jewel in his head:[1]
    And this our life exempt from public haunt
    Finds tongues in trees, books in the running brooks,
    Sermons in stones and good in every thing.
    I would not change it.
Ami.   Happy is your Grace,

---

[1] *precious jewel in his head*] Cf. Lyly's *Euphues*: "The foule Toade hath a faire stone in his head" (ed. Arber, p. 53). The ignorant popular belief, that a toad carried a precious stone in its head, which was universal in Shakespeare's day, is apparently derived from the fact that a stone or gem, chiefly found in Egypt, is of the brownish gray colour of toads, and is therefore called a batrachite or toadstone. Pliny in his *Natural History* (Book 32) ascribes to a bone in the toad's head curative and other properties, but does not suggest that a gem is ever found there. In his description elsewhere of the toad-stones of Egypt he only notes their association with toads in the way of colour.

That can translate the stubbornness of fortune
Into so quiet and so sweet a style.

DUKE S.   Come, shall we go and kill us venison?
And yet it irks me the poor dappled fools,
Being native burghers of this desert city,
Should in their own confines with forked heads[2]
Have their round haunches gored.

FIRST LORD.   Indeed, my lord,
The melancholy Jaques grieves at that,
And, in that kind, swears you do more usurp
Than doth your brother that hath banish'd you.
To-day my Lord of Amiens and myself
Did steal behind him as he lay along
Under an oak whose antique root peeps out
Upon the brook that brawls along this wood:
To the which place a poor sequester'd stag,
That from the hunter's aim had ta'en a hurt,
Did come to languish, and indeed, my lord,
The wretched animal heaved forth such groans,
That their discharge did stretch his leathern coat
Almost to bursting, and the big round tears
Coursed one another down his innocent nose
In piteous chase; and thus the hairy fool,
Much marked of the melancholy Jaques,
Stood on the extremest verge of the swift brook,
Augmenting it with tears.

DUKE S.   But what said Jaques?
Did he not moralize[3] this spectacle?

FIRST LORD.   O, yes, into a thousand similes.
First, for his weeping into the needless stream;
"Poor deer," quoth he, "thou makest a testament
As worldlings do, giving thy sum of more
To that which had too much": then, being there alone,
Left and abandon'd of his velvet friends;
"'T is right," quoth he; "thus misery doth part
The flux of company": anon a careless herd,
Full of the pasture, jumps along by him
And never stays to greet him; "Ay," quoth Jaques,

---

[2]*forked heads*] arrow heads. Roger Ascham, in *Toxophilus* (ed. Arber, p. 135), mentions
that arrow heads, "having two points stretching forwards," are commonly called "fork
heads." Cf. *Lear*, I, i, 143, where the arrow-head is called "the fork."

[3]*moralize*] Cf. Cotgrave, *Fr.-Eng. Dict.*: "Moraliser: To *morralize*, to expound morrally,
to give a morall sence vnto." See also *infra*, II, vii, 29: "*moral* on the time."

"Sweep on, you fat and greasy citizens;
'T is just the fashion: wherefore do you look
Upon that poor and broken bankrupt there?"
Thus most invectively he pierceth through
The body of the country, city, court,
Yea, and of this our life; swearing that we
Are mere usurpers, tyrants and what's worse,
To fright the animals and to kill them up[4]
In their assign'd and native dwelling-place.

DUKE S.   And did you leave him in this contemplation?

SEC. LORD.   We did, my lord, weeping and commenting
Upon the sobbing deer.

DUKE S.   Show me the place:
I love to cope[5] him in these sullen fits,
For then he's full of matter.

FIRST LORD.   I'll bring you to him straight.   [*Exeunt.*

SCENE II. *A Room in the Palace.*

Enter DUKE FREDERICK, *with* Lords

DUKE F.   Can it be possible that no man saw them?
It cannot be: some villains of my court
Are of consent and sufferance in this.

FIRST LORD.   I cannot hear of any that did see her.
The ladies, her attendants of her chamber,
Saw her a-bed, and in the morning early
They found the bed untreasured of their mistress.

SEC. LORD.   My lord, the roynish[1] clown, at whom so oft
Your Grace was wont to laugh, is also missing.
Hisperia, the princess' gentlewoman,
Confesses that she secretly o'erheard

---

[4]*kill . . . up*] Intensitive of "kill," *i.e.* exterminate. Cf. Adlington's *Apuleius' Golden Asse,* 1582, fo. 159: "*Killed up* with colde."

[5]*cope*] meet with, encounter. Cf. *Venus and Adonis,* 889: "They all strain courtesy who shall *cope* him first."

---

[1]*roynish*] scurvy. Cognate forms "roynous" and "roignous," both meaning "coarse," figure in the *Romaunt of the Rose,* ll. 987, 6193. The word seems adapted from the French. Cotgrave's *Fr.-Eng. Dict.* has "rougneux," which is interpreted "scabbie, mangie," and "scuruie." Cf. *Macb.,* I, iii, 6: "*rump-fed ronyon* [mangy creature]."

Your daughter and her cousin much commend
The parts and graces of the wrestler
That did but lately foil the sinewy Charles;
And she believes, wherever they are gone,
That youth is surely in their company.

DUKE F.   Send to his brother; fetch that gallant hither;
If he be absent, bring his brother to me;
I'll make him find him: do this suddenly,
And let not search and inquisition quail[2]
To bring again these foolish runaways.   [*Exeunt.*

SCENE III. *Before Oliver's House.*

Enter ORLANDO *and* ADAM, *meeting*

ORL.   Who's there?

ADAM.   What, my young master? O my gentle master!
O my sweet master! O you memory
Of old Sir Rowland! why, what make you here?
Why are you virtuous? why do people love you?
And wherefore are you gentle, strong and valiant?
Why would you be so fond to overcome
The bonny priser[1] of the humorous Duke?
Your praise is come too swiftly home before you.
Know you not, master, to some kind of men
Their graces serve them but as enemies?
No more do yours: your virtues, gentle master,
Are sanctified and holy traitors to you.
O, what a world is this, when what is comely
Envenoms him that bears it!

ORL.   Why, what's the matter?

ADAM.   O unhappy youth!
Come not within these doors; within this roof
The enemy of all your graces lives:

---

[2]*quail*] grow faint, slacken in effort.

[1]*bonny priser*] strong prizefighter (*i.e.*, contender for a prize). The word *bonny* is the
reading of all the Folios, and is doubtless right. The epithet is frequently used in the
sense of "strong" as well as in that of "comely." Warburton's widely adopted correction,
boney, i.e., "muscular," is unnecessary.

Your brother—no, no brother; yet the son—
Yet not the son, I will not call him son,
Of him I was about to call his father,—
Hath heard your praises, and this night he means
To burn the lodging where you use to lie
And you within it: if he fail of that,
He will have other means to cut you off.
I overheard him and his practices.
This is no place;[2] this house is but a butchery:
Abhor it, fear it, do not enter it.

ORL.   Why, whither, Adam, wouldst thou have me go?

ADAM.   No matter whither, so you come not here.

ORL.   What, wouldst thou have me go and beg my food?
Or with a base and boisterous sword enforce
A thievish living on the common road?
This I must do, or know not what to do:
Yet this I will not do, do how I can;
I rather will subject me to the malice
Of a diverted blood[3] and bloody brother.

ADAM.   But do not so. I have five hundred crowns,
The thrifty hire I saved under your father,
Which I did store to be my foster-nurse
When service should in my old limbs lie lame,
And unregarded age in corners thrown:
Take that, and He that doth the ravens feed,
Yea, providently caters for the sparrow,
Be comfort to my age! Here is the gold;
All this I give you. Let me be your servant:
Though I look old, yet I am strong and lusty;
For in my youth I never did apply
Hot and rebellious liquors in my blood,
Nor did not with unbashful forehead woo
The means of weakness and debility;
Therefore my age is as a lusty winter,
Frosty, but kindly: let me go with you;
I'll do the service of a younger man
In all your business and necessities.

ORL.   O good old man, how well in thee appears
The constant service of the antique world,
When service sweat for duty, not for meed!

---

[2]*This is no place*] Cf. *Lover's Complaint*, 82: "Love made him her *place*, [*i.e.*, her home, place to dwell in]."
[3]*diverted blood*] blood (or natural affection) turned from the course of nature.

Thou art not for the fashion of these times,
Where none will sweat but for promotion,
And having that do choke their service up
Even with the having: it is not so with thee.
But, poor old man, thou prunest a rotten tree,
That cannot so much as a blossom yield
In lieu of all thy pains and husbandry.
But come thy ways; we'll go along together,
And ere we have thy youthful wages spent,
We'll light upon some settled low content.

ADAM.　Master, go on, and I will follow thee,
To the last gasp, with truth and loyalty.
From seventeen[4] years till now almost fourscore
Here lived I, but now live here no more.
At seventeen years many their fortunes seek;
But at fourscore it is too late a week:
Yet fortune cannot recompense me better
Than to die well and not my master's debtor.　　　*[Exeunt.*

SCENE IV. *The Forest of Arden.*

Enter ROSALIND *for* GANYMEDE, CELIA *for* ALIENA, *and* TOUCHSTONE

ROS.　O Jupiter, how weary[1] are my spirits!

TOUCH.　I care not for my spirits, if my legs were not weary.

ROS.　I could find in my heart to disgrace my man's apparel and to cry
like a woman; but I must comfort the weaker vessel, as doublet
and hose[2] ought to show itself courageous to petticoat: therefore,
courage, good Aliena.

CEL.　I pray you, bear with me; I cannot go no further.

TOUCH.　For my part, I had rather bear with you than bear you: yet I
should bear no cross,[3] if I did bear you; for I think you have no
money in your purse.

---

[4]*seventeen*] This is Rowe's emendation for the *seventy* of the Folios.

---

[1]*weary*] Theobald's emendation of the *merry* of the Folios.
[2]*doublet and hose*] the chief features of male attire in Shakespeare's day.
[3]*bear no cross*] a quibble on the two meanings of the phrase, viz., "endure hardship" and
"carry a coin," specifically known as a "cross," from the stamp upon it of a cross. Cf. 2
Hen. IV, I, ii, 212–213: "you are too impatient to *bear crosses.*"

Ros.   Well, this is the forest of Arden.

Touch.   Ay, now am I in Arden; the more fool I; when I was at home, I was in a better place: but travellers must be content.

Ros.   Ay, be so, good Touchstone.

Enter Corin *and* Silvius

      Look you, who comes here; a young man and an old in solemn talk.

Cor.   That is the way to make her scorn you still.

Sil.   O Corin, that thou knew'st how I do love her!

Cor.   I partly guess; for I have loved ere now.

Sil.   No, Corin, being old, thou canst not guess,
Though in thy youth thou wast as true a lover
As ever sigh'd upon a midnight pillow:
But if thy love were ever like to mine,—
As sure I think did never man love so,—
How many actions most ridiculous
Hast thou been drawn to by thy fantasy?[4]

Cor.   Into a thousand that I have forgotten.

Sil.   O, thou didst then ne'er love so heartily!
If thou remember'st not the slightest folly
That ever love did make thee run into,
Thou hast not loved:
Or if thou hast not sat as I do now,
Wearing thy hearer in thy mistress' praise,
Thou hast not loved:
Or if thou hast not broke from company
Abruptly, as my passion now makes me,
Thou hast not loved.
O Phebe, Phebe, Phebe!   [*Exit.*

Ros.   Alas, poor shepherd! searching of thy wound, I have by hard adventure found mine own.

Touch.   And I mine. I remember, when I was in love I broke my sword upon a stone and bid him take that for coming a-night to Jane Smile: and I remember the kissing of her batlet[5] and the cow's dugs that her pretty chopt[6] hands had milked: and I remember the wooing of a peascod instead of her; from whom I took two cods and, giving her them again, said with weeping tears

---

[4]*fantasy*] Used like the cognate form "fancy" in the sense of affection or love.

[5]*batlet*] Thus the Second and later Folios. The First Folio reads *batler*, which there seems no reason for changing. Neither form is met elsewhere. The reference is to the bat or flat wooden instrument (sometimes called a washing-beetle) with which clothes are beaten by the laundress. Cf. Levins's *Manipulus*, 1570, p. 38: "To *battle* clothes. Excutere."

[6]*chopt*] chapped. Cf. *Sonnet* lxii, 10: "*chopp'd* with tann'd antiquity."

"Wear these for my sake." We that are true lovers run into strange capers; but as all is mortal in nature, so is all nature in love mortal in folly.[7]

ROS.   Thou speakest wiser than thou art ware of.

TOUCH.   Nay, I shall ne'er be ware of mine own wit till I break my shins against it.

ROS.   Jove, Jove! this shepherd's passion
Is much upon my fashion.

TOUCH.   And mine; but it grows something stale with me.

CEL.   I pray you, one of you question yond man
If he for gold will give us any food:
I faint almost to death.

TOUCH.   Holla, you clown!

ROS.   Peace, fool: he's not thy kinsman.

COR.   Who calls?

TOUCH.   Your betters, sir.

COR.   Else are they very wretched.

ROS.   Peace, I say. Good even to you, friend.

COR.   And to you, gentle sir, and to you all.

ROS.   I prithee, shepherd, if that love or gold
Can in this desert place buy entertainment,
Bring us where we may rest ourselves and feed:
Here's a young maid with travel much oppress'd
And faints for succour.

COR.   Fair sir, I pity her
And wish, for her sake more than for mine own,
My fortunes were more able to relieve her;
But I am shepherd to another man
And do not shear the fleeces that I graze:
My master is of churlish disposition
And little recks to find the way to heaven
By doing deeds of hospitality:
Besides, his cote, his flocks and bounds of feed
Are now on sale, and at our sheepcote now,
By reason of his absence, there is nothing
That you will feed on; but what is, come see,
And in my voice[8] most welcome shall you be.

ROS.   What is he that shall buy his flock and pasture?

COR.   That young swain that you saw here but erewhile,
That little cares for buying any thing.

ROS.   I pray thee, if it stand with honesty,

---

[7]*mortal in folly*] "Mortal" is here a slang intensitive meaning "excessive," "extravagant," with the implied suggestion that folly deals death to love.

[8]*in my voice*] as far as my voice or vote has power to bid you welcome.

Buy thou the cottage, pasture and the flock,
  And thou shalt have to pay for it of us.
CEL.   And we will mend thy wages. I like this place,
  And willingly could waste my time in it.
COR.   Assuredly the thing is to be sold:
  Go with me: if you like upon report
  The soil, the profit and this kind of life,
  I will your very faithful feeder[9] be
  And buy it with your gold right suddenly.   [*Exeunt.*

SCENE V. *The Forest.*

Enter AMIENS, JAQUES, *and others*

SONG

AMI.   Under the greenwood tree
                              Who loves to lie with me,
                              And turn[1] his merry note
                              Unto the sweet bird's throat,
                    Come hither, come hither, come hither:
                              Here shall he see
                              No enemy
                        But winter and rough weather.

JAQ.   More, more, I prithee, more.
AMI.   It will make you melancholy, Monsieur Jaques.
JAQ.   I thank it. More, I prithee, more. I can suck melancholy out of
    a song, as a weasel sucks eggs. More, I prithee, more.
AMI.   My voice is ragged: I know I cannot please you.
JAQ.   I do not desire you to please me; I do desire you to sing. Come,
    more; another stanzo:[2] call you 'em stanzos?
AMI.   What you will, Monsieur Jaques.

---

[9]*feeder*] This word in the sense of "servant" is not uncommon, and various suggested
changes are unnecessary.

[1]*turn*] This is the reading of the Folios, and the word clearly means "adapt." Cf. Hall's
Satires, VI, i: "Martiall *turns* his merry note." Rowe's widely accepted emendation,
tunes, may be rejected.
[2]*stanzo*] Cotgrave, *Fr.-Eng. Dict.*, gives the form "stanzo" (for stanza) when interpret-
ing the French "stance." In *L. L. L.*, IV, ii, 99, "stanze" is read in the original editions,—the First Folio and First Quarto,—and "stanza" in the later Folios. There is an
obvious uncertainty as to the right form.

JAQ.   Nay, I care not for their names; they owe me nothing.[3] Will you
sing?

AMI.   More at your request than to please myself.

JAQ.   Well then, if ever I thank any man, I'll thank you; but that they
call compliment is like the encounter of two dog-apes, and when
a man thanks me heartily, methinks I have given him a penny and
he renders me the beggarly thanks. Come, sing; and you that will
not, hold your tongues.

AMI.   Well, I'll end the song. Sirs, cover[4] the while; the Duke will
drink under this tree. He hath been all this day to look you.

JAQ.   And I have been all this day to avoid him. He is too disputable
for my company: I think of as many matters as he; but I give
heaven thanks, and make no boast of them. Come, warble, come.

SONG

Who doth ambition shun,   [*All together here.*
And loves to live i' the sun,
Seeking the food he eats,
And pleased with what he gets,
Come hither, come hither, come hither:
Here shall he see
No enemy
But winter and rough weather.

JAQ.   I'll give you a verse to this note, that I made yesterday in despite
of my invention.

AMI.   And I'll sing it.

JAQ.   Thus it goes:—

If it do come to pass
That any man turn ass,
Leaving his wealth and ease
A stubborn will to please,
Ducdame, ducdame, ducdame:[5]
Here shall he see
Gross fools as he,
And if he will come to me.

[3] *names . . . owe me nothing*] an allusion to the use of the Latin "nomina" in the common sense of "details of debt." Cooper's *Thesaurus*, 1573, defines "Nomina" as "the names of debtes owen."

[4] *cover*] lay the cloth.

[5] *Ducdame*] In all probability a nonsensical parody of the conventional burden of an unidentified popular song. Cf. in *All's Well*, I, iii, 69, the clown's senseless sing-song "Fond done, done fond" in his ditty of Helen of Greece. Attempts have been made to connect "ducdame" with like-sounding words in Latin, Italian, French, Gaelic, Welsh, Greek, and Romany.

AMI.   What's that "ducdame"?

JAQ.   'T is a Greek invocation, to call fools into a circle. I'll go sleep, if I can; if I cannot, I'll rail against all the first-born of Egypt.[6]

AMI.   And I'll go seek the Duke: his banquet is prepared.

                                                                    [*Exeunt severally.*

SCENE VI. *The Forest.*

Enter ORLANDO *and* ADAM

ADAM.   Dear master, I can go no further; O, I die for food! Here lie I down, and measure out my grave. Farewell, kind master.

ORL.   Why, how now, Adam! no greater heart in thee? Live a little; comfort a little; cheer thyself a little. If this uncouth forest yield any thing savage, I will either be food for it or bring it for food to thee. Thy conceit is nearer death than thy powers. For my sake be comfortable; hold death awhile at the arm's end: I will here be with thee presently; and if I bring thee not something to eat, I will give thee leave to die: but if thou diest before I come, thou art a mocker of my labour. Well said! thou lookest cheerly, and I'll be with thee quickly. Yet thou liest in the bleak air: come, I will bear thee to some shelter; and thou shalt not die for lack of a dinner, if there live any thing in this desert. Cheerly, good Adam!   [*Exeunt.*

SCENE VII. *The Forest.*

A table set out. *Enter* DUKE SENIOR, AMIENS, *and* Lords *like outlaws*

DUKE S.   I think he be transform'd into a beast;
     For I can no where find him like a man.

FIRST LORD.   My lord, he is but even now gone hence:
     Here was he merry, hearing of a song.

----

[6]*the first-born of Egypt*] high-born persons.

DUKE S.   If he, compact of jars, grow musical,
    We shall have shortly discord in the spheres.[1]
    Go, seek him: tell him I would speak with him.

Enter JAQUES

FIRST LORD.   He saves my labour by his own approach.
DUKE S.   Why, how now, monsieur! what a life is this,
    That your poor friends must woo your company?
    What, you look merrily!
JAQ.   A fool, a fool! I met a fool i' the forest,
    A motley[2] fool; a miserable world!
    As I do live by food, I met a fool;
    Who laid him down and bask'd him in the sun,
    And rail'd on Lady Fortune in good terms,
    In good set terms, and yet a motley fool.
    "Good morrow, fool," quoth I. "No, sir," quoth he,
    "Call me not fool till heaven hath sent me fortune:"
    And then he drew a dial from his poke,[3]
    And, looking on it with lack-lustre eye,
    Says very wisely, "It is ten o'clock:
    Thus we may see," quoth he, "how the world wags:
    'T is but an hour ago since it was nine;
    And after one hour more 't will be eleven;
    And so, from hour to hour, we ripe and ripe,
    And then, from hour to hour, we rot and rot;
    And thereby hangs a tale." When I did hear
    The motley fool thus moral[4] on the time,
    My lungs began to crow like chanticleer,
    That fools should be so deep-contemplative;
    And I did laugh sans intermission

---

[1]*spheres*] The common belief in the music of the spheres is well illustrated in *Merch. of Ven.*, V, i, 60–61: "There's not the smallest orb which thou behold'st But in his motion like an angel sings."

[2]*motley*] a reference to the conventional parti-coloured or patchwork dress of the professional fool. "Mottled" would be the modern expression. A species of variegated cloth seems to have borne in the trade the name of "motley." Cf. line 34, *infra*, "*Motley's* the only wear," and 43, "a *motley* coat."

[3]*dial from his poke*] It was common among the lower orders to carry in the "poke" or pocket a sundial in the form of a metal ring about two inches in diameter, which was so marked and contrived that sunlight falling upon it indicated the hour of day. A specimen of a pocket dial of the Elizabethan period is preserved in the Museum at Shakespeare's birthplace, Stratford-upon-Avon.

[4]*moral*] Cf. II, i, 44, *supra*, "*moralize* this spectacle." There seems little doubt that "moral on" is a verb meaning "moralize on." The suggestion that "moral" is here used adjectivally offers an awkward construction.

An hour by his dial. O noble fool!
A worthy fool! Motley's the only wear.

DUKE S. What fool is this?

JAQ. O worthy fool! One that hath been a courtier,
And says, if ladies be but young and fair,
They have the gift to know it: and in his brain,
Which is as dry as the remainder biscuit
After a voyage, he hath strange places cramm'd[5]
With observation, the which he vents
In mangled forms. O that I were a fool!
I am ambitious for a motley coat.

DUKE S. Thou shalt have one.

JAQ.   It is my only suit;[6]
Provided that you weed your better judgements
Of all opinion that grows rank in them
That I am wise. I must have liberty
Withal, as large a charter as the wind,[7]
To blow on whom I please; for so fools have;
And they that are most galled with my folly,
They most must laugh. And why, sir, must they so?
The "why" is plain as way to parish church:
He that a fool doth very wisely hit
Doth very foolishly, although he smart,
Not to seem senseless of the bob:[8] if not,
The wise man's folly is anatomized
Even by the squandering glances[9] of the fool.
Invest me in my motley; give me leave
To speak my mind, and I will through and through
Cleanse the foul body of the infected world,
If they will patiently receive my medicine.

DUKE S. Fie on thee! I can tell what thou wouldst do.

JAQ. What, for a counter,[10] would I do but good?

DUKE S. Most mischievous foul sin, in chiding sin:

---

[5]*he hath strange places cramm'd*] he hath collected from observation or study a mass of
strange topics, allusions, passages from books. Cf. the use of the Latin word "loci" and
the Greek "τόποι."

[6]*my only suit*] a quibble on the two meanings of the word "petition" and "dress."

[7]*as large a charter as the wind*] Cf. *Hen. V,* I, i, 48: "The *air,* a *charter'd libertine,* is still."

[8]*Not to . . . bob*] The Folios omit the words *not to,* which Theobald first supplied. They
are necessary to the sense. The general meaning is that the wise man, though he may
smart under a fool's taunt, ought to ignore the "bob" or rap of a fool's comment.

[9]*squandering glances*] random shots.

[10]*counter*] a thing of no value; a metal disc, of no intrinsic value, used in making
calculations.

For thou thyself hast been a libertine,
As sensual as the brutish sting[11] itself;
And all the embossed sores and headed evils,
That thou with license of free foot[12] hast caught,
Wouldst thou disgorge into the general world.

JAQ.   Why, who cries out on pride,
That can therein tax any private party?
Doth it not flow as hugely as the sea,
Till that the weary very means do ebb?[13]
What woman in the city do I name,
When that I say the city-woman bears
The cost of princes on unworthy shoulders?
Who can come in and say that I mean her,
When such a one as she such is her neighbour?
Or what is he of basest function,
That says his bravery is not on my cost,
Thinking that I mean him, but therein suits
His folly to the mettle of my speech?[14]
There then; how then? what then? Let me see wherein
My tongue hath wrong'd him: if it do him right,
Then he hath wrong'd himself; if he be free,
Why then my taxing like a wild-goose flies,
Unclaim'd of any man. But who comes here?

Enter ORLANDO, *with his sword drawn*

ORL.   Forbear, and eat no more.
JAQ.   Why, I have eat none yet.
ORL.   Nor shalt not, till necessity be served.
JAQ.   Of what kind should this cock come of?
DUKE S.   Art thou thus bolden'd, man, by thy distress?
Or else a rude despiser of good manners,
That in civility thou seem'st so empty?
ORL.   You touch'd my vein at first: the thorny point
Of bare distress hath ta'en from me the show

---

[11]*brutish sting*] animal impulse.

[12]*with license of free foot*] gadding about with no restraint.

[13]*Till . . . ebb*] This is the original reading. It means that pride flows on like the tidal sea
till its "very means," or sustaining forces, becoming weary or exhausted, ebb or decay.
Singer's emendation, *the wearer's very means*, is not happy.

[14]*Or what . . . speech?*] The general meaning is that one finds men in the lowest position in life taking a foolish pride in showy apparel who, if they hear a censorious ob-
server denounce the vanity of spending money on dress, retort that the critic does not
pay for what they wear; the critic's censure is intended to have no particular or per-
sonal application, but such a reply is a safe sign that the cap fits.

       Of smooth civility: yet am I inland[15] bred
       And know some nurture. But forbear, I say:
       He dies that touches any of this fruit
       Till I and my affairs are answered.

JAQ.   An you will not be answered with reason, I must die.

DUKE S.   What would you have? Your gentleness shall force,
       More than your force move us to gentleness.

ORL.   I almost die for food; and let me have it.

DUKE S.   Sit down and feed, and welcome to our table.

ORL.   Speak you so gently? Pardon me, I pray you:
       I thought that all things had been savage here;
       And therefore put I on the countenance
       Of stern commandment. But whate'er you are
       That in this desert inaccessible,
       Under the shade of melancholy boughs,
       Lose and neglect the creeping hours of time;
       If ever you have look'd on better days,
       If ever been where bells have knoll'd to church,
       If ever sat at any good man's feast,
       If ever from your eyelids wiped a tear
       And know what 't is to pity and be pitied,
       Let gentleness my strong enforcement be:
       In the which hope I blush, and hide my sword.

DUKE S.   True is it that we have seen better days,
       And have with holy bell been knoll'd to church,
       And sat at good men's feasts, and wiped our eyes
       Of drops that sacred pity hath engender'd:
       And therefore sit you down in gentleness
       And take upon command[16] what help we have
       That to your wanting may be minister'd.

ORL.   Then but forbear your food a little while,
       Whiles, like a doe, I go to find my fawn
       And give it food. There is an old poor man,
       Who after me hath many a weary step
       Limp'd in pure love: till he be first sufficed,
       Oppress'd with two weak evils, age and hunger,
       I will not touch a bit.

DUKE S.   Go find him out,
       And we will nothing waste till you return.

ORL.   I thank ye; and be blest for your good comfort!   [Exit.

---

[15]*inland*] civilized, refined, the converse of "outlandish." Cf. III, ii, 322, *infra*: "an *inland* man."

[16]*upon command*] at your command.

DUKE S.   Thou seest we are not all alone unhappy:
    This wide and universal theatre
    Presents more woeful pageants than the scene
    Wherein we play in.
JAQ.   All the world's a stage,[17]
    And all the men and women merely players:
    They have their exits and their entrances;
    And one man in his time plays many parts,
    His acts being seven ages. At first the infant,
    Mewling and puking in the nurse's arms.
    Then the whining school-boy, with his satchel
    And shining morning face, creeping like snail
    Unwillingly to school. And then the lover,
    Sighing like furnace,[18] with a woeful ballad
    Made to his mistress' eyebrow. Then a soldier,
    Full of strange oaths, and bearded like the pard,
    Jealous in honour, sudden and quick in quarrel,
    Seeking the bubble reputation
    Even in the cannon's mouth. And then the justice,
    In fair round belly with good capon[19] lined,
    With eyes severe and beard of formal cut,
    Full of wise saws and modern instances;[20]
    And so he plays his part. The sixth age shifts
    Into the lean and slipper'd pantaloon,
    With spectacles on nose and pouch on side,
    His youthful hose, well saved, a world too wide
    For his shrunk shank; and his big manly voice,
    Turning again toward childish treble, pipes
    And whistles in his sound. Last scene of all,
    That ends this strange eventful history,
    Is second childishness and mere oblivion,

---

[17]*All . . . stage*] Cf. *Merch. of Ven.*, I, i, 77–78: "I hold the world but as the world, Gratiano; A stage, where every man must play a part." The comparison of the world to a stage was a commonplace in Greek, Latin, and modern European literature. The Globe Theatre bore the proverbial motto, "Totus mundus agit histrionem." The division of man's life into seven parts or ages, which Shakespeare likens to acts of a play, is found in the Greek writings of the physician Hippocrates and of the late Greek philosopher Proclus, and was generally accepted by philosophers, poets, and artists of the European Renaissance.

[18]*Sighing like furnace*] Cf. *Cymb.*, I, vi, 65–66: "he [*i.e.*, a Frenchman in love] *furnaces* The thick *sighs* from him."

[19]*the justice . . . capon*] Capons formed gifts which suitors were in the habit of offering justices of the peace. Cf. Wither's *Christmas Carol*, lines 41, 42: "Now poor men to the *justices* With *capons* make their arrants [*i.e.*, errands]."

[20]*modern instances*] trite or commonplace maxims or anecdotes.

Sans teeth, sans eyes, sans taste, sans every thing.

Re-enter ORLANDO, *with* ADAM

DUKE S.   Welcome. Set down your venerable burthen,
   And let him feed.
ORL.   I thank you most for him.
ADAM.   So had you need:
   I scarce can speak to thank you for myself.
DUKE S.   Welcome; fall to: I will not trouble you
   As yet, to question you about your fortunes.
   Give us some music; and, good cousin, sing.

SONG

AMI.   Blow, blow, thou winter wind,
                    Thou art not so unkind
                       As man's ingratitude;
                    Thy tooth is not so keen,
                    Because thou art not seen,
                       Although thy breath be rude.
         Heigh-ho! sing, heigh-ho! unto the green holly:
         Most friendship is feigning, most loving mere folly:
                    Then, heigh-ho, the holly!
                       This life is most jolly.

                    Freeze, freeze, thou bitter sky,
                    That does not bite so nigh
                       As benefits forgot:
                    Though thou the waters warp,
                    Thy sting is not so sharp
                       As friend remember'd not.
         Heigh-ho! sing, &c.

DUKE S.   If that you were the good Sir Rowland's son,
   As you have whisper'd faithfully you were,
   And as mine eye doth his effigies[21] witness
   Most truly limn'd and living in your face,
   Be truly welcome hither: I am the Duke
   That loved your father: the residue of your fortune,
   Go to my cave and tell me. Good old man,
   Thou art right welcome as thy master is.
   Support him by the arm. Give me your hand,
   And let me all your fortunes understand.   [*Exeunt.*

---

[21]*effigies*] The accent in this word, which must be pronounced trisyllabically, falls on
the second syllable.

ACT III.

SCENE I. *A Room in the Palace.*

Enter DUKE FREDERICK, Lords, *and* OLIVER

DUKE FREDERICK.   Not see him since? Sir, sir, that cannot be:
    But were I not the better part made mercy,
    I should not seek an absent argument
    Of my revenge, thou present. But look to it:
    Find out thy brother, wheresoe'er he is;
    Seek him with candle; bring him dead or living
    Within this twelvemonth, or turn thou no more
    To seek a living in our territory:
    Thy lands and all things that thou dost call thine
    Worth seizure do we seize into our hands,
    Till thou canst quit thee by thy brother's mouth
    Of what we think against thee.
OLI.   O that your Highness knew my heart in this!
    I never loved my brother in my life.
DUKE F.   More villain thou. Well, push him out of doors;
    And let my officers of such a nature
    Make an extent upon[1] his house and lands:
    Do this expediently and turn him going.   [*Exeunt.*

---

[1]*Make an extent upon, etc.*] In strict legal phraseology the process of "making an extent," *i.e.*, executing the writ "extendi facias," consisted in appraising the value of property to its full extent as a preliminary to its summary seizure. The process ordinarily followed a sentence of forfeiture of which in the present instance Shakespeare gives no hint. The phrase is very commonly met with in Elizabethan plays in the loose significance, as here, of taking forcible possession of property.

SCENE II. *The Forest.*

Enter ORLANDO, *with a paper*

ORL.   Hang there, my verse, in witness of my love:
     And thou, thrice-crowned queen of night,[1] survey
   With thy chaste eye, from thy pale sphere above,
     Thy huntress' name that my full life doth sway.
   O Rosalind! these trees shall be my books
     And in their barks my thoughts I'll character;
   That every eye which in this forest looks
     Shall see thy virtue witness'd every where.
   Run, run, Orlando; carve on every tree
   The fair, the chaste and unexpressive[2] she.   [*Exit.*

Enter CORIN *and* TOUCHSTONE

COR.   And how like you this shepherd's life, Master Touchstone?

TOUCH.   Truly, shepherd, in respect of itself, it is a good life; but in respect that it is a shepherd's life, it is naught. In respect that it is solitary, I like it very well; but in respect that it is private, it is a very vile life. Now, in respect it is in the fields, it pleaseth me well; but in respect it is not in the court, it is tedious. As it is a spare life, look you, it fits my humour well; but as there is no more plenty in it, it goes much against my stomach. Hast any philosophy in thee, shepherd?

COR.   No more but that I know the more one sickens the worse at ease he is; and that he that wants money, means and content is without three good friends; that the property of rain is to wet and fire to burn; that good pasture makes fat sheep, and that a great cause of the night is lack of the sun; that he that hath learned no wit by nature nor art may complain of good breeding[3] or comes of a very dull kindred.

---

[1] *thrice-crowned queen of night*] Luna, or the moon, was believed in classical mythology to rule three realms,—earth, heaven, where she was known as "Diana," and the infernal regions, where she was known as "Hecate." Chapman, in his *Hymn to Night* (1594), describes how the goddess with "triple forehead" controls earth, seas, and hell. Cf. *Mids. N. Dr.,* V, i, 391: "the *triple* Hecate's team."

[2] *unexpressive*] inexpressible; a common usage. Cf. Milton's *Lycidas,* 176: "The *unexpressive* nuptial song."

[3] *good breeding*] *i.e.,* the want of good breeding; a common manner of speech in Elizabethan English.

TOUCH. Such a one is a natural philosopher. Wast ever in court, shepherd?

COR. No, truly.

TOUCH. Then thou art damned.

COR. Nay, I hope.

TOUCH. Truly, thou art damned, like an ill-roasted egg all on one side.

COR. For not being at court? Your reason.

TOUCH. Why, if thou never wast at court, thou never sawest good manners; if thou never sawest good manners, then thy manners must be wicked; and wickedness is sin, and sin is damnation. Thou art in a parlous state, shepherd.

COR. Not a whit, Touchstone: those that are good manners at the court are as ridiculous in the country as the behaviour of the country is most mockable at the court. You told me you salute not at the court, but you kiss[4] your hands: that courtesy would be uncleanly, if courtiers were shepherds.

TOUCH. Instance, briefly; come, instance.

COR. Why, we are still handling our ewes, and their fells, you know, are greasy.

TOUCH. Why, do not your courtier's hands sweat? and is not the grease of a mutton as wholesome as the sweat of a man? Shallow, shallow. A better instance, I say; come.

COR. Besides, our hands are hard.

TOUCH. Your lips will feel them the sooner. Shallow again. A more sounder instance, come.

COR. And they are often tarred over with the surgery of our sheep; and would you have us kiss tar? The courtier's hands are perfumed with civet.

TOUCH. Most shallow man! thou worms-meat, in respect of a good piece of flesh indeed! Learn of the wise, and perpend: civet is of a baser birth than tar, the very uncleanly flux of a cat. Mend the instance, shepherd.

COR. You have too courtly a wit for me: I'll rest.

TOUCH. Wilt thou rest damned? God help thee, shallow man! God make incision in thee! thou art raw.[5]

COR. Sir, I am a true labourer: I earn that I eat, get that I wear, owe no man hate, envy no man's happiness, glad of other men's good, content with my harm, and the greatest of my pride is to see my ewes graze and my lambs suck.

---

[4]*but you kiss*] without kissing.

[5]*God make incision . . . raw*] A reference to blood-letting, which was the accepted method of treating diseases alike of mind or body. "Raw" seems used in a double sense of "ignorant" and "suffering from a flesh wound," which requires medical treatment.

TOUCH.   That is another simple sin in you, to bring the ewes and the
     rams together and to offer to get your living by the copulation of
     cattle; to be bawd to a bell-wether, and to betray a she-lamb of a
     twelvemonth to a crooked-pated, old, cuckoldly ram, out of all
     reasonable match. If thou beest not damned for this, the devil
     himself will have no shepherds; I cannot see else how thou
     shouldst 'scape.

COR.   Here comes young Master Ganymede, my new mistress's brother.

Enter ROSALIND, *with a paper, reading*

ROS.   From the east to western Ind,
                  No jewel is like Rosalind.
                  Her worth, being mounted on the wind,
                  Through all the world bears Rosalind.
                  All the pictures fairest lined
                  Are but black to Rosalind.
                  Let no face be kept in mind
                  But the fair of Rosalind.

TOUCH.   I'll rhyme you so eight years together, dinners and suppers
     and sleeping-hours excepted: it is the right butter-women's rank[6]
     to market.

ROS.   Out, fool!

TOUCH.   For a taste:

                  If a hart do lack a hind,
                  Let him seek out Rosalind.
                  If the cat will after kind,
                  So be sure will Rosalind.
                  Winter garments must be lined,
                  So must slender Rosalind.
                  They that reap must sheaf and bind;
                  Then to cart with Rosalind.
                  Sweetest nut hath sourest rind,
                  Such a nut is Rosalind.
                  He that sweetest rose will find,
                  Must find love's prick and Rosalind.

[6]*rank*] This, the original reading, has been much questioned, and the numerous suggested substitutes for *rank* include *rate, rack, canter*, and others. It is clear that the
sense required is that of a jog trot or ambling pace, such as characterises butter-women
on their way to market. Such a meaning may possibly be deducible from the women's
practice of riding or walking in file or *rank*. Cf. Pettie's translation of Guazzo's, *Civil
Conversation* (1586): "All the women in the towne runne thether *of a ranke*, as it were
in procession." But much is to be said for the emendation *rack*, which was in common
use for a horse's jogging method of progression.

This is the very false gallop[7] of verses: why do you infect yourself
with them?

ROS.   Peace, you dull fool! I found them on a tree.

TOUCH.   Truly, the tree yields bad fruit.

ROS.   I'll graff it with you, and then I shall graff it with a medlar: then
it will be the earliest fruit[8] i' the country; for you'll be rotten ere
you be half ripe, and that's the right virtue of the medlar.

TOUCH.   You have said; but whether wisely or no, let the forest judge.

Enter CELIA, *with a writing*

ROS.   Peace!
Here comes my sister, reading: stand aside.

CEL. [*reads*]   Why should this a desert be?
               For it is unpeopled? No;
          Tongues I'll hang on every tree,
               That shall civil sayings show:
          Some, how brief the life of man
               Runs his erring pilgrimage,
          That the stretching of a span
               Buckles in his sum of age;
          Some, of violated vows
               'Twixt the souls of friend and friend:
          But upon the fairest boughs,
               Or at every sentence end,
          Will I Rosalinda write,
               Teaching all that read to know
          The quintessence of every sprite
               Heaven would in little[9] show.
          Therefore Heaven Nature charged
               That one body should be fill'd
          With all graces wide-enlarged:
               Nature presently distill'd
          Helen's cheek, but not her heart,
               Cleopatra's majesty,

---

[7]*false gallop*] Cf. Nashe's *Foure Letters*, "I would trot *a false gallop* through the rest of
his ragged *verses*." The term technically means the jerky amble in which the horse puts
the left foot before the right. Shakespeare, in *1 Hen. IV*, III, i, 134–135, likens "minc-
ing poetry" to the "forced gait of a shuffling nag."

[8]*earliest fruit*] The medlar is now one of the latest fruits to ripen. The circumstance that
it rots ere it ripens argues a premature precocity, which may justify Rosalind's quibbling argument.

[9]*in little*] The train of thought has here astrological significance, and "in little" probably refers to the "microcosm, the little world of man," which is a miniature reflection
of the stars. "A picture *in little*," as in *Hamlet*, II, ii, 362, was a common synonym for
a miniature painting. But there is no such reference here.

         Atalanta's better part,[10]
           Sad Lucretia's modesty.
         Thus Rosalind of many parts
           By heavenly synod was devised;
         Of many faces, eyes and hearts,
           To have the touches dearest prized.
      Heaven would that she these gifts should have,
      And I to live and die her slave.

Ros.   O most gentle pulpiter![11] what tedious homily of love have you wearied your parishioners withal, and never cried "Have patience, good people"!

Cel.   How now! back, friends! Shepherd, go off a little. Go with him, sirrah.

Touch.   Come, shepherd, let us make an honourable retreat; though not with bag and baggage, yet with scrip and scrippage.

                             [*Exeunt* Corin *and* Touchstone.

Cel.   Didst thou hear these verses?

Ros.   O, yes, I heard them all, and more too; for some of them had in them more feet than the verses would bear.

Cel.   That's no matter: the feet might bear the verses.

Ros.   Ay, but the feet were lame and could not bear themselves without the verse and therefore stood lamely in the verse.

Cel.   But didst thou hear without wondering how thy name should be hanged and carved upon these trees?

Ros.   I was seven of the nine days out of the wonder before you came; for look here what I found on a palm-tree. I was never so be-rhymed since Pythagoras' time, that I was an Irish rat,[12] which I can hardly remember.

Cel.   Trow you who hath done this?

Ros.   Is it a man?

---

[10]*Atalanta's better part*] Ovid declares himself unable to decide whether Atalanta more excelled in swiftness of foot or in beauty of face (*Met.*, X, 562–563). In line 260, *infra*, reference is made to "Atalanta's heels," the first of her two distinctive characteristics. At this place Shakespeare probably had in mind the charm of feature which Ovid puts to her credit.

[11]*pulpiter*] *i.e.*, preacher. This is Spedding's ingenious substitute for *Jupiter* of the Folios. But Rosalind has already made one appeal to Jupiter (II, iv, 1), and has twice called on Jove (II, iv, 56), while she makes a passing reference to the god at III, ii, 221, *infra*. Irrelevant use of these expletives of adjuration seems in keeping with her character, and the old reading may possibly be right.

[12]*be-rhymed . . . Irish rat*] Cf. Jonson's *Poetaster*, Dialogue to the Reader, 150–151: "*Rime* 'hem to death, as they doe *Irish rats* In drumming tunes." The superstitious belief that rats can be rhymed to death seems to be cherished by the peasantry of France as well as of Ireland.

CEL. And a chain, that you once wore, about his neck. Change you colour?

ROS. I prithee, who?

CEL. O Lord, Lord! it is a hard matter for friends to meet; but mountains may be removed with earthquakes and so encounter.

ROS. Nay, but who is it?

CEL. Is it possible?

ROS. Nay, I prithee now with most petitionary vehemence, tell me who it is.

CEL. O wonderful, wonderful, and most wonderful wonderful! and yet again wonderful, and after that, out of all hooping![13]

ROS. Good my complexion![14] dost thou think, though I am caparisoned like a man, I have a doublet and hose in my disposition? One inch of delay more is a South-sea of discovery;[15] I prithee, tell me who is it quickly, and speak apace. I would thou couldst stammer, that thou mightst pour this concealed man out of thy mouth, as wine comes out of a narrow-mouthed bottle, either too much at once, or none at all. I prithee, take the cork out of thy mouth that I may drink thy tidings.

CEL. So you may put a man in your belly.

ROS. Is he of God's making?[16] What manner of man? Is his head worth a hat? or his chin worth a beard?

CEL. Nay, he hath but a little beard.

ROS. Why, God will send more, if the man will be thankful: let me stay the growth of his beard, if thou delay me not the knowledge of his chin.

CEL. It is young Orlando, that tripped up the wrestler's heels and your heart both in an instant.

ROS. Nay, but the devil take mocking: speak sad brow and true maid.[17]

CEL. I' faith, coz, 't is he.

[13]*out of all hooping!*] beyond all the limits of wonder which shouting can adequately express.

[14]*Good my complexion!*] This exclamation seems a nervous and involuntary appeal to Rosalind's feminine tell-tale complexion. The inversion of the epithet "good," which is very common in Elizabethan English, somewhat obscures the meaning, which amounts in effect to nothing more than an ebullition of anxiety lest her girl's face shall betray her.

[15]*One inch of delay more is a South-sea of discovery*] The slightest delay in satisfying my curiosity will expose me to the uncertainties and perplexities of an exploring voyage in some great unknown ocean like the unexplored South-sea or Pacific Ocean.

[16]*of God's making?*] The implied alternative is "a man of his tailor's making." Cf. *Lear*, II, ii, 50: "nature disclaims in thee: a tailor made thee."

[17]*speak . . . maid*] speak in all seriousness and truth. Cf. for the construction 258, *infra*, "I *answer you right painted cloth*," and *K. John*, II, i, 462: "He *speaks plain cannon fire*, and smoke and bounce."

Ros.   Orlando?

Cel.   Orlando.

Ros.   Alas the day! what shall I do with my doublet and hose? What did he when thou sawest him? What said he? How looked he? Wherein went he?[18] What makes he here? Did he ask for me? Where remains he? How parted he with thee? and when shalt thou see him again? Answer me in one word.

Cel.   You must borrow me Gargantua's mouth[19] first: 't is a word too great for any mouth of this age's size. To say ay and no to these particulars is more than to answer in a catechism.

Ros.   But doth he know that I am in this forest and in man's apparel? Looks he as freshly as he did the day he wrestled?

Cel.   It is as easy to count atomies[20] as to resolve the propositions of a lover; but take a taste of my finding him, and relish it with good observance. I found him under a tree, like a dropped acorn.

Ros.   It may well be called Jove's tree,[21] when it drops forth such fruit.

Cel.   Give me audience, good madam.

Ros.   Proceed.

Cel.   There lay he, stretched along, like a wounded knight.

Ros.   Though it be pity to see such a sight, it well becomes the ground.

Cel.   Cry "holla"[22] to thy tongue, I prithee; it curvets unseasonably. He was furnished like a hunter.

Ros.   O, ominous! he comes to kill my heart.[23]

Cel.   I would sing my song without a burden: thou bringest me out of tune.

Ros.   Do you not know I am a woman? when I think, I must speak. Sweet, say on.

Cel.   You bring me out. Soft! comes he not here?

Enter ORLANDO *and* JAQUES

Ros.   'T is he: slink by, and note him.

---

[18]*Wherein went he?*] How did he go dressed?

[19]*Gargantua's mouth*] Gargantua, Rabelais' giant, swallows five pilgrims with their staves in a salad (Bk. I, ch. 38). Cf. Cotgrave's *Fr.-Engl. Dict.*, "Gargantua. Great throat, Rab."

[20]*atomies*] The Third and Fourth Folios read *atomes*, which Rowe changed to *atoms*. "Atomies" is used again in III, v, 13, *infra*.

[21]*Jove's tree*] Latin poets call the oak "Jove's tree." Shakespeare here seems to have borrowed direct from Golding's Ovid, *Met.*, I, 106: "The *acornes dropt* on ground from *Joves brode tree* in feelde."

[22]*"holla"*] stop! Cf. *Venus and Adonis*, 283–284: "What recketh he the rider's angry stir, His flattering 'Holla,' or his 'Stand, I say'?"

[23]*heart*] A common quibble between "heart" and "hart."

JAQ.   I thank you for your company; but, good faith, I had as lief have been myself alone.

ORL.   And so had I; but yet, for fashion sake,
I thank you too for your society.

JAQ.   God buy you:[24] let's meet as little as we can.

ORL.   I do desire we may be better strangers.

JAQ.   I pray you, mar no more trees with writing love-songs in their barks.

ORL.   I pray you, mar no moe[25] of my verses with reading them ill-favouredly.

JAQ.   Rosalind is your love's name?

ORL.   Yes, just.

JAQ.   I do not like her name.

ORL.   There was no thought of pleasing you when she was christened.

JAQ.   What stature is she of?

ORL.   Just as high as my heart.

JAQ.   You are full of pretty answers. Have you not been acquainted with goldsmiths' wives, and conned them out of rings?[26]

ORL.   Not so; but I answer you right painted cloth,[27] from whence you have studied your questions.

JAQ.   You have a nimble wit: I think 't was made of Atalanta's heels.[28] Will you sit down with me? and we two will rail against our mistress the world, and all our misery.

ORL.   I will chide no breather[29] in the world but myself, against whom I know most faults.

JAQ.   The worst fault you have is to be in love.

ORL.   'T is a fault I will not change for your best virtue. I am weary of you.

JAQ.   By my troth, I was seeking for a fool when I found you.

ORL.   He is drowned in the brook: look but in, and you shall see him.

JAQ.   There I shall see mine own figure.

ORL.   Which I take to be either a fool or a cipher.

---

[24]*God buy you*] *buy* is the reading of the Folios. It is equivalent to "God b' wi' you," *i.e.*, "God be with you." Jaques repeats it, IV, i, 28, *infra*, and Touchstone in V, iv, 37.

[25]*moe*] This is the reading of the First Folio, which the later Folios change to the modern *more*.

[26]*goldsmiths' . . . rings*] Goldsmiths dealt largely at the time in rings on which were inscribed posies or mottoes.

[27]*right painted cloth*] Painted cloth was the term applied to cheap tapestries, on which tales from scripture or from popular literature were represented together with moral maxims or mottoes. Labels bearing brief speeches were sometimes attached to the mouths of the figures. Such speeches Orlando charges Jaques with studying. Cf., for a similar construction, line 199, *supra*, "*speak sad brow* and true maid."

[28]*Atalanta's heels*] Cf. note on line 137, *supra* (see footnote 10).

[29]*breather*] Cf. *Sonnet* lxxxi, 12: "When all the *breathers of this world* are dead."

JAQ.   I'll tarry no longer with you: farewell, good Signior Love.

ORL.   I am glad of your departure: adieu, good Monsieur Melancholy.

                                                [Exit JAQUES.

ROS.   [*Aside to* CELIA] I will speak to him like a saucy lackey, and under that habit play the knave with him. Do you hear, forester?

ORL.   Very well: what would you?

ROS.   I pray you, what is 't o'clock?

ORL.   You should ask me what time o' day: there's no clock in the forest.

ROS.   Then there is no true lover in the forest; else sighing every minute and groaning every hour would detect the lazy foot of Time as well as a clock.

ORL.   And why not the swift foot of Time? had not that been as proper?

ROS.   By no means, sir: Time travels in divers paces with divers persons. I'll tell you who Time ambles withal, who Time trots withal, who Time gallops withal and who he stands still withal.

ORL.   I prithee, who doth he trot withal?

ROS.   Marry, he trots hard with a young maid between the contract of her marriage and the day it is solemnized: if the interim be but a se'nnight, Time's pace is so hard that it seems the length of seven year.

ORL.   Who ambles Time withal?

ROS.   With a priest that lacks Latin, and a rich man that hath not the gout; for the one sleeps easily because he cannot study, and the other lives merrily because he feels no pain; the one lacking the burden of lean and wasteful learning, the other knowing no burden of heavy tedious penury: these Time ambles withal.

ORL.   Who doth he gallop withal?

ROS.   With a thief to the gallows; for though he go as softly as foot can fall, he thinks himself too soon there.

ORL.   Who stays it still withal?

ROS.   With lawyers in the vacation; for they sleep between term and term and then they perceive not how Time moves.

ORL.   Where dwell you, pretty youth?

ROS.   With this shepherdess, my sister: here in the skirts of the forest, like fringe upon a petticoat.

ORL.   Are you native of this place?

ROS.   As the cony that you see dwell where she is kindled.

ORL.   Your accent is something finer than you could purchase in so removed a dwelling.

ROS.   I have been told so of many: but indeed an old religious uncle

of mine taught me to speak, who was in his youth an inland[30]
man; one that knew courtship too well, for there he fell in love. I
have heard him read many lectures against it, and I thank God I
am not a woman, to be touched with so many giddy offences as he
hath generally taxed their whole sex withal.

ORL. Can you remember any of the principal evils that he laid to the
charge of women?

ROS. There were none principal; they were all like one another as
half-pence are, every one fault seeming monstrous till his fellow-
fault came to match it.

ORL. I prithee, recount some of them.

ROS. No, I will not cast away my physic but on those that are sick.
There is a man haunts the forest, that abuses our young plants
with carving Rosalind on their barks; hangs odes upon hawthorns
and elegies on brambles; all, forsooth, deifying the name of
Rosalind: if I could meet that fancy-monger, I would give him
some good counsel, for he seems to have the quotidian of love[31]
upon him.

ORL. I am he that is so love-shaked: I pray you, tell me your remedy.

ROS. There is none of my uncle's marks upon you: he taught me how
to know a man in love; in which cage[32] of rushes I am sure you are
not prisoner.

ORL. What were his marks?

ROS. A lean cheek, which you have not; a blue eye[33] and sunken,
which you have not; an unquestionable[34] spirit, which you have
not; a beard neglected, which you have not; but I pardon you for
that, for simply your having in beard is a younger brother's revenue: then your hose should be ungartered, your bonnet unbanded,[35] your sleeve unbuttoned, your shoe untied and every
thing about you demonstrating a careless desolation; but you are
no such man; you are rather point-device in your accoutrements,
as loving yourself than seeming the lover of any other.

---

[30]*inland*] refined. Cf. II, vii, 96, *supra*, "*inland* bred."

[31]*fancy-monger . . . quotidian of love*] Cf. Lyly's *Euphues* (p. 66): "If euer she haue been
taken with the feuer of *fancie* [*i.e.*, love], she will help his ague, who by his *quotidian
fit* [*i.e.*, daily recurring paroxysm of fever] is conuerted into phrensie."

[32]*cage*] often used for "prison." Rosalind mockingly suggests that Orlando's prison has
rushes for bars, and is no serious impediment.

[33]*blue eye*] eye with a dark circle around it. Cf. *Tempest*, I, ii, 269: "*blue-eyed* hag."

[34]*unquestionable*] averse to conversation. Cf. *Hamlet*, I, iv, 43, "Thou comest in such a
questionable shape," where "questionable" means "inciting to conversation," "willing
to be conversed with."

[35]*bonnet unbanded*] Hats without hatbands were at the time regarded as signs of sloven-
liness in dress.

ORL.   Fair youth, I would I could make thee believe I love.

ROS.   Me believe it! you may as soon make her that you love believe
       it; which, I warrant, she is apter to do than to confess she does: that
       is one of the points in the which women still give the lie to their
       consciences. But, in good sooth, are you he that hangs the verses
       on the trees, wherein Rosalind is so admired?

ORL.   I swear to thee, youth, by the white hand of Rosalind, I am that
       he, that unfortunate he.

ROS.   But are you so much in love as your rhymes speak?

ORL.   Neither rhyme nor reason can express how much.

ROS.   Love is merely a madness; and, I tell you, deserves as well a dark
       house and a whip as madmen do:[36] and the reason why they are
       not so punished and cured is, that the lunacy is so ordinary that
       the whippers are in love too. Yet I profess curing it by counsel.

ORL.   Did you ever cure any so?

ROS.   Yes, one, and in this manner. He was to imagine me his love,
       his mistress; and I set him every day to woo me: at which time
       would I, being but a moonish youth, grieve, be effeminate,
       changeable, longing and liking; proud, fantastical, apish, shallow,
       inconstant, full of tears, full of smiles; for every passion something
       and for no passion truly any thing, as boys and women are for the
       most part cattle of this colour: would now like him, now loathe
       him; then entertain him, then forswear him; now weep for him,
       then spit at him; that I drave my suitor from his mad humour of
       love to a living[37] humour of madness; which was, to forswear the
       full stream of the world and to live in a nook merely monastic.
       And thus I cured him; and this way will I take upon me to wash
       your liver as clean as a sound sheep's heart, that there shall not be
       one spot of love in 't.

ORL.   I would not be cured, youth.

ROS.   I would cure you, if you would but call me Rosalind and come
       every day to my cote and woo me.

ORL.   Now, by the faith of my love, I will: tell me where it is.

ROS.   Go with me to it and I'll show it you: and by the way you shall
       tell me where in the forest you live. Will you go?

ORL.   With all my heart, good youth.

ROS.   Nay, you must call me Rosalind. Come, sister, will you go?
                                                        [*Exeunt.*

---

[36]*a dark house and a whip as madmen do*] this was the ordinary treatment of lunatics at
    the time. Cf. Malvolio's experience in *Tw. Night*, V, i.

[37]*mad . . . living*] unreasoning . . . real or actual.

SCENE III. *The Forest.*

Enter TOUCHSTONE *and* AUDREY; JAQUES *behind*

TOUCH.   Come apace, good Audrey: I will fetch up your goats, Audrey. And how, Audrey? am I the man yet? doth my simple feature content you?

AUD.   Your features![1] Lord warrant us! what features?

TOUCH.   I am here with thee and thy goats, as the most capricious poet, honest Ovid, was among the Goths.[2]

JAQ. [*Aside*] O knowledge ill-inhabited, worse than Jove in a thatched house![3]

TOUCH.   When a man's verses cannot be understood, nor a man's good wit seconded with the forward child, understanding, it strikes a man more dead than a great reckoning in a little room.[4] Truly, I would the gods had made thee poetical.

AUD.   I do not know what "poetical" is: is it honest in deed and word? is it a true thing?

TOUCH.   No, truly; for the truest poetry is the most feigning; and lovers are given to poetry, and what they swear in poetry may be said as lovers they do feign.

AUD.   Do you wish then that the gods had made me poetical?

TOUCH.   I do, truly; for thou swearest to me thou art honest: now, if thou wert a poet, I might have some hope thou didst feign.

AUD.   Would you not have me honest?

TOUCH.   No, truly, unless thou wert hard-favoured; for honesty coupled to beauty is to have honey a sauce to sugar.

JAQ. [*Aside*]   A material fool!

AUD.   Well, I am not fair; and therefore I pray the gods make me honest.

---

[1]*feature . . . features?*] This word was used in the three senses of (1) comeliness, (2) the build of the body, and (3) any part of the face. Touchstone apparently employs it in the first sense, and Audrey in the last. It is possible that there is an implied pun in Audrey's "what features?" on the word "faitor," *i.e.*, a villain, with which "feature" might easily be confused in pronunciation.

[2]*capricious . . . Goths*] "Capricious" is of course from the Latin "caper," a goat. "Goths" was so pronounced as to make the pun on "goats" quite clear. As a matter of history, Ovid was banished to the land of the Getae.

[3]*Jove . . . house*] The reference is to the thatched cottage of the peasants Philemon and Baucis, who entertained Jove unawares, according to Ovid, *Metam.*, VIII, 630, *seq.* There is another allusion to the story in *Much Ado*, II, i, 82–83: (D. Pedro.) "My visor is *Philemon's roof*; within the house is *Jove.* (Hero.) Why then, your visor should be *thatched.*"

[4]*great reckoning . . . room*] a heavy bill for a narrow accommodation.

TOUCH.   Truly, and to cast away honesty upon a foul slut were to put
     good meat into an unclean dish.

AUD.   I am not a slut, though I thank the gods I am foul.[5]

TOUCH.   Well, praised be the gods for thy foulness! sluttishness may
     come hereafter. But be it as it may be, I will marry thee, and to
     that end I have been with Sir Oliver Martext the vicar of the next
     village, who hath promised to meet me in this place of the forest
     and to couple us.

JAQ. [*Aside*]   I would fain see this meeting.

AUD.   Well, the gods give us joy!

TOUCH.   Amen. A man may, if he were of a fearful heart, stagger in
     this attempt; for here we have no temple but the wood, no assem-
     bly but horn-beasts. But what though? Courage! As horns are odi-
     ous, they are necessary. It is said, "many a man knows no end of
     his goods:" right; many a man has good horns, and knows no end
     of them. Well, that is the dowry of his wife; 't is none of his own
     getting. Horns?—even so:—poor men alone?[6] No, no; the noblest
     deer hath them as huge as the rascal. Is the single man therefore
     blessed? No: as a walled town is more worthier than a village, so is
     the forehead of a married man more honourable than the bare
     brow of a bachelor; and by how much defence[7] is better than no
     skill, by so much is a horn more precious than to want. Here
     comes Sir Oliver.

Enter SIR OLIVER MARTEXT

     Sir Oliver Martext, you are well met: will you dispatch us here
     under this tree, or shall we go with you to your chapel?

SIR OLI.   Is there none here to give the woman?

TOUCH.   I will not take her on gift of any man.

SIR OLI.   Truly, she must be given, or the marriage is not lawful.

JAQ.   Proceed, proceed: I'll give her.

TOUCH.   Good even, good Master What-ye-call 't: how do you, sir?
     You are very well met: God 'ild[8] you for your last company:
     I am very glad to see you: even a toy in hand here, sir: nay, pray
     be covered.

JAQ.   Will you be married, motley?

---

[5]*foul*] the word meant "plain" or "homely," more frequently than "base" or "dirty." It
     was the ordinary antithesis of "fair."

[6]*Horns? . . . alone?*] The Folios read: *hornes, euen so poore men alone*. Theobald intro-
     duced the punctuation adopted in the text, which makes the passage intelligible.

[7]*defence*] art of fencing. Cf. *Hamlet*, IV, vii, 97: "art and exercise in your *defence*".

[8]*God 'ild*] God yield or reward you. The phrase is repeated by Touchstone, V, iv, 53,
     infra. Cf. *Ant. and Cleop.*, IV, ii, 33: "And the *gods yield* you for 't."

Touch.   As the ox hath his bow,[9] sir, the horse his curb and the fal-
    con her bells, so man hath his desires; and as pigeons bill, so wed-
    lock would be nibbling.
Jaq.   And will you, being a man of your breeding, be married under a
    bush like a beggar? Get you to church, and have a good priest that
    can tell you what marriage is: this fellow will but join you together
    as they join wainscot; then one of you will prove a shrunk panel,
    and like green timber warp, warp.
Touch. [*Aside*]   I am not in the mind but I were better to be married
    of him than of another: for he is not like to marry me well; and not
    being well married, it will be a good excuse for me hereafter to
    leave my wife.
Jaq.   Go thou with me, and let me counsel thee.
Touch.   Come, sweet Audrey:
    We must be married, or we must live in bawdry.
    Farewell, good Master Oliver: not,—

> O sweet Oliver,[10]
> O brave Oliver,
> Leave me not behind thee:

but,—

> Wind away,[11]
> Begone, I say,
> I will not to wedding with thee.

[*Exeunt* Jaques, Touchstone, *and* Audrey.
Sir Oli.   'T is no matter: ne'er a fantastical knave of them all shall
    flout me out of my calling.   [*Exit.*

---

[9]*bow*] literally the bow-shaped piece of wood, which fitted into the yoke beneath the
    neck of oxen, but here apparently used for the yoke itself.
[10]*O sweet Oliver*] This was the opening line of a very popular ballad. Only the two lines
    ("O swete Olyuer Leaue me not behind the[e]") survive elsewhere—in the license for
    the publication of the ballad granted by the Stationers' Company to Richard Jones, 6
    August, 1584.
[11]*Wind away*] Wend away, depart.

SCENE IV. *The Forest.*

Enter ROSALIND *and* CELIA

ROS.   Never talk to me; I will weep.

CEL.   Do, I prithee; but yet have the grace to consider that tears do
       not become a man.

ROS.   But have I not cause to weep?

CEL.   As good cause as one would desire; therefore weep.

ROS.   His very hair is of the dissembling colour.

CEL.   Something browner than Judas's:[1] marry, his kisses are Judas's
       own children.

ROS.   I' faith, his hair is of a good colour.

CEL.   An excellent colour: your chestnut was ever the only colour.

ROS.   And his kissing is as full of sanctity as the touch of holy bread.

CEL.   He hath bought a pair of cast[2] lips of Diana: a nun of winter's
       sisterhood kisses not more religiously; the very ice of chastity is in
       them.

ROS.   But why did he swear he would come this morning, and comes
       not?

CEL.   Nay, certainly, there is no truth in him.

ROS.   Do you think so?

CEL.   Yes; I think he is not a pick-purse nor a horse-stealer; but for his
       verity in love, I do think him as concave as a covered goblet[3] or a
       worm-eaten nut.

ROS.   Not true in love?

CEL.   Yes, when he is in; but I think he is not in.

ROS.   You have heard him swear downright he was.

CEL.   "Was" is not "is": besides, the oath of a lover is no stronger than
       the word of a tapster; they are both the confirmer of false reckon-
       ings. He attends here in the forest on the Duke your father.

ROS.   I met the Duke yesterday and had much question with him: he
       asked me of what parentage I was; I told him, of as good as he; so
       he laughed and let me go. But what talk we of fathers, when there
       is such a man as Orlando?

CEL.   O, that's a brave man! he writes brave verses, speaks brave

---

[1]*browner than Judas's*] Judas was invariably credited with red hair and beard.

[2]*cast*] This is the reading of the First Folio, but the other Folios read *chast, i.e.,* chaste.
"Cast" was frequently applied to apparel in the sense of "cast off," "left off." This epithet is more in keeping with Celia's banter than the conventional "chaste," which the
mention of Diana naturally suggests.

[3]*concave . . . goblet*] a goblet when empty was kept covered.

words, swears brave oaths and breaks them bravely, quite traverse, athwart the heart of his lover; as a puisny[4] tilter, that spurs his horse but on one side, breaks his staff[5] like a noble goose: but all's brave that youth mounts and folly guides. Who comes here?

Enter CORIN

COR.   Mistress and master, you have oft inquired
      After the shepherd that complain'd of love,
      Who you saw sitting by me on the turf,
      Praising the proud disdainful shepherdess
      That was his mistress.
CEL.   Well, and what of him?
COR.   If you will see a pageant truly play'd,
      Between the pale complexion of true love
      And the red glow of scorn and proud disdain,
      Go hence a little and I shall conduct you,
      If you will mark it.
ROS.   O come, let us remove:
      The sight of lovers feedeth those in love.
      Bring us to this sight, and you shall say
      I'll prove a busy actor in their play.   [*Exeunt.*

SCENE V. *Another Part of the Forest.*

Enter SILVIUS *and* PHEBE

SIL.   Sweet Phebe, do not scorn me; do not, Phebe;
      Say that you love me not, but say not so
      In bitterness. The common executioner,
      Whose heart the accustom'd sight of death makes hard,
      Falls not the axe upon the humbled neck

---

[4]*puisny*] This is the old reading. Capell and later editors substitute the more modern form *puny*. It is used here not in the modern sense of "diminutive," but in that of "having the skill of a novice," "unskilled." The word comes through the French from the Latin "postnatus," "younger-born."

[5]*breaks his staff*] To break a staff in a tournament across ("quite traverse, athwart," l. 38) the body of an adversary, and not at push of point, was an accepted sign of clumsy incompetence. Cf. *All's Well*, II, i, 66, "Good faith, *across*," and *Much Ado*, V, i, 136–137: "this last [staff] was broke *cross*."

    But first begs pardon: will you sterner be
    Than he that dies and lives[1] by bloody drops?

Enter ROSALIND, CELIA, *and* CORIN, *behind*

PHE.   I would not be thy executioner:
    I fly thee, for I would not injure thee.
    Thou tell'st me there is murder in mine eye:
    'T is pretty, sure, and very probable,
    That eyes, that are the frail'st and softest things,
    Who shut their coward gates on atomies,[2]
    Should be call'd tyrants, butchers, murderers!
    Now I do frown on thee with all my heart;
    And if mine eyes can wound, now let them kill thee:
    Now counterfeit to swoon; why now fall down;
    Or if thou canst not, O, for shame, for shame,
    Lie not, to say mine eyes are murderers!
    Now show the wound mine eye hath made in thee:
    Scratch thee but with a pin, and there remains
    Some scar of it; lean but upon a rush,
    The cicatrice and capable impressure[3]
    Thy palm some moment keeps; but now mine eyes,
    Which I have darted at thee, hurt thee not,
    Nor, I am sure, there is no force in eyes
    That can do hurt.
SIL.   O dear Phebe,
    If ever,—as that ever may be near,—
    You meet in some fresh cheek the power of fancy,
    Then shall you know the wounds invisible
    That love's keen arrows make.
PHE.   But till that time
    Come not thou near me: and when that time comes,
    Afflict me with thy mocks, pity me not;
    As till that time I shall not pity thee.
ROS.   And why, I pray you? Who might be your mother,
    That you insult, exult, and all at once,
    Over the wretched? What though you have no beauty,—
    As, by my faith, I see no more in you
    Than without candle may go dark to bed,—

---

[1] *dies and lives*] This is a common inversion of the more ordinary phrase "lives and dies,"
i.e., subsists from the cradle to the grave. Cf. Barclay's *Ship of Fooles*, 1570, f. 67: "He
is a foole, and so shall he *dye and live*."
[2] *atomies*] Cf. III, ii, 217, *supra*.
[3] *The cicatrice . . . impressure*] The scar, or mark, and perceptible or sensible impression.

Must you be therefore proud and pitiless?
Why, what means this? Why do you look on me?
I see no more in you than in the ordinary
Of nature's sale-work.[4] 'Od's my little life,
I think she means to tangle my eyes too!
No, faith, proud mistress, hope not after it:
'T is not your inky brows, your black silk hair,
Your bugle[5] eyeballs, nor your cheek of cream,
That can entame my spirits to your worship.
You foolish shepherd, wherefore do you follow her,
Like foggy south, puffing with wind and rain?[6]
You are a thousand times a properer man
Than she a woman: 't is such fools as you
That makes the world full of ill-favour'd children:
'T is not her glass, but you, that flatters her;
And out of you she sees herself more proper
Than any of her lineaments can show her.
But, mistress, know yourself: down on your knees,
And thank heaven, fasting, for a good man's love:
For I must tell you friendly in your ear,
Sell when you can: you are not for all markets:
Cry the man mercy; love him; take his offer:
Foul is most foul, being foul to be a scoffer.[7]
So take her to thee, shepherd: fare you well.

PHE.   Sweet youth, I pray you, chide a year together:
       I had rather hear you chide than this man woo.

ROS.   He's fallen in love with your foulness and she'll fall in love with
       my anger. If it be so, as fast as she answers thee with frowning
       looks, I'll sauce her with bitter words. Why look you so upon me?

PHE.   For no ill will I bear you.

ROS.   I pray you, do not fall in love with me,
       For I am falser than vows made in wine:
       Besides, I like you not. If you will know my house,
       'T is at the tuft of olives here hard by.
       Will you go, sister? Shepherd, ply her hard.
       Come, sister. Shepherdess, look on him better,
       And be not proud: though all the world could see,

---

[4]*sale-work*] ready-made goods.
[5]*bugle*] black, from the tube-shaped glass bead, commonly of that colour, used to ornament wearing apparel.
[6]*foggy south . . . rain*] The foggy southern quarter of the sky, which generates wind and
rain. Cf. *Rom. and Jul.*, I, iv, 103: "the *dewdropping south*."
[7]*Foul . . . scoffer*] An ugly woman exaggerates her ugliness when she grows scornful.

None could be so abused in sight as he.
Come, to our flock.   [*Exeunt* ROSALIND, CELIA, *and* CORIN.

PHE.   Dead shepherd, now I find thy saw of might,
"Who ever loved that loved not at first sight?"[8]

SIL.   Sweet Phebe,—

PHE.   Ha, what say'st thou, Silvius?

SIL.   Sweet Phebe, pity me.

PHE.   Why, I am sorry for thee, gentle Silvius.

SIL.   Wherever sorrow is, relief would be:
If you do sorrow at my grief in love,
By giving love your sorrow and my grief
Were both extermined.

PHE.   Thou hast my love: is not that neighbourly?

SIL.   I would have you.

PHE.   Why, that were covetousness.
Silvius, the time was that I hated thee,
And yet it is not that I bear thee love;
But since that thou canst talk of love so well,
Thy company, which erst was irksome to me,
I will endure, and I'll employ thee too:
But do not look for further recompense
Than thine own gladness that thou art employ'd.

SIL.   So holy and so perfect is my love,
And I in such a poverty of grace,
That I shall think it a most plenteous crop
To glean the broken ears after the man
That the main harvest reaps: loose now and then
A scatter'd smile, and that I'll live upon.

PHE.   Know'st thou the youth that spoke to me erewhile?

SIL.   Not very well, but I have met him oft;
And he hath bought the cottage and the bounds
That the old carlot[9] once was master of.

PHE.   Think not I love him, though I ask for him;
'T is but a peevish boy; yet he talks well;
But what care I for words? yet words do well
When he that speaks them pleases those that hear.
It is a pretty youth: not very pretty:

---

[8]*Dead shepherd . . . sight*] The "dead shepherd" is Christopher Marlowe, who died in 1593. The line, "Who ever loved," etc., is from Marlowe's popular translation of the pseudo-Musaeus' Greek poem, *Hero and Leander* (Sest. I, 1. 176), first printed in 1598.

[9]*carlot*] Apparently a diminutive of "carl," churl, peasant. No other example of the word is found.

But, sure, he's proud, and yet his pride becomes him:
He'll make a proper man: the best thing in him
Is his complexion; and faster than his tongue
Did make offence his eye did heal it up.
He is not very tall; yet for his years he's tall:
His leg is but so so; and yet 't is well:
There was a pretty redness in his lip,
A little riper and more lusty red
Than that mix'd in his cheek; 't was just the difference
Betwixt the constant red and mingled damask.[10]
There be some women, Silvius, had they mark'd him
In parcels as I did, would have gone near
To fall in love with him: but, for my part,
I love him not nor hate him not; and yet
I have more cause to hate him than to love him:
For what had he to do to chide at me?
He said mine eyes were black and my hair black;
And, now I am remember'd, scorn'd at me:
I marvel why I answer'd not again:
But that's all one; omittance is no quittance.[11]
I'll write to him a very taunting letter,
And thou shalt bear it: wilt thou, Silvius?

SIL.   Phebe, with all my heart.

PHE.   I'll write it straight;
The matter 's in my head and in my heart:
I will be bitter with him and passing short.
Go with me, Sylvius.

                                                    [*Exeunt.*

---

[10]*mingled damask*] Cf. *Sonnet* cxxx, 5: "I have seen roses *damask'd*, red and white."
[11]*omittance is no quittance*] Milton, *Paradise Lost*, X, 53, varies this expression thus:
"Forbearance is no quittance." Quittance means discharge.

ACT IV.

Scene I. *The Forest.*

Enter ROSALIND, CELIA, *and* JAQUES

JAQUES.   I prithee, pretty youth, let me be better acquainted with thee.

ROS.   They say you are a melancholy fellow.

JAQ.   I am so; I do love it better than laughing.

ROS.   Those that are in extremity of either are abominable fellows,
and betray themselves to every modern censure[1] worse than
drunkards.

JAQ.   Why, 't is good to be sad and say nothing.

ROS.   Why then, 't is good to be a post.

JAQ.   I have neither the scholar's melancholy, which is emulation; nor
the musician's, which is fantastical; nor the courtier's, which is
proud; nor the soldier's, which is ambitious; nor the lawyer's,
which is politic; nor the lady's, which is nice; nor the lover's,
which is all these: but it is a melancholy of mine own, com-
pounded of many simples, extracted from many objects; and indeed the sundry contemplation of my travels, in which my often
rumination wraps me in a most humorous sadness.

ROS.   A traveller! By my faith, you have great reason to be sad: I fear
you have sold your own lands to see other men's; then, to have
seen much, and to have nothing, is to have rich eyes[2] and poor
hands.

JAQ.   Yes, I have gained my experience.

ROS.   And your experience makes you sad: I had rather have a fool to
make me merry than experience to make me sad; and to travel for
it too!

Enter ORLANDO

[1]*modern censure*] common, ordinary judgment.
[2]*rich eyes*] Cf. *All's Well*, V, iii, 16–17: "the survey Of *richest eyes.*"

287

ORL. Good day and happiness, dear Rosalind!

JAQ. Nay, then, God buy you,[3] an you talk in blank verse. [*Exit.*

ROS. Farewell, Monsieur Traveller: look you lisp and wear strange suits; disable all the benefits of your own country; be out of love with your nativity and almost chide God for making you that countenance you are; or I will scarce think you have swam in a gondola.[4] Why, how now, Orlando! where have you been all this while? You a lover! An you serve me such another trick, never come in my sight more.

ORL. My fair Rosalind, I come within an hour of my promise.

ROS. Break an hour's promise in love! He that will divide a minute into a thousand parts, and break but a part of the thousandth part of a minute in the affairs of love, it may be said of him that Cupid hath clapped him o' the shoulder, but I'll warrant him heart-whole.

ORL. Pardon me, dear Rosalind.

ROS. Nay, an you be so tardy, come no more in my sight: I had as lief be wooed of a snail.

ORL. Of a snail?

ROS. Ay, of a snail; for though he comes slowly, he carries his house on his head; a better jointure, I think, than you make a woman: besides, he brings his destiny with him.

ORL. What's that?

ROS. Why, horns, which such as you are fain to be beholding to your wives for: but he comes armed in his fortune and prevents the slander of his wife.

ORL. Virtue is no horn-maker; and my Rosalind is virtuous.

ROS. And I am your Rosalind.

CEL. It pleases him to call you so; but he hath a Rosalind of a better leer than you.

ROS. Come, woo me, woo me; for now I am in a holiday humour and like enough to consent. What would you say to me now, an I were your very very Rosalind?

ORL. I would kiss before I spoke.

ROS. Nay, you were better speak first; and when you were gravelled for lack of matter, you might take occasion to kiss. Very good orators, when they are out, they will spit; and for lovers lacking—God warn us!—matter, the cleanliest shift is to kiss.

ORL. How if the kiss be denied?

ROS. Then she puts you to entreaty and there begins new matter.

[3]*God buy you*] Cf. III, ii, 242, *supra.*

[4]*swam in a gondola*] been on a visit to Venice, the fashionable goal of contemporary travel.

ORL.   Who could be out, being before his beloved mistress?

ROS.   Marry, that should you, if I were your mistress, or I should think my honesty ranker than my wit.

ORL.   What, of my suit?

ROS.   Not out of your apparel, and yet out of your suit. Am not I your Rosalind?

ORL.   I take some joy to say you are, because I would be talking of her.

ROS.   Well, in her person, I say I will not have you.

ORL.   Then in mine own person I die.

ROS.   No, faith, die by attorney.[5] The poor world is almost six thousand years old, and in all this time there was not any man died in his own person, videlicet, in a love-cause. Troilus had his brains dashed out with a Grecian club; yet he did what he could to die before, and he is one of the patterns of love. Leander, he would have lived many a fair year, though Hero had turned nun, if it had not been for a hot midsummer night; for, good youth, he went but forth to wash him in the Hellespont and being taken with the cramp was drowned: and the foolish chroniclers[6] of that age found it was "Hero of Sestos." But these are all lies: men have died from time to time and worms have eaten them, but not for love.

ORL.   I would not have my right Rosalind of this mind; for, I protest, her frown might kill me.

ROS.   By this hand, it will not kill a fly. But come, now I will be your Rosalind in a more coming-on disposition, and ask me what you will, I will grant it.

ORL.   Then love me, Rosalind.

ROS.   Yes, faith, will I, Fridays and Saturdays and all.

ORL.   And wilt thou have me?

ROS.   Ay, and twenty such.

ORL.   What sayest thou?

ROS.   Are you not good?

ORL.   I hope so.

ROS.   Why then, can one desire too much of a good thing? Come, sister, you shall be the priest and marry us. Give me your hand, Orlando. What do you say, sister?

ORL.   Pray thee, marry us.

CEL.   I cannot say the words.

ROS.   You must begin, "Will you, Orlando—"

---

[5]*by attorney*] by deputy. Cf. *Rich. III*, V, iii, 83: "I, *by attorney*, bless thee from thy mother."

[6]*chroniclers*] This is the reading of the Folios. It was needlessly changed by Hanmer to *coroners*, which the use of the word "found," *i.e.* "gave the finding or verdict," only speciously supports.

CEL.   Go to. Will you, Orlando, have to wife this Rosalind?

ORL.   I will.

ROS.   Ay, but when?

ORL.   Why now; as fast as she can marry us.

ROS.   Then you must say "I take thee, Rosalind, for wife."

ORL.   I take thee, Rosalind, for wife.

ROS.   I might ask you for your commission; but I do take thee, Orlando, for my husband: there's a girl goes before the priest;[7] and certainly a woman's thought runs before her actions.

ORL.   So do all thoughts; they are winged.

ROS.   Now tell me how long you would have her after you have possessed her.

ORL.   For ever and a day.

ROS.   Say "a day," without the "ever." No, no, Orlando, men are April when they woo, December when they wed: maids are May when they are maids, but the sky changes when they are wives. I will be more jealous of thee than a Barbary cock-pigeon[8] over his hen, more clamorous than a parrot against rain, more new-fangled[9] than an ape, more giddy in my desires than a monkey: I will weep for nothing, like Diana in the fountain,[10] and I will do that when you are disposed to be merry; I will laugh like a hyen, and that when thou art inclined to sleep.

ORL.   But will my Rosalind do so?

ROS.   By my life, she will do as I do.

ORL.   O, but she is wise.

ROS.   Or else she could not have the wit to do this: the wiser, the way-warder: make the doors upon a woman's wit and it will out at the casement; shut that and 't will out at the key-hole; stop that, 't will fly with the smoke out at the chimney.

ORL.   A man that had a wife with such a wit, he might say "Wit, whither wilt?"[11]

ROS.   Nay, you might keep that check for it till you met your wife's wit going to your neighbour's bed.

ORL.   And what wit could wit have to excuse that?

---

[7]*there 's a girl . . . priest*] Rosalind admits that the bride is anticipating the part in the ceremony that belongs to Celia, who acts as priest.

[8]*Barbary cock-pigeon*] This bird, now known as a "barb," is of black colour, and was introduced from North Africa. Cf. *2 Hen. IV*, II, iv, 94: "*Barbary* hen."

[9]*new-fangled*] fond of what is new. Cf. Cotgrave's *Fr.-Eng. Dict.*: "Fantastique, humorous, *new-fangled*, giddie, skittish."

[10]*like . . . fountain*] A possible allusion to an "alabaster image of Diana," which, according to Stow, was set up near the cross at West Cheap, London, with "water conveyed from the Thames prilling from her naked breast."

[11]*Wit, whither wilt?*] Cf. I, ii, 51, *supra*.

Ros.   Marry, to say she came to seek you there. You shall never take
  her without her answer, unless you take her without her tongue.
  O, that woman that cannot make her fault her husband's occasion,[12] let her never nurse her child herself, for she will breed it
  like a fool!

ORL.   For these two hours, Rosalind, I will leave thee.

Ros.   Alas, dear love, I cannot lack thee two hours!

ORL.   I must attend the Duke at dinner: by two o'clock I will be with
  thee again.

Ros.   Ay, go your ways, go your ways; I knew what you would prove:
  my friends told me as much, and I thought no less: that flattering
  tongue of yours won me: 't is but one cast away, and so, come,
  death! Two o'clock is your hour?

ORL.   Ay, sweet Rosalind.

Ros.   By my troth, and in good earnest, and so God mend me, and by
  all pretty oaths that are not dangerous, if you break one jot of your
  promise or come one minute behind your hour, I will think you
  the most pathetical[13] break-promise, and the most hollow lover,
  and the most unworthy of her you call Rosalind, that may be chosen out of the gross band of the unfaithful: therefore beware my
  censure and keep your promise.

ORL.   With no less religion than if thou wert indeed my Rosalind: so
  adieu.

Ros.   Well, Time is the old justice that examines all such offenders,
  and let Time try: adieu.   [*Exit* ORLANDO.

CEL.   You have simply misused our sex in your love-prate: we must
  have your doublet and hose plucked over your head, and show the
  world what the bird hath done to her own nest.

Ros.   O coz, coz, coz, my pretty little coz, that thou didst know how
  many fathom deep I am in love! But it cannot be sounded: my affection hath an unknown bottom, like the bay of Portugal.[14]

CEL.   Or rather, bottomless; that as fast as you pour affection in, it
  runs out.

Ros.   No, that same wicked bastard of Venus that was begot of
  thought, conceived of spleen, and born of madness, that blind

---

[12]*make . . . occasion*] represent her fault to be occasioned by her husband, or make her
  fault the opportunity of taking advantage of her husband. The reading, though often
  questioned, is probably right.
[13]*pathetical*] The word, though often meaning "impassioned," or "persuasive," seems to
  acquire here a touch of scorn, and is almost equivalent to "pitiful." Cf. *L. L. L.*, IV, i,
  141: "A most *pathetical* wit."
[14]*bay of Portugal*] Sailors bestowed this title on the sea off the Portuguese coast between
  Oporto and Cintra. The water there attained a depth of 1400 fathoms within 42 miles
  of the shore.

rascally boy that abuses every one's eyes because his own are out,
let him be judge how deep I am in love. I'll tell thee, Aliena, I cannot be out of the sight of Orlando: I'll go find a shadow[15] and sigh
till he come.

CEL.   And I'll sleep.   [*Exeunt.*

SCENE II. *The Forest.*

Enter JAQUES, Lords, *and* Foresters

JAQ.   Which is he that killed the deer?

A LORD.   Sir; it was I.

JAQ.   Let 's present him to the Duke, like a Roman conqueror; and it
        would do well to set the deer's horns upon his head, for a branch
        of victory. Have you no song, forester, for this purpose?

FOR.   Yes, sir.

JAQ.   Sing it: 't is no matter how it be in tune, so it make noise enough.

SONG

FOR.   What shall he have that kill'd the deer?
                    His leather skin and horns to wear.
                        Then sing him home:[1]

                                [*The rest shall bear this burden.*
                    Take thou no scorn to wear the horn;
                    It was a crest ere thou wast born:
                        Thy father's father wore it,
                        And thy father bore it:
                    The horn, the horn, the lusty horn
                    Is not a thing to laugh to scorn.   [*Exeunt.*

---

[15]*shadow*] shade, or shady place. Cf. *Tempest*, IV, i, 66–67: "Broom-groves, Whose
  shadow the dismissed bachelor loves."

[1]*Then sing him home:*] In the Folios these words, together with those here printed as the
appended stage direction, form a single line of the song. Theobald first made the
change which is adopted here. A few editors read, *They sing him home,* and include
these words along with those which follow in the stage direction. The song appears
with music in John Hilton's *Catch that catch can,* 1652. The particular words with
which this note deals are all omitted. Hilton is doubtfully identified with a famous musician of the same name, who was Shakespeare's contemporary.

SCENE III. *The Forest.*

Enter ROSALIND *and* CELIA

ROS.   How say you now? Is it not past two o'clock? and here much
     Orlando![1]

CEL.   I warrant you, with pure love and troubled brain, he hath ta'en his
     bow and arrows and is gone forth to sleep. Look, who comes here.

Enter SILVIUS

SIL.   My errand is to you, fair youth;
     My gentle Phebe bid me give you this:
     I know not the contents: but, as I guess
     By the stern brow and waspish action
     Which she did use as she was writing of it,
     It bears an angry tenour: pardon me;
     I am but as a guiltless messenger.

ROS.   Patience herself would startle at this letter
     And play the swaggerer; bear this, bear all:
     She says I am not fair, that I lack manners;
     She calls me proud, and that she could not love me,
     Were man as rare as phœnix.[2] 'Od's my will!
     Her love is not the hare that I do hunt:
     Why writes she so to me? Well, shepherd, well,
     This is a letter of your own device.

SIL.   No, I protest, I know not the contents:
     Phebe did write it.

ROS.   Come, come, you are a fool,
     And turn'd into the extremity of love.
     I saw her hand: she has a leathern hand,
     A freestone-colour'd[3] hand; I verily did think
     That her old gloves were on, but 't was her hands:
     She has a huswife's hand; but that's no matter:
     I say she never did invent this letter;
     This is a man's invention and his hand.

---

[1]*and here much Orlando*] An ironical use of "much," implying just the opposite of what
the word means: "we find much of, a great deal of, Orlando here," *i.e.*, "he is not here
at all." Cf. the colloquialism, "I shall get much [*verè*—nothing] by that."

[2]*as rare as phœnix*] The phœnix is commonly described in classical poetry as unique.
Cf. Ovid's *Amores*, II, vi, 54, "vivax phœnix, *unica* semper avis." Cf. *Tempest*, III, iii,
23: "There is one tree, the phœnix' throne; *one phœnix*."

[3]*freestone-colour'd*] brownish yellow, like bath brick.

SIL.   Sure, it is hers.

ROS.   Why, 't is a boisterous and a cruel style,
      A style for challengers; why, she defies me,
      Like Turk to Christian: women's gentle brain
      Could not drop forth such giant-rude invention,
      Such Ethiope[4] words, blacker in their effect
      Than in their countenance. Will you hear the letter?

SIL.   So please you, for I never heard it yet;
      Yet heard too much of Phebe's cruelty.

ROS.   She Phebes me: mark how the tyrant writes.

[*Reads*]   Art thou god to shepherd turn'd,
                    That a maiden's heart hath burn'd?

      Can a woman rail thus?

SIL.   Call you this railing?

ROS.   [*reads*]

                  Why, thy godhead laid apart,
                  Warr'st thou with a woman's heart?

      Did you ever hear such railing?

                  Whiles the eye of man did woo me,
                  That could do no vengeance to me.

      Meaning me a beast.

                  If the scorn of your bright eyne
                  Have power to raise such love in mine,
                  Alack, in me what strange effect
                  Would they work in mild aspect![5]
                  Whiles you chid me, I did love;
                  How then might your prayers move!
                  He that brings this love to thee
                  Little knows this love in me:
                  And by him seal up thy mind;[6]
                  Whether that thy youth and kind[7]
                  Will the faithful offer take
                  Of me and all that I can make;
                  Or else by him my love deny,
                  And then I'll study how to die.

---

[4]*Ethiope*] this is the only example of the adjectival use of this word, which is frequently
found elsewhere as a noun, meaning "a swarthy person."

[5]*aspect*] This word, which is always accented on the last syllable in Shakespeare, is here
an astrological term denoting the appearance of the planets. Cf. *Wint. Tale*, II, i,
106–107: "the heavens look With an *aspéct* more favourable."

[6]*seal up thy mind*] seal up your decision, and send it back by him.

[7]*youth and kind*] youth and nature, the natural sentiment of youth.

SIL.   Call you this chiding?
CEL.   Alas, poor shepherd!
ROS.   Do you pity him? no, he deserves no pity. Wilt thou love such
     a woman? What, to make thee an instrument and play false strains
     upon thee! not to be endured! Well, go your way to her, for I see
     love hath made thee a tame snake, and say this to her: that if she
     love me, I charge her to love thee; if she will not, I will never have
     her unless thou entreat for her. If you be a true lover, hence, and
     not a word; for here comes more company.   [*Exit* SILVIUS.

Enter OLIVER

OLI.   Good morrow, fair ones: pray you, if you know,
     Where in the purlieus of this forest stands
     A sheep-cote fenced about with olive-trees?
CEL.   West of this place, down in the neighbour bottom:
     The rank of osiers by the murmuring stream
     Left on your right hand brings you to the place.
     But at this hour the house doth keep itself;
     There 's none within.
OLI.   If that an eye may profit by a tongue,
     Then should I know you by description;
     Such garments and such years: "The boy is fair,
     Of female favour, and bestows himself[8]
     Like a ripe sister:[9] the woman low,
     And browner than her brother." Are not you
     The owner of the house I did inquire for?
CEL.   It is no boast, being ask'd, to say we are.
OLI.   Orlando doth commend him to you both,
     And to that youth he calls his Rosalind
     He sends this bloody napkin.[10] Are you he?
ROS.   I am: what must we understand by this?
OLI.   Some of my shame; if you will know of me
     What man I am, and how, and why, and where
     This handkercher was stain'd.
CEL.   I pray you, tell it.
OLI.   When last the young Orlando parted from you

---

[8]*bestows himself*] deports himself, behaves, as in 2 *Hen. IV*, II, ii, 163–164: "How might
we see Falstaff *bestow himself* to-night in his true colours."

[9]*Like a ripe sister*] This, the original reading, leaves the line metrically imperfect. A syllable seems lacking after "sister." But such an irregularity is not uncommon. With a
view to correcting the metre, and removing the ambiguity of "ripe sister," *right forester*"
has been substituted. "Like a ripe sister" may be correct, and may mean that Rosalind
treats Celia like a mature, elder kinswoman.

[10]*napkin*] This is the "handkercher" or "handkerchief" of line 96, *infra*.

He left a promise to return again
Within an hour, and pacing through the forest,
Chewing the food of sweet and bitter fancy,
Lo, what befel! he threw his eye aside,
And mark what object did present itself:
Under an oak,[11] whose boughs were moss'd with age
And high top bald with dry antiquity,
A wretched ragged man, o'ergrown with hair,
Lay sleeping on his back: about his neck
A green and gilded snake had wreathed itself,
Who with her head nimble in threats approach'd
The opening of his mouth; but suddenly,
Seeing Orlando, it unlink'd itself,
And with indented glides[12] did slip away
Into a bush: under which bush's shade
A lioness, with udders all drawn dry,
Lay couching, head on ground, with catlike watch,
When that the sleeping man should stir; for 't is
The royal disposition of that beast
To prey on nothing that doth seem as dead:
This seen, Orlando did approach the man
And found it was his brother, his elder brother.

CEL. O, I have heard him speak of that same brother;
And he did render him the most unnatural
That lived amongst men.

OLI.   And well he might so do,
For well I know he was unnatural.

ROS. But, to Orlando: did he leave him there,
Food to the suck'd and hungry lioness?

OLI. Twice did he turn his back and purposed so;
But kindness, nobler ever than revenge,
And nature, stronger than his just occasion,[13]
Made him give battle to the lioness,
Who quickly fell before him: in which hurtling
From miserable slumber I awaked.

CEL. Are you his brother?

ROS.   Was 't you he rescued?

---

[11]*oak*] The Folios insert *old* before *oak,* but metrical considerations almost compel its
omission, which Pope first proposed.

[12]*indented glides*] sinuous glidings. Cf. "*indented* wave" of the movement of the serpent
in Milton's *Paradise Lost*, IX, 496.

[13]*just occasion*] the just ground which would have warranted Orlando in abandoning
his brother.

CEL.   Was 't you that did so oft contrive to kill him?
OLI.   'T was I; but 't is not I: I do not shame
 To tell you what I was, since my conversion
 So sweetly tastes, being the thing I am.
ROS.   But, for the bloody napkin?
OLI.   By and by.
 When from the first to last betwixt us two
 Tears our recountments had most kindly bathed,
 As[14] how I came into that desert place;
 In brief, he led me to the gentle Duke,
 Who gave me fresh array and entertainment,
 Committing me unto my brother's love;
 Who led me instantly unto his cave,
 There stripp'd himself, and here upon his arm
 The lioness had torn some flesh away,
 Which all this while had bled; and now he fainted
 And cried, in fainting, upon Rosalind.
 Brief, I recover'd him, bound up his wound;
 And, after some small space, being strong at heart,
 He sent me hither, stranger as I am,
 To tell this story, that you might excuse
 His broken promise, and to give this napkin,
 Dyed in his blood, unto the shepherd youth
 That he in sport doth call his Rosalind.
          [ROSALIND *swoons.*

CEL.   Why, how now, Ganymede! sweet Ganymede!
OLI.   Many will swoon when they do look on blood.
CEL.   There is more in it. Cousin Ganymede!
OLI.   Look, he recovers.
ROS.   I would I were at home.
CEL.   We'll lead you thither.
 I pray you, will you take him by the arm?
OLI.   Be of good cheer, youth: you a man! you lack a man's heart.
ROS.   I do so, I confess it. Ah, sirrah, a body would think this was well
 counterfeited! I pray you, tell your brother how well I counter-
 feited. Heigh-ho!
OLI.   This was not counterfeit: there is too great testimony in your
 complexion that it was a passion of earnest.
ROS.   Counterfeit, I assure you.
OLI.   Well then, take a good heart and counterfeit to be a man.
ROS.   So I do: but, i' faith, I should have been a woman by right.

---

[14]As] As for instance.

CEL.   Come, you look paler and paler: pray you, draw homewards.
      Good sir, go with us.
OLI.   That will I, for I must bear answer back
      How you excuse my brother, Rosalind.
ROS.   I shall devise something: but, I pray you, commend my coun-
      terfeiting to him. Will you go?   [*Exeunt.*

ACT V.

SCENE I. *The Forest.*

Enter TOUCHSTONE *and* AUDREY

TOUCHSTONE.   We shall find a time, Audrey; patience, gentle Audrey.

AUD.   Faith, the priest was good enough, for all the old gentleman's saying.

TOUCH.   A most wicked Sir Oliver, Audrey, a most vile Martext. But, Audrey, there is a youth here in the forest lays claim to you.

AUD.   Ay, I know who 't is: he hath no interest in me in the world: here comes the man you mean.

TOUCH.   It is meat and drink[1] to me to see a clown: by my troth, we that have good wits have much to answer for; we shall be flouting; we cannot hold.[2]

Enter WILLIAM

WILL.   Good even, Audrey.

AUD.   God ye good even, William.

WILL.   And good even to you, sir.

TOUCH.   Good even, gentle friend. Cover thy head, cover thy head; nay, prithee, be covered. How old are you, friend?

WILL.   Five and twenty, sir.

TOUCH.   A ripe age. Is thy name William?

WILL.   William, sir.

TOUCH.   A fair name. Wast born i' the forest here?

WILL.   Ay, sir, I thank God.

TOUCH.   "Thank God;" a good answer. Art rich?

WILL.   Faith, sir, so so.

---

[1]*meat and drink*] a proverbial expression implying something very congenial. Cf. *M. Wives*, I, i, 268: "That's *meat and drink* to me."

[2]*hold*] restrain (*sc.* our wit).

299

TOUCH. "So so" is good, very good, very excellent good; and yet it is not; it is but so so. Art thou wise?

WILL. Ay, sir, I have a pretty wit.

TOUCH. Why, thou sayest well. I do now remember a saying, "The fool doth think he is wise, but the wise man knows himself to be a fool." The heathen philosopher, when he had a desire to eat a grape, would open his lips when he put it into his mouth; meaning thereby that grapes were made to eat and lips to open. You do love this maid?

WILL. I do, sir.

TOUCH. Give me your hand. Art thou learned?

WILL. No, sir.

TOUCH. Then learn this of me: to have, is to have; for it is a figure in rhetoric that drink, being poured out of a cup into a glass, by filling the one doth empty the other; for all your writers do consent that ipse is he: now, you are not ipse, for I am he.

WILL. Which he, sir?

TOUCH. He, sir, that must marry this woman. Therefore, you clown, abandon,—which is in the vulgar leave,—the society,—which in the boorish is company,—of this female,—which in the common is woman; which together is, abandon the society of this female, or, clown, thou perishest; or, to thy better understanding, diest; or, to wit, I kill thee, make thee away, translate thy life into death, thy liberty into bondage: I will deal in poison with thee, or in bastinado,[3] or in steel; I will bandy[4] with thee in faction; I will o'er-run thee with policy; I will kill thee a hundred and fifty ways: therefore tremble, and depart.

AUD. Do, good William.

WILL. God rest you merry, sir.   [*Exit.*

Enter CORIN

COR. Our master and mistress seeks you; come, away, away!

TOUCH. Trip, Audrey! trip, Audrey! I attend, I attend.   [*Exeunt.*

---

[3]*bastinado*] cudgelling. Cf. Florio's *Ital.-Eng. Dict.:* "A *bastonado*, or cudgell-blow."
[4]*bandy*] The word literally means "to toss from side to side like a tennis-ball"; but it is here synonymous with "contend" or "fight."

SCENE II. *The Forest.*

Enter ORLANDO *and* OLIVER

ORL.   Is 't possible that on so little acquaintance you should like her? that but seeing you should love her? and loving woo? and, wooing, she should grant? and will you persever to enjoy her?

OLI.   Neither call the giddiness of it in question, the poverty of her, the small acquaintance, my sudden wooing, nor her sudden consenting; but say with me, I love Aliena; say with her that she loves me; consent with both that we may enjoy each other: it shall be to your good; for my father's house and all the revenue that was old Sir Rowland's will I estate upon you, and here live and die a shepherd.

ORL.   You have my consent. Let your wedding be to-morrow: thither will I invite the Duke and all's contented followers. Go you and prepare Aliena; for look you, here comes my Rosalind.

Enter ROSALIND

ROS.   God save you, brother.

OLI.   And you, fair sister.[1]   [*Exit.*

ROS.   O, my dear Orlando, how it grieves me to see thee wear thy heart in a scarf![2]

ORL.   It is my arm.

ROS.   I thought thy heart had been wounded with the claws of a lion.

ORL.   Wounded it is, but with the eyes of a lady.

ROS.   Did your brother tell you how I counterfeited to swoon when he showed me your handkercher?

ORL.   Ay, and greater wonders than that.

ROS.   O, I know where you are: nay, 't is true: there was never any thing so sudden but the fight of two rams, and Caesar's thrasonical brag of "I came, saw, and overcame:" for your brother and my sister no sooner met but they looked; no sooner looked but they loved; no sooner loved but they sighed; no sooner sighed but they asked one another the reason; no sooner knew the reason but they sought the remedy: and in these degrees have they made a pair of stairs to marriage which they will climb incontinent, or

---

[1]*fair sister*] Rosalind is still disguised, and, as far as is known, Oliver believes her to be a boy. But he enters into Orlando's humour, and calls her "sister" in the spirit of Act IV, Sc. i. Cf. IV, iii, 86, where Oliver has already likened the boy Rosalind to "a *ripe sister.*"

[2]*in a scarf*] in a sling.

else be incontinent before marriage: they are in the very wrath of love and they will together; clubs cannot part them.

ORL. They shall be married to-morrow, and I will bid the Duke to the nuptial.[3] But, O, how bitter a thing it is to look into happiness through another man's eyes! By so much the more shall I to-morrow be at the height of heart-heaviness, by how much I shall think my brother happy in having what he wishes for.

ROS. Why then, to-morrow I cannot serve your turn for Rosalind?

ORL. I can live no longer by thinking.

ROS. I will weary you then no longer with idle talking. Know of me then, for now I speak to some purpose, that I know you are a gentleman of good conceit: I speak not this that you should bear a good opinion of my knowledge, insomuch I say I know you are; neither do I labour for a greater esteem than may in some little measure draw a belief from you, to do yourself good and not to grace me. Believe then, if you please, that I can do strange things: I have, since I was three year old, conversed with a magician, most profound in his art and yet not damnable. If you do love Rosalind so near the heart as your gesture cries it out, when your brother marries Aliena, shall you marry her: I know into what straits of fortune she is driven; and it is not impossible to me, if it appear not inconvenient to you, to set her before your eyes to-morrow human as she is and without any danger.

ORL. Speakest thou in sober meanings?

ROS. By my life, I do; which I tender dearly, though I say I am a magician.[4] Therefore, put you in your best array; bid your friends; for if you will be married to-morrow, you shall; and to Rosalind, if you will.

Enter SILVIUS *and* PHEBE

Look, here comes a lover of mine and a lover of hers.

PHE. Youth, you have done me much ungentleness,
To show the letter that I writ to you.

ROS. I care not if I have: it is my study
To seem despiteful and ungentle to you:
You are there followed by a faithful shepherd;
Look upon him, love him; he worships you.

PHE. Good shepherd, tell this youth what 't is to love.

SIL. It is to be all made of sighs and tears;

---

[3]*nuptial*] Shakespeare invariably uses the singular. The plural, "nuptials," is a more modern usage. Conversely he employs "funerals" where we use "funeral."

[4]*By my life . . . magician*] By statute law, 5 Eliz., Cap. 16, practisers of witchcraft were liable to punishment by death.

        And so am I for Phebe.

PHE.   And I for Ganymede.

ORL.   And I for Rosalind.

ROS.   And I for no woman.

SIL.   It is to be all made of faith and service;
        And so am I for Phebe.

PHE.   And I for Ganymede.

ORL.   And I for Rosalind.

ROS.   And I for no woman.

SIL.   It is to be all made of fantasy,
        All made of passion, and all made of wishes;
        All adoration, duty, and observance,[5]
        All humbleness, all patience, and impatience,
        All purity, all trial, all observance;
        And so am I for Phebe.

PHE.   And so am I for Ganymede.

ORL.   And so am I for Rosalind.

ROS.   And so am I for no woman.

PHE.   If this be so, why blame you me to love you?

SIL.   If this be so, why blame you me to love you?

ORL.   If this be so, why blame you me to love you?

ROS.   Why do you speak too, "Why blame you me to love you?"

ORL.   To her that is not here, nor doth not hear.

ROS.   Pray you, no more of this; 't is like the howling of Irish wolves against the moon.[6] [*To Sil.*] I will help you, if I can: [*To Phe.*] I would love you, if I could. To-morrow meet me all together. [*To Phe.*] I will marry you, if ever I marry woman, and I'll be married to-morrow: [*To Orl.*] I will satisfy you, if ever I satisfied man, and you shall be married to-morrow: [*To Sil.*] I will content you, if what pleases you contents you, and you shall be married to-morrow. [*To Orl.*] As you love Rosalind, meet: [*To Sil.*] as you love Phebe, meet: and as I love no woman, I'll meet. So, fare you well: I have left you commands.

SIL.   I'll not fail, if I live.

PHE.   Nor I.

ORL.   Nor I.   [*Exeunt.*

---

[5] *observance*] The repetition of this word at the end of the next line but one below suggests that one or other of the two "observances" is wrongly printed. The word seems somewhat more closely connected with "adoration" and "duty" as here, than with "purity" and "trial" as in line 91. Malone suggested *obedience* in the second place. Others prefer Ritson's conjecture of *obeisance*.

[6] *howling . . . moon*] Cf. Lodge's *Romance of Rosalynd*: "Thou barkest with the *wolves* of Syria *against the moone*." Wolves abounded in Ireland, and the substitution of the epithet *Irish* for *of Syria* is quite natural.

SCENE III. *The Forest.*

Enter TOUCHSTONE *and* AUDREY

TOUCH.   To-morrow is the joyful day, Audrey; to-morrow will we be
   married.

AUD.   I do desire it with all my heart; and I hope it is no dishonest desire to desire to be a woman of the world.[1] Here come two of the
   banished Duke's pages.

Enter two Pages

FIRST PAGE.   Well met, honest gentleman.

TOUCH.   By my troth, well met. Come, sit, sit, and a song.

SEC. PAGE.   We are for you: sit i' the middle.

FIRST PAGE.   Shall we clap into 't roundly,[2] without hawking or spit-
   ting or saying we are hoarse, which are the only prologues to a bad
   voice?

SEC. PAGE.   I' faith, i' faith; and both in a tune, like two gipsies on a
   horse.

SONG

It was a lover and his lass,[3]
  With a hey, and a ho, and a hey nonino,
That o'er the green corn-field did pass
  In the spring time, the only pretty ring time,[4]

When birds do sing, hey ding a ding, ding:
Sweet lovers love the spring.

Between the acres of the rye,[5]
  With a hey, and a ho, and a hey nonino,
These pretty country folks would lie,
  In spring time, &c.

[1] *a woman of the world*] a married woman. Cf. *Much Ado*, II, i, 287. In *All's Well*, I, iii,
18, "To go *to the world*" means "to get married."

[2] *clap into 't roundly*] strike up the song straight away. Cf. *Much Ado*, III, iv, 38: "*Clap's*
into 'Light o' love.'"

[3] *seq. It was a lover, etc.*] The music of this song is found with the words in a volume of
MS. music in the Advocates' Library, Edinburgh, which seems to date from the early
part of the seventeenth century.

[4] *ring time*] The Folios read *rang time*, for which the Edinburgh MS. of the song substitutes *ring time, i.e.,* wedding time, which is obviously right.

[5] *Between the acres of the rye*] The reference seems to be to balks or banks of un-
ploughed turf which, in the common-field system of agriculture prevailing in
Elizabethan England, divided the acre strips of land from one another.

> This carol they began that hour,
>   With a hey, and a ho, and a hey nonino,
> How that a life was but a flower
>   In spring time, &c.
>
> And therefore take the present time,
>   With a hey, and a ho, and a hey nonino;
> For love is crowned with the prime
>   In spring time, &c.

TOUCH.   Truly, young gentlemen, though there was no great matter
    in the ditty, yet the note was very untuneable.[6]
FIRST PAGE.   You are deceived, sir: we kept time, we lost not our time.
TOUCH.   By my troth, yes; I count it but time lost to hear such a fool-
    ish song. God buy you;[7] and God mend your voices! Come,
    Audrey.   [*Exeunt.*

SCENE IV. *The Forest.*

Enter DUKE SENIOR, AMIENS, JAQUES, ORLANDO, OLIVER, *and* CELIA

DUKE S.   Dost thou believe, Orlando, that the boy
    Can do all this that he hath promised?
ORL.   I sometimes do believe, and sometimes do not;
    As those that fear they hope, and know they fear.[1]

Enter ROSALIND, SILVIUS, *and* PHEBE

ROS.   Patience once more, whiles our compact is urged:
    You say, if I bring in your Rosalind,
    You will bestow her on Orlando here?
DUKE S.   That would I, had I kingdoms to give with her.
ROS.   And you say, you will have her, when I bring her?

---

[6]*untuneable*] This is the reading of the Folios, for which Theobald substituted *untime-
able.* The change seems hardly necessary. "Out of *tune*" and "out of *time*" meant precisely the same thing.
[7]*God buy you*] God be with you. Cf. III, ii, 242.

[1]*fear they hope, and know they fear*] This, the original reading, has been often questioned, but no satisfactory substitute has been suggested. Orlando seeks to express the
extremity of his perplexity between hope and fear; he would seem to compare his lot
with those who have grave misgivings about what they hope, and their only sure knowledge is that they have misgivings.

ORL.   That would I, were I of all kingdoms king.

Ros.   You say, you'll marry me, if I be willing?

PHE.   That will I, should I die the hour after.

Ros.   But if you do refuse to marry me,
       You'll give yourself to this most faithful shepherd?

PHE.   So is the bargain.

Ros.   You say, that you'll have Phebe, if she will?

SIL.   Though to have her and death were both one thing.

Ros.   I have promised to make all this matter even.
       Keep you your word, O Duke, to give your daughter;
       You yours, Orlando, to receive his daughter:
       Keep your word, Phebe, that you'll marry me,
       Or else refusing me, to wed this shepherd:
       Keep your word, Silvius, that you'll marry her,
       If she refuse me: and from hence I go,
       To make these doubts all even.

                          [*Exeunt* ROSALIND *and* CELIA.

DUKE S.   I do remember in this shepherd boy
          Some lively touches of my daughter's favour.

ORL.   My lord, the first time that I ever saw him
       Methought he was a brother to your daughter:
       But, my good lord, this boy is forest-born,
       And hath been tutor'd in the rudiments
       Of many desperate studies by his uncle,
       Whom he reports to be a great magician,
       Obscured in the circle of this forest.

Enter TOUCHSTONE *and* AUDREY

JAQ.   There is, sure, another flood toward,[2] and these couples are com-
       ing to the ark. Here comes a pair of very strange beasts, which in
       all tongues are called fools.

TOUCH.   Salutation and greeting to you all!

JAQ.   Good my lord, bid him welcome: this is the motley-minded gen-
       tleman that I have so often met in the forest: he hath been a
       courtier, he swears.

TOUCH.   If any man doubt that, let him put me to my purgation. I
       have trod a measure; I have flattered a lady; I have been politic
       with my friend, smooth with mine enemy; I have undone three
       tailors; I have had four quarrels, and like to have fought one.

JAQ.   And how was that ta'en up?

---

[2]*toward*] imminent. Cf. *Hamlet*, V, ii, 356–357: "O proud death, What feast is *toward*
in thine eternal cell."

TOUCH. Faith, we met, and found the quarrel was upon the seventh cause.[3]

JAQ. How seventh cause? Good my lord, like this fellow.

DUKE S. I like him very well.

TOUCH. God 'ild you,[4] sir; I desire you of the like. I press in here, sir, amongst the rest of the country copulatives, to swear and to forswear; according as marriage binds and blood breaks: a poor virgin, sir, an ill-favoured thing, sir, but mine own; a poor humour of mine, sir, to take that that no man else will: rich honesty dwells like a miser, sir, in a poor house; as your pearl in your foul oyster.

DUKE S. By my faith, he is very swift and sententious.

TOUCH. According to the fool's bolt, sir, and such dulcet diseases.[5]

JAQ. But, for the seventh cause; how did you find the quarrel on the seventh cause?

TOUCH. Upon a lie seven times removed:—bear your body more seeming, Audrey:—as thus, sir. I did dislike[6] the cut of a certain courtier's beard: he sent me word, if I said his beard was not cut well, he was in the mind it was: this is called the Retort Courteous. If I sent him word again "it was not well cut," he would send me word, he cut it to please himself: this is called the Quip Modest. If again "it was not well cut," he disabled my judgement: this is called the Reply Churlish. If again "it was not well cut," he would answer, I spake not true: this is called the Reproof Valiant. If again "it was not well cut," he would say, I lie: this is called the Countercheck Quarrelsome: and so to the Lie Circumstantial and the Lie Direct.

JAQ. And how oft did you say his beard was not well cut?

TOUCH. I durst go no further than the Lie Circumstantial, nor he durst not give me the Lie Direct; and so we measured swords and parted.

JAQ. Can you nominate in order now the degrees of the lie?

---

[3]*seventh cause*] This is explained at line 65, *infra*, as "a lie seven times removed." The duel ordinarily was caused by a quarrel in which one man gave the other the lie. Touchstone distinguishes, *infra*, seven modes in which a lie may be given, ranging from the "Retort Courteous" to the "Lie Direct." Shakespeare drew very literally this account of such gradations of the lie from the popular handbook on the subject of fencing and duelling by Vincent Saviolo, an Italian fencing master of London, whose work, called "Vincentio Saviolo his Practise," was published in 1595.

[4]*God 'ild you*] God reward you. See footnote 8 on III, iii, 65, *supra*.

[5]*dulcet diseases*] Probably this is intentional nonsense with some such suggestion as "charming disagreeablenesses." Johnson too seriously proposed to read *discourses* for *diseases*.

[6]*dislike*] The word is often used, as here, not merely for entertaining, but also for expressing, dislike. Cf. *Meas. for Meas.*, I, ii, 17: "I never heard any soldier *dislike* it."

TOUCH.   O sir, we quarrel in print, by the book;[7] as you have books for good manners:[8] I will name you the degrees. The first, the Retort Courteous; the second, the Quip Modest; the third, the Reply Churlish; the fourth, the Reproof Valiant; the fifth, the Countercheck Quarrelsome; the sixth, the Lie with Circumstance; the seventh, the Lie Direct. All these you may avoid but the Lie Direct; and you may avoid that too, with an If. I knew when seven justices could not take up a quarrel, but when the parties were met themselves, one of them thought but of an If, as, "If you said so, then I said so"; and they shook hands and swore brothers. Your If is the only peace-maker; much virtue in If.

JAQ.   Is not this a rare fellow, my lord? he's as good at any thing and yet a fool.

DUKE S.   He uses his folly like a stalking-horse[9] and under the presentation of that he shoots his wit.

Enter HYMEN, ROSALIND, *and* CELIA

Still Music

HYM.   Then is there mirth in heaven,
            When earthly things made even
                Atone together.
            Good Duke, receive thy daughter:
            Hymen from heaven brought her,
                Yea, brought her hither,
            That thou mightst join her hand[10] with his
            Whose heart within his bosom is.

ROS.   To you I give myself, for I am yours.
            To you I give myself, for I am yours.

DUKE S.   If there be truth in sight, you are my daughter.

ORL.   If there be truth in sight, you are my Rosalind.

PHE.   If sight and shape be true,
            Why then, my love adieu!

ROS.   I'll have no father, if you be not he:
            I'll have no husband, if you be not he:
            Nor ne'er wed woman, if you be not she.

---

[7]*by the book*] An allusion probably to the book by Saviolo mentioned in footnote 3 on line 49, *supra*.

[8]*books for good manners*] There were many such. Cf. Hugh Rhodes' *Boke of Nurture*, or *Schole of good Manners* (1550?), and Sir Thomas Hoby's *The Courtyer* (1561).

[9]*stalking-horse*] Cf. Drayton's *Polyolbion*, Song 25: "One underneath his horse to get a shoot doth *stalk*."

[10]*her hand*] This is the reading of the Third and Fourth Folios. The First and Second Folios read *his hand*, obviously in error.

HYM.   Peace, ho! I bar confusion:
       'T is I must make conclusion
       Of these most strange events:
       Here's eight that must take hands
       To join in Hymen's bands,
         If truth holds true contents.
       You and you no cross shall part:
       You and you are heart in heart:
       You to his love must accord,
       Or have a woman to your lord:
       You and you are sure together,
       As the winter to foul weather.
       Whiles a wedlock-hymn we sing,
       Feed yourselves with questioning;
       That reason wonder may diminish,
       How thus we met, and these things finish.

SONG

      Wedding is great Juno's crown:
        O blessed bond of board and bed!
      'T is Hymen peoples every town;
        High wedlock then be honoured:
      Honour, high honour and renown,
      To Hymen, god of every town!

DUKE S.   O my dear niece, welcome thou art to me!
    Even daughter, welcome, in no less degree.
PHE.   I will not eat my word, now thou art mine;
    Thy faith my fancy to thee doth combine.

Enter JAQUES DE BOYS[11]

JAQ. DE B.   Let me have audience for a word or two:
    I am the second son of old Sir Rowland,
    That bring these tidings to this fair assembly.
    Duke Frederick, hearing how that every day
    Men of great worth resorted to this forest,
    Address'd a mighty power; which were on foot,
    In his own conduct, purposely to take
    His brother here and put him to the sword:
    And to the skirts of this wild wood he came;
    Where meeting with an old religious man,
    After some question with him, was converted
    Both from his enterprise and from the world;

[11]*Jaques de Boys*] See footnote 2 on I, i, 4.

His crown bequeathing to his banish'd brother,
And all their lands restored to them[12] again
That were with him exiled. This to be true,
I do engage my life.

DUKE S.   Welcome, young man;
Thou offer'st fairly to thy brothers' wedding:
To one his lands withheld; and to the other
A land itself at large, a potent dukedom.
First, in this forest let us do those ends
That here were well begun and well begot:
And after, every of this happy number,
That have endured shrewd[13] days and nights with us,
Shall share the good of our returned fortune,
According to the measure of their states.
Meantime, forget this new-fallen dignity,
And fall into our rustic revelry.
Play, music! And you, brides and bridegrooms all,
With measure heap'd in joy, to the measures fall.

JAQ.   Sir, by your patience. If I heard you rightly,
The Duke hath put on a religious life
And thrown into neglect the pompous court?

JAQ. DE B.   He hath.

JAQ.   To him will I: out of these convertites
There is much matter to be heard and learn'd.
[*To Duke S.*] You to your former honour I bequeath;
Your patience and your virtue well deserves it:
[*To Orl.*] You to a love, that your true faith doth merit:
[*To Oli.*] You to your land, and love, and great allies:
[*To Sil.*] You to a long and well-deserved bed:
[*To Touch.*] And you to wrangling; for thy loving voyage
Is but for two months victuall'd. So, to your pleasures:
I am for other than for dancing measures.

DUKE S.   Stay, Jaques, stay.

JAQ.   To see no pastime I: what you would have
I'll stay to know at your abandon'd cave.   [*Exit.*

DUKE S.   Proceed, proceed: we will begin these rites,
As we do trust they'll end, in true delights.   [A *dance.*

---

[12]*them*] This is Rowe's correction of the original reading *him*.
[13]*shrewd*] evil, disastrous. Cf. *Merch. of Ven.*, III, ii, 246: "There are some *shrewd* contents in yon same paper."

EPILOGUE

ROS.　It is not the fashion to see the lady the epilogue; but it is no more unhandsome than to see the lord the prologue. If it be true that good wine needs no bush,[1] 't is true that a good play needs no epilogue: yet to good wine they do use good bushes; and good plays prove the better by the help of good epilogues. What a case am I in then, that am neither a good epilogue, nor cannot insinuate with you in the behalf of a good play! I am not furnished like a beggar, therefore to beg will not become me: my way is to conjure you; and I'll begin with the women. I charge you, O women, for the love you bear to men, to like as much of this play as please you: and I charge you, O men, for the love you bear to women, — as I perceive by your simpering, none of you hates them, — that between you and the women the play may please. If I were a woman[2] I would kiss as many of you as had beards that pleased me, complexions that liked me and breaths that I defied not: and, I am sure, as many as have good beards or good faces or sweet breaths will, for my kind offer, when I make curtsy, bid me farewell.

[*Exeunt.*

---

[1]*bush*] It was customary for tavern-keepers and vintners to hang a *bush* of holly or ivy outside their houses, usually attached to the signboard.
[2]*If I were a woman*] The part of Rosalind, according to the practice of the Elizabethan stage, was played by a boy.

The Merry Wives of Windsor

The Merry Wives of Windsor

The Merry Wives of Windsor is an unusual example of Shakespeare's comedic talent. Virtually his only play that portrays middle-class country life in any way, it also is the only one set in Windsor, where it was probably first performed. The setting of the farce is at once understandable since it was supposedly written at the express request of Queen Elizabeth I after she had seen the performances of both parts of *Henry IV*. The queen had grown so enamored of Falstaff that she commanded Shakespeare to write a play detailing the character's exploits in love. Not only did the skillful dramatist comply with her order, but he is also said to have completed it in a fortnight. The first recorded mention of this can be found in John Dennis's preface to the 1702 adaptation of the play.

One of Shakespeare's great comedies, *The Merry Wives of Windsor* might have been written as early as 1597, as its first performance is thought to have occurred during the Feast of St. George, which was the initiation ceremony for the newly elected Knights of the Garter. An early version of the play, entered into the Stationers' Register in January 1602, was later discovered to be a "bad quarto," a mangled form of the play reconstructed from memory by one of the actors. The authoritative text of the play was first published in 1623 in the First Folio, a collected edition of Shakespeare's plays.

Unlike many of Shakespeare's works, *The Merry Wives of Windsor* owes little of its plot to previous writers. If conjecture can be believed—that Shakespeare wrote and performed the play all within fourteen days—then one can only assume that the dramatist must have revived events and characters from previous plays, perhaps ones already owned by his theatre company. Although no specific source is known, some critics infer that the comic devices in the play correspond with Italian popular comedy of the time, specifically Straparola's *Le Tredici Piacevoli Notte,* which was then available in English translations.

SUSAN RATTINER

Dramatis Personæ[1]

SIR JOHN FALSTAFF.

FENTON, a gentleman.

SHALLOW, a country justice.

SLENDER, cousin to Shallow.

FORD,
PAGE, } two gentlemen dwelling at Windsor.

WILLIAM PAGE, a boy, son to Page.

SIR HUGH EVANS, a Welsh parson.

DOCTOR CAIUS, a French physician.

HOST of the Garter Inn.

BARDOLPH,
PISTOL, } sharpers attending on Falstaff.
NYM,

ROBIN, page to Falstaff.

SIMPLE, servant to Slender.

RUGBY, servant to Doctor Caius.

MISTRESS FORD.

MISTRESS PAGE.

ANNE PAGE, her daughter.

MISTRESS QUICKLY, servant to Doctor Caius.

Servants to Page, Ford, etc.

SCENE—*Windsor, and the neighbourhood*

---

[1]An imperfect sketch of this play was first published in quarto in 1602, and was reissued in 1619. A complete version first appeared in the First Folio of 1623, and this was reissued in a Third Quarto in 1630. The Folio first divided the text into acts and scenes. But there is no list of "dramatis personæ." This was first supplied by Nicholas Rowe in his edition of Shakespeare's works, 1709.

ACT I.

SCENE I. *Windsor. Before Page's House.*

Enter JUSTICE SHALLOW, SLENDER, *and* SIR HUGH EVANS

SHALLOW.   Sir Hugh, persuade me not; I will make a Star-chamber matter[1] of it: if he were twenty Sir John Falstaffs, he shall not abuse Robert Shallow, esquire.

SLEN.   In the county of Gloucester, justice of peace and "Coram."[2]

SHAL.   Ay, cousin Slender, and "Custalorum."

SLEN.   Ay, and "Rato-lorum" too; and a gentleman born, master parson; who writes himself "Armigero, in any bill, warrant, quittance, or obligation, "Armigero."

SHAL.   Ay, that I do; and have done any time these three hundred years.

SLEN.   All his successors gone before him hath done 't; and all his ancestors that come after him may: they may give the dozen white luces[3] in their coat.

SHAL.   It is an old coat.

EVANS.   The dozen white louses[4] do become an old coat well; it agrees well, passant; it is a familiar beast to man, and signifies love.

---

[1]*Star-chamber matter*] Matter for the Court of Star Chamber, which had cognizance of all riots.

[2]*"Coram"*] Slender here and in his next speech is confusedly recalling the official Latin titles of a justice of the peace. The word "quorum," which he mispronounces "coram," was prominent in the formal commission, which also designated a justice "custos rotulorum." Justice Shallow would sign his attestations "*Coram* me Roberto Shallow, *armigero*" (*i.e.* arms-bearer, esquire).

[3]*dozen white luces*] "Luce" was the name commonly applied to a full-grown and ageing pike. Shallow is a caricature sketch of Sir Thomas *Lucy* of Charlecote, who is reputed to have punished Shakespeare in his youth for poaching in his park. Sir Thomas bore on his heraldic shield three *luces* hauriant argent.

[4]*louses*] Sir Hugh's punning confusion of "luce" with "louse" ("a familiar beast to man") implies that he pronounced the two words alike.

SHAL. The luce is the fresh fish; the salt fish is an old coat.[5]

SLEN. I may quarter,[6] coz.

SHAL. You may, by marrying.

EVANS. It is marring indeed, if he quarter it.

SHAL. Not a whit.

EVANS. Yes, py'r lady; if he has a quarter of your coat, there is but three skirts for yourself, in my simple conjectures: but that is all one. If Sir John Falstaff have committed disparagements unto you, I am of the church, and will be glad to do my benevolence to make atonements and compremises between you.

SHAL. The council[7] shall hear it; it is a riot.

EVANS. It is not meet the council hear a riot; there is no fear of Got in a riot: the council, look you, shall desire to hear the fear of Got, and not to hear a riot; take your vizaments in that.[8]

SHAL. Ha! o' my life, if I were young again, the sword should end it.

EVANS. It is petter that friends is the sword, and end it: and there is also another device in my prain, which peradventure prings goot discretions with it:—there is Anne Page, which is daughter to Master Thomas Page,[9] which is pretty virginity.

SLEN. Mistress Anne Page? She has brown hair, and speaks small[10] like a woman.

EVANS. It is that fery person for all the orld, as just as you will desire; and seven hundred pounds of moneys, and gold and silver, is her grandsire upon his death's-bed (Got deliver to a joyful resurrections!) give, when she is able to overtake seventeen years old: it were a goot motion if we leave our pribbles and prabbles,[11] and desire a marriage between Master Abraham and Mistress Anne Page.

SLEN. Did her grandsire leave her seven hundred pound?

EVANS. Ay, and her father is make her a petter penny.

[5]These lines are difficult to explain. Shallow, by way of denying Evans's suggestion of agreement between "luces" and "an old coat," points out that the pike, which lives in *fresh* water, can have no staleness about it; such an attribute is only possible in *salted* fish (of the sea), which can therefore be alone identified with an old cast-off coat.

[6]*quarter*] a technical term in heraldry; used as a verb, it means to fill a compartment of a shield with armorial bearings other than those of one's father—*e.g.* those of one's wife.

[7]*council*] the star-chamber, which was a committee of the privy council.

[8]*take . . . that*] be sure of that. "Vizaments" is a blunder for "advisements" counsels, deliberations.

[9]*Thomas Page*] This is the original reading. Elsewhere, II, i, and V, v, Page is called "George." "Thomas" is probably an oversight of the author.

[10]*speaks small*] speaks in a low voice.

[11]*pribbles and prabbles*] The Welshman's mispronunciation of bribble-brabble, a common reduplicated form of "brabble," discordant babble, vain chatter.

SLEN.   I know the young gentlewoman; she has good gifts.

EVANS.   Seven hundred pounds and possibilities is goot gifts.

SHAL.   Well, let us see honest Master Page. Is Falstaff there?

EVANS.   Shall I tell you a lie? I do despise a liar as I do despise one that
is false, or as I despise one that is not true. The knight, Sir John, is
there; and, I beseech you, be ruled by your well-willers. I will peat
the door for Master Page. [*Knocks*] What, hoa! Got pless your
house here!

PAGE. [*within*]   Who's there?

Enter PAGE

EVANS.   Here is Got's plessing, and your friend, and Justice Shallow;
and here young Master Slender, that peradventures shall tell you
another tale, if matters grow to your likings.

PAGE.   I am glad to see your worships well. I thank you for my venison, Master Shallow.

SHAL.   Master Page, I am glad to see you: much good do it your good
heart! I wished your venison better; it was ill killed. How doth
good Mistress Page?—and I thank you always with my heart, la!
with my heart.

PAGE.   Sir, I thank you.

SHAL.   Sir, I thank you; by yea and no, I do.

PAGE.   I am glad to see you, good Master Slender.

SLEN.   How does your fallow greyhound, sir? I heard say he was out-
run on Cotsall.[12]

PAGE.   It could not be judged, sir.

SLEN.   You'll not confess, you'll not confess.

SHAL.   That he will not. 'T is your fault; 't is your fault; 't is a good dog.

PAGE.   A cur, sir.

SHAL.   Sir, he's a good dog, and a fair dog: can there be more said? he
is good and fair. Is Sir John Falstaff here?

PAGE.   Sir, he is within; and I would I could do a good office between
you.

EVANS.   It is spoke as a Christians ought to speak.

SHAL.   He hath wronged me, Master Page.

PAGE.   Sir, he doth in some sort confess it.

SHAL.   If it be confessed, it is not redressed: is not that so, Master Page?
He hath wronged me; indeed he hath; at a word, he hath, believe
me: Robert Shallow, esquire, saith, he is wronged.

PAGE.   Here comes Sir John.

---

[12]*Cotsall*] The local pronunciation of Cotswold. On the Cotswold hills, in
Gloucestershire, coursing matches and meetings for rural sports were frequently held.

Enter Sir John Falstaff, Bardolph, Nym, *and* Pistol

Fal.   Now, Master Shallow, you'll complain of me to the king?

Shal.   Knight, you have beaten my men, killed my deer, and broke open my lodge.

Fal.   But not kissed your keeper's daughter?

Shal.   Tut, a pin! this shall be answered.

Fal.   I will answer it straight; I have done all this. That is now answered.

Shal.   The council shall know this.

Fal.   'T were better for you if it were known in counsel:[13] you'll be laughed at.

Evans.   Pauca verba, Sir John; Goot worts.[14]

Fal.   Goot worts! good cabbage. Slender, I broke your head: what matter have you against me?

Slen.   Marry, sir, I have matter in my head against you; and against your cony-catching rascals, Bardolph, Nym, and Pistol.

Bard.   You Banbury cheese![15]

Slen.   Ay, it is no matter.

Pist.   How now, Mephostophilus![16]

Slen.   Ay, it is no matter.

Nym.   Slice, I say! pauca, pauca: slice![17] that's my humour.

Slen.   Where's Simple, my man? Can you tell, cousin?

Evans.   Peace, I pray you. Now let us understand. There is three umpires in this matter, as I understand; that is, Master Page, fidelicet Master Page; and there is myself, fidelicet myself; and the three party is, lastly and finally, mine host of the Garter.

Page.   We three, to hear it and end it between them.

Evans.   Fery goot: I will make a prief of it in my note-book; and we will afterwards ork upon the cause with as great discreetly as we can.

Fal.   Pistol!

Pist.   He hears with ears.

Evans.   The tevil and his tam! what phrase is this, "He hears with ear"? why, it is affectations.

Fal.   Pistol, did you pick Master Slender's purse?

Slen.   Ay, by these gloves, did he, or I would I might never come in

---

[13]*known in counsel*] kept secret.

[14]*worts*] vegetables, of which the "cole-wort" or cabbage is one of the commonest species.

[15]*Banbury cheese*] flat, thin cheese.

[16]*Mephostophilus*] A probable reference to Marlowe's tragedy of *Dr. Faustus.*

[17]*Slice . . . pauca*] Nym echoes Evans' exclamation "pauca verba." "Slice" is a characteristic allusion to the sword.

mine own great chamber again else, of seven groats in mill-sixpences, and two Edward shovel-boards, that cost me two shilling and two pence a-piece[18] of Yead[19] Miller, by these gloves.

FAL. Is this true, Pistol?

EVANS. No; it is false, if it is a pick-purse.

PIST. Ha, thou mountain-foreigner! Sir John and master mine,
I combat challenge of this latten bilbo.[20]
Word of denial in thy labras[21] here!
Word of denial: froth and scum, thou liest!

SLEN. By these gloves, then, 't was he.

NYM. Be avised, sir, and pass good humours: I will say "marry trap"[22] with you, if you run the nuthook's humour on me; that is the very note of it.

SLEN. By this hat, then, he in the red face had it; for though I cannot remember what I did when you made me drunk, yet I am not altogether an ass.

FAL. What say you, Scarlet and John?[23]

BARD. Why, sir, for my part, I say the gentleman had drunk himself out of his five sentences.

EVANS. It is his five senses: fie, what the ignorance is!

BARD. And being fap,[24] sir, was, as they say, cashiered; and so conclusions passed the careires.[25]

SLEN. Ay, you spake in Latin then too; but 't is no matter: I'll ne'er be drunk whilst I live again, but in honest, civil, godly company, for this trick: if I be drunk, I'll be drunk with those that have the fear of God, and not with drunken knaves.

EVANS. So Got udge me, that is a virtuous mind.

FAL. You hear all these matters denied, gentlemen; you hear it.

---

[18]*seven groats . . . a-piece*] groats, *i.e.* four-penny pieces, were coins of very old standing; milled or stamped sixpences were first coined in 1561. "Edward shovel-boards" were broad and heavy shilling-pieces of Edward VI's reign, and came to be used as counters or discs in the popular game of shovel-board, which in principle resembles the more modern game of "squayles." Slender's words indicate that the value of Edward VI's shillings had greatly appreciated; but his figures are not to be depended on. Seven groats (of four-pence each) could not be converted into sixpence's.

[19]*Yead*] A colloquial form of Ned.

[20]*latten bilbo*] Slender is compared to a sword blade.

[21]*labras*] Pistol bombastically uses the Spanish word for lips.

[22]*I will say "marry trap"*] I will catch you (cry quits with you), if you play the "nuthook" (*i.e.* constable or catchpole) with me.

[23]*Scarlet and John*] The names of two followers of Robin Hood. "Scarlet" alludes to Bardolph's red face.

[24]*fap*] drunken; probably from "vappa," a drunken person.

[25]*passed the careires*] galloped on at full speed; a technical term of the equestrian menage, or art of riding.

Enter ANNE PAGE, *with wine*; MISTRESS FORD *and* MISTRESS PAGE, *following*

PAGE. Nay, daughter, carry the wine in; we'll drink within.

> [*Exit* ANNE PAGE.

SLEN. O heaven! this is Mistress Anne Page.

PAGE. How now, Mistress Ford!

FAL. Mistress Ford, by my troth, you are very well met: by your leave, good mistress.   [*Kisses her.*

PAGE. Wife, bid these gentlemen welcome. Come, we have a hot venison pasty to dinner: come, gentlemen, I hope we shall drink down all unkindness.

> [*Exeunt all except* SHAL., SLEN., *and* EVANS.

SLEN. I had rather than forty shillings I had my Book of Songs and Sonnets[26] here.

Enter SIMPLE

How now, Simple! where have you been? I must wait on myself, must I? You have not the Book of Riddles[27] about you, have you?

SIM. Book of Riddles! why, did you not lend it to Alice Shortcake upon All-hallowmas last, a fortnight afore Michaelmas?[28]

SHAL. Come, coz; come, coz; we stay for you. A word with you, coz; marry, this, coz: there is, as 't were, a tender, a kind of tender, made afar off by Sir Hugh here. Do you understand me?

SLEN. Ay, sir, you shall find me reasonable; if it be so, I shall do that that is reason.

SHAL. Nay, but understand me.

SLEN. So I do, sir.

EVANS. Give ear to his motions, Master Slender: I will description the matter to you, if you be capacity of it.

SLEN. Nay, I will do as my cousin Shallow says: I pray you, pardon me; he's a justice of peace in his country, simple though I stand here.

EVANS. But that is not the question: the question is concerning your marriage.

[26]*Book of Songs and Sonnets*] Slender seeks amatory verse wherewith to court Anne Page. The book he specifies is probably the popular poetic miscellany, generally called *Tottel's Miscellany*, but really entitled *Songes and Sonnetes*, 1557. An eighth edition appeared in 1587.

[27]*Book of Riddles*] *The Booke of Mery Riddles* was very popular in the 16th and 17th centuries, though no edition earlier than that of 1600 seems to be extant.

[28]*All-hallowmas last . . . Michaelmas*] Slender seems to confuse Michaelmas (29 September) with Martlemas or Martinmas (11 November). All-hallowmas (All Saints, 1 November) comes some five weeks after Michaelmas, but ten days "afore" Martlemas.

SHAL.   Ay, there's the point, sir.

EVANS.   Marry, is it; the very point of it; to Mistress Anne Page.

SLEN.   Why, if it be so, I will marry her upon any reasonable demands.

EVANS.   But can you affection the 'oman? Let us command to know that of your mouth or of your lips; for divers philosophers hold that the lips is parcel of the mouth. Therefore, precisely, can you carry your good will to the maid?

SHAL.   Cousin Abraham Slender, can you love her?

SLEN.   I hope, sir, I will do as it shall become one that would do reason.

EVANS.   Nay, Got's lords and his ladies! you must speak possitable, if you can carry her your desires towards her.

SHAL.   That you must. Will you, upon good dowry, marry her?

SLEN.   I will do a greater thing than that, upon your request, cousin, in any reason.

SHAL.   Nay, conceive me, conceive me, sweet coz: what I do is to pleasure you, coz. Can you love the maid?

SLEN.   I will marry her, sir, at your request: but if there be no great love in the beginning, yet heaven may decrease it upon better acquaintance, when we are married and have more occasion to know one another; I hope, upon familiarity will grow more contempt: but if you say, "Marry her," I will marry her; that I am freely dissolved, and dissolutely.

EVANS.   It is a fery discretion answer; save the fall is in the ort[29] "dissolutely:" the ort is, according to our meaning, "resolutely:" his meaning is good.

SHAL.   Ay, I think my cousin meant well.

SLEN.   Ay, or else I would I might be hanged, la!

SHAL.   Here comes fair Mistress Anne.

Re-enter ANNE PAGE

Would I were young for your sake, Mistress Anne!

ANNE.   The dinner is on the table; my father desires your worships' company.

SHAL.   I will wait on him, fair Mistress Anne.

EVANS.   Od's plessed will! I will not be absence at the grace.

[*Exeunt* SHALLOW *and* EVANS.

ANNE.   Will 't please your worship to come in, sir?

SLEN.   No, I thank you, forsooth, heartily; I am very well.

---

[29]*fall . . . ort*] Fall is a mispronunciation of "fault," as "ort" is of "word."

ANNE.   The dinner attends you, sir.

SLEN.   I am not a-hungry, I thank you, forsooth. Go, sirrah, for all you
are my man, go wait upon my cousin Shallow. [*Exit* SIMPLE.] A
justice of peace sometime may be beholding to his friend for a
man. I keep but three men and a boy yet, till my mother be dead:
but what though? yet I live like a poor gentleman born.

ANNE.   I may not go in without your worship: they will not sit till you
come.

SLEN.   I' faith, I'll eat nothing; I thank you as much as though I did.

ANNE.   I pray you, sir, walk in.

SLEN.   I had rather walk here, I thank you. I bruised my shin th' other
day with playing at sword and dagger with a master of fence; three
veneys for a dish of stewed prunes;[30] and, by my troth, I cannot
abide the smell of hot meat since. Why do your dogs bark so? be
there bears i' the town?

ANNE.   I think there are, sir; I heard them talked of.

SLEN.   I love the sport well; but I shall as soon quarrel at it as any man
in England. You are afraid, if you see the bear loose, are you not?

ANNE.   Ay, indeed, sir.

SLEN.   That's meat and drink[31] to me, now. I have seen Sackerson[32]
loose twenty times, and have taken him by the chain; but, I warrant you, the women have so cried and shrieked at it, that it
passed: but women, indeed, cannot abide 'em; they are very ill-
favoured rough things.

Re-enter PAGE

PAGE.   Come, gentle Master Slender, come; we stay for you.

SLEN.   I'll eat nothing, I thank you, sir.

PAGE.   By cock and pie, you shall not choose, sir! come, come.

SLEN.   Nay, pray you, lead the way.

PAGE.   Come on, sir.

SLEN.   Mistress Anne, yourself shall go first.

ANNE.   Not I, sir; pray you, keep on.

SLEN.   Truly, I will not go first; truly, la! I will not do you that wrong.

ANNE.   I pray you, sir.

SLEN.   I'll rather be unmannerly than troublesome. You do yourself
wrong, indeed, la!   [*Exeunt.*

---

[30]*three veneys . . . prunes*] The wager for which the fencing-match was played was a dish
of stewed prunes to be paid to him who scored three "veneys" (*i.e.* hits).

[31]*meat and drink*] a common proverbial phrase, expressing infinite satisfaction.

[32]*Sackerson*] The name of a far-famed performing bear, which was a chief attraction, at
the date of the performance of this play, at the Paris Garden in Southwark.

SCENE II. *The Same.*

Enter SIR HUGH EVANS *and* SIMPLE

EVANS.   Go your ways, and ask of Doctor Caius' house which is the
way: and there dwells one Mistress Quickly, which is in the manner of his nurse, or his dry nurse, or his cook, or his laundry, his
washer, and his wringer.

SIM.   Well, sir.

EVANS.   Nay, it is petter yet. Give her this letter; for it is a 'oman that
altogether's acquaintance[1] with Mistress Anne Page: and the letter
is, to desire and require her to solicit your master's desires to
Mistress Anne Page. I pray you, be gone: I will make an end of my
dinner; there's pippins and cheese to come.   [*Exeunt.*

SCENE III. *A Room in the Garter Inn.*

Enter FALSTAFF, HOST, BARDOLPH, NYM, PISTOL, *and* ROBIN

FAL.   Mine host of the Garter!

HOST.   What say my bully-rook? speak scholarly and wisely.

FAL.   Truly, mine host, I must turn away some of my followers.

HOST.   Discard, bully Hercules; cashier: let them wag; trot, trot.

FAL.   I sit at ten pounds a week.

HOST.   Thou 'rt an emperor, Cæsar, Keisar, and Pheezar. I will entertain Bardolph; he shall draw, he shall tap: said I well, bully
Hector?

FAL.   Do so, good mine host.

HOST.   I have spoke; let him follow. [*To* BARD.] Let me see thee froth
and lime:[1] I am at a word; follow.   [*Exit.*

FAL.   Bardolph, follow him. A tapster is a good trade: an old cloak
makes a new jerkin; a withered serving-man a fresh tapster. Go;
adieu.

BARD.   It is a life that I have desired: I will thrive.

PIST.   O base Hungarian[2] wight! wilt thou the spigot wield?
                                                      [*Exit* BARDOLPH.

---

[1]*that altogether's acquaintance*] that is fully acquainted with.

[1]*froth and lime*] The host invites Bardolph to try his hand as a tapster, whose function
it was to make the beer "froth and lime," *i.e.* sparkle by covertly introducing *lime* into
the glass.

[2]*Hungarian*] The earlier Quartos read *Gongarian*. Steevens quoted without reference a
line from an unidentified old play, "O base Gongarian! wilt thou the distaff wield?" But
the epithet "Hungarian" was often used in the sense of "swaggering" or "bombastic."

NYM.   He was gotten in drink: is not the humour conceited?

FAL.   I am glad I am so acquit of this tinder-box: his thefts were too open; his filching was like an unskilful singer; he kept not time.

NYM.   The good humour is to steal at a minute's rest.[3]

PIST.   "Convey," the wise it call. "Steal!" foh! a fico for the phrase!

FAL.   Well, sirs, I am almost out at heels.

PIST.   Why, then, let kibes ensue.

FAL.   There is no remedy; I must cony-catch; I must shift.

PIST.   Young ravens must have food.

FAL.   Which of you know Ford of this town?

PIST.   I ken the wight: he is of substance good.

FAL.   My honest lads, I will tell you what I am about.

PIST.   Two yards, and more.

FAL.   No quips now, Pistol! Indeed, I am in the waist two yards about; but I am now about no waste; I am about thrift. Briefly, I do mean to make love to Ford's wife: I spy entertainment in her; she discourses, she carves, she gives the leer of invitation: I can construe the action of her familiar style; and the hardest voice of her behaviour, to be Englished rightly, is "I am Sir John Falstaff's."

PIST.   He hath studied her will, and translated her will,[4] out of honesty into English.

NYM.   The anchor is deep: will that humour pass?

FAL.   Now, the report goes she has all the rule of her husband's purse: he hath a legion of angels.

PIST.   As many devils entertain; and "To her, boy," say I.

NYM.   The humour rises; it is good: humour me the angels.

FAL.   I have writ me here a letter to her: and here another to Page's wife, who even now gave me good eyes too, examined my parts with most judicious œillades;[5] sometimes the beam of her view gilded my foot, sometimes my portly belly.

PIST.   Then did the sun on dunghill shine.

NYM.   I thank thee for that humour.

FAL.   O, she did so course o'er my exteriors with such a greedy intention, that the appetite of her eye did seem to scorch me up like a burning-glass! Here's another letter to her: she bears the purse too;

---

[3]*at a minute's rest*] This, the original reading, has been ingeniously altered by many editors to *at a minim's rest.* "Minim" is the shortest note in music. "At a minim's rest" would mean "with the utmost rapidity."

[4]*will . . . will*] This is the reading of the First Folio. The earlier Quartos read *well* for the first *will* and omit the second phrase. *Will* in both cases is doubtless right.

[5]*œillades*] A French word meaning "amorous glances," very occasionally met with in Elizabethan literature.

she is a region in Guiana,[6] all gold and bounty. I will be cheaters[7]
to them both, and they shall be exchequers to me; they shall be
my East and West Indies, and I will trade to them both. Go bear
thou this letter to Mistress Page; and thou this to Mistress Ford: we
will thrive, lads, we will thrive.

PIST.   Shall I sir Pandarus of Troy become,
    And by my side wear steel? then, Lucifer take all!

NYM.   I will run no base humour: here, take the humour-letter: I will
    keep the haviour of reputation.

FAL. [*To* ROBIN]   Hold, sirrah, bear you these letters tightly;
    Sail like my pinnace to these golden shores.
    Rogues, hence, avaunt! vanish like hailstones, go;
    Trudge, plod away o' the hoof; seek shelter, pack!
    Falstaff will learn the humour of the age,
    French thrift, you rogues; myself and skirted page.
                                    [*Exeunt* FALSTAFF *and* ROBIN.

PIST.   Let vultures gripe thy guts! for gourd and fullam holds,
    And high and low[8] beguiles the rich and poor:
    Tester I'll have in pouch when thou shalt lack,
    Base Phrygian Turk!

NYM.   I have operations which be humours of revenge.

PIST.   Wilt thou revenge?

NYM.   By welkin and her star!

PIST.   With wit or steel?

NYM.   With both the humours, I:
    I will discuss the humour of this love to Page.

PIST.   And I to Ford shall eke unfold
            How Falstaff, varlet vile,
        His dove will prove, his gold will hold,
            And his soft couch defile.

NYM.   My humour shall not cool: I will incense Page to deal with
    poison; I will possess him with yellowness,[9] for the revolt of mine[10]
    is dangerous: that is my true humour.

---

[6]*a region in Guiana*] An allusion to Sir Walter Ralegh's recent exploration of Guiana,
of which he published an account in 1595.

[7]*cheaters*] A punning quibble on "cheaters" and "escheaters," officers of the Exchequer.

[8]*gourd . . . low*] "Gourd," "fullam," "high [men]" and "low [men]" were all cant terms
for loaded dice in common use by sharpers.

[9]*yellowness*] the traditional colour of jealousy.

[10]*revolt of mine*] This is the original reading. Theobald suggested *revolt of mien* (*i.e.*
change of complexion), which does not add much point to Nym's threat. The
Cambridge editors suggest that "anger" is omitted after "mine." Most probably Nym
merely means to say in his grandiloquent jargon "my revolt," *i.e.* "my purpose of re-
nouncing allegiance to Falstaff."

PIST.   Thou art the Mars of malecontents: I second thee; troop on.
                                                                [*Exeunt.*

SCENE IV. *A Room in Doctor Caius's House.*

Enter MISTRESS QUICKLY, SIMPLE, *and* RUGBY

QUICK.   What, John Rugby! I pray thee, go to the casement, and see
    if you can see my master, Master Doctor Caius, coming. If he do,
    i' faith, and find any body in the house, here will be an old abus-
    ing of God's patience and the king's English.

RUG.   I'll go watch.

QUICK.   Go; and we'll have a posset for 't soon at night, in faith, at the
    latter end of a sea-coal fire. [*Exit* RUGBY.] An honest, willing, kind
    fellow, as ever servant shall come in house withal; and, I warrant
    you, no tell-tale nor no breed-bate: his worst fault is, that he is
    given to prayer; he is something peevish that way: but nobody but
    has his fault; but let that pass. Peter Simple, you say your name is?

SIM.   Ay, for fault of a better.

QUICK.   And Master Slender's your master?

SIM.   Ay, forsooth.

QUICK.   Does he not wear a great round beard, like a glover's paring-
    knife?

SIM.   No, forsooth: he hath but a little wee face,[1] with a little yellow
    beard,—a Cain-coloured[2] beard.

QUICK.   A softly-sprighted man, is he not?

SIM.   Ay, forsooth: but he is as tall a man of his hands[3] as any is be-
    tween this and his head; he hath fought with a warrener.

QUICK.   How say you?—O, I should remember him: does he not hold
    up his head, as it were, and strut in his gait?

SIM.   Yes, indeed, does he.

QUICK.   Well, heaven send Anne Page no worse fortune! Tell Master

---

[1]*wee face*] This is the original reading. Capell needlessly substituted *whey-face* (meaning "pale-faced"), as in *Macb.*, V, iii. In the Second Quarto (in the preceding speech,
which the Folio alters), Dame Quickly applies to Slender's beard the epithet "whay
coloured," but *wee* is quite appropriate to the context.

[2]*Cain-coloured*] The early Quartos read "*Kane* colored," which tends to justify the popular emendation "*Cane*-coloured" for the First Folio reading "*Caine*-colored." "*Cane*-
coloured beard" would be much the same as "straw-colour beard" in *Mids. N. Dr.*, I,
ii. If "*Cain*-coloured" be retained, there would be a reference to the red colour of
Cain's beard in current pictorial illustrations of Scriptural history.

[3]*as tall a man of his hands*] In Florio's *Italian Dictionary*, 1598, "manesco" is interpreted as "readie or nimble-handed; *a tall man of his hands.*"

Parson Evans I will do what I can for your master: Anne is a good
girl, and I wish—

Re-enter RUGBY

RUG.   Out, alas! here comes my master.

QUICK.   We shall all be shent. Run in here, good young man; go into
this closet: he will not stay long. [*Shuts* SIMPLE *in the closet.*]
What, John Rugby! John! what, John, I say! Go, John, go inquire
for my master; I doubt he be not well, that he comes not home.

[*Singing*] And down, down, adown-a, &c.

Enter DOCTOR CAIUS

CAIUS.   Vat is you sing? I do not like des toys. Pray you, go and vetch
me in my closet un boitier vert,—a box, a green-a box: do intend
vat I speak? a green-a box.

QUICK.   Ay, forsooth; I'll fetch it you. [*Aside*] I am glad he went not in
himself: if he had found the young man, he would have been
horn-mad.

CAIUS.   Fe, fe, fe, fe! ma foi, il fait fort chaud. Je m'en vais à la cour,—
la grande affaire.

QUICK.   Is it this, sir?

CAIUS.   Oui; mette le au mon pocket: dépêcne, quickly. Vere is dat
knave Rugby?

QUICK.   What, John Rugby! John!

RUG.   Here, Sir!

CAIUS.   You are John Rugby, and you are Jack Rugby. Come, take-a
your rapier, and come after my heel to the court.

RUG.   'T is ready, sir, here in the porch.

CAIUS.   By my trot, I tarry too long. Od's me! Qu'ai-j'oublié! dere is
some simples in my closet, dat I vill not for the varld I shall leave
behind.

QUICK.   Ay me, he'll find the young man there, and be mad!

CAIUS.   O diable, diable! vat is in my closet? Villain! larron! [*Pulling*
SIMPLE *out.*] Rugby, my rapier!

QUICK.   Good master, be content.

CAIUS.   Wherefore shall I be content-a?

QUICK.   The young man is an honest man.

CAIUS.   What shall de honest man do in my closet? dere is no honest
man dat shall come in my closet.

QUICK.   I beseech you, be not so phlegmatic. Here the truth of it: he
came of an errand to me from Parson Hugh.

CAIUS.   Vell.

SIM.   Ay, forsooth; to desire her to—

QUICK. Peace, I pray you.

CAIUS. Peace-a your tongue. Speak-a your tale.

SIM. To desire this honest gentlewoman, your maid, to speak a good word to Mistress Anne Page for my master in the way of marriage.

QUICK. This is all, indeed, la! but I'll ne'er put my finger in the fire, and need not.

CAIUS. Sir Hugh send-a you? Rugby, baille[4] me some paper. Tarry you a little-a while.   [*Writes.*

QUICK. [*Aside to* SIMPLE] I am glad he is so quiet: if he had been throughly moved, you should have heard him so loud and so melancholy. But notwithstanding, man, I'll do you your master what good I can: and the very yea and the no is, the French doctor, my master,—I may call him my master, look you, for I keep his house; and I wash, wring, brew, bake, scour, dress meat and drink, make the beds, and do all myself,—

SIM. [*Aside to* QUICKLY] 'T is a great charge to come under one body's hand.

QUICK. [*Aside to* SIMPLE] Are you avised o' that? you shall find it a great charge: and to be up early and down late;—but notwithstanding,—to tell you in your ear; I would have no words of it,— my master himself is in love with Mistress Anne Page: but notwithstanding that, I know Anne's mind,—that's neither here nor there.

CAIUS. You jack'nape, give-a this letter to Sir Hugh; by gar, it is a shallenge: I will cut his troat in de park; and I will teach a scurvy jack-a-nape priest to meddle or make. You may be gone; it is not good you tarry here.—By gar, I will cut all his two stones; by gar, he shall not have a stone to throw at his dog.   [*Exit* SIMPLE.

QUICK. Alas, he speaks but for his friends.

CAIUS. It is no matter-a ver dat:—do not you tell-a me dat I shall have Anne Page for myself?—By gar, I vill kill de Jack priest; and I have appointed mine host of de Jarteer to measure our weapon.—By gar, I will myself have Anne Page.

QUICK. Sir, the maid loves you, and all shall be well. We must give folks leave to prate: what, the good-jer![5]

CAIUS. Rugby, come to the court with me. By gar, if I have not Anne Page, I shall turn your head out of my door. Follow my heels, Rugby.   [*Exeunt* CAIUS *and* RUGBY.

QUICK. You shall have An fool's-head of your own.[6] No, I know Anne's mind for that: never a woman in Windsor knows more of

---

[4]*baille*] French for "give, deliver."

[5]*what, the good-jer!*] a common expletive expressive of surprise; "in the name of fortune!"

[6]*fool's-head . . . own*] make a fool of yourself.

Anne's mind than I do; nor can do more than I do with her, I
thank heaven.

FENT. [*Within*]   Who's within there? ho!

QUICK.   Who's there, I trow? Come near the house, I pray you.

Enter FENTON

FENT.   How now, good woman! how dost thou?

QUICK.   The better that it pleases your good worship to ask.

FENT.   What news? how does pretty Mistress Anne?

QUICK.   In truth, sir, and she is pretty, and honest, and gentle; and one
that is your friend, I can tell you that by the way; I praise heaven
for it.

FENT.   Shall I do any good, think'st thou? shall I not lose my suit?

QUICK.   Troth, sir, all is in his hands above: but notwithstanding,
Master Fenton, I'll be sworn on a book, she loves you. Have not
your worship a wart above your eye?

FENT.   Yes, marry, have I; what of that?

QUICK.   Well, thereby hangs a tale:—good faith, it is such another
Nan; but, I detest, an honest maid as ever broke bread:—we had
an hour's talk of that wart.—I shall never laugh but in that maid's
company!—But, indeed, she is given too much to allicholy and
musing: but for you—well, go to.

FENT.   Well, I shall see her to-day. Hold, there's money for thee; let
me have thy voice in my behalf: if thou seest her before me, commend me.

QUICK.   Will I? i' faith, that we will; and I will tell your worship more
of the wart the next time we have confidence; and of other wooers.

FENT.   Well, farewell; I am in great haste now.

QUICK.   Farewell to your worship. [*Exit* FENTON.] Truly, an honest
gentleman: but Anne loves him not; for I know Anne's mind as
well as another does.—Out upon 't! what have I forgot?   [*Exit.*

ACT II.

Scene I. *Before Page's House.*

Enter Mistress Page, *with a letter*.

Mistress Page.   What, have I scaped love-letters in the holiday-time
of my beauty, and am I now a subject for them? Let me see.

[*Reads.*

"Ask me no reason why I love you; for though Love use Reason for his
physician, he admits him not for his counsellor. You are not young, no
more am I; go to, then, there's sympathy: you are merry, so am I; ha, ha!
then there's more sympathy: you love sack, and so do I; would you desire
better sympathy? Let it suffice thee, Mistress Page,—at the least, if the
love of soldier can suffice,—that I love thee. I will not say, pity me,—'t
is not a soldier-like phrase; but I say, love me. By me,

> Thine own true knight,
> By day or night,
> Or any kind of light,
> With all his might
> For thee to fight,   John Falstaff."

What a herod of Jewry is this! O wicked, wicked world! One that
is well-nigh worn to pieces with age to show himself a young gallant! What an unweighed behaviour hath this Flemish drunkard
picked—with the devil's name!—out of my conversation, that he
dares in this manner assay me? Why, he hath not been thrice in
my company! What should I say to him? I was then frugal of my
mirth: Heaven forgive me! Why, I'll exhibit a bill in the parlia-
ment for the putting down of men. How shall I be revenged
on him? for revenged I will be, as sure as his guts are made of
puddings.

Enter Mistress Ford

Mrs Ford.   Mistress Page! trust me, I was going to your house.

MRS PAGE.   And, trust me, I was coming to you. You look very ill.

MRS FORD.   Nay, I'll ne'er believe that; I have to show to the contrary.

MRS PAGE.   Faith, but you do, in my mind.

MRS FORD.   Well, I do, then; yet, I say, I could show you to the contrary. O Mistress Page, give me some counsel!

MRS PAGE.   What's the matter, woman?

MRS FORD.   O woman, if it were not for one trifling respect, I could come to such honour!

MRS PAGE.   Hang the trifle, woman! take the honour. What is it?— dispense with trifles;—what is it?

MRS FORD.   If I would but go to hell for an eternal moment or so, I could be knighted.

MRS PAGE.   What? thou liest! Sir Alice Ford! These knights will hack;[1] and so thou shouldst not alter the article of thy gentry.

MRS FORD.   We burn daylight:[2]—here, read, read; perceive how I might be knighted. I shall think the worse of fat men, as long as I have an eye to make difference of men's liking: and yet he would not swear; praised women's modesty; and gave such orderly and well-behaved reproof to all uncomeliness, that I would have sworn his disposition would have gone to the truth of his words; but they do no more adhere and keep place together than the Hundredth Psalm to the tune of "Green Sleeves."[3] What tempest, I trow, threw this whale, with so many tuns of oil in his belly, ashore at Windsor? How shall I be revenged on him? I think the best way were to entertain him with hope, till the wicked fire of lust have melted him in his own grease. Did you ever hear the like?

MRS PAGE.   Letter for letter, but that the name of Page and Ford differs! To thy great comfort in this mystery of ill opinions, here's the twin-brother of thy letter: but let thine inherit first; for, I protest,

---

[1]*hack*] commonly explained in the unsupported sense of "grow hackneyed," "pall," "get too common," with a reference to James I's indiscriminate creation of knights (at a date later than the first draft of the play). There seems no point in the suggestion that "hack" is used here in its ordinary sense of "mutilate," "cut off," in allusion to the ceremonial degradation of unworthy knights by cutting off their spurs, the special emblem of chivalry. "Hack" undoubtedly appears in its ordinary sense of "mutilate," *infra*, III, i, but in a later scene it recurs in quite a different and apparently a ribald sense in IV, i, where Mrs. Quickly says a boy is taught by his master "*to hick and to hack*, which they'll do fast enough of themselves, and to call 'horum' (*i.e.* whore)." "Hack" or "hackney" was a slang name for a loose woman, and hence a verb meaning "to have dealings with loose women" is deducible. It is possible that Mrs. Page here intends some such quibbling allusion.

[2]*We burn daylight*] to lose time.

[3]*the tune of "Green Sleeves"*] One of the most popular ballads of Shakespeare's day.

mine never shall. I warrant he hath a thousand of these letters, writ with blank space for different names,—sure, more,—and these are of the second edition: he will print them, out of doubt; for he cares not what he puts into the press, when he would put us two. I had rather be a giantess, and lie under Mount Pelion. Well, I will find you twenty lascivious turtles ere one chaste man.

MRS FORD.   Why, this is the very same; the very hand, the very words. What doth he think of us?

MRS PAGE.   Nay, I know not: it makes me almost ready to wrangle with mine own honesty. I'll entertain myself like one that I am not acquainted withal; for, sure, unless he know some strain[4] in me, that I know not myself, he would never have boarded me in this fury.

MRS FORD.   "Boarding," call you it? I'll be sure to keep him above deck.

MRS PAGE.   So will I: if he come under my hatches, I'll never to sea again. Let's be revenged on him: let's appoint him a meeting; give him a show of comfort in his suit, and lead him on with a fine-baited delay, till he hath pawned his horses to mine host of the Garter.

MRS FORD.   Nay, I will consent to act any villany against him, that may not sully the chariness of our honesty. O, that my husband saw this letter! it would give eternal food to his jealousy.

MRS PAGE.   Why, look where he comes; and my good man too: he's as far from jealousy as I am from giving him cause; and that, I hope, is an unmeasurable distance.

MRS FORD.   You are the happier woman.

MRS PAGE.   Let's consult together against this greasy knight. Come hither.   [*They retire.*

Enter FORD, *with* PISTOL, *and* PAGE, *with* NYM

FORD.   Well, I hope it be not so.

PIST.   Hope is a curtal dog in some affairs:
         Sir John affects thy wife.

FORD.   Why, sir, my wife is not young.

PIST.   He wooes both high and low, both rich and poor,
         Both young and old, one with another, Ford;
    -    He loves the gallimaufry:[5] Ford, perpend.

FORD.   Love my wife!

---

[4]*some strain*] some natural disposition (to sensuality).
[5]*gallimaufry*] This word, which is from the French, properly means "a stew or hash" of mixed meats. Pistol applies it to a promiscuous assembly of persons.

PIST.   With liver burning hot. Prevent, or go thou,
Like Sir Actæon he, with Ringwood[6] at thy heels:
O, odious is the name!

FORD.   What name, sir?

PIST.   The horn, I say. Farewell.
Take heed; have open eye; for thieves do foot by night:
Take heed, ere summer comes, or cuckoo-birds do sing.
Away, Sir Corporal Nym!—
Believe it, Page; he speaks sense.   [*Exit.*

FORD. [*Aside*]   I will be patient; I will find out this.

NYM. [*To* PAGE]   And this is true; I like not the humour of lying. He
hath wronged me in some humours: I should have borne the hu-
moured letter to her; but I have a sword, and it shall bite upon my
necessity. He loves your wife; there's the short and the long. My
name is Corporal Nym; I speak, and I avouch; 't is true: my name
is Nym, and Falstaff loves your wife. Adieu. I love not the humour
of bread and cheese; and there's the humour of it. Adieu.   [*Exit.*

PAGE.   "The humour of it," quoth 'a! here's a fellow frights English out
of his wits.

FORD.   I will seek out Falstaff.

PAGE.   I never heard such a drawling, affecting rogue.

FORD.   If I do find it:—well.

PAGE.   I will not believe such a Cataian,[7] though the priest o' the town
commended him for a true man.

FORD.   'T was a good sensible fellow:—well.

PAGE.   How now, Meg!

[MRS PAGE *and* MRS FORD *come forward.*

MRS PAGE.   Whither go you, George? Hark you.

MRS FORD.   How now, sweet Frank! why art thou melancholy?

FORD.   I melancholy! I am not melancholy. Get you home, go.

MRS FORD.   Faith, thou hast some crotchets in thy head. Now, will
you go, Mistress Page?

MRS PAGE.   Have with you. You'll come to dinner, George? [*Aside to*
MRS FORD] Look who comes yonder: she shall be our messenger
to this paltry knight.

MRS FORD. [*Aside to* MRS PAGE]   Trust me, I thought on her: she'll fit
it.

---

[6]*Sir Actæon . . . Ringwood*] The story of Actæon, an ardent hunter, who for defying
Diana, goddess of the chase, was turned by her into a stag, is told by Ovid. Ovid gives
the names of Actæon's hounds, the last being called "Hylactor." Golding, in his translation of Ovid's *Metamorphoses*, renders the name "Hylactor" by "*Ringwood.*" This is
clear proof of Shakespeare's indebtedness to Golding in this passage. Actæon's transformation to a horned stag is noticed below, III, ii: "a secure and wilful *Actæon.*"

[7]*Cataian*] Literally, a native of Cathay or China, but often used for "thief" or "sharper."

Enter MISTRESS QUICKLY

MRS PAGE. You are come to see my daughter Anne?

QUICK. Ay, forsooth; and, I pray, how does good Mistress Anne?

MRS PAGE. Go in with us and see: we have an hour's talk with you.
                    [*Exeunt* MRS PAGE, MRS FORD, *and* MRS QUICKLY.

PAGE. How now, Master Ford!

FORD. You heard what this knave told me, did you not?

PAGE. Yes: and you heard what the other told me?

FORD. Do you think there is truth in them?

PAGE. Hang 'em, slaves! I do not think the knight would offer it: but these that accuse him in his intent towards our wives are a yoke of his discarded men; very rogues, now they be out of service.

FORD. Were they his men?

PAGE. Marry, were they.

FORD. I like it never the better for that. Does he lie at the Garter?

PAGE. Ay, marry, does he. If he should intend this voyage toward my wife, I would turn her loose to him; and what he gets more of her than sharp words, let it lie on my head.

FORD. I do not misdoubt my wife; but I would be loath to turn them together. A man may be too confident: I would have nothing lie on my head: I cannot be thus satisfied.

PAGE. Look where my ranting host of the Garter comes: there is either liquor in his pate, or money in his purse, when he looks so merrily.

Enter HOST

   How now, mine host!

HOST. How now, bully-rook! thou 'rt a gentleman. Cavaleiro-justice, I say!

Enter SHALLOW

SHAL. I follow, mine host, I follow. Good even and twenty, good Master Page! Master Page, will you go with us? we have sport in hand.

HOST. Tell him, cavaleiro-justice; tell him, bully-rook.

SHAL. Sir, there is a fray to be fought between Sir Hugh the Welsh priest and Caius the French doctor.

FORD. Good mine host o' the Garter, a word with you.
                    [*Drawing him aside.*

HOST. What say'st thou, my bully-rook?

SHAL. [*To* PAGE] Will you go with us to behold it? My merry host hath had the measuring of their weapons; and, I think, hath appointed them contrary places; for, believe me, I hear the parson is no jester. Hark, I will tell you what our sport shall be.

                                     [*They converse apart.*

HOST.   Hast thou no suit against my knight, my guest-cavaleire?

FORD.   None, I protest: but I'll give you a pottle of burnt sack[8] to give me recourse to him, and tell him my name is Brook; only for a jest.

HOST.   My hand, bully; thou shalt have egress and regress;—said I well?—and thy name shall be Brook. It is a merry knight. Will you go, An-heires?[9]

SHAL.   Have with you, mine host.

PAGE.   I have heard the Frenchman hath good skill in his rapier.

SHAL.   Tut, sir, I could have told you more. In these times you stand on distance, your passes, stoccadoes, and I know not what: 't is the heart, Master Page; 't is here, 't is here. I have seen the time, with my long sword I would have made you four tall fellows skip like rats.

HOST.   Here, boys, here, here! shall we wag?

PAGE.   Have with you. I had rather hear them scold than fight.

                              [*Exeunt* HOST, SHAL., *and* PAGE.

FORD.   Though Page be a secure fool, and stands so firmly on his wife's frailty,[10] yet I cannot put off my opinion so easily: she was in his company at Page's house; and what they made there, I know not. Well, I will look further into 't: and I have a disguise to sound Falstaff. If I find her honest, I lose not my labour; if she be otherwise, 't is labour well bestowed.   [*Exit.*

SCENE II. *A Room in The Garter Inn.*

Enter FALSTAFF *and* PISTOL

FAL.   I will not lend thee a penny.

PIST.   Why, then the world 's mine oyster,
         Which I with sword will open.

---

[8]*burnt sack*] apparently sack heated by dipping a red-hot iron in the liquid.

[9]*An-heires*] This is the reading of the early editions, and is an obvious misprint. Theobald substituted *myn-heers* (*i.e.* the Dutch word for "gentlemen," which was not unfamiliar in colloquial English). It seems more probable that the host used the word "hearts" or "my hearts," *i.e.* brave fellows. This is the host's greeting in like circumstances, III, ii, *infra* ("Farewell, my *hearts*").

[10]*stands . . . frailty*] Malone explains "has such perfect confidence in his unchaste wife," Ford being supposed to credit every woman with frailty. Theobald read *fealty* for *frailty*, and thus removed the ambiguity, which was probably intentional on the author's part.

FAL.. Not a penny. I have been content, sir, you should lay my countenance to pawn: I have grated upon[1] my good friends for three re-
prieves for you and your coach-fellow Nym; or else you had
looked through the grate,[2] like a geminy of baboons. I am damned
in hell for swearing to gentlemen my friends, you were good soldiers and tall fellows; and when Mistress Bridget lost the handle of
her fan, I took 't upon mine honour thou hadst it not.

PIST. Didst not thou share? hadst thou not fifteen pence?

FAL. Reason, you rogue, reason: think'st thou I'll endanger my soul
gratis? At a word, hang no more about me, I am no gibbet for you.
Go. A short knife and a throng![3] — To your manor of Pickt-hatch![4]
Go. You'll not bear a letter for me, you rogue! you stand upon
your honour! Why, thou unconfinable baseness, it is as much as I
can do to keep the terms of my honour precise: I, I, I myself sometimes, leaving the fear of God on the left hand, and hiding mine
honour in my necessity, am fain to shuffle, to hedge, and to lurch;
and yet you, rogue, will ensconce your rags, your cat-a-mountain
looks, your red-lattice phrases,[5] and your bold-beating[6] oaths,
under the shelter of your honour! You will not do it, you!

PIST. I do relent: what would thou more of man?

Enter ROBIN

ROB. Sir, here's a woman would speak with you.

FAL. Let her approach.

Enter MISTRESS QUICKLY

QUICK. Give your worship good morrow.

FAL. Good morrow, good wife.

QUICK. Not so, an 't please your worship.

FAL. Good maid, then.

QUICK. I'll be sworn;
    As my mother was, the first hour I was born.

FAL. I do believe the swearer. What with me?

---

[1]*grated upon*] worried, annoyed.

[2]*through the grate*] sc. of the prison cell.

[3]*A short knife . . . throng*] Falstaff ironically recommends the short knife which cut-
purses were wont to turn to account in a throng or crowd.

[4]*Pickt-hatch*] The name of a street in Clerkenwell, London, which was notoriously fre-
quented by loose characters. The name seems to mean a hatch (*i.e.* wicket, gate, half
door) with pikes or spikes fastened at the top. Some of the houses in the street were
thus distinguished.

[5]*red-lattice phrases*] tavern parlour talk.

[6]*bold-beating*] hectoring, braggadocio-like. For this, the original reading, Hanmer ingeniously suggested *bull-baiting*.

QUICK.   Shall I vouchsafe your worship a word or two?

FAL.   Two thousand, fair woman: and I'll vouchsafe thee the hearing.

QUICK.   There is one Mistress Ford, sir:—I pray, come a little nearer
this ways:—I myself dwell with Master Doctor Caius,—

FAL.   Well, on: Mistress Ford, you say,—

QUICK.   Your worship says very true:—I pray your worship, come a little nearer this ways.

FAL.   I warrant thee, nobody hears;—mine own people, mine own
people.

QUICK.   Are they so? God bless them, and make them his servants!

FAL.   Well, Mistress Ford;—what of her?

QUICK.   Why, sir, she's a good creature.—Lord, Lord! your worship's
a wanton! Well, heaven forgive you and all of us, I pray!

FAL.   Mistress Ford;—come, Mistress Ford,—

QUICK.   Marry, this is the short and the long of it; you have brought
her into such a canaries[7] as 't is wonderful. The best courtier of
them all, when the court lay at Windsor, could never have
brought her to such a canary. Yet there has been knights, and
lords, and gentlemen, with their coaches; I warrant you, coach
after coach, letter after letter, gift after gift; smelling so sweetly, all
musk, and so rushling, I warrant you, in silk and gold; and in such
alligant terms; and in such wine and sugar of the best and the
fairest, that would have won any woman's heart; and, I warrant
you, they could never get an eye-wink of her: I had myself twenty
angels given me this morning; but I defy all angels—in any such
sort, as they say—but in the way of honesty: and, I warrant you,
they could never get her so much as sip on a cup with the proud-
est of them all: and yet there has been earls, nay, which is more,
pensioners;[8] but, I warrant you, all is one with her.

FAL.   But what says she to me? be brief, my good she-Mercury.

QUICK.   Marry, she hath received your letter; for the which she thanks
you a thousand times; and she gives you to notify, that her husband will be absence from his house between ten and eleven.

FAL.   Ten and eleven.

QUICK.   Ay, forsooth; and then you may come and see the picture, she
says, that you wot of: Master Ford, her husband, will be from
home. Alas, the sweet woman leads an ill life with him! he's a very
jealousy man: she leads a very frampold life with him, good heart.

FAL.   Ten and eleven. Woman, commend me to her; I will not fail
her.

---

[7]*canaries*] a dance with a very quick step. Mrs. Quickly confused the word with
"quandary."

[8]*pensioners*] gentlemen of the sovereign's body guard.

QUICK.   Why, you say well. But I have another messenger to your worship. Mistress Page hath her hearty commendations to you, too:
and let me tell you in your ear, she's as fartuous a civil modest
wife, and one, I tell you, that will not miss you morning nor
evening prayer, as any is in Windsor, whoe'er be the other: and
she bade me tell your worship that her husband is seldom from
home; but, she hopes, there will come a time. I never knew a
woman so dote upon a man: surely, I think you have charms, la;
yes, in truth.

FAL.   Not I, I assure thee: setting the attraction of my good parts aside,
I have no other charms.

QUICK.   Blessing on your heart for 't!

FAL.   But, I pray thee, tell me this: has Ford's wife and Page's wife acquainted each other how they love me?

QUICK.   That were a jest indeed! they have not so little grace, I hope:
that were a trick indeed! But Mistress Page would desire you to
send her your little page, of all loves:[9] her husband has a marvellous infection to the little page; and, truly, Master Page is an honest man. Never a wife in Windsor leads a better life than she does:
do what she will, say what she will, take all, pay all, go to bed when
she list, rise when she list, all is as she will: and, truly, she deserves
it; for if there be a kind woman in Windsor, she is one. You must
send her your page; no remedy.

FAL.   Why, I will.

QUICK.   Nay, but do so, then: and, look you, he may come and go between you both; and, in any case, have a nay-word,[10] that you may
know one another's mind, and the boy never need to understand
any thing; for 't is not good that children should know any wickedness: old folks, you know, have discretion, as they say, and know
the world.

FAL.   Fare thee well: commend me to them both: there's my purse; I
am yet thy debtor. Boy, go along with this woman. [*Exeunt*
MISTRESS QUICKLY *and* ROBIN.] This news distracts me!

PIST.   This punk is one of Cupid's carriers:
Clap on more sails; pursue; up with your fights:[11]
Give fire: she is my prize, or ocean whelm them all!   [*Exit.*

FAL.   Say'st thou so, old Jack? go thy ways; I'll make more of thy old
body than I have done. Will they yet look after thee? Wilt thou,

---

[9]*of all loves*] In *Othello*, III, i, the Quarto reading, "Desire you *of all loves*," is altered
in the Folios to *for loves sake*, the obvious meaning of the very common expression.

[10]*nay-word*] pass word.

[11]*fights*] "fighting sails," or screens which were hung round the decks of ships in action;
a technical term in nautical treatises.

after the expense of so much money, be now a gainer? Good body, I thank thee. Let them say 't is grossly done; so it be fairly done, no matter.

Enter BARDOLPH

BARD.   Sir John, there's one Master Brook below would fain speak with you, and be acquainted with you; and hath sent your worship a morning's draught of sack.

FAL.   Brook is his name?

BARD.   Ay, sir.

FAL.   Call him in. [*Exit* BARDOLPH.] Such Brooks are welcome to me, that o'erflow such liquor. Ah, ha! Mistress Ford and Mistress Page, have I encompassed you? go to; via!

Re-enter BARDOLPH, *with* FORD *disguised*

FORD.   Bless you, sir!

FAL.   And you, sir! Would you speak with me?

FORD.   I make bold to press with so little preparation upon you.

FAL.   You're welcome. What's your will?—Give us leave, drawer.
                                                        [*Exit* BARDOLPH.

FORD.   Sir, I am a gentleman that have spent much; my name is Brook.

FAL.   Good Master Brook, I desire more acquaintance of you.

FORD.   Good Sir John, I sue for yours: not to charge you; for I must let you understand I think myself in better plight for a lender than you are: the which hath something emboldened me to this un-seasoned intrusion; for they say, if money go before, all ways do lie open.

FAL.   Money is a good soldier, sir, and will on.

FORD.   Troth, and I have a bag of money here troubles me: if you will help to bear it, Sir John, take all, or half, for easing me of the carriage.

FAL.   Sir, I know not how I may deserve to be your porter.

FORD.   I will tell you, sir, if you will give me the hearing.

FAL.   Speak, good Master Brook: I shall be glad to be your servant.

FORD.   Sir, I hear you are a scholar,—I will be brief with you,—and you have been a man long known to me, though I had never so good means, as desire, to make myself acquainted with you. I shall discover a thing to you, wherein I must very much lay open mine own imperfection: but, good Sir John, as you have one eye upon my follies, as you hear them unfolded, turn another into the reg-ister of your own; that I may pass with a reproof the easier, sith you yourself know how easy it is to be such an offender.

FAL. Very well, sir; proceed.

FORD. There is a gentlewoman in this town; her husband's name is Ford.

FAL. Well, sir.

FORD. I have long loved her, and, I protest to you, bestowed much on her; followed her with a doting observance; engrossed opportunities to meet her, fee'd every slight occasion that could but niggardly give me sight of her; not only bought many presents to give her, but have given largely to many to know what she would have given; briefly, I have pursued her as love hath pursued me; which hath been on the wing of all occasions. But whatsoever I have merited, either in my mind or in my means, meed, I am sure, I have received none; unless experience be a jewel that I have purchased at an infinite rate, and that hath taught me to say this:

> "Love like a shadow flies when substance love pursues;
> Pursuing that that flies, and flying what pursues."

FAL. Have you received no promise of satisfaction at her hands?

FORD. Never.

FAL. Have you importuned her to such a purpose?

FORD. Never.

FAL. Of what quality was your love, then?

FORD. Like a fair house built on another man's ground; so that I have lost my edifice by mistaking the place where I erected it.

FAL. To what purpose have you unfolded this to me?

FORD. When I have told you that, I have told you all. Some say, that though she appear honest to me, yet in other places she enlargeth her mirth so far that there is shrewd construction made of her. Now, Sir John, here is the heart of my purpose: you are a gentleman of excellent breeding, admirable discourse, of great admittance, authentic in your place and person, generally allowed[12] for your many war-like, court-like, and learned preparations.

FAL. O, sir!

FORD. Believe it, for you know it. There is money; spend it, spent it; spend more; spend all I have; only give me so much of your time in exchange of it, as to lay an amiable siege to the honesty of this Ford's wife: use your art of wooing; win her to consent to you: if any man may, you may as soon as any.

FAL. Would it apply well to the vehemency of your affection, that I

---

[12]*of great admittance . . . allowed*] being admitted into or fitted for great society, holding a position of recognized authority and importance, and being generally allowed or commended, etc.

should win what you would enjoy? Methinks you prescribe to
yourself very preposterously.

FORD.   O, understand my drift. She dwells so securely on the excellency of her honour, that the folly of my soul dares not present itself: she is too bright to be looked against. Now, could I come to
her with any detection in my hand, my desires had instance and
argument to commend themselves: I could drive her then from
the ward of her purity, her reputation, her marriage-vow, and a
thousand other her defences, which now are too too strongly em-
battled against me. What say you to 't, Sir John?

FAL.   Master Brook, I will first make bold with your money; next, give
me your hand; and last, as I am a gentleman, you shall, if you will,
enjoy Ford's wife.

FORD.   O good sir!

FAL.   I say you shall.

FORD.   Want no money, Sir John; you shall want none.

FAL.   Want no Mistress Ford, Master Brook; you shall want none. I
shall be with her, I may tell you, by her own appointment; even as
you came in to me, her assistant, or go-between, parted from me:
I say I shall be with her between ten and eleven; for at that time
the jealous rascally knave her husband will be forth. Come you to
me at night; you shall know how I speed.

FORD.   I am blest in your acquaintance. Do you know Ford, sir?

FAL.   Hang him, poor cuckoldly knave! I know him not:—yet I wrong
him to call him poor; they say the jealous wittolly knave hath
masses of money; for the which his wife seems to me well-
favoured. I will use her as the key of the cuckoldly rogue's coffer;
and there's my harvest-home.

FORD.   I would you knew Ford, sir, that you might avoid him, if you
saw him.

FAL.   Hang him, mechanical salt-butter rogue![13] I will stare him out
of his wits; I will awe him with my cudgel: it shall hang like a me-
teor o'er the cuckold's horns. Master Brook, thou shalt know I will
predominate over the peasant, and thou shalt lie with his wife.
Come to me soon at night. Ford's a knave, and I will aggravate his
style;[14] thou, Master Brook, shalt know him for knave and cuckold. Come to me soon at night.   [*Exit.*

FORD.   What a damned Epicurean rascal is this! My heart is ready to
crack with impatience. Who says this is improvident jealousy? my
wife hath sent to him; the hour is fixed; the match is made. Would

---

[13]*mechanical salt-butter rogue*] an artisan, who never tasted anything but salt butter.
[14]*aggravate his style*] add more titles (*i.e.* "knave" and "cuckold") to those he already
enjoys.

any man have thought this? See the hell of having a false woman! My bed shall be abused, my coffers ransacked, my reputation gnawn at; and I shall not only receive this villanous wrong, but stand under the adoption of abominable terms, and by him that does me this wrong. Terms! names!—Amaimon[15] sounds well; Lucifer, well; Barbason,[16] well; yet they are devils' additions, the names of fiends: but Cuckold! Wittol!—Cuckold! the devil himself hath not such a name. Page is an ass, a secure ass: he will trust his wife; he will not be jealous. I will rather trust a Fleming with my butter, Parson Hugh the Welshman with my cheese, an Irishman with my aqua-vitæ[17] bottle, or a thief to walk my ambling gelding, than my wife with herself: then she plots, then she ruminates, then she devises; and what they think in their hearts they may effect, they will break their hearts but they will effect. God be praised for my jealousy!—Eleven o'clock the hour. I will prevent this, detect my wife, be revenged on Falstaff, and laugh at Page. I will about it; better three hours too soon than a minute too late. Fie, fie, fie! cuckold! cuckold! cuckold! [*Exit.*

SCENE III. A *Field Near Windsor.*

Enter CAIUS *and* RUGBY

CAIUS.   Jack Rugby!

RUG.   Sir?

CAIUS.   Vat is de clock, Jack?

RUG.   'T is past the hour, sir, that Sir Hugh promised to meet.

CAIUS.   By gar, he has save his soul, dat he is no come; he has pray his Pible well, dat he is no come: by gar, Jack Rugby, he is dead already, if he be come.

RUG.   He is wise, sir; he knew your worship would kill him, if he came.

CAIUS.   By gar, de herring is no dead so as I vill kill him. Take your rapier, Jack; I vill tell you how I vill kill him.

RUG.   Alas, sir, I cannot fence.

CAIUS.   Villainy, take your rapier.

RUG.   Forbear; here's company.

---

[15]*Amaimon*] The name of a demon or sprite, which figures in Reginald Scot's *Discovery of Witchcraft.*

[16]*Barbason*] represents Scot's fiend of hell called "Barbatos.

[17]*aqua-vitæ*] Usquebaugh, strong spirits, with indulgence in which Irishmen were commonly credited.

Enter HOST, SHALLOW, SLENDER, *and* PAGE

HOST.   Bless thee, bully doctor!

SHAL.   Save you, Master Doctor Gaius!

PAGE.   Now, good master doctor!

SLEN.   Give you good morrow, sir.

CAIUS.   Vat be all you, one, two, tree, four, come for?

HOST.   To see thee fight, to see thee foin, to see thee traverse; to see thee here, to see thee there; to see thee pass thy punto, thy stock, thy reverse, thy distance, thy montant.[1] Is he dead, my Ethiopian? is he dead, my Francisco? ha, bully! What says my Æsculapius? my Galen? my heart of elder?[2] ha! is he dead, bully-stale? is he dead?

CAIUS.   By gar, he is de coward Jack priest of de vorld; he is not show his face.

HOST.   Thou art a Castalion-King-Urinal.[3] Hector of Greece, my boy!

CAIUS.   I pray you, bear vitness that me have stay six or seven, two, tree hours for him, and he is no come.

SHAL.   He is the wiser man, master doctor: he is a curer of souls, and you a curer of bodies; if you should fight, you go against the hair of your professions. Is it not true, Master Page?

PAGE.   Master Shallow, you have yourself been a great fighter, though now a man of peace.

SHAL.   Bodykins, Master Page, though I now be old, and of the peace, if I see a sword out, my finger itches to make one. Though we are justices, and doctors, and churchmen, Master Page, we have some salt of our youth in us; we are the sons of women, Master Page.

PAGE.   'T is true, Master Shallow.

SHAL.   It will be found so, Master Page. Master Doctor Caius, I am come to fetch you home. I am sworn of the peace: you have shewed yourself a wise physician, and Sir Hugh hath shewn himself a wise and patient churchman. You must go with me, master doctor.

HOST.   Pardon, guest-justice.—A word, Mounseur Mock-water.

---

[1] *to see . . . montant*] Mine Host rattles off a long series of fencing terms. Thus "foin" is to "thrust"; "traverse" is to "parry"; "punto" and "stock" *i.e.* stoccato, both mean "thrust"; "reverse" is a backhanded stroke; "distance" is the space between the antagonists; "montant," or "montanto," is a direct blow.

[2] *my heart of elder*] a burlesque parody of "heart of oak"; the elder-tree's heart is of pith.

[3] *Castalion-King-Urinal*] This is the reading of the Folios. But the meaning is improved by the commonly accepted change, *Castilian, King-urinal!* "Castilian" was an epithet commonly applied to a braggadocio. In vulgar talk Elizabethan doctors were often jeered at for their professional practice of inspecting urine. The like intention is apparent in the host's insolent exclamations "bully-stale" and "Mock water" *i.e.* "Muck-water."

CAIUS. Mock-vater! vat is dat?

HOST. Mock-water, in our English tongue, is valour, bully.

CAIUS. By gar, den, I have as much mock-vater as de Englishman.— Scurvy jack-dog priest! by gar, me vill cut his ears.

HOST. He will clapper-claw thee tightly, bully.

CAIUS. Clapper-de-claw! vat is dat?

HOST. That is, he will make thee amends.

CAIUS. By gar, me do look he shall clapper-de-claw me; for, by gar, me vill have it.

HOST. And I will provoke him to 't, or let him wag.

CAIUS. Me tank you for dat.

HOST. And, moreover, bully,—But first, master guest, and Master Page, and eke Cavaleiro Slender, go you through the town to Frogmore. [*Aside to them.*

PAGE. Sir Hugh is there, is he?

HOST. He is there: see what humour he is in; and I will bring the doctor about by the fields. Will it do well?

SHAL. We will do it.

PAGE, SHAL., and SLEN. Adieu, good master doctor.

[*Exeunt* PAGE, SHAL., *and* SLEN.

CAIUS. By gar, me vill kill de priest; for he speak for a jack-an-ape to Anne Page.

HOST. Let him die: sheathe thy impatience, throw cold water on thy choler: go about the fields with me through Frogmore: I will bring thee where Mistress Anne Page is, at a farm-house a-feasting; and thou shalt woo her. Cried I aim?[4] said I well?

CAIUS. By gar, me dank you vor dat: by gar, I love you; and I shall procure-a you de good guest, de earl, de knight, de lords, de gentlemen, my patients.

HOST. For the which I will be thy adversary toward Anne Page. Said I well?

CAIUS. By gar, 't is good; vell said.

HOST. Let us wag, then.

CAIUS. Come at my heels, Jack Rugby. [*Exeunt.*

---

[4]*Cried I aim?*] This is Douce's ingenious emendation for the Folio reading *Cride-game.* The earlier Quartos read *cried game.* "To cry aim," *i.e.* to stand beside the archer and to suggest the direction of his aim, is a technical phrase in archery. The host asks if he has not given the doctor good advice in his suit.

ACT III.

Scene I. A *Field Near Frogmore*.

Enter Sir Hugh Evans *and* Simple

Evans. I pray you now, good Master Slender's serving-man, and
friend Simple by your name, which way have you looked for
Master Caius, that calls himself doctor of physic?

Sim. Marry, sir, the pittie-ward,[1] the park-ward, every way; old
Windsor way, and every way but the town way.

Evans. I most fehemently desire you you will also look that way.

Sim. I will, sir.   [*Exit.*

Evans. Pless my soul, how full of chollors I am, and trempling of
mind!—I shall be glad if he have deceived me.—How melan-
cholies I am!—I will knog his urinals about his knave's costard
when I have goot opportunities for the ork.—Pless my soul!—

[*Sings.*

> To shallow rivers, to whose falls
> Melodious birds sings madrigals;
> There will we make our peds of roses,
> And a thousand fragrant posies.[2]
> To shallow—

Mercy on me! I have a great dispositions to cry.   [*Sings.*

---

[1] *pittie-ward*] This word, which is altered in the second and later Folios to *pitty-wary*, has
not been satisfactorily explained. The early emendation *city-ward* circumvents the dif-
ficulty. The suggestion that the word is equivalent to "pitwards," towards the pit, *i.e.* a
sawpit or gravel pit (in or about Windsor), is speciously supported by the mention of
"a sawpit," *infra*, IV, iv; of "a pit hard by Herne's oak," V, iii; and of "the pit," V, iv.
From the fact that medieval Bristol was credited by William of Worcester with a street
called "Via de Pyttey," and with a gate called "Pyttey Gate," it may be that a like name
was applied to some thoroughfare of Elizabethan Windsor.

[2] *To shallow rivers, etc.*] These four lines form part of the lyric "Come live with me and
be my love" (assigned to Christopher Marlowe), which was first printed in Jaggard's pi-
ratical miscellany called "*The Passionate Pilgrime*, By W. Shakespeare, 1599."

> Melodious birds sing madrigals—
> Whenas I sat in Pabylon[3]—
> And a thousand vagram posies.
> To shallow &c.

Re-enter SIMPLE

SIM.   Yonder he is coming, this way, Sir Hugh.
EVANS.   He's welcome.—   [*Sings.*

> To shallow rivers, to whose falls—

Heaven prosper the right!—What weapons is he?
SIM.   No weapons, sir. There comes my master, Master Shallow, and another gentleman, from Frogmore, over the style, this way.
EVANS.   Pray you, give me my gown; or else keep it in your arms.

Enter PAGE, SHALLOW, *and* SLENDER

SHAL.   How now, master parson! Good morrow, good Sir Hugh. Keep a gamester from the dice, and a good student from his book, and it is wonderful.
SLEN. [*Aside*]   Ah, sweet Anne Page!
PAGE.   Save you, good Sir Hugh!
EVANS.   Pless you from his mercy sake, all of you!
SHAL.   What, the sword and the word! do you study them both, master parson?
PAGE.   And youthful still! in your doublet and hose this raw rheumatic day!
EVANS.   There is reasons and causes for it.
PAGE.   We are come to you to do a good office, master parson.
EVANS.   Fery well: what is it?
PAGE.   Yonder is a most reverend gentleman, who, belike having received wrong by some person, is at most odds with his own gravity and patience that ever you saw.
SHAL.   I have lived fourscore years and upward; I never heard a man of his place, gravity, and learning, so wide of his own respect.
EVANS.   What is he?
PAGE.   I think you know him; Master Doctor Caius, the renowned French physician.

---

[3]*Whenas I sat in Pabylon*] This is an interpolation into Marlowe's poem. Sir Hugh in his confusion jumbles his quotations. There is doubtless a reminiscence of *Ps.* cxxxvii, 1: "By the waters of Babylon we sat down and wept." But it should be noted that in the First (imperfect) Quarto of the play (1602) Evans prefixes to his repetition of Marlowe's lines the words (omitted in the Folio), "There dwelt a man in Babylon." That is the first line of another popular contemporary ballad known as *The Ballad of Constant Susanna.*

EVANS.   Got's will, and his passion of my heart! I had as lief you would
tell me of a mess of porridge.

PAGE.   Why?

EVANS.   He has no more knowledge in Hibocrates and Galen,—and
he is a knave besides; a cowardly knave as you would desires to be
acquainted withal.

PAGE.   I warrant you, he's the man should fight with him.

SLEN. [*Aside*]   O sweet Anne Page!

SHAL.   It appears so, by his weapons. Keep them asunder: here comes
Doctor Caius.

Enter HOST, CAIUS, *and* RUGBY

PAGE.   Nay, good master parson, keep in your weapon.

SHAL.   So do you, good master doctor.

HOST.   Disarm them, and let them question: let them keep their
limbs whole, and hack our English.

CAIUS.   I pray you, let-a me speak a word with your ear. Verefore vill
you not meet-a me?

EVANS. [*Aside to* CAIUS]   Pray you, use your patience: in good time.

CAIUS.   By gar, you are de coward, de Jack dog, John ape.

EVANS. [*Aside to* CAIUS]   Pray you, let us not be laughing-stocks to
other men's humours; I desire you in friendship, and I will one
way or other make you amends. [*Aloud*] I will knog your urinals
about your knave's cogscomb for missing your meetings and
appointments.

CAIUS.   Diable!—Jack Rugby,—mine host de Jarteer,—have I not stay
for him to kill him? have I not, at de place I did appoint?

EVANS.   As I am a Christians soul, now, look you, this is the place appointed: I'll be judgement by mine host of the Garter.

HOST.   Peace, I say, Gallia and Gaul, French and Welsh, soul-curer
and body-curer!

CAIUS.   Ay, dat is very good; excellent.

HOST.   Peace, I say! hear mine host of the Garter. Am I politic? am I
subtle? am I a Machiavel? Shall I lose my doctor? no; he gives me
the potions and the motions. Shall I lose my parson, my priest, my
Sir Hugh? no; he gives me the proverbs and the no-verbs. Give me
thy hand, terrestrial; so. Give me thy hand, celestial; so. Boys of
art, I have deceived you both; I have directed you to wrong places:
your hearts are mighty, your skins are whole, and let burnt sack be
the issue. Come, lay their swords to pawn. Follow me, lads of
peace; follow, follow, follow.

SHAL.   Trust me, a mad host. Follow, gentlemen, follow.

SLEN. [*Aside*]   O sweet Anne Page!

                               [*Exeunt* SHAL., SLEN.; PAGE, *and* HOST.

CAIUS.   Ha, do I perceive dat? have you make-a de sot of us, ha, ha?

EVANS.   This is well; he has made us his vlouting-stog.[4]—I desire you that we may be friends; and let us knog our prains together to be revenge on this same scall,[5] scurvy, cogging companion, the host of the Garter.

CAIUS.   By gar, with all my heart. He promise to bring me where is Anne Page; by gar, he deceive me too.

EVANS.   Well, I will smite his noddles. Pray you, follow.   [*Exeunt.*

SCENE II. *The Street, in Windsor.*

Enter MISTRESS PAGE *and* ROBIN

MRS PAGE.   Nay, keep your way, little gallant; you were wont to be a follower, but now you are a leader. Whether had you rather lead mine eyes, or eye your master's heels?

ROB.   I had rather, forsooth, go before you like a man than follow him like a dwarf.

MRS PAGE.   O, you are a flattering boy: now I see you'll be a courtier.

Enter FORD

FORD.   Well met, Mistress Page. Whither go you?

MRS PAGE.   Truly, sir, to see your wife. Is she at home?

FORD.   Ay; and as idle as she may hang together,[1] for want of company. I think, if your husbands were dead, you two would marry.

MRS PAGE.   Be sure of that,—two other husbands.

FORD.   Where had you this pretty weathercock?

MRS PAGE.   I cannot tell what the dickens his name is my husband had him of.—What do you call your knight's name, sirrah?

ROB.   Sir John Falstaff.

FORD.   Sir John Falstaff!

MRS PAGE.   He, he; I can never hit on 's name. There is such a league between my good man and he!—Is your wife at home indeed?

FORD.   Indeed she is.

MRS PAGE.   By your leave, sir: I am sick till I see her.

                                   [*Exeunt* MRS PAGE *and* ROBIN.

---

[4]*vlouting-stog*] Evans' mispronunciation of "flouting-stock," *i.e.* butt.

[5]*scall*] "Scall" is equivalent to "scald," and means much the same as "scurvy," the word which follows.

---

[1]*as idle as she may hang together*] as idle as one can possibly be: a colloquialism equivalent to the modern slang "as idle as she can stick."

FORD.   Has Page any brains? hath he any eyes? hath he any thinking? Sure, they sleep; he hath no use of them. Why, this boy will carry a letter twenty mile, as easy as a cannon will shoot point-blank twelve score.[2] He pieces out his wife's inclination; he gives her folly motion and advantage: and now she's going to my wife, and Falstaff's boy with her. A man may hear this shower sing in the wind.[3] And Falstaff's boy with her! Good plots, they are laid; and our revolted wives share damnation together. Well; I will take him, then torture my wife, pluck the borrowed veil of modesty from the so seeming Mistress Page, divulge Page himself for a secure and wilful Actæon; and to these violent proceedings all my neighbours shall cry aim.[4] [*Clock heard.*] The clock gives me my cue, and my assurance bids me search: there I shall find Falstaff: I shall be rather praised for this than mocked; for it is as positive as the earth is firm that Falstaff is there: I will go.

Enter PAGE, SHALLOW, SLENDER, HOST, SIR HUGH EVANS, CAIUS, *and* RUGBY

SHAL., PAGE, &C.   Well met, Master Ford.
FORD.   Trust me, a good knot:[5] I have good cheer at home; and I pray you all go with me.
SHAL.   I must excuse myself, Master Ford.
SLEN.   And so must I, sir: we have appointed to dine with Mistress Anne, and I would not break with her for more money than I'll speak of.
SHAL.   We have lingered about a match between Anne Page and my cousin Slender, and this day we shall have our answer.
SLEN.   I hope I have your good will, father Page.
PAGE.   You have, Master Slender; I stand wholly for you:—but my wife, master doctor, is for you altogether.
CAIUS.   Ay, be-gar; and de maid is love-a me: my nursh-a Quickly tell me so mush.
HOST.   What say you to young Master Fenton? he capers, he dances, he has eyes of youth, he writes verses, he speaks holiday,[6] he smells April and May: he will carry 't, he will carry 't; 't is in his buttons;[7] he will carry 't.

---

[2]*twelve score*] twelve score yards.
[3]*may hear this shower . . . wind*] A phrase implying the coming of a storm, which is often heralded by a whistling or singing note in the rising wind.
[4]*cry aim*] give encouragement.
[5]*a good knot*] a welcome gathering of friends.
[6]*speaks holiday*] uses choice phrases.
[7]*in his buttons*] altogether in his compass or ability.

PAGE.   Not by my consent, I promise you. The gentleman is of no having:[8] he kept company with the wild prince and Poins;[9] he is of too
high a region;[10] he knows too much. No, he shall not knit a knot
in his fortunes with the finger of my substance: if he take her, let
him take her simply; the wealth I have waits on my consent, and
my consent goes not that way.

FORD.   I beseech you heartily, some of you go home with me to dinner: besides your cheer, you shall have sport; I will show you a
monster. Master doctor, you shall go; so shall you, Master Page;
and you, Sir Hugh.

SHAL.   Well, fare you well: we shall have the freer wooing at Master
Page's.   [*Exeunt* SHAL. *and* SLEN.

CAIUS.   Go home, John Rugby; I come anon.   [*Exit* RUGBY.

HOST.   Farewell, my hearts: I will to my honest knight Falstaff, and
drink canary with him.   [*Exit.*

FORD. [*Aside*]   I think I shall drink in pipe-wine[11] first with him; I'll
make him dance. Will you go, gentles?

ALL.   Have with you to see this monster.   [*Exeunt.*

SCENE III. *A Room in Ford's House.*

Enter MISTRESS FORD *and* MISTRESS PAGE

MRS FORD.   What, John! What, Robert!
MRS PAGE.   Quickly, quickly!—is the buck-basket[1]—
MRS FORD.   I warrant. What, Robin, I say!

Enter Servants *with a basket*

MRS PAGE.   Come, come, come.
MRS FORD.   Here, set it down.
MRS PAGE.   Give your men the charge; we must be brief.

---

[8]*no having*] no property or fortune.
[9]*the wild prince and Poins*] Prince Hal, afterwards Henry V, and his favourite companion Poins, both of whom are leading characters in the two parts of *Hen. IV.*
[10]*too high a region*] too high a rank, too highly placed. "Region" is often applied to the
highest layers of the atmospheric air.
[11]*drink in pipe-wine*] There is a pun on the word "pipe," which is employed in the double sense of an instrument used for dance-music and a liquid-measure. Similarly, "canary" is both a dance and a wine. The meaning is to the same effect as that of the next
sentence: "I'll make him dance." "Drink in" is equivalent to "drink." "Pipe-wine" is
literally wine drawn from the pipe (or barrel of two hogsheads).

---

[1]*buck-basket*] The basket in which dirty clothes were sent to be "bucked," or washed by
the thorough process commonly known as "bucking."

MRS FORD.   Marry, as I told you before, John and Robert, be ready
       here hard by in the brew-house; and when I suddenly call you,
       come forth, and; without any pause or staggering, take this basket
       on your shoulders: that done, trudge with it in all haste, and carry
       it among the whitsters in Datchet-mead, and there empty it in the
       muddy ditch close by the Thames side.
MRS PAGE.   You will do it?
MRS FORD.   I ha' told them over and over; they lack no direction. Be
       gone, and come when you are called.   [Exeunt Servants.
MRS PAGE.   Here comes little Robin.

Enter ROBIN

MRS FORD.   How now, my eyas-musket! what news with you?
ROB.   My master, Sir John, is come in at your backdoor, Mistress
       Ford, and requests your company.
MRS PAGE.   You little Jack-a-Lent,[2] have you been true to us?
ROB.   Ay, I'll be sworn. My master knows not of your being here, and
       hath threatened to put me into everlasting liberty, if I tell you of
       it; for he swears he'll turn me away.
MRS PAGE.   Thou 'rt a good boy: this secrecy of thine shall be a tailor
       to thee, and shall make thee a new doublet and hose. I'll go hide
       me.
MRS FORD.   Do so. Go tell thy master I am alone. [Exit ROBIN.]
       Mistress Page, remember you your cue.
MRS PAGE.   I warrant thee; if I do not act it, hiss me.   [Exit.
MRS FORD.   Go to, then: we'll use this unwholesome humidity, this
       gross watery pumpion; we'll teach him to know turtles from jays.[3]

Enter FALSTAFF

FAL.   "Have I caught" thee, "my heavenly jewel?"[4] Why, now let me
       die, for I have lived long enough: this is the period of my ambi-
       tion: O this blessed hour!
MRS FORD.   O sweet Sir John!
FAL.   Mistress Ford, I cannot cog, I cannot prate, Mistress Ford. Now
       shall I sin in my wish: I would thy husband were dead: I'll speak it
       before the best lord; I would make thee my lady.
MRS FORD.   I your lady, Sir John! alas, I should be a pitiful lady!

[2]Jack-a-Lent] a puppet, at which, during Lent, children at play flung sticks or stones.
[3]turtles from jays] faithful wives from loose women. In Italian putta means both jay and
    harlot.
[4]"Have I caught" . . . "my heavenly jewel?"] These words form the first line of the sec-
    ond song in Sir Philip Sidney's Astrophel and Stella (first published in 1591). The early
    Quartos of the play rightly omit thee.

FAL.   Let the court of France show me such another. I see how thine
   eye would emulate the diamond: thou hast the right arched
   beauty of the brow that becomes the ship-tire, the tire-valiant, or
   any tire of Venetian admittance.[5]

MRS FORD.   A plain kerchief, Sir John: my brows become nothing
   else; nor that well neither.

FAL.   By the Lord, thou art a traitor to say so: thou wouldst make an
   absolute courtier; and the firm fixture of thy foot would give an excellent motion to thy gait in a semi-circled farthingale. I see what
   thou wert, if Fortune thy foe[6] were not, Nature thy friend. Come,
   thou canst not hide it.

MRS FORD.   Believe me, there's no such thing in me.

FAL.   What made me love thee? let that persuade thee there's something extraordinary in thee. Come, I cannot cog, and say thou art
   this and that, like a many of these lisping hawthorn-buds, that
   come like women in men's apparel, and smell like Bucklersbury[7]
   in simple time; I cannot: but I love thee; none but thee; and thou
   deservest it.

MRS FORD.   Do not betray me, sir. I fear you love Mistress Page.

FAL.   Thou mightst as well say I love to walk by the Counter-gate,[8]
   which is as hateful to me as the reek of a lime-kiln.

MRS FORD.   Well, heaven knows how I love you; and you shall one
   day find it.

FAL.   Keep in that mind; I'll deserve it.

MRS FORD.   Nay, I must tell you, so you do; or else I could not be in
   that mind.

ROB. [*Within*]   Mistress Ford, Mistress Ford! here's Mistress Page at
   the door, sweating, and blowing, and looking wildly, and would
   needs speak with you presently.

---

[5]*the ship-tire . . . of Venetian admittance*] Falstaff refers to three kinds of headdress,
firstly that shaped like a ship, secondly "the tire-valiant," and lastly that of the quality
held in esteem at Venice, in the Venetian fashion. The "tire-valiant" is not easy to explain. The early Quartos read "tire-vellet" (*i.e.* velvet), which makes good sense.
Stubbes in his *Anatomie of Abuses*, denounces with heat velvet ornaments for the
head. "Tire-valiant" can only mean headdress of very "brave" *i.e.* showy, design.

[6]*Fortune thy foe*] "Fortune my foe" are the opening words of a popular ballad deploring
the caprices of Fortune. It is found in early ballad collections, and runs to twenty-two
stanzas. The opening line runs, "*Fortune my foe*, why dost thou frown on me?"

[7]*Bucklersbury*] A street at the east end of Cheapside, London, which was full of apothe-
caries' shops and was redolent of medicinal herbs or simples in early summer, when
they were freshly stored.

[8]*Counter-gate*] the gate of the gaol. Two prisons in the city of London were known respectively as the Wood Street *Counter*, the Poultry *Counter*. "The *Counter*" was the
title of the gaol in Southwark.

FAL.   She shall not see me: I will ensconce me behind the arras.[9]

MRS FORD.   Pray you, do so: she's a very tattling woman.

[FALSTAFF *hides himself.*

Re-enter MISTRESS PAGE *and* ROBIN

What's the matter? how now!

MRS PAGE.   O Mistress Ford, what have you done? You're shamed, you're overthrown, you're undone for ever!

MRS FORD.   What's the matter, good Mistress Page?

MRS PAGE.   O well-a-day, Mistress Ford! having an honest man to your husband, to give him such cause of suspicion!

MRS FORD.   What cause of suspicion?

MRS PAGE.   What cause of suspicion! Out upon you! how am I mistook in you!

MRS FORD.   Why, alas, what's the matter?

MRS PAGE.   Your husband's coming hither, woman, with all the officers in Windsor, to search for a gentleman that he says is here now in the house, by your consent, to take an ill advantage of his absence: you are undone.

MRS FORD.   'T is not so, I hope.

MRS PAGE.   Pray heaven it be not so, that you have such a man here! but 't is most certain your husband's coming, with half Windsor at his heels, to search for such a one. I come before to tell you. If you know yourself clear, why, I am glad of it; but if you have a friend here, convey, convey him out. Be not amazed; call all your senses to you; defend your reputation, or bid farewell to your good life for ever.

MRS FORD.   What shall I do? There is a gentleman my dear friend; and I fear not mine own shame so much as his peril: I had rather than a thousand pound he were out of the house.

MRS PAGE.   For shame! never stand "you had rather" and "you had rather:" your husband's here at hand; bethink you of some conveyance: in the house you cannot hide him. O, how have you deceived me! Look, here is a basket: if he be of any reasonable stature, he may creep in here; and throw foul linen upon him, as if it were going to bucking: or,—it is whiting-time,[10]—send him by your two men to Datchet-mead.

MRS FORD.   He's too big to go in there. What shall I do?

FAL. [*Coming forward*]   Let me see 't, let me see 't, O, let me see 't!— I'll in, I'll in.—Follow your friend's counsel.—I'll in.

[9]*the arras*] the tapestry which hung from wooden rods at a little distance from the wall of the room.

[10]*whiting-time*] bleaching-time, spring-time.

Mrs Page.   What, Sir John Falstaff! Are these your letters, knight?

Fal.   I love thee.[11]—Help me away.—Let me creep in here.—I'll
never—   [*Gets into the basket; they cover him with foul linen*.

Mrs Page.   Help to cover your master, boy.—Call your men, Mistress
Ford.—You dissembling knight!

Mrs Ford.   What, John! Robert! John!   [*Exit* Robin.

Re-enter Servants

Go take up these clothes here quickly.—Where's the cowl-staff?
look, how you drumble!—Carry them to the laundress in Datchet-
mead; quickly, come.

Enter Ford, Page, Caius, *and* Sir Hugh Evans

Ford.   Pray you, come near: if I suspect without cause, why then
make sport at me; then let me be your jest; I deserve it.—How
now! whither bear you this?

Serv.   To the laundress, forsooth.

Mrs Ford.   Why, what have you to do whither they bear it? You were
best meddle with buck-washing.

Ford.   Buck!—I would I could wash myself of the buck!—Buck,
buck, buck! Ay, buck; I warrant you, buck; and of the season too,
it shall appear. [*Exeunt* Servants *with the basket*.] Gentlemen, I
have dreamed to-night; I'll tell you my dream. Here, here, here be
my keys: ascend my chambers; search, seek, find out: I'll warrant
we'll unkennel the fox. Let me stop this way first. [*Locking the
door*.] So, now uncape.[12]

Page.   Good Master Ford, be contented: you wrong yourself too
much.

Ford.   True, Master Page. Up, gentlemen; you shall see sport anon:
follow me, gentlemen.   [*Exit*.

Evans.   This is fery fantastical humours and jealousies.

Caius.   By gar, 't is no the fashion of France; it is not jealous in
France.

Page.   Nay, follow him, gentlemen; see the issue of his search.
                    [*Exeunt* Page, Caius, *and* Evans.

Mrs Page.   Is there not a double excellency in this?

Mrs Ford.   I know not which pleases me better, that my husband is
deceived, or Sir John.

[11]*I love thee*] Malone and most of his successors add from the early Quartos, *and none
but thee*. The words sound like a quotation from some old song. Falstaff had already
told Mrs. Ford "I love thee; none but thee."

[12]*uncape*] No other example of this word is found. The meaning is obviously "uncou-
ple" (of hounds in hunting). "Cape" was occasionally used in the sense of "collar."

Mrs Page.   What a taking was he in when your husband asked who
    was in the basket!

Mrs Ford.   I am half afraid he will have need of washing; so throw-
    ing him into the water will do him a benefit.

Mrs Page.   Hang him, dishonest rascal! I would all of the same strain
    were in the same distress.

Mrs Ford.   I think my husband hath some special suspicion of
    Falstaff's being here; for I never saw him so gross in his jealousy till
    now.

Mrs Page.   I will lay a plot to try that; and we will yet have more tricks
    with Falstaff: his dissolute disease will scarce obey this medicine.

Mrs Ford.   Shall we send that foolish carrion,[13] Mistress Quickly, to
    him, and excuse his throwing into the water; and give him another
    hope, to betray him to another punishment?

Mrs Page.   We will do it: let him be sent for tomorrow, eight o'clock,
    to have amends.

Re-enter Ford, Page, Caius, *and* Sir Hugh Evans

Ford.   I cannot find him: may be the knave bragged of that he could
    not compass.

Mrs Page. [*Aside to* Mrs Ford]   Heard you that?

Mrs Ford.   You use me well,[14] Master Ford, do you?

Ford.   Ay, I do so.

Mrs Ford.   Heaven make you better than your thoughts!

Ford.   Amen!

Mrs Page.   You do yourself mighty wrong, Master Ford.

Ford.   Ay, ay; I must bear it.

Evans.   If there be any pody in the house, and in the chambers, and
    in the coffers, and in the presses, heaven forgive my sins at the day
    of judgement!

Caius.   By gar, nor I too: there is no bodies.

Page.   Fie, fie, Master Ford! are you not ashamed? What spirit, what
    devil suggests this imagination? I would not ha' your distemper in
    this kind for the wealth of Windsor Castle.

Ford.   'T is my fault, Master Page: I suffer for it.

Evans.   You suffer for a pad conscience: your wife is as honest a
    'omans as I will desires among five thousand, and five hundred
    too.

Caius.   By gar, I see 't is an honest woman.

Ford.   Well, I promised you a dinner.—Come, come, walk in the
    Park: I pray you, pardon me; I will hereafter make known to you

---

[13]*carrion*] a term of contempt.

[14]*You use me well*] Theobald prefixed the words *Ay, ay; peace*: from the early Quartos.

why I have done this.—Come, wife; come, Mistress Page.—I pray
you, pardon me; pray heartily pardon me.

PAGE. Let's go in, gentlemen; but, trust me, we'll mock him. I do invite you to-morrow morning to my house to breakfast: after, we'll
a-birding together; I have a fine hawk for the bush. Shall it be so?

FORD. Any thing.

EVANS. If there is one, I shall make two in the company.

CAIUS. If there be one or two, I shall make-a the turd.

FORD. Pray you, go, Master Page.

EVANS. I pray you now, remembrance to-morrow on the lousy knave,
mine host.

CAIUS. Dat is good; by gar, with all my heart!

EVANS. A lousy knave, to have his gibes and his mockeries!

[*Exeunt.*

Scene IV. *A Room in Page's House.*

Enter FENTON *and* ANNE PAGE

FENT. I see I cannot get thy father's love;
  Therefore no more turn me to him, sweet Nan.

ANNE. Alas, how then?

FENT.   Why, thou must be thyself.
  He doth object I am too great of birth;
  And that, my state being gall'd with my expense,
  I seek to heal it only by his wealth:
  Besides these, other bars he lays before me,—
  My riots past, my wild societies;[1]
  And tells me 't is a thing impossible
  I should love thee but as a property.

ANNE. May be he tells you true.

FENT. No, heaven so speed me in my time to come!
  Albeit I will confess thy father's wealth
  Was the first motive that I woo'd thee, Anne:
  Yet, wooing thee, I found thee of more value
  Than stamps in gold[2] or sums in sealed bags;
  And 't is the very riches of thyself
  That now I aim at.

ANNE.   Gentle Master Fenton,
  Yet seek my father's love; still seek it, sir:

[1]*societies*] associates, companions.
[2]*stamps in gold*] coins.

If opportunity and humblest suit
Cannot attain it, why, then,—hark you hither!

[*They converse apart.*

Enter SHALLOW, SLENDER, *and* MISTRESS QUICKLY

SHAL.   Break their talk, Mistress Quickly: my kinsman shall speak for
himself.

SLEN.   I'll make a shaft or a bolt[3] on 't: 'slid, 't is but venturing.

SHAL.   Be not dismayed.

SLEN.   No, she shall not dismay me: I care not for that, but that I am
afeard.

QUICK.   Hark ye; Master Slender would speak a word with you.

ANNE.   I come to him. [*Aside*] This is my father's choice.
O, what a world of vile ill-favour'd faults
Looks handsome in three hundred pounds a-year!

QUICK.   And how does good Master Fenton? Pray you, a word with
you.

SHAL.   She's coming; to her, coz. O boy, thou hadst a father!

SLEN.   I had a father, Mistress Anne; my uncle can tell you good jests
of him. Pray you, uncle, tell Mistress Anne the jest, how my father
stole two geese out of a pen, good uncle.

SHAL.   Mistress Anne, my cousin loves you.

SLEN.   Ay, that I do; as well as I love any woman in Gloucestershire.

SHAL.   He will maintain you like a gentlewoman.

SLEN.   Ay, that I will, come cut and long-tail,[4] under the degree of a
squire.

SHAL.   He will make you a hundred and fifty pounds ointure.

ANNE.   Good Master Shallow, let him woo for himself.

SHAL.   Marry, I thank you for it; I thank you for that good comfort. She
calls you, coz: I'll leave you.

ANNE.   Now, Master Slender,—

SLEN.   Now, good Mistress Anne,—

ANNE.   What is your will?

SLEN.   My will! od's heartlings, that's a pretty jest indeed! I ne'er made
my will yet, I thank heaven; I am not such a sickly creature, I give
heaven praise.

ANNE.   I mean, Master Slender, what would you with me?

SLEN.   Truly, for mine own part, I would little or nothing with you.
Your father and my uncle hath made motions: if it be my luck, so;

---

[3]*shaft or a bolt*] proverbial expression for "I'll do it one way or another." A shaft was a
long, slender arrow; a bolt, a short, thick one.

[4]*come cut and long-tail*] whatever come, alluding to dogs with short and long tails;
equivalent to "bob-tag and rag-tail."

if not, happy man be his dole![5] They can tell you how things go
better that I can: you may ask your father; here he comes.

Enter PAGE *and* MISTRESS PAGE

PAGE.   Now, Master Slender: love him, daughter Anne.—
    Why, how now! what does Master Fenton here?
    You wrong me, sir, thus still to haunt my house:
    I told you, sir, my daughter is disposed of.
FENT.   Nay, Master Page, be not impatient.
MRS PAGE.   Good Master Fenton, come not to my child.
PAGE.   She is no match for you.
FENT.   Sir, will you hear me?
PAGE.   No, good Master Fenton.
    Come, Master Shallow; come, son Slender, in.
    Knowing my mind, you wrong me, Master Fenton.
               [Exeunt PAGE, SHAL., *and* SLEN.
QUICK.   Speak to Mistress Page.
FENT.   Good Mistress Page, for that I love your daughter
    In such a righteous fashion as I do,
    Perforce, against all checks, rebukes and manners,
    I must advance the colours of my love,
    And not retire: let me have your good will.
ANNE.   Good mother, do not marry me to yond fool.
MRS PAGE.   I mean it not; I seek you a better husband.
QUICK.   That's my master, master doctor.
ANNE.   Alas, I had rather be set quick i' the earth,
    And bowl'd to death with turnips!
MRS PAGE.   Come, trouble not yourself. Good Master Fenton,
    I will not be your friend nor enemy:
    My daughter will I question how she loves you,
    And as I find her, so am I affected.
    Till then farewell, sir: she must needs go in;
    Her father will be angry.
FENT.   Farewell, gentle mistress: farewell, Nan.
               [Exeunt MRS PAGE *and* ANNE.
QUICK.   This is my doing now: "Nay," said I, "will you cast away your
    child on a fool, and a physician?[6] Look on Master Fenton:" this is
    my doing.

---

[5] *happy man be his dole*] good fortune go with you.
[6] *a fool, and a physician*] The two words were constantly brought together colloquially,
apparently in vague allusion to the proverbial phrase, "A man of forty is either a fool
or his own physician." Some editors read *or* for *and*.

FENT. I thank thee; and I pray thee, once to-night
　　　　Give my sweet Nan this ring: there's for thy pains.
QUICK.　Now heaven send thee good fortune! [*Exit* FENTON.] A kind
　　　　heart he hath: a woman would run through fire and water for such
　　　　a kind heart. But yet I would my master had Mistress Anne; or I
　　　　would Master Slender had her; or, in sooth, I would Master
　　　　Fenton had her: I will do what I can for them all three; for so I
　　　　have promised, and I'll be as good as my word; but speciously[7] for
　　　　Master Fenton. Well, I must of another errand to Sir John Falstaff
　　　　from my two mistresses: what a beast am I to slack it!　　[*Exit*.

SCENE V. *A Room in the Garter Inn.*

Enter FALSTAFF *and* BARDOLPH

FAL.　Bardolph, I say,—
BARD.　Here, sir.
FAL.　Go fetch me a quart of sack; put a toast in 't. [*Exit* BARD.] Have
　　　　I lived to be carried in a basket, like a barrow of butcher's offal,
　　　　and to be thrown in the Thames? Well, if I be served such another
　　　　trick, I'll have my brains ta'en out, and buttered, and give them to
　　　　a dog for a new-year's gift. The rogues slighted me into the river
　　　　with as little remorse as they would have drowned a blind bitch's
　　　　puppies,[1] fifteen i' the litter: and you may know by my size that I
　　　　have a kind of alacrity in sinking; if the bottom were as deep as
　　　　hell, I should down. I had been drowned, but that the shore was
　　　　shelvy and shallow,—a death that I abhor; for the water swells a
　　　　man; and what a thing should I have been when I had been
　　　　swelled! I should have been a mountain of mummy.

Re-enter BARDOLPH *with sack*

BARD.　Here's Mistress Quickly, sir, to speak with you.
FAL.　Come, let me pour in some sack to the Thames water; for my
　　　　belly's as cold as if I had swallowed snowballs for pills to cool the
　　　　reins. Call her in.
BARD.　Come in, woman!

Enter MISTRESS QUICKLY

QUICK.　By your leave; I cry you mercy: give your worship good
　　　　morrow.

[7]*speciously*] blunder for "especially."

[1]*blind bitch's puppies*] a colloquial inversion for a "bitch's blind puppies."

FAL. Take away these chalices. Go brew me a pottle of sack finely.

BARD. With eggs, sir?

FAL. Simple of itself; I'll no pullet-sperm in my brewage. [*Exit* BARDOLPH.] How now!

QUICK. Marry, sir, I come to your worship from Mistress Ford.

FAL. Mistress Ford! I have had ford enough; I was thrown into the ford; I have my belly full of ford.

QUICK. Alas the day! good heart, that was not her fault: she does so take on with[2] her men; they mistook their erection.[3]

FAL. So did I mine, to build upon a foolish woman's promise.

QUICK. Well, she laments, sir, for it, that it would yearn your heart to see it. Her husband goes this morning a-birding; she desires you once more to come to her between eight and nine: I must carry her word quickly: she'll make you amends, I warrant you.

FAL. Well, I will visit her: tell her so; and bid her think what a man is: let her consider his frailty, and then judge of my merit.

QUICK. I will tell her.

FAL. Do so. Between nine and ten, sayest thou?

QUICK. Eight and nine, sir.

FAL. Well, be gone: I will not miss her.

QUICK. Peace be with you, sir. [*Exit.*

FAL. I marvel I hear not of Master Brook; he sent me word to stay within: I like his money well.—O, here he comes.

Enter FORD

FORD. Bless you, sir!

FAL. Now, Master Brook,—you come to know what hath passed between me and Ford's wife?

FORD. That, indeed, Sir John, is my business.

FAL. Master Brook, I will not lie to you: I was at her house the hour she appointed me.

FORD. And sped you, sir?

FAL. Very ill-favouredly, Master Brook.

FORD. How so, sir? Did she change her determination?

FAL. No, Master Brook; but the peaking Cornuto her husband, Master Brook, dwelling in a continual 'larum of jealousy, comes me in the instant of our encounter, after we had embraced, kissed, protested, and, as it were, spoke the prologue of our comedy; and at his heels a rabble of his companions, thither provoked and instigated by his distemper, and, forsooth, to search his house for his wife's love.

---

[2]*take on with*] rage at, get in a passion with.
[3]*erection*] blunder for "direction."

FORD. What, while you were there?

FAL. While I was there.

FORD. And did he search for you, and could not find you?

FAL. You shall hear. As good luck would have it, comes in one
Mistress Page; gives intelligence of Ford's approach; and, in her
invention and Ford's wife's distraction, they conveyed me into a
buck-basket.

FORD. A buck-basket!

FAL. By the Lord, a buck-basket!—rammed me in with foul shirts and
smocks, socks, foul stockings, greasy napkins; that, Master Brook,
there was the rankest compound of villanous smell that ever offended nostril.

FORD. And how long lay you there?

FAL. Nay, you shall hear, Master Brook, what I have suffered to bring
this woman to evil for your good. Being thus crammed in the basket, a couple of Ford's knaves, his hinds, were called forth by their
mistress to carry me in the name of foul clothes to Datchet-lane:
they took me on their shoulders; met the jealous knave their master in the door, who asked them once or twice what they had in
their basket: I quaked for fear, lest the lunatic knave would have
searched it; but fate, ordaining he should be a cuckold, held his
hand. Well: on went he for a search, and away went I for foul
clothes. But mark the sequel, Master Brook: I suffered the pangs
of three several deaths; first, an intolerable fright, to be detected
with[4] a jealous rotten bell-wether; next, to be compassed, like a
good bilbo,[5] in the circumference of a peck, hilt to point, heel to
head, and then, to be stopped in, like a strong distillation, with
stinking clothes that fretted in their own grease: think of that,—a
man of my kidney,—think of that,—that am as subject to heat as
butter; a man of continual dissolution and thaw: it was a miracle
to 'scape suffocation. And in the height of this bath, when I was
more than half stewed in grease, like a Dutch dish, to be thrown
into the Thames, and cooled, glowing hot, in that surge, like a
horse-shoe; think of that,—hissing hot,—think of that, Master
Brook.

FORD. In good sadness,[6] sir, I am sorry that for my sake you have suffered all this. My suit, then, is desperate; you'll undertake her no
more?

FAL. Master Brook, I will be thrown into Etna, as I have been into

---

[4]*detected with*] detected by.

[5]*bilbo*] the blade of a bilbo, *i.e.* a Spanish sword from Bilbao, which was extremely flexible and elastic.

[6]*In good sadness*] In sober earnest.

Thames, ere I will leave her thus. Her husband is this morning gone a-birding: I have received from her another embassy of meeting; 'twixt eight and nine is the hour, Master Brook.

FORD. 'T is past eight already, sir.

FAL. Is it? I will then address me to my appointment. Come to me at your convenient leisure, and you shall know how I speed; and the conclusion shall be crowned with your enjoying her. Adieu. You shall have her, Master Brook; Master Brook, you shall cuckold Ford. [*Exit.*

FORD. Hum! ha! is this a vision? is this a dream? do I sleep? Master Ford, awake! awake, Master Ford! there's a hole made in your best coat, Master Ford. This 't is to be married! this 't is to have linen and buck-baskets! Well, I will proclaim myself what I am: I will now take the lecher; he is at my house; he cannot 'scape me; 't is impossible he should; he cannot creep into a halfpenny purse,[7] nor into a pepper-box: but, lest the devil that guides him should aid him, I will search impossible places. Though what I am I cannot avoid, yet to be what I would not shall not make me tame: if I have horns to make one mad, let the proverb go with me,—I'll be horn-mad. [*Exit.*

---

[7]*halfpenny purse*] The halfpenny, which was of silver, was a very small coin.

ACT IV.

Scene I. A *Street*.

Enter Mistress Page, Mistress Quickly, *and* William

MRS PAGE. Is he at Master Ford's already, think'st thou?

QUICK. Sure he is by this, or will be presently: but, truly, he is very courageous[1] mad about his throwing into the water. Mistress Ford desires you to come suddenly.

MRS PAGE. I'll be with her by and by; I'll but bring my young man here to school. Look, where his master comes; 't is a playing-day, I see.

Enter Sir Hugh Evans

How now, Sir Hugh! no school to-day?

EVANS. No; Master Slender is let the boys leave to play.

QUICK. Blessing of his heart!

MRS PAGE. Sir Hugh, my husband says my son profits nothing in the world at his book. I pray you, ask him some questions in his accidence.

EVANS. Come hither, William; hold up your head; come.

MRS PAGE. Come on, sirrah; hold up your head; answer your master, be not afraid.

EVANS. William, how many numbers is in nouns?

WILL. Two.

QUICK. Truly, I thought there had been one number more, because they say, "Od's nouns."

EVANS. Peace your tattlings! What is "fair," William?

WILL. Pulcher.

QUICK. Polecats! there are fairer things than polecats, sure.

EVANS. You are a very simplicity 'oman: I pray you, peace.—What is "lapis," William?

---

[1]*courageous*] apparently a blunder for "outrageous."

WILL.   A stone.

EVANS.   And what is "a stone," William?

WILL.   A pebble.

EVANS.   No, it is "lapis": I pray you, remember in your prain.

WILL.   Lapis.

EVANS.   That is a good William. What is he, William, that does lend articles?

WILL.   Articles are borrowed of the pronoun, and be thus declined, "Singulariter, nominativo, hic, hæc, hoc.

EVANS.   Nominativo, hig, hag, hog; pray you, mark: genitivo, hujus. Well, what is your accusative case?

WILL.   Accusativo, hinc.

EVANS.   I pray you, have your remembrance, child; accusativo, hung, hang, hog.

QUICK.   "Hang-hog" is Latin for bacon, I warrant you.

EVANS.   Leave your prabbles,[2] 'oman.—What is the focative case, William?

WILL.   O,—vocativo, O.

EVANS.   Remember, William; focative is caret.

QUICK.   And that's a good root.

EVANS.   'Oman, forbear.

MRS PAGE.   Peace!

EVANS.   What is your genitive case plural, William?

WILL.   Genitive case!

EVANS.   Ay.

WILL.   Genitive,—horum, harum, horum.

QUICK.   Vengeance of Jenny's case! fie on her! never name her, child, if she be a whore.

EVANS.   For shame, 'oman.

QUICK.   You do ill to teach the child such words:—he teaches him to hick and to hack,[3] which they'll do fast enough of themselves, and to call "horum":—fie upon you!

EVANS.   'Oman, art thou lunatics? hast thou no understandings for thy cases, and the numbers of the genders? Thou art as foolish Christian creatures as I would desires.

MRS PAGE.   Prithee, hold thy peace.

EVANS.   Show me now, William, some declensions of your pronouns.

WILL.   Forsooth, I have forgot.

EVANS.   It is qui, quæ, quod: if you forget your "quies," your "quæs,"

---

[2]*prabbles*] chatter.
[3]*hick and to hack*] apparently used in a somewhat ribald significance.

and your "quods," you must be preeches.[4] Go your ways, and play; go.

MRS PAGE.   He is a better scholar than I thought he was.

EVANS.   He is a good sprag memory. Farewell, Mistress Page.

MRS PAGE.   Adieu, good Sir Hugh.   [*Exit* SIR HUGH.
Get you home, boy. Come, we stay too long.   [*Exeunt.*

SCENE II. *A Room in Ford's House.*

Enter FALSTAFF *and* MISTRESS FORD

FAL.   Mistress Ford, your sorrow hath eaten up my sufferance. I see you are obsequious in your love,[1] and I profess requital to a hair's breadth; not only, Mistress Ford, in the simple office of love, but in all the accoutrement, complement, and ceremony of it. But are you sure of your husband now?

MRS FORD.   He's a-birding, sweet Sir John.

MRS PAGE. [*Within*]   What, ho, gossip Ford! what, ho!

MRS FORD.   Step into the chamber, Sir John.   [*Exit* FALSTAFF.

Enter MISTRESS PAGE

MRS PAGE.   How now, sweetheart! who's at home besides yourself?

MRS FORD.   Why, none but mine own people.

MRS PAGE.   Indeed!

MRS FORD.   No, certainly. [*Aside to her*] Speak louder.

MRS PAGE.   Truly, I am so glad you have nobody here.

MRS FORD.   Why?

MRS PAGE.   Why, woman, your husband is in his old lunes[2] again: he so takes on yonder with[3] my husband; so rails against all married mankind; so curses all Eve's daughters, of what complexion soever; and so buffets himself on the forehead, crying, "Peer out, peer out!"[4] that any madness I ever yet beheld seemed but tameness, civility, and patience, to this his distemper he is in now: I am glad the fat knight is not here.

MRS FORD.   Why, does he talk of him?

---

[4]*preeches*] breeches: breeched, *i.e.* flogged.

[1]*your sorrow . . . love*] your grief has blotted out the memory of my sufferings. I see your devotion (to me) is seriously meant (of the seriousness attaching to funereal rites or obsequies).

[2]*lunes*] "Lunes" means "fits of lunacy."

[3]*takes on . . . with*] gets in a passion with.

[4]*Peer out, peer out!*] Horns, make your appearance, come forth!

MRS PAGE.   Of none but him; and swears he was carried out, the last
time he searched for him, in a basket; protests to my husband he
is now here; and hath drawn him and the rest of their company
from their sport, to make another experiment of his suspicion: but
I am glad the knight is not here; now he shall see his own foolery.

MRS FORD.   How near is he, Mistress Page?

MRS PAGE.   Hard by, at street end; he will be here anon.

MRS FORD.   I am undone!—the knight is here.

MRS PAGE.   Why, then, you are utterly shamed, and he's but a dead
man. What a woman are you!—Away with him, away with him!
better shame than murder.

MRS FORD.   Which way should he go? how should I bestow him?
Shall I put him into the basket again?

Re-enter FALSTAFF

FAL.   No, I'll come no more i' the basket. May I not go out ere he
come?

MRS PAGE.   Alas, three of Master Ford's brothers watch the door with
pistols, that none shall issue out; otherwise you might slip away ere
he came. But what make you here?

FAL.   What shall I do?—I'll creep up into the chimney.

MRS FORD.   There they always use to discharge their birding-pieces.
Creep into the kiln-hole.

FAL.   Where is it?

MRS FORD.   He will seek there, on my word. Neither press, coffer,
chest, trunk, well, vault, but he hath an abstract[5] for the remembrance of such places, and goes to them by his note: there is no
hiding you in the house.

FAL.   I'll go out, then.

MRS PAGE.   If you go out in your own semblance, you die, Sir John.
Unless you go out disguised,—

MRS FORD.   How might we disguise him?

MRS PAGE.   Alas the day, I know not! There is no woman's gown big
enough for him; otherwise he might put on a hat, a muffler, and
a kerchief, and so escape.

FAL.   Good hearts, devise something: any extremity rather than a mischief.

MRS FORD.   My maid's aunt, the fat woman of Brentford, has a gown
above.

MRS PAGE.   On my word, it will serve him; she's as big as he is: and
there's her thrummed hat,[6] and her muffler too. Run up, Sir John.

[5]*abstract*] short list or inventory.
[6]*thrummed hat*] hat made of coarse yarn.

MRS FORD.   Go, go, sweet Sir John: Mistress Page and I will look some linen for your head.

MRS PAGE.   Quick, quick! we'll come dress you straight: put on the gown the while.   [*Exit* FALSTAFF.

MRS FORD.   I would my husband would meet him in this shape: he cannot abide the old woman of Brentford; he swears she's a witch; forbade her my house, and hath threatened to beat her.

MRS PAGE.   Heaven guide him to thy husband's cudgel, and the devil guide his cudgel afterwards!

MRS FORD.   But is my husband coming?

MRS PAGE.   Ay, in good sadness,[7] is he; and talks of the basket too, howsoever he hath had intelligence.

MRS FORD.   We'll try that; for I'll appoint my men to carry the basket again, to meet him at the door with it, as they did last time.

MRS PAGE.   Nay, but he'll be here presently: let's go dress him like the witch of Brentford.

MRS FORD.   I'll first direct my men what they shall do with the basket. Go up; I'll bring linen for him straight.   [*Exit*.

MRS PAGE.   Hang him, dishonest varlet! we cannot misuse him enough. We'll leave a proof, by that which we will do,
Wives may be merry, and yet honest too:
We do not act that often jest and laugh;
'Tis old, but true,—Still swine eats all the draff.   [*Exit*.

Re-enter MISTRESS FORD *with two* Servants

MRS FORD.   Go, sirs, take the basket again on your shoulders: your master is hard at door; if he bid you set it down, obey him: quickly, dispatch.   [*Exit*.

FIRST SERV.   Come, come, take it up.

SEC. SERV.   Pray heaven it be not full of knight again.

FIRST SERV.   I hope not; I had as lief bear so much lead.

Enter FORD, PAGE, SHALLOW, CAIUS, *and* SIR HUGH EVANS

FORD.   Ay, but if it prove true, Master Page, have you any way then to unfool me again? Set down the basket, villain! Somebody call my wife. Youth in a basket!—O you pandarly rascals! there's a knot, a ging, a pack,[8] a conspiracy against me: now shall the devil be shamed.—What, wife, I say!—Come, come forth! Behold what honest clothes you send forth to bleaching!

PAGE.   Why, this passes, Master Ford; you are not to go loose any longer; you must be pinioned.

---

[7]*in good sadness*] in sober earnest.
[8]*a knot, a ging, a pack*] an assembly, a gang, a crowd.

EVANS.   Why, this is lunatics! this is mad as a mad dog!
SHAL.   Indeed, Master Ford, this is not well, indeed.
FORD.   So say I too, sir.

Re-enter MISTRESS FORD

   Come hither, Mistress Ford; Mistress Ford, the honest woman,
   the modest wife, the virtuous creature, that hath the jealous fool
   to her husband! I suspect without cause, mistress, do I?
MRS FORD.   Heaven be my witness you do, if you suspect me in any
   dishonesty.
FORD.   Well said, brazen-face! hold it out.[9] Come forth, sirrah!
                                        [*Pulling clothes out of the basket.*
PAGE.   This passes!
MRS FORD.   Are you not ashamed? let the clothes alone.
FORD.   I shall find you anon.
EVANS.   'T is unreasonable! Will you take up your wife's clothes?
   Come away.
FORD.   Empty the basket, I say!
MRS FORD.   Why, man, why?
FORD.   Master Page, as I am a man, there was one conveyed out of my
   house yesterday in this basket: why may not he be there again? In
   my house I am sure he is: my intelligence is true; my jealousy is
   reasonable. Pluck me out all the linen.
MRS FORD.   If you find a man there, he shall die a flea's death.
PAGE.   Here's no man.
SHAL.   By my fidelity, this is not well, Master Ford; this wrongs you.
EVANS.   Master Ford, you must pray, and not follow the imaginations
   of your own heart: this is jealousies.
FORD.   Well, he's not here I seek for.
PAGE.   No, nor nowhere else but in your brain.
FORD.   Help to search my house this one time. If I find not what I
   seek, show no colour for my extremity;[10] let me for ever be your
   table-sport; let them say of me, "As jealous as Ford, that searched
   a hollow walnut for his wife's leman." Satisfy me once more; once
   more search with me.
MRS FORD.   What, ho, Mistress Page! come you and the old woman
   down; my husband will come into the chamber.
FORD.   Old woman! what old woman's that?
MRS FORD.   Why, it is my maid's aunt of Brentford.
FORD.   A witch, a quean, an old cozening quean! Have I not forbid
     her my house? She comes of errands, does she? We are simple

---

[9]*hold it out*] keep it up.
[10]*show no colour . . . extremity*] admit no reasonable pretext for my extreme courses.

men: we do not know what's brought to pass under the profession
of fortune-telling. She works by charms, by spells, by the figure,[11]
and such daubery[12] as this is, beyond our element: we know nothing. Come down, you witch, you hag, you; come down, I say!

MRS FORD.   Nay, good, sweet husband!—Good gentlemen, let him
not strike the old woman.

Re-enter FALSTAFF *in woman's clothes, and* MISTRESS PAGE

MRS PAGE.   Come, Mother Prat: come, give me your hand.

FORD.   I'll prat her. [*Beating him*] Out of my door, you witch, you
hag,[13] you baggage, you polecat, you ronyon! out, out! I'll conjure
you, I'll fortune-tell you.   [*Exit* FALSTAFF.

MRS PAGE.   Are you not ashamed? I think you have killed the poor
woman.

MRS FORD.   Nay, he will do it. 'T is a goodly credit for you.

FORD.   Hang her, witch!

EVANS.   By yea and no, I think the 'oman is a witch indeed: I like
not when a 'oman has a great peard; I spy a great peard under his
muffler.

FORD.   Will you follow, gentlemen? I beseech you, follow; see but the
issue of my jealousy: if I cry out thus upon no trial, never trust me
when I open again.[14]

PAGE.   Let's obey his humour a little further: come, gentlemen.
                          [*Exeunt* FORD, PAGE, SHAL., CAIUS, *and* EVANS.

MRS PAGE.   Trust me, he beat him most pitifully.

MRS FORD.   Nay, by the mass, that he did not; he beat him most un-
pitifully methought.

MRS PAGE.   I'll have the cudgel hallowed and hung o'er the altar; it
hath done meritorious service.

MRS FORD.   What think you? may we, with the warrant of woman-
hood and the witness of a good conscience, pursue him with any
further revenge?

MRS PAGE.   The spirit of wantonness is, sure, scared out of him: if the
devil have him not in fee-simple, with fine and recovery, he will
never, I think, in the way of waste, attempt us again.

MRS FORD.   Shall we tell our husbands how we have served him?

---

[11]*by the figure*] by casting the figure, by calculating the horoscope.

[12] *daubery*] cheating. The verb "daub" is similarly used.

[13]*hag*] This is the reading of the Third and later Folios. The First and Second Folios
read *rag*. But *hag* has already been used. "Rag" was, however, occasionally employed
as a term of contempt.

[14]*cry out . . . again*] The expression is drawn from hunting, in which the hounds cry out
when they find the scent. "Open" means "open mouth," "give tongue."

MRS PAGE.   Yes, by all means; if it be but to scrape the figures[15] out of your husband's brains. If they can find in their hearts the poor unvirtuous fat knight shall be any further afflicted, we two will still be the ministers.

MRS FORD.   I'll warrant they'll have him publicly shamed: and methinks there would be no period to the jest, should he not be publicly shamed.

MRS PAGE.   Come, to the forge with it, then; shape it: I would not have things cool.   [*Exeunt.*

SCENE III. *A Room in the Garter Inn.*

Enter HOST *and* BARDOLPH

BARD.   Sir, the Germans desire to have three of your horses: the duke himself will be to-morrow at court, and they are going to meet him.

HOST.   What duke should that be comes so secretly? I hear not of him in the court. Let me speak with the gentlemen: they speak English?

BARD.   Ay, sir; I'll call them to you.

HOST.   They shall have my horses; but I'll make them pay; I'll sauce them: they have had my house a week at command; I have turned away my other guests: they must come off; I'll sauce them. Come.   [*Exeunt.*

SCENE IV. *A Room in Ford's House.*

Enter PAGE, FORD, MISTRESS PAGE, MISTRESS FORD, *and* SIR HUGH EVANS

EVANS.   'T is one of the best discretions of a 'oman as ever I did look upon.

PAGE.   And did he send you both these letters at an instant?

MRS PAGE.   With a quarter of an hour.

FORD.   Pardon me, wife. Henceforth do what thou wilt;
    I rather will suspect the sun with cold
    Than thee with wantonness: now doth thy honour stand,
    In him that was of late an heretic,
    As firm as faith.

---

[15]*figures*] imaginary forms, ideas.

PAGE.   'T is well, 't is well; no more:
 Be not as extreme in submission
 As in offence.
 But let our plot go forward: let our wives
 Yet once again, to make us public sport,
 Appoint a meeting with this old fat fellow,
 Where we may take him, and disgrace him for it.

FORD. There is no better way than that they spoke of.

PAGE. How? to send him word they'll meet him in the Park at midnight? Fie, fie! he'll never come.

EVANS. You say he has been thrown in the rivers, and has been grievously peaten, as an old 'oman: methinks there should be terrors in
 him that he should not come; methinks his flesh is punished, he
 shall have no desires.

PAGE. So think I too.

MRS FORD. Devise but how you'll use him when he comes,
 And let us two devise to bring him thither.

MRS PAGE. There is an old tale goes that Herne the hunter,
 Sometime a keeper here in Windsor forest,
 Doth all the winter-time, at still midnight,
 Walk round about an oak, with great ragg'd horns;
 And there he blasts the tree, and takes the cattle,[1]
 And makes milch-kine yield blood, and shakes a chain
 In a most hideous and dreadful manner:
 You have heard of such a spirit; and well you know
 The superstitious idle-headed eld
 Received, and did deliver to our age,
 This tale of Herne the hunter for a truth.

PAGE. Why, yet there want not many that do fear
 In deep of night to walk by this Herne's oak:
 But what of this?

MRS FORD. Marry, this is our device;
 That Falstaff at that oak shall meet with us.[2]

PAGE. Well, let it not be doubted but he'll come:
 And in this shape when you have brought him thither,
 What shall be done with him? what is your plot?

MRS PAGE. That likewise have we thought upon, and thus:
 Nan Page my daughter and my little son
 And three or four more of their growth we'll dress

---

[1]*takes the cattle*] strikes the cattle with disease.

[2]*Marry . . . us*] This speech is given far more explicitly in the First and early Quartos, and thence most editors derive a third line, *Disguis'd like Herne with huge horns on his head.* Some such insertion seems necessary to explain the next speech.

    Like urchins, ouphes and fairies, green and white,
    With rounds of waxen tapers on their heads,
    And rattles in their hands: upon a sudden,
    As Falstaff, she, and I, are newly met,
    Let them from forth a sawpit rush at once
    With some diffused song: upon their sight,
    We two in great amazedness will fly:
    Then let them all encircle him about,
    And, fairy-like, to pinch[3] the unclean knight;
    And ask him why, that hour of fairy revel,
    In their so sacred paths he dares to tread
    In shape profane.

MRS FORD.   And till he tell the truth,
    Let the supposed fairies pinch him sound,
    And burn him with their tapers.

MRS PAGE.   The truth being known,
    We'll all present ourselves, dis-horn the spirit,
    And mock him home to Windsor.

FORD.   The children must
    Be practised well to this, or they'll ne'er do 't.

EVANS.   I will teach the children their behaviours; and I will be like a
    jack-an-apes also, to burn the knight with my taber.

FORD.   That will be excellent. I'll go buy them vizards.

MRS PAGE.   My Nan shall be the queen of all the fairies,
    Finely attired in a robe of white.

PAGE.   That silk will I go buy. [*Aside*] And in that time
    . Shall Master Slender steal my Nan away,
    And marry her at Eton. Go send to Falstaff straight.

FORD.   Nay, I'll to him again in name of Brook:
    He'll tell me all his purpose: sure, he'll come.

MRS PAGE.   Fear not you that. Go get us properties
    And tricking for our fairies.

EVANS.   Let us about it: it is admirable pleasures and fery honest
    knaveries.   [*Exeunt* PAGE, FORD, *and* EVANS.

MRS PAGE.   Go, Mistress Ford,
    Send quickly to Sir John, to know his mind.   [*Exit* MRS FORD.
    I'll to the doctor: he hath my good will,
    And none but he, to marry with Nan Page.
    That Slender, though well landed, is an idiot;
    And he my husband best of all affects.

---

[3]*to pinch*] This is the Folio reading, for which editors have substituted *to-pinch*, where "to" is regarded as an intensive prefix. Such a form is found elsewhere.

The doctor is well money'd, and his friends
Potent at court: he, none but he, shall have her,
Though twenty thousand worthier come to crave her.   [*Exit.*

SCENE V. A *Room in the Garter Inn.*

Enter HOST *and* SIMPLE

HOST.   What wouldst thou have, boor? what, thickskin? speak,
     breathe, discuss; brief, short, quick, snap.

SIM.   Marry, sir, I come to speak with Sir John Falstaff from Master
     Slender.

HOST.   There's his chamber, his house, his castle, his standing-bed,
     and truckle-bed; 't is painted about with the story of the Prodigal,
     fresh and new. Go knock and call; he'll speak like an Anthropo-
     phaginian[1] unto thee: knock, I say.

SIM.   There's an old woman, a fat woman, gone up into his chamber:
     I'll be so bold as stay, sir, till she come down; I come to speak with
     her, indeed.

HOST.   Ha! a fat woman! the knight may be robbed: I'll call.—Bully
     knight! bully Sir John! speak from thy lungs military: art thou
     there? it is thine host, thine Ephesian,[2] calls.

FAL. [*Above*]   How now, mine host!

HOST.   Here's a Bohemian-Tartar[3] tarries the coming down of thy fat
     woman. Let her descend, bully, let her descend; my chambers are
     honourable: fie! privacy? fie!

Enter FALSTAFF

FAL.   There was, mine host, an old fat woman even now with me; but
     she's gone.

SIM.   Pray you, sir, was 't not the wise woman of Brentford?

FAL.   Ay, marry, was it, muscle-shell:[4] what would you with her?

SIM.   My master, sir, Master Slender, sent to her, seeing her go thor-
     ough the streets, to know, sir, whether one Nym, sir, that beguiled
     him of a chain, had the chain or no.

---

[1]*Anthropophaginian*] "Anthropophagi" was the accepted term for man-eaters or canni-
bals. "Anthropophaginian" is mine host's invention, and is coined on the analogy of
"Carthaginian."

[2]*Ephesian*] This word has much the same significance in Elizabethan slang as
"Corinthian," *i.e.*, a good fellow, a man of mettle.

[3]*Bohemian-Tartar*] a grandiloquent periphrasis for "gipsy."

[4]*muscle-shell*] Simple's lips are agape, like the shells of a mussel.

FAL.   I spake with the old woman about it.

SIM.   And what says she, I pray, sir?

FAL.   Marry, she says that the very same man that beguiled Master Slender of his chain cozened him of it.

SIM.   I would I could have spoken with the woman herself; I had other things to have spoken with her too from him.

FAL.   What are they? let us know.

HOST.   Ay, come; quick.

SIM.   I may not conceal[5] them, sir.

HOST.   Conceal them, or thou diest.

SIM.   Why, sir, they were nothing but about Mistress Anne Page; to know if it were my master's fortune to have her or no.

FAL.   'T is, 't is his fortune.

SIM.   What, sir?

FAL.   To have her, or no. Go; say the woman told me so.

SIM.   May I be bold to say so, sir?

FAL.   Ay, sir; like who more bold.

SIM.   I thank your worship: I shall make my master glad with these tidings.   [*Exit.*

HOST.   Thou art clerkly, thou art clerkly, Sir John. Was there a wise woman with thee?

FAL.   Ay, that there was, mine host; one that hath taught me more wit than ever I learned before in my life; and I paid nothing for it neither, but was paid[6] for my learning.

Enter BARDOLPH

BARD.   Out, alas, sir! cozenage, mere cozenage!

HOST.   Where be my horses? speak well of them, varletto.

BARD.   Run away with the cozeners: for so soon as I came beyond Eton, they threw me off, from behind one of them, in a slough of mire; and set spurs and away, like three German devils, three Doctor Faustuses.[7]

HOST.   They are gone but to meet the duke, villain: do not say they be fled, Germans are honest men.

Enter SIR HUGH EVANS

EVANS.   Where is mine host?

HOST.   What is the matter, sir?

EVANS.   Have a care of your entertainments: there is a friend of mine

---

[5]*conceal*] blunder for "reveal."

[6]*was paid*] was paid out, punished, beaten.

[7]*Faustuses*] a probable reference to Marlowe's tragedy of *Dr. Faustus.*

come to town, tells me there is three cozen-germans[8] that has cozened all the hosts of Readins, of Maidenhead, of Colebrook, of horses and money. I tell you for good will, look you: you are wise, and full of gibes and vlouting-stocks,[9] and 't is not convenient you should be cozened. Fare you well.   [Exit.

Enter DOCTOR CAIUS

CAIUS.   Vere is mine host de Jarteer?
HOST.   Here, master doctor, in perplexity and doubtful dilemma.
CAIUS.   I cannot tell vat is dat: but it is tell-a me dat you make grand preparation for a duke de Jamany: by my trot, dere is no duke dat the court is known to come. I tell you for good vill: adieu.   [Exit.
HOST.   Hue and cry, villain, go!—Assist me, knight.—I am undone!— Fly, run, hue and cry, villain!—I am undone!

[Exeunt HOST *and* BARD.

FAL.   I would all the world might be cozened; for I have been cozened and beaten too. If it should come to the ear of the court, how I have been transformed, and how my transformation hath been washed and cudgelled, they would melt me out of my fat drop by drop, and liquor fishermen's boots with me: I warrant they would whip me with their fine wits till I were as crest-fallen as a dried pear. I never prospered since I forswore myself at primero. Well, if my wind were but long enough to say my prayers, I would repent.

Enter MISTRESS QUICKLY

Now, whence come you?
QUICK.   From the two parties, forsooth.
FAL.   The devil take one party, and his dam the other! And so they shall be both bestowed. I have suffered more for their sakes, more than the villanous inconstancy of man's disposition is able to bear.
QUICK.   And have not they suffered? Yes, I warrant; speciously[10] one of them; Mistress Ford, good heart, is beaten black and blue, that you cannot see a white spot about her.

---

[8]*there is three cozen-germans*] There is a plain reference here to a contemporary episode of historic importance. The First Quarto reads, *there is three sorts of cosen garmombles.* "Garmombles" seems to be a burlesque rendering of the German name "Mompelgard." In 1592 Frederick, Duke of Wirtemberg, who was well known in England during his stay by his subordinate title of Count Mompelgard, was granted official permission to requisition post-horses free of charge—a grant which offended innkeepers. Count Mompelgard seems to have actually visited inns at Reading, Maidenhead, and Colebrook, the places mentioned in the text.
[9]*vlouting-stocks*] flouts.
[10]*speciously*] blunder for "especially."

FAL. What tell'st thou me of black and blue? I was beaten myself into
all the colours of the rainbow; and I was like to be apprehended
for the witch of Brentford: but that my admirable dexterity of wit,
my counterfeiting the action of an old woman, delivered me, the
knave constable had set me i' the stocks, i' the common stocks, for
a witch.

QUICK. Sir, let me speak with you in your chamber: you shall hear
how things go; and, I warrant, to your content. Here is a letter will
say somewhat. Good hearts, what ado here is to bring you together! Sure, one of you does not serve heaven well, that you are
so crossed.

FAL. Come up into my chamber. [*Exeunt.*

SCENE VI. *The Same. Another Room in the Garter Inn.*

Enter FENTON *and* HOST

HOST. Master Fenton, talk not to me; my mind is heavy: I will give
over all.

FENT. Yet hear me speak. Assist me in my purpose,
And, as I am a gentleman, I'll give thee
A hundred pound in gold more than your loss.

HOST. I will hear you, Master Fenton; and I will at the least keep your
counsel.

FENT. From time to time I have acquainted you
With the dear love I bear to fair Anne Page;
Who mutually hath answer'd my affection,
So far forth as herself might be her chooser,
Even to my wish: I have a letter from her
Of such contents as you will wonder at;
The mirth whereof so larded with my matter,
That neither singly can be manifested,
Without the show of both; fat Falstaff[1]
Hath a great scene: the image of the jest
I'll show you here at large. Hark, good mine host.
To-night at Herne's oak, just 'twixt twelve and one,
Must my sweet Nan present the Fairy Queen;
The purpose why, is here: in which disguise,
While other jests are something rank on foot,
Her father hath commanded her to slip

---

[1]*fat Falstaff*] The earlier Quartos insert *wherein* before *fat Falstaff*. The insertion seems
necessary to complete the line.

Away with Slender, and with him at Eton
Immediately to marry: she hath consented:
Now, sir,
Her mother, even strong against that match,
And firm for Doctor Caius, hath appointed
That he shall likewise shuffle her away,
While other sports are tasking of their minds,
And at the deanery, where a priest attends,
Straight marry her: to this her mother's plot
She seemingly obedient likewise hath
Made promise to the doctor. Now, thus it rests:
Her father means she shall be all in white;
And in that habit, when Slender sees his time
To take her by the hand and bid her go,
She shall go with him: her mother hath intended,
The better to denote her to the doctor,—
For they must all be mask'd and vizarded,—
That quaint in green she shall be loose enrobed,
With ribands pendent, flaring 'bout her head;
And when the doctor spies his vantage ripe,
To pinch her by the hand, and, on that token,
The maid hath given consent to go with him.

HOST.   Which means she to deceive, father or mother?
FENT.   Both, my good host, to go along with me:
And here it rests,—that you'll procure the vicar
To stay for me at church 'twixt twelve and one,
And, in the lawful name of marrying,
To give our hearts united ceremony.[2]

HOST.   Well, husband your device; I'll to the vicar:
Bring you the maid, you shall not lack a priest.
FENT.   So shall I evermore be bound to thee;
Besides, I'll make a present recompence.   [*Exeunt.*

---

[2]*united ceremony*] uniting ceremony, ceremony of union.

ACT V.

SCENE I. *A Room in the Garter Inn.*

Enter FALSTAFF *and* MISTRESS QUICKLY

FALSTAFF. Prithee, no more prattling; go. I'll hold. This is the third
   time; I hope good luck lies in odd numbers. Away! go. They say
   there is divinity in odd numbers, either in nativity, chance, or
   death. Away!

QUICK. I'll provide you a chain; and I'll do what I can to get you a
   pair of horns.

FAL. Away, I say; time wears: hold up your head, and mince.[1]

[*Exit* MRS QUICKLY.

Enter FORD

   How now, Master Brook! Master Brook, the matter will be known
   to-night, or never. Be you in the Park about midnight, at Herne's
   oak, and you shall see wonders.

FORD. Went you not to her yesterday, sir, as you told me you had
   appointed?

FAL. I went to her, Master Brook, as you see, like a poor old man: but
   I came from her, Master Brook, like a poor old woman. That same
   knave Ford, her husband, hath the finest mad devil of jealousy in
   him, Master Brook, that ever governed frenzy. I will tell you:—he
   beat me grievously, in the shape of a woman; for in the shape of
   man, Master Brook, I fear not Goliath with a weaver's beam; because I know also life is a shuttle.[2] I am in haste; go along with me:
   I'll tell you all, Master Brook. Since I plucked geese,[3] played truant, and whipped top, I knew not what 't was to be beaten till
   lately. Follow me: I'll tell you strange things of this knave Ford, on

---

[1]*mince*] walk with affected gait, with short steps.
[2]*life is a shuttle*] Cf. *Job*, vii, 6: "My days are swifter than a weaver's *shuttle*."
[3]*plucked geese*] stripped living geese of their feathers as boys were wont to do.

whom to-night I will be revenged, and I will deliver his wife into your hand. Follow. Strange things in hand, Master Brook! Follow.

[*Exeunt.*

SCENE II. *Windsor Park.*

Enter PAGE, SHALLOW, *and* SLENDER

PAGE.   Come, come; we'll couch i' the castle-ditch till we see the light of our fairies. Remember, son Slender, my daughter.

SLEN.   Ay, forsooth; I have spoke with her, and we have a nay-word how to know one another: I come to her in white, and cry, "mum;" she cries "budget;"[1] and by that we know one another.

SHAL.   That's good too: but what needs either your "mum" or her "budget"? the white will decipher her well enough. It hath struck ten o'clock.

PAGE.   The night is dark; light and spirits will become it well. Heaven prosper our sport! No man means evil but the devil, and we shall know him by his horns. Let's away; follow me.   [*Exeunt.*

SCENE III. *A Street Leading to the Park.*

Enter MISTRESS PAGE, MISTRESS FORD, *and* DOCTOR CAIUS

MRS PAGE.   Master Doctor, my daughter is in green: when you see your time, take her by the hand, away with her to the deanery, and dispatch it quickly. Go before into the Park: we two must go together.

CAIUS.   I know vat I have to do. Adieu.

MRS PAGE.   Fare you well, sir. [*Exit* CAIUS.] My husband will not rejoice so much at the abuse of Falstaff as he will chafe at the doctor's marrying my daughter: but 't is no matter; better a little chiding than a great deal of heart-break.

MRS FORD.   Where is Nan now and her troop of fairies, and the Welsh devil Hugh?

MRS PAGE.   They are all couched in a pit hard by Herne's oak, with obscured lights; which, at the very instant of Falstaff's and our meeting, they will at once display to the night.

MRS FORD.   That cannot choose but amaze him.

---

[1] "*mum*" . . . "*budget*"] Both were whispered exclamations implying the need of keeping secrets.

MRS PAGE.   If he be not amazed, he will be mocked; if he be amazed, he will every way be mocked.

MRS FORD.   We'll betray him finely.

MRS PAGE.   Against such lewdsters and their lechery
Those that betray them do no treachery.

MRS FORD.   The hour draws on. To the oak, to the oak!   [*Exeunt.*

SCENE IV. *Windsor Park.*

Enter SIR HUGH EVANS *disguised, with others as Fairies*

EVANS.   Trib, trib, fairies; come; and remember your parts: be pold, I pray you; follow me into the pit; and when I give the watch-'ords, do as I pid you: come, come; trib, trib.   [*Exeunt.*

SCENE V. *Another Part of the Park.*

Enter FALSTAFF *disguised as Herne*

FAL.   The Windsor bell hath struck twelve; the minute draws on. Now, the hot-blooded gods assist me! Remember, Jove, thou wast a bull for thy Europa; love set on thy horns. O powerful love! that, in some respects, makes a beast a man; in some other, a man a beast. You were also, Jupiter, a swan for the love of Leda. O omnipotent Love! how near the god drew to the complexion of a goose! A fault done first in the form of a beast;—O Jove, a beastly fault! And then another fault in the semblance of a fowl;—think on 't, Jove; a foul fault! When gods have hot backs, what shall poor men do? For me, I am here a Windsor stag; and the fattest, I think, i' the forest. Send me a cool rut-time, Jove, or who can blame me to piss my tallow?—Who comes here? my doe?

Enter MISTRESS FORD *and* MISTRESS PAGE

MRS FORD.   Sir John! art thou there, my deer? my male deer?

FAL.   My doe with the black scut! Let the sky rain potatoes; let it thunder to the tune of Green Sleeves, hail kissing-comfits,[1] and snow eringoes;[2] let there come a tempest of provocation, I will shelter me here.

---

[1]*kissing-comfits*] perfumed sugar plums, which made the breath sweet.
[2]*rain potatoes*] Potatoes and "eringoes" (the candied root of the sea holly) were in early days reckoned aphrodisiacs. Potatoes and eringoes are frequently mentioned together by Elizabethan dramatists in the same significance as in the text.

MRS FORD.   Mistress Page is come with me, sweetheart.
FAL.   Divide me like a bribe buck,[3] each a haunch: I will keep my
     sides to myself, my shoulders for the fellow of this walk,[4] and my
     horns I bequeath your husbands. Am I a woodman, ha? Speak I
     like Herne the hunter? Why, now is Cupid a child of conscience;
     he makes restitution. As I am a true spirit, welcome!

                                                        [*Noise within.*

MRS PAGE.   Alas, what noise?
MRS FORD.   Heaven forgive our sins!
FAL.   What should this be?
MRS FORD. }
MRS PAGE. } Away, away!   [*They run off.*
FAL.   I think the devil will not have me damned, lest the oil that's in
     me should set hell on fire; he would never else cross me thus.

Enter SIR HUGH EVANS, *disguised as before;* PISTOL, *as Hobgoblin;*
    MISTRESS QUICKLY, ANNE PAGE, *and others, as Fairies, with*
    tapers.[5]

QUICK.   Fairies, black, grey, green, and white,
         You moonshine revellers, and shades of night,
         You orphan heirs of fixed destiny,[6]
         Attend your office and your quality.
         Crier Hobgoblin, make the fairy oyes.
PIST.   Elves, list your names; silence, you airy toys.
         Cricket, to Windsor chimneys shalt thou leap:
         Where fires thou find'st unraked and hearths unswept,
         There pinch the maids as blue as bilberry:
         Our radiant queen hates sluts and sluttery.
FAL.   They are fairies; he that speaks to them shall die:
         I'll wink and couch: no man their works must eye.

                                          [*Lies down upon his face.*

EVANS.   Where's Bede?[7] Go you, and where you find a maid
         That, ere she sleep, has thrice her prayers said,
         Raise up the organs of her fantasy;
         Sleep she as sound as careless infancy:

---

[3]*bribe buck*] Theobald's emendation of the early reading, *brib'd buck.* It probably means
 a buck of the fine quality bred for giving away as bribes or presents.
[4]*the fellow of this walk*] the forester or gamekeeper.
[5]*Enter . . . tapers*] In the early Quartos this stage direction reads thus: "Enter Sir Hugh
 like a Satyre, and boyes drest like Fayries, Mistresse Quickly, like the queene of
 Fayries; they sing a song about him and afterward speake."
[6]*orphan heirs . . . destiny*] miraculously conceived inheritors of immortality.
[7]*Bede*] This is the name given to the fairy messenger in the Folios. The early Quartos
 read *Pead,* which is probably more in keeping with Sir Hugh's ordinary dialect.

But those as sleep and think not on their sins,
Pinch them, arms, legs, backs, shoulders, sides, and shins.
QUICK.   About, about;
Search Windsor Castle, elves, within and out:
Strew good luck, ouphes, on every sacred room;
That it may stand till the perpetual doom,
In state as wholesome as in state 't is fit,
Worthy the owner, and the owner it.
The several chairs of order look you scour
With juice of balm and every precious flower:
Each fair instalment[8] coat, and several crest,
With loyal blazon, evermore be blest!
And nightly, meadow-fairies, look you sing,
Like to the Garter's compass, in a ring:
Th' expressure that it bears, green let it be,
More fertile-fresh than all the field to see;
And *Honi soit qui mal y pense* write
In emerald tufts, flowers purple, blue, and white;
Like sapphire, pearl, and rich embroidery,
Buckled below fair knighthood's bending knee:
Fairies use flowers for their charactery.[9]
Away; disperse: but till 't is one o'clock,
Our dance of custom round about the oak
Of Herne the hunter, let us not forget.
EVANS.   Pray you, lock hand in hand; yourselves in order set;
And twenty glow-worms shall our lanterns be,
To guide our measure round about the tree
But, stay; I smell a man of middle-earth.[10]
FAL.   Heavens defend me from that Welsh fairy, lest he transform me
to a piece of cheese!
PIST.   Vile worm, thou wast o'erlook'd even in thy birth.
QUICK.   With trial-fire touch me his finger-end:
If he be chaste, the flame will back descend,
And turn him[11] to no pain; but if he start,
It is the flesh of a corrupted heart.
PIST.   A trial, come.
EVANS.   Come, will this wood take fire?
                              [*They burn him with their tapers.*

---

[8]*instalment*] The word which commonly means "installation" seems to signify here the "stall" of a knight of the Garter.

[9]*charactery*] written cipher; often used in the sense of "shorthand."

[10]*middle*] a conventional poetic epithet. In the current astronomical system the earth was the *middle* region of the universe, of which the upper region was the home of God and the lower region the abode of the fairies.

[11]*turn him*] put him, a common contemporary usage.

FAL. Oh, Oh, Oh!
QUICK. Corrupt, corrupt, and tainted in desire!
    About him, fairies; sing a scornful rhyme;
    And, as you trip, still pinch him to your time.

SONG

> Fie on sinful fantasy![12]
> Fie on lust and luxury![13]
> Lust is but a bloody fire,[14]
> Kindled with unchaste desire,
> Fed in heart, whose flames aspire,
> As thoughts do blow them, higher and higher.
>   Pinch him, fairies, mutually;
>   Pinch him for his villany;
> Pinch him, and burn him, and turn him about,
> Till candles and starlight and moonshine be out.

During this song they pinch FALSTAFF. DOCTOR CAIUS *comes one way,
and steals away a boy in green;* SLENDER *another way, and takes
off a boy in white; and* FENTON *comes, and steals away* MRS
ANNE PAGE. *A noise of hunting is heard within. All the Fairies run
away.* FALSTAFF *pulls off his buck's head, and rises.*[15]

Enter PAGE, FORD, MISTRESS PAGE *and* MISTRESS FORD

PAGE. Nay, do not fly; I think we have watch'd you now:
    Will none but Herne the hunter serve your turn?
MRS PAGE. I pray you, come, hold up the jest no higher.
    Now, good Sir John, how like you Windsor wives?
    See you these, husband? do not these fair yokes[16]
    Become the forest better than the town?
FORD. Now, sir, who's a cuckold now? Master Brook, Falstaff's
    a knave, a cuckoldly knave; here are his horns, Master Brook:
    and, Master Brook, he hath enjoyed nothing of Ford's but his buck-
    basket, his cudgel, and twenty pounds of money, which must be
    paid to Master Brook; his horses are arrested for it, Master Brook.

---

[12]*fantasy*] love.
[13]*luxury*] lasciviousness, incontinence.
[14]*bloody fire*] fire of blood.
[15]*During this song . . . rises*] This stage direction is absent from the First Folio, but it figures in the early Quartos, whence Theobald and succeeding editors have borrowed it.
[16]*fair yokes*] This is the reading of the First Folio, which the Second and later Folios changed to *okes, i.e.* oaks. The reference, of course, is to the horns, which sometimes take a shape resembling yokes for cattle. It is less reasonable to identify the horns with the branches of an oak tree.

MRS FORD. Sir John, we have had ill luck; we could never meet. I will never take you for my love again; but I will always count you my deer.

FAL. I do begin to perceive that I am made an ass.

FORD. Ay, and an ox too: both the proofs are extant.

FAL. And these are not fairies? I was three or four times in the thought they were not fairies: and yet the guiltiness of my mind, the sudden surprise of my powers, drove the grossness of the foppery into a received belief, in despite of the teeth of[17] all rhyme and reason, that they were fairies. See now how wit may be made a Jack-a-Lent, when 't is upon ill employment!

EVANS. Sir John Falstaff, serve Got, and leave your desires, and fairies will not pinse you.

FORD. Well said, fairy Hugh.

EVANS. And leave you your jealousies too, I pray you.

FORD. I will never mistrust my wife again, till thou art able to woo her in good English.

FAL. Have I laid my brain in the sun and dried it, that it wants matter to prevent so gross o'erreaching as this? Am I ridden with a Welsh goat too? shall I have a coxcomb of frize?[18] 'T is time I were choked with a piece of toasted cheese.

EVANS. Seese is not good to give putter; your pelly is all putter.

FAL. "Seese" and "putter"? Have I lived to stand at the taunt of one that makes fritters of English? This is enough to be the decay of lust and late-walking through the realm.

MRS PAGE. Why, Sir John, do you think, though we would have thrust virtue out of our hearts by the head and shoulders, and have given ourselves without scruple to hell, that ever the devil could have made you our delight?

FORD. What, a hodge-pudding? a bag of flax?

MRS PAGE. A puffed man?

PAGE. Old, cold, withered, and of intolerable entrails?

FORD. And one that is as slanderous as Satan?

PAGE. And as poor as Job?

FORD. And as wicked as his wife?

EVANS. And given to fornications, and to taverns, and sack, and wine, and metheglins, and to drinkings, and swearings, and starings, pribbles and prabbles?

FAL. Well, I am your theme: you have the start of me; I am dejected;

---

[17]*despite of the teeth of*] An emphatic conjunction of "despite" and "in the teeth of."

[18]*a coxcomb of frize*] A professional fool's cap made of the rough woollen cloth which was a leading Welsh manufacture.

I am not able to answer the Welsh flannel: ignorance itself is a plummet o'er me:[19] use me as you will.

FORD.   Marry, sir, we'll bring you to Windsor, to one Master Brook, that you have cozened of money, to whom you should have been a pandar: over and above that you have suffered, I think to repay that money will be a biting affliction.

PAGE.   Yet be cheerful, knight: thou shalt eat a posset to-night at my house; where I will desire thee to laugh at my wife, that now laughs at thee: tell her Master Slender hath married her daughter.

MRS PAGE.   [Aside]   Doctors doubt that: if Anne Page be my daughter, she is, by this, Doctor Caius' wife.

Enter SLENDER

SLEN.   Whoa, ho! ho, father Page!
PAGE.   Son, how now! how now, son! have you dispatched?
SLEN.   Dispatched! I'll make the best in Gloucestershire know on 't; would I were hanged, la, else!
PAGE.   Of what, son?
SLEN.   I came yonder at Eton to marry Mistress Anne Page, and she's a great lubberly boy. If it had not been i' the church, I would have swinged him, or he should have swinged me. If I did not think it had been Anne Page, would I might never stir!—and 't is a post-master's boy.
PAGE.   Upon my life, then, you took the wrong.
SLEN.   What need you tell me that? I think so, when I took a boy for a girl. If I had been married to him, for all he was in woman's apparel, I would not have had him.
PAGE.   Why, this is your own folly. Did not I tell you how you should know my daughter by her garments?
SLEN.   I went to her in white, and cried "mum," and she cried "budget," as Anne and I had appointed; and yet it was not Anne, but a postmaster's boy.
MRS PAGE.   Good George, be not angry: I knew of your purpose; turned my daughter into green; and, indeed, she is now with the doctor at the deanery, and there married.

Enter CAIUS

CAIUS.   Vere is Mistress Page? By gar, I am cozened: I ha' married un garçon, a boy; un paysan, by gar, a boy; it is not Anne Page: by gar, I am cozened.
MRS PAGE.   Why, did you take her in green?

---

[19]*ignorance . . . plummet o'er me*] ignorance, helplessness overcomes me with its leaden weight. "Plummet" is the weight of lead attached to the "plumbline."

CAIUS. Ay, by gar, and 't is a boy: by gar, I'll raise all Windsor.

[Exit.

FORD. This is strange. Who hath got the right Anne?
PAGE. My heart misgives me:—here comes Master Fenton.

Enter FENTON *and* ANNE PAGE

How now, Master Fenton!
ANNE. Pardon, good father! good my mother, pardon!
PAGE. Now, mistress, how chance you went not with Master Slender?
MRS PAGE. Why went you not with master doctor, maid?
FENT. You do amaze her: hear the truth of it.
You would have married her most shamefully,
Where there was no proportion held in love.
The truth is, she and I, long since contracted,
Are now so sure that nothing can dissolve us.
The offence is holy that she hath committed;
And this deceit loses the name of craft,
Of disobedience, or unduteous title;
Since therein she doth evitate and shun
A thousand irreligious cursed hours,
Which forced marriage would have brought upon her.
FORD. Stand not amazed; here is no remedy:
In love the heavens themselves do guide the state;
Money buys lands, and wives are sold by fate.
FAL. I am glad, though you have ta'en a special stand[20] to strike at me,
that your arrow hath glanced.
PAGE. Well, what remedy? Fenton, heaven give thee joy!
What cannot be eschew'd must be embraced.
FAL. When night-dogs run, all sorts of deer are chased.
MRS PAGE. Well, I will muse no further. Master Fenton,
Heaven give you many, many merry days!
Good husband, let us every one go home,
And laugh this sport o'er by a country fire;
Sir John and all.
FORD.   Let it be so. Sir John,
To Master Brook you yet shall hold your word;
For he to-night shall lie with Mistress Ford.

[Exeunt.

---

[20]*stand*] a hiding place in the forest, whence the huntsman aims his arrow at the deer.

DOVER · THRIFT · EDITIONS

POETRY

LA VITA NUOVA, Dante Alighieri. 56pp. 41915-0

101 GREAT AMERICAN POEMS, The American Poetry & Literacy Project (ed.). (Available in U.S. only.) 96pp. 40158-8

ENGLISH ROMANTIC POETRY: An Anthology, Stanley Appelbaum (ed.). 256pp. 29282-7

DOVER BEACH AND OTHER POEMS, Matthew Arnold. 112pp. 28037-3

SELECTED POEMS FROM "FLOWERS OF EVIL," Charles Baudelaire. 64pp. 28450-6

BHAGAVADGITA, Bhagavadgita. 112pp. 27782-8

THE BOOK OF PSALMS, King James Bible. 128pp. 27541-8

IMAGIST POETRY: AN ANTHOLOGY, Bob Blaisdell (ed.). 176pp. (Available in U.S. only.) 40875-2

IRISH VERSE: AN ANTHOLOGY, Bob Blaisdell (ed.). 160pp. 41914-2

BLAKE'S SELECTED POEMS, William Blake. 96pp. 28517-0

SONGS OF INNOCENCE AND SONGS OF EXPERIENCE, William Blake. 64pp. 27051-3

THE CLASSIC TRADITION OF HAIKU: An Anthology, Faubion Bowers (ed.). 96pp. 29274-6

TO MY HUSBAND AND OTHER POEMS, Anne Bradstreet (Robert Hutchinson, ed.). 80pp. 41408-6

BEST POEMS OF THE BRONTË SISTERS (ed. by Candace Ward), Emily, Anne, and Charlotte Brontë. 64pp. 29529-X

SONNETS FROM THE PORTUGUESE AND OTHER POEMS, Elizabeth Barrett Browning. 64pp. 27052-1

MY LAST DUCHESS AND OTHER POEMS, Robert Browning. 128pp. 27783-6

POEMS AND SONGS, Robert Burns. 96pp. 26863-2

SELECTED POEMS, George Gordon, Lord Byron. 112pp. 27784-4

JABBERWOCKY AND OTHER POEMS, Lewis Carroll. 64pp. 41582-1

SELECTED CANTERBURY TALES, Geoffrey Chaucer. 144pp. 28241-4

THE RIME OF THE ANCIENT MARINER AND OTHER POEMS, Samuel Taylor Coleridge. 80pp. 27266-4

WAR IS KIND AND OTHER POEMS, Stephen Crane. 64pp. 40424-2

THE CAVALIER POETS: An Anthology, Thomas Crofts (ed.). 80pp. 28766-1

SELECTED POEMS, Emily Dickinson. 64pp. 26466-1

SELECTED POEMS, John Donne. 96pp. 27788-7

SELECTED POEMS, Paul Laurence Dunbar. 80pp. 29980-5

"THE WASTE LAND" AND OTHER POEMS, T. S. Eliot. 64pp. (Available in U.S. only.) 40061-1

THE CONCORD HYMN AND OTHER POEMS, Ralph Waldo Emerson. 64pp. 29059-X

THE RUBÁIYÁT OF OMAR KHAYYÁM: FIRST AND FIFTH EDITIONS, Edward FitzGerald. 64pp. 26467-X

A BOY'S WILL AND NORTH OF BOSTON, Robert Frost. 112pp. (Available in U.S. only.) 26866-7

THE ROAD NOT TAKEN AND OTHER POEMS, Robert Frost. 64pp. (Available in U.S. only.) 27550-7

HARDY'S SELECTED POEMS, Thomas Hardy. 80pp. 28753-X

"GOD'S GRANDEUR" AND OTHER POEMS, Gerard Manley Hopkins. 80pp. 28729-7

A SHROPSHIRE LAD, A. E. Housman. 64pp. 26468-8

LYRIC POEMS, John Keats. 80pp. 26871-3

GUNGA DIN AND OTHER FAVORITE POEMS, Rudyard Kipling. 80pp. 26471-8

SNAKE AND OTHER POEMS, D. H. Lawrence. 64pp. 40647-4

DOVER · THRIFT · EDITIONS

PLAYS

THE MIKADO, William Schwenck Gilbert. 64pp. 27268-0

FAUST, PART ONE, Johann Wolfgang von Goethe. 192pp. 28046-2

THE INSPECTOR GENERAL, Nikolai Gogol. 80pp. 28500-6

SHE STOOPS TO CONQUER, Oliver Goldsmith. 80pp. 26867-5

A DOLL'S HOUSE, Henrik Ibsen. 80pp. 27062-9

GHOSTS, Henrik Ibsen. 64pp. 29852-3

HEDDA GABLER, Henrik Ibsen. 80pp. 26469-6

THE WILD DUCK, Henrik Ibsen. 96pp. 41116-8

VOLPONE, Ben Jonson. 112pp. 28049-7

DR. FAUSTUS, Christopher Marlowe. 64pp. 28208-2

THE MISANTHROPE, Molière. 64pp. 27065-3

ANNA CHRISTIE, Eugene O'Neill. 80pp. 29985-6

BEYOND THE HORIZON, Eugene O'Neill. 96pp. 29085-9

THE EMPEROR JONES, Eugene O'Neill. 64pp. 29268-1

THE LONG VOYAGE HOME AND OTHER PLAYS, Eugene O'Neill. 80pp. 28755-6

RIGHT YOU ARE, IF YOU THINK YOU ARE, Luigi Pirandello. 64pp. (Not available in Europe or United Kingdom.) 29576-1

SIX CHARACTERS IN SEARCH OF AN AUTHOR, Luigi Pirandello. 64pp. (Not available in Europe or United Kingdom.) 29992-9

PHÈDRE, Jean Racine. 64pp. 41927-4

HANDS AROUND, Arthur Schnitzler. 64pp. 28724-6

ANTONY AND CLEOPATRA, William Shakespeare. 128pp. 40062-X

AS YOU LIKE IT, William Shakespeare. 80pp. 40432-3

HAMLET, William Shakespeare. 128pp. 27278-8

HENRY IV, William Shakespeare. 96pp. 29584-2

JULIUS CAESAR, William Shakespeare. 80pp. 26876-4

KING LEAR, William Shakespeare. 112pp. 28058-6

LOVE'S LABOUR'S LOST, William Shakespeare. 64pp. 41929-0

MACBETH, William Shakespeare. 96pp. 27802-6

MEASURE FOR MEASURE, William Shakespeare. 96pp. 40889-2

THE MERCHANT OF VENICE, William Shakespeare. 96pp. 28492-1

A MIDSUMMER NIGHT'S DREAM, William Shakespeare. 80pp. 27067-X

MUCH ADO ABOUT NOTHING, William Shakespeare. 80pp. 28272-4

OTHELLO, William Shakespeare. 112pp. 29097-2

RICHARD III, William Shakespeare. 112pp. 28747-5

ROMEO AND JULIET, William Shakespeare. 96pp. 27557-4

THE TAMING OF THE SHREW, William Shakespeare. 96pp. 29765-9

THE TEMPEST, William Shakespeare. 96pp. 40658-X

TWELFTH NIGHT; OR, WHAT YOU WILL, William Shakespeare. 80pp. 29290-8

ARMS AND THE MAN, George Bernard Shaw. 80pp. (Not available in Europe or United Kingdom.) 26476-9

HEARTBREAK HOUSE, George Bernard Shaw. 128pp. (Not available in Europe or United Kingdom.) 29291-6

PYGMALION, George Bernard Shaw. 96pp. (Available in U.S. only.) 28222-8

THE RIVALS, Richard Brinsley Sheridan. 96pp. 40433-1

THE SCHOOL FOR SCANDAL, Richard Brinsley Sheridan. 96pp. 26687-7

ANTIGONE, Sophocles. 64pp. 27804-2

OEDIPUS AT COLONUS, Sophocles. 64pp. 40659-8

OEDIPUS REX, Sophocles. 64pp. 26877-2

DOVER · THRIFT · EDITIONS

PLAYS

ELECTRA, Sophocles. 64pp. 28482-4

MISS JULIE, August Strindberg. 64pp. 27281-8

THE PLAYBOY OF THE WESTERN WORLD AND RIDERS TO THE SEA, J. M. Synge. 80pp. 27562-0

THE DUCHESS OF MALFI, John Webster. 96pp. 40660-1

THE IMPORTANCE OF BEING EARNEST, Oscar Wilde. 64pp. 26478-5

LADY WINDERMERE'S FAN, Oscar Wilde. 64pp. 40078-6

BOXED SETS

FAVORITE JANE AUSTEN NOVELS: *Pride and Prejudice, Sense and Sensibility* and *Persuasion* (Complete and Unabridged), Jane Austen. 800pp. 29748-9

BEST WORKS OF MARK TWAIN: Four Books, Dover. 624pp. 40226-6

EIGHT GREAT GREEK TRAGEDIES: Six Books, Dover. 480pp. 40203-7

FIVE GREAT ENGLISH ROMANTIC POETS, Dover. 496pp. 27893-X

FIVE GREAT PLAYS, Dover. 368pp. 27179-X

47 GREAT SHORT STORIES: Stories by Poe, Chekhov, Maupassant, Gogol, O. Henry, and Twain, Dover. 688pp. 27178-1

GREAT AFRICAN-AMERICAN WRITERS: Seven Books, Dover. 704pp. 29995-3

GREAT AMERICAN NOVELS, Dover. 720pp. 28665-7

GREAT ENGLISH NOVELS, Dover. 704pp. 28666-5

GREAT IRISH WRITERS: Five Books, Dover. 672pp. 29996-1

GREAT MODERN WRITERS: Five Books, Dover. 720pp. (Available in U.S. only.) 29458-7

GREAT WOMEN POETS: 4 Complete Books, Dover. 256pp. (Available in U.S. only.) 28388-7

MASTERPIECES OF RUSSIAN LITERATURE: Seven Books, Dover. 880pp. 40665-2

SEVEN GREAT ENGLISH VICTORIAN POETS: Seven Volumes, Dover. 592pp. 40204-5

SIX GREAT AMERICAN POETS: Poems by Poe, Dickinson, Whitman, Longfellow, Frost, and Millay, Dover. 512pp. (Available in U.S. only.) 27425-X

38 SHORT STORIES BY AMERICAN WOMEN WRITERS: Five Books, Dover. 512pp. 29459-5

26 GREAT TALES OF TERROR AND THE SUPERNATURAL, Dover. 608pp. (Available in U.S. only.) 27891-3

All books complete and unabridged. All 5³⁄₁₆" x 8¹⁄₄," paperbound. Available at your book dealer, online at **www.doverpublications.com**, or by writing to Dept. GI, Dover Publications, Inc., 31 East 2nd Street, Mineola, NY 11501. For current price information or for free catalogs (please indicate field of interest), write to Dover Publications or log on to **www.doverpublications.com** and see every Dover book in print. Dover publishes more than 500 books each year on science, elementary and advanced mathematics, biology, music, art, literary history, social sciences, and other areas.